Mo Mowlam

Mo Mowlam was born in 1949 and educated at Coundon Court Comprehensive School, Coventry and the Universities of Durham and Iowa. She taught in America at the Universities of Wisconsin and Florida, before returning to teach at Newcastle University and to join the staff of Northern College, Barnsley. She became an MP in 1987, member of the Shadow Cabinet in 1992 and Northern Ireland Secretary in 1997. She resigned as Cabinet Office Minister and MP in 2001. She lives in Redcar and London with her husband, Jon Norton.

Mo Mowlam

Momentum

The Struggle for Peace,
Politics and the People

CORONET BOOKS
Hodder & Stoughton

First published in Great Britain in 2002
by Hodder and Stoughton
First published in paperback in 2003
by Hodder and Stoughton
A division of Hodder Headline

A Coronet paperback

8

A CIP catalogue record for this title
is available from the British Library

ISBN 978-0-340-79395-4

Typeset in Monotype Sabon by
Rowland Phototypesetting Ltd,
Bury St Edmunds, Suffolk
Printed and bound in Great Britain by
Clays Ltd, St Ives plc

Hodder and Stoughton
A division of Hodder Headline
338 Euston Road
London NW1 3BH

In memory of two mums, mine and Nigel's

History, despite its wrenching pain, cannot be unlived, and if faced with courage, need not be lived again.

Maya Angelou

Contents

Illustrations

Preface

When I became Secretary of State for N. Ireland, I was already becoming well-known as a politician, partly because I was a woman who had fought a brain tumour, and partly because of my manner, which was not that of most politicians. After a while as Secretary of State my popularity grew, I think because we made some progress against expectations, and people like a good-news story with a human angle. Lots of people wrote, phoned and stopped me in the street to say words to the effect: 'Well done, Mo, you are doing a grand job.' I tried talking to them about what was going on but rarely got very far.

This experience reinforced an existing view, which I had held from when I taught political science in the USA and at Newcastle University. There was not a great deal of interest in the problems being fought over in N. Ireland: most students viewed it as part of the course that had to be learnt. There were some exceptions – those students who had become politicized on the left or the right. From the left most argued that in N. Ireland a minority, the Catholics, were being oppressed by the Protestants and the British and were fighting for their liberation. From the right most argued there was an unruly mob, the minority, who were using violence to achieve their aims and should be opposed by all the might of the British state. It was as simple and as crude as this.

These opposing views were held by a small proportion of the general public. The vast majority did not want to know what was going on. They were aware of the violence but it was not their problem.

It is difficult to write a readable book on N. Ireland. I have started to read a number and have not finished them. Attempting, and rightly so, to set out the detailed and complicated facts involved and to represent the varying points of view and the different interpretations of the same event often makes the book difficult to read. I have written this book from my own perspective. I could find no other way to do it. It is my perspective on the marches and the talks and how we got to where we have. One of the difficulties is illustrated by my use of N. Ireland throughout the book. North is preferred by the nationalists as it suggests the north of the whole of Ireland; Northern is preferred by the unionists, signifying that it is part of the UK.

I have tried to make it a fun and enjoyable book to read, writing primarily for the general reader and not the specialist. I have enjoyed writing it. I haven't written a book before and when I started my keyboard skills were limited. They still are. I can open a file, type quickly enough, save and print. Jon, my husband, has usually been on hand when the text disappears, shrinks or covers only half the screen. When major disasters have happened, the Computer Repair Centre has been on call. Even with their skills they couldn't find 10,000 words I managed to erase a couple of months into writing. I have written every morning six days a week for six months, with the odd day off when tiredness took its toll.

I hope that people will have the same enjoyment in reading the book that I had in writing it. I hope they gain some understanding of why the violence took place and why and how great efforts have been made by many people to achieve peace and make it last.

It is far from over yet, but I hope people in N. Ireland and in the south in the Republic are far enough down the road to peace that despite the many hurdles ahead and the violence and deaths to come that movement continues to be forward and not backward. We must work hard for generations to come to help and not to interfere in the efforts of the people of N. Ireland, as ultimately it is they who will bring the peace and a better future, both north and south.

What I have read and found useful is the work of David McKittrick, David McVea and Eamonn Mallie on general politics; Dominic Bryan and Neil Jarman on the marches; Chris McCrudden on equality; Conor Gearty on civil liberties; and Paul Bew on history.

For the sake of completeness the book also includes my time in opposition preparing for government and how I left N. Ireland to go to the Cabinet Office. The work that I did there particularly on drugs, genetically modified foods and reform of government is included too. My story ends with what I learnt, why I left and what I am planning to do now.

This book was made possible by the work and actions of many people. Let me start with my husband Jon, and with Nigel Warner. Jon has me for better or worse since our marriage in 1995. Nigel and I worked together through thick and thin for more than eight years. Both were invaluable in the help they gave in writing this book. It wouldn't have been the same without them – many, many thanks to them both.

Many other people helped with providing facts and figures as I went along. I would especially like to thank Tracey Temple, Miles Beale, Robert Cayzer, John Fuller, Arlene McCreight, Ken Lindsay, Bill Jeffrey, Jonathan Stephens, Conor Gearty and particularly John McKervill. Also John Harrison, photographer in Belfast, Doug Moodie of the *Gazette* on Teesside and *North News* who helped with the photos.

I would also like to thank the people of Redcar (and all my staff there) who made it possible by electing and supporting me throughout the years.

Those who participated in the talks process showed a courage and commitment to lasting peace that I will never forget, and I thank them all. Many others – civil servants, the police, the army, the voluntary sector, business people and trade unionists – played their part, usually away from the glare of publicity. And of course the media. Despite an up-and-down relationship with them, I have many good friends in the press and on TV and radio who at times as reporters, editors or commentators did their best to move the peace process forward.

Finally I would like to thank those from overseas who worked to make progress. Without George Mitchell it would not have been possible. Likewise his co-chairs in the talks, Hari Holkeri and John de Chastelain. From the US: the Clintons, Bill and Hillary, Madeleine Albright, Jim Lyons; from Europe, Monika Wulf-Mathies and Presidents Santer and Gil Robles; from South Africa, Nelson Mandela; and many, many others from across the world all gave support and encouragement to the peacemakers at times when they needed it most.

But above all I want to thank the people of N. Ireland and the Irish Republic. Many of them have given years of their lives to help bring about peace and will never be properly thanked for all they have done, and many have lost loved ones and will always feel their loss. They helped to educate me and by voting yes in the 1998 referendum helped give the peace process the momentum it needed.

Whether in Belfast or in the Cabinet Office in London I enjoyed working with many colleagues, including the Ministers Adam Ingram, Paul Murphy, Tony Worthington, Alf Dubs, John McFall, George Howarth, Ian McCartney, Graham Stringer, Margaret Jay and Charlie Falconer, as well as Ivor Roberts, Chris Maccabe and a host of civil servants, my parliamentary private secretaries Helen Jackson and Margaret Moran, my special advisers Nigel, Andrew Lappin and Anna Healy, and expert advisers Mike Trace and Louise Casey.

Thanks to you all.

Mo Mowlam
February 2002

I
Go For It

I gave up smoking in December 1996. We were having Christmas, Jon and I with his children, H and Freddie, in Glandore, County Cork, Ireland. It was not the first time we had been to Cork – thanks to the generosity of a good friend, Margaret Jay, we had visited a number of times before. We had had some wonderful trips there, walking, boating, dancing, singing and just relaxing and having fun. We had decided to do something different for the New Year, so we set off by car for Dingle Bay across the Kerry hills. It might not have been the wisest of decisions as Jon had a bad cold and a twisted ankle, so to say the least he was not very mobile. But Margaret and her husband Mike had arrived and we didn't want to outstay our welcome.

I too had a bad cold and cough, and like every other time I was ill I gave up smoking, but for some reason this time it worked – goodness knows why. I can only put it down to the wonderful Cork air, which is almost mystical in its softness and beauty. Ironically, I stopped smoking just a few weeks before I had any idea that I had a tumour.

We set off across the hills of Kerry, a sunny, fresh day. The views were spectacular as we climbed the hills and hit the snow line. Increasingly as I drove along it became impossible to tell what was road and what was not; it was very scary as a real blizzard began in earnest. When we reached the top of the pass I would have turned round, if it had been possible, but the road was so narrow, the snow so deep and the drop so precipitous that there was no option but to go straight on. Having got down the other side and into Tralee without a cigarette I felt I could give up. Since then, I have only had two cigarettes, both during the final negotiations of the Good Friday Agreement in 1998.

We stayed in Tralee as the snow was too bad for us to try and get to Dingle Bay. Tralee I am sure has a lot of interesting entertainments, but between Christmas and New Year there was very little on offer. In fact the only places open apart from the odd shop were the bars. Having visited all the bars that take families, we finally left the town with two children who could play a fair game of pool, darts not so well (the dart board was a bit high for them), but pretty whiz at cards and dominoes. I thought then that this experience would help if and when they went to college; and later, when H obtained the grades to get her into Trinity in Dublin, I thought her well prepared.

We returned to London via the ferry to Swansea. There had been quite a swell, which had kept us awake as we listened to the creaking ship. Fred staggered off as we landed in Wales feeling sick. We headed back to London in the car, but soon had to stop to allow Fred to throw up at the side of the road. Jon helped him, as I can't handle sick, and at the same time he jokingly told Fred that he should not worry about being sick – it was a natural reaction to being in Wales. Fred, for some reason, although he was only nine, has always remembered these words. He cannot resist telling this story whenever we have Welsh friends over.

When I got back to London I realized I had forgotten that I had a scan booked at the Charing Cross Hospital in Hammersmith. I had been ill on and off throughout 1996, nothing so debilitating that I had to stop work for any length of time, just a series of colds, flu, bad coughs and sore throats. I assumed I was just run down. In July I had a bad attack of bronchitis and the doctor came out to see me. I wasn't worried, as I had had an annual attack of bronchitis ever since I was a child. My mother used to worry that I would become immune to the yearly intake of penicillin. It became an annual joke at the House of Commons. Dennis Turner, an MP with a generous spirit and good humour, used to offer to rub my chest with whiskey and honey. The closest he ever got was to make such a concoction for me to drink.

The doctor noticed what I had been ignoring for some time, that occasionally my right hand would shake uncontrollably. I said it was nothing, but I agreed that if it did not go away I would see him again. Inevitably I ignored both him and the arm. Later in the year a good friend of mine, another doctor, and I were together in Redcar, my constituency in Cleveland. She also noticed the shaking hand and insisted, as she was no longer in general practice, that I go and see a friend of hers when I returned to London the following week. (Interestingly my friend had given up general practice to do a counselling course as she had decided that most of her patients, particularly the women, needed counselling rather than medical help.) Obediently I saw her friend and hence had the scan arranged for early in January 1997.

Kate, my assistant from the House of Commons office, came with me. They did the scan twice, for some reason, though I was not worried – I didn't really register why they had done it a second time. The scan itself was such a horrible experience, as I was totally enclosed and unable to move. To cope with my feelings of panic I did what I would do many times in the future: I set myself a problem to take my mind off the claustrophobia. As I sat waiting to see the doctor it slowly dawned on me that they had done it a second time because they had seen something abnormal and wanted to be sure. As I have done all my life with a difficult situation, I ignored it until I had to act. I suppose I learnt this living with an alcoholic father.

I saw a number of doctors, and luckily found two I could relate to; one a young surgeon who was very kind and straightforward, Dr Peterson, and the other a consultant who understood me right away and is now a firm friend, Dr Glaser. Jon, having been called by Kate, came to the hospital, so all three of us heard the news of what the scans revealed together. I remember Jon as calm, although I know now that inside this was far from how he was feeling. The young surgeon was very clear. He said it was serious, exactly how serious it was difficult to say until he had got into my skull and had a look. Amazingly, we listened as though this was a perfectly normal situation, although the news we were being given was pretty devastating. We left with instructions to return for the operation to investigate the nature of the tumour in four or five days' time.

We gathered our thoughts at the Café Rouge across the road from the hospital in Hammersmith. Such a normal setting for such an abnormal meeting. Basically we agreed that there was nothing we could do until we knew the exact nature of the tumour. Kate said she would clear the diary for the time I would be having the operation and we would take it from there. We did not mention the possibility of my having a stroke when the investigative operation – the biopsy – took place. Our overall calm hid varying degrees of panic.

I am very good at coping with difficult situations – by burying them until I have to deal with them. Or, as people that know me put it, I have a great ability to avoid what I don't want to face up to. Growing up, I would shoot upstairs immediately a meal had finished to do my homework. Often I actually did the work; just as often I would settle down with a good novel instead. I used to cover all my books in brown paper to protect them, and also so no one would know whether I was reading a history textbook or *Black Beauty*. My sister Jean says my homework became a great excuse to avoid doing the washing-up and drying-up after dinner. Growing up in a family with an alcoholic had its problems. I learnt to live with stress and just keep going. A useful lesson for the N. Ireland peace talks! I often used to worry in my teens and twenties about drinking too much. The experts always say that children of alcoholics often turn out as drinkers too. My worry was increased by my mum always saying how like him I was. I have always enjoyed a drink, but now I have turned fifty I know I have avoided following in his footsteps. We coped as a family. Money was short, but thanks to my mother we managed. She worked hard all her life to keep us together, often doing two jobs. It was never easy. I very rarely brought friends home in case he was wandering around half dressed, or in a drunken state, slurring his words, or worse had fallen over and gone to sleep. Things got easier when my brother was old enough and strong enough to stand up to him. I coped by closing off the difficult times and do not find it easy going back and writing and talking about them. Sadly my father died in 1979. He had been suffering from cancer, but I was never sure whether the alcohol or the cancer got him first. We all miss him.

My main concern on being told about the tumour was whether it was so serious that if we won the election I would be too ill to take part in government. I had spent so much of my adult life either in Parliament, teaching politics or practising it that not to achieve government would have been crushing. I believe now that the determination to make government was the crucial medicine that kept me going through the dark days of the radiotherapy and steroids. Jon, I think, found it disturbing that this idea was so overwhelming. With hindsight I can see why.

I also wanted to keep the news of the tumour from friends and the public because I instinctively knew from other difficult times in my life that I coped best if I emotionally buried the problem. For that reason, I also didn't tell my mother. When eventually I told her she was hurt, but I couldn't have got through emotionally as well as I did if I had had to find the strength to answer to loved ones and friends about how I felt all the time. On the same grounds I didn't tell my sister. It would have been a weight for her to carry along with her work, family and looking after Mum on a day-to-day basis, which was demanding enough in itself. It wasn't too difficult not telling other folk because everyone I knew was fixated on the election. If calls came in it was quite reasonable that I was either sleeping or campaigning, and so I didn't have to lie about being unavailable. I think it was a difficult time for the people I did tell, such as Jon and Kate, because they had to be the public face. Did I feel bad about not telling others? No, not in terms of coping, and when the news began to break in the press I just told the truth, which seemed to satisfy most people.

The hardest week (I was very fortunate it was only a week; some people have to wait a lot longer in other hospitals) was between knowing I had a tumour and not knowing the seriousness of it. Would we be on holiday in the summer as if all was normal again? Would I be well enough to be in government? Would I still be alive in a couple of months or not? The week of not knowing was a tough one. Jon and I saw no point in engaging in 'what if' questions, but equally there was a clear understanding between us that this was potentially shattering. Once we understood the basics we cuddled a lot and carried on as normal, though it is possible that our intake of whiskey went up that week. My main memory is going with Jon to see *Evita* at the cinema. We had neither of us realized that Evita herself had died of cancer.

Dr Glaser, now my regular, was good. He talked to me a lot and understood why I wanted to keep it quiet. There was also no problem with the staff. At this point I was a relatively well known Opposition politician, but nothing to get excited about. I was worried about news leakage in the form of another doctor who had treated a colleague from Parliament, Jean (Baroness) Denton, who had also been diagnosed with a brain tumour. Ironically she was in N. Ireland as a Minister in the Major administration, a highly respected one. She was doing an excellent job in getting industry interested in investing in N. Ireland, for which her contacts from her time working at Rover were no doubt useful. When I entered government I entertained the idea of keeping her officially involved, because in N. Ireland jobs would be a crucial element in any future agreement. People would need to see some progress, some positive changes if they were to have a belief that any peace process could work. However the idea was treated with horror by both the newly appointed Ministers and the civil servants. Her doctor took an interest in my case, as he had recognized me when I went in for my scan. Fortunately Dr Glaser managed to handle him without me getting involved. I kept in touch with Jean during her last few years and witnessed her steady decline. When she died in February 2001, I spoke at her funeral in Battersea. It was very sad. She is a constant reminder to me of how lucky I have been.

I went into hospital about a week after the initial scan just wanting to get the operation over. I knew what the bottom line was. In the frank and very helpful discussion we had had with the surgeon about the operation to ascertain the state of the tumour, I knew that it could result in a stroke and, worse, that it could reveal that the tumour would be fatal. I think Jon found my stay in hospital worse than I did. I slept most of the time, and while he waited for me to wake up he would look at people in the other beds in the ward – at least one of whom died during the time I was there.

I closed my mind to what was going on. Until I knew what the damage was, I slept as much as I could to avoid thinking about it. I had odd moments of panic – was this going to be the end for me? But I used to talk myself down from those scary moments, telling myself to wait until I knew what the facts were. I also found that if my brain would not switch off I could think of holidays and relive in my head the best bits. I also told myself that I had made the right decision not to tell people because I found coping by myself so much easier.

The relief I felt when I learnt that it was not going to be life-threatening was incredible – although of course I knew that my condition was still quite serious. I was offered radiotherapy now or after the election. I decided to get it out of the way, as I felt this would interfere least in my being able to get on with what I hoped would be my job in N. Ireland. Luckily I did not have to have chemotherapy. The moment when the weight of dread was lifted was one I will never forget. I had not allowed myself to believe that I was going to die. On the way back home that day Jon's sense of relief was evident in his face and every bone in his body. Kate, who kept her emotions in more than anybody, even smiled. She was always there gently helping and thinking about what needed to be done. She managed the whole of the work front, which was not easy. She more than anybody got me through.

At the first of many visits to the hospital I had a face mask fitted to hold me still during the radiotherapy. The mask was very constricting, and again I had to think of holidays to stop me panicking when it was put on. I learnt to cope with this and the scans by arriving every morning for the radiotherapy with an idea or problem to think about and sweets to suck. A lot of people who have written to me about radiotherapy say that for them the claustrophobic experience of the mask was worse than having their hair fall out. For me it was all much the same degree of hell.

One technique I developed to distract me during the radio-therapy – which was very thought-consuming and therefore very useful – was to go back in my mind through my time in Parliament. I always started with my arrival at Westminster in 1987. I had walked in through the main car entrance and was walking along the pavement edge – the cobbles are lethal on heels – eating an ice-cream when I was told off by one of the security police because it was undignified behaviour. I think a lot has changed in Parliament since then. Thankfully it has become less 'dignified' in that way, less stuffy. My memories of the first year are happy ones. I made a lot of good friends, among MPs and House staff. The penguins, as I used to call the Parliamentary messengers in their long coats and stockings, slowly relaxed and on the long nights of voting were always ready for a joke and a laugh. I found it a very comfortable and warm working environment. Yes, some of the facilities are poor and the lack of a crèche is appalling (particularly for the hundreds of female staff members), but I was very content. It is a great club to be a member of.

I was privileged to be appointed early on to the Public Accounts Committee, which is important for holding Whitehall accountable. When I joined, Bob Sheldon (then MP for Ashton-under-Lyne) was chair of the committee. I learnt a lot from him and admired him. We left the House at the same time, in 2001, he taking with him a breadth of knowledge and experience which it is difficult to replicate. I also learnt a lot about other departments in government and how government actually worked. I was a very junior member on the committee, but was treated as an equal by the other members, although not always by some of the civil servants that came before us. One recollection is when the permanent secretary from Agriculture came before us to give evidence. When it was my turn to ask a question, the permanent secretary asked in a very patronizing tone how he should address me, Miss or Ms. I replied, 'Just call me doctor.' The word obviously went around because after that I never got any similar stupidities from others who came before the committee.

Then, as the radiotherapy machine continued to hum, I would turn my mind to the time when Neil Kinnock called me in to see him – more formally than he sometimes did – to offer me a job as a junior shadow Minister for N. Ireland. Neil was very keen to promote women and give them experience so that he had a balanced ministerial team. I have never been sure why he chose me. I have always believed, but have no idea if it is true, that Neil offered the then shadow Secretary of State for N. Ireland, Kevin McNamara, three names to choose from. In a recent debate in the Parliamentary Labour party (PLP) we had discussed the Labour party's position on abortion. All three women on the list for the N. Ireland job were pro a woman's right to choose, and I had argued in the PLP for such a right, but I had also supported a free vote. A free vote meant it would be harder to get through, but I could not justify forcing members of the PLP who were devout Catholics to vote against their strongly held beliefs. I have always thought that that's why Kevin – himself a Catholic – gave me the job.

By the time I got this far into my Parliamentary career, the scan was usually over.

When I knew exactly what was going on I told two other people. The first was Nigel, my political adviser who had been with me since 1992. We had worked together on a whole range of policies which my shadow ministerial positions had thrown up. These included public service reform, the City, the arts and media, and of course N. Ireland. Our futures were and still are bound together and he had a right to know. When Jon first told him, 'They've found something in Mo's brain, but they are not sure what it is,' Nigel replied, 'It's probably a list of things to do.' (As you will discover, I love lists.) I knew that when he was told what was going on he would file it away and that would be that.

The other person I told was Tony Blair. I asked for a meeting but he called on the phone instead. I told him I had been diagnosed with a benign brain tumour, that I was having radiotherapy and coping well and that it was not a problem. I considered it a private matter, but I felt I had an obligation to tell him. He asked how I was and I told him that I was fine and going to be okay. He was solicitous and concerned but when I reassured him he thanked me and asked that I keep him informed. He obviously had enough on his mind with the election so close that my reassurances were enough to satisfy him.

As the weeks went by, coping with the treatment got tougher and tougher. I used to arrive home knackered and just crawl into bed. Apart from when he was putting a whiskey in my hand and saying good night, Jon says, we didn't really talk for most of February and March that year.

I remember my last public engagement with hair was in February 1997 at the fiftieth birthday party in Glasgow of my old friend Adam Ingram (MP for East Kilbride), a robust Glaswegian. Adam and I had entered the House of Commons at the same time, and he is one of my closest friends in politics. The evening did not start well. I was coming from a Labour party event by train and had arranged to meet Jon, H and Freddie at Glasgow station. They had flown up earlier and hired a car. We were all going to drive from central Glasgow to attend the party in East Kilbride. Unfortunately neither Jon nor I knew that Glasgow has two railway stations. He was therefore at one of them with the kids waiting for me, while I was at the other waiting for them. We eventually met between the two as we had finally worked out the problem, and arrived late at the community hall where the party was under way. The main event of the evening was just starting – a *This Is Your Life*-type entertainment, with Adam sitting in a grand chair, as people from his past emerged to recount embarrassing stories of his youth. After the main event I did a little Scottish dancing, which I enjoyed, and then sat and watched Fred, who danced the night away with a whole selection of Scottish MPs' wives.

At the time there were dire warnings coming from some of N. Ireland's unionists suggesting that unless I was more understanding towards them after the election there would be violence. I sat at the party thinking about this, but I was too tired to be anything but determined to resist in the face of such blatant threats. With hindsight that was the right response.

Jon departed for Jordan on business in the middle of February. It was only for a week but I missed him terribly. Not so much for the witty conversation – we communicated more by grunts at this stage – as for his constant, solid presence, which was a comfort when I was feeling down. The radiotherapy at times made me feel slightly sick. But Kate used to look after me so well I could get through the tough days. She or Nigel would always be there, supported by Katherine and Sarah, who also worked in my office at the time. Kate would always have chocolate, water and jellybabies ready for me or would just let me sleep in the car or train, waking me up in time to wash my face, put on some perfume and learn the name of the town and the name of the group I was meeting or the person I was campaigning for. Then she would get me out of the train at the right station, and steer me in the direction of the welcoming party. And off I would go.

The radiotherapy took its toll not just by sapping my energy, but also by taking my hair. The worst was avoided on advice from my hairdresser, Anthony Yacomine – I just cut it all off. This was a very helpful piece of advice that I have passed on to other women who have written or phoned me to share their experiences on how to cope. It was particularly valuable because it gave me at least some control over what was happening and stopped me feeling a complete victim. Anthony was a great support to me at this time. Like most women I dreaded the hair loss, and his practical help and advice were invaluable. He made it less of a big deal. He is a Glaswegian Italian, warm, sensitive, honest and direct, a good person whom I never thought of as a supportive friend until I realized that I always felt so much more positive after seeing him. When I first told him of the impending hair loss he immediately went into action. He told me to buy a wig early on and explained that he would cut it in the same style as my hair. This he did, although it required quite a radical change in hairstyle, from long and on my shoulders to a variation on a pudding-bowl cut.

It became harder and harder not to tell H. She would often wander into our bedroom or bathroom early in the morning or late at night, and hiding my baldness was becoming absurd. So Jon told her what was wrong and that I was going to be okay. She didn't seem to worry. Mid-teens are not easy; and, as she was a victim of divorce, having to please four adults rather than just two must sometimes have seemed an unfair burden. She has always been very attentive and kind. Despite telling H, we decided not to tell Fred as he was still very young. But we need not have worried – he found out soon enough, simply by walking into our bedroom one morning and noticing I had no hair. We talked about it, and that was that. Apart from him trying on my wig and poncing about in it, all was well.

Both H and Freddie were a great help during this time, without them necessarily being aware of it. Just by being there they were a tremendous incentive not to get depressed or fall asleep. They seemed to accept that for most of the time I was either campaigning or sleeping. Also they were company and support for Jon, who had by now spent the best part of the year living with someone who was not really there. H particularly, being that bit older and very close to her dad, was marvellous. I remember coming home once and they were sitting on the settee chatting away like a couple of oldies. They get on well, and H was a real support to Jon during this time. She always watched out for Fred. Even when he was driving her mad and she didn't want to see him, you knew that if he was in trouble she would be there for him. I think she carried a feeling of responsibility from the early days of the divorce. I often thought the hardest part of divorce is the exchange of kids from one parent to the other. I still have images in my head of H taking Fred's hand as they left the car to go back to mum. At least we had cars. I often see single men in Redcar at the weekend having time with their child. Out of their hostel or one-room flat they walk them along the sea front trying to be dad – little money and no transport to do anything else. It is a heartbreaking sight.

Only afterwards did I realize how supportive Jon had been, with very little response from me. It was during the previous general election in 1992 that Jon and I had got together. We had met each other in the 1980s when Jon was both a socialist and an international banker in the City, a rare combination. I used to call him a banker-wanker and still do. He was then trying to encourage support for the Labour party among his City colleagues – a difficult and, some suggested, a dangerous task if promotion is desired. He set up an organization called the Smithfield Group, which arranged regular meetings in the crypt of St Mary-le-Bow Church in Cheapside, where he invited Labour MPs to come and speak. Few were keen, but among those that did go were Paul Boateng, Ken Livingstone, John Prescott, Diane Abbott and me.

As shadow spokesperson for the City and Financial Affairs I also became an active member of the fund-raising 1000 Club, of which Jon was also a founder member along with the novelist Ken Follett. This was an attempt to raise funds from wealthy middle-class supporters of the Labour party. It was called the 1000 Club because the aim was to raise £1000 from a thousand people every year. This was a very useful initiative and was one of the first steps to try and widen the base of the party. The Smithfield Group was founded to try and create more understanding between the party and the City, rather than just settle for a knee-jerk reaction of prejudice on both sides. It was a big hill to climb, as evidenced by the few MPs who were willing to attend, but this was the small beginnings of a broader initiative in the party, which became known as the prawn-cocktail offensive. During this time of eating for Labour I gained a lot of confidence. Eating lunch in boardroom after boardroom I learnt much about the City, but I also learnt how lacking in confidence even the most powerful men can be under their cover of arrogance. Crack a joke at their expense, ask the other woman present how many lunches she had attended (the answer was, always, this is the first), and the men would become slightly less overbearing. Humour made them more human.

After our initial meetings Jon and I talked occasionally, mostly about City matters. We got on, but that was all to begin with. He was married, and a couple of years earlier I had had a serious affair with a married man ending in a lot of pain all round which had decided me never to go down that path again. In the run-up to the 1992 election I was excited and busy and, though I was also lonely, I decided there was no point in moping around: I would just have to get out and spend time with people.

I had a very well kitted-out kitchen in my flat at Black Prince Road in Kennington, close to Parliament, but dinner parties were not on as I couldn't cook. My mother had come down from Coventry to London when I moved into the flat and she worked hard buying carpets, furniture and everything a flat needed – something she enjoyed doing. As a result it looked very smart. I lodged there during the week, returning every weekend to Redcar. Driving back to Redcar on a Thursday night was fine if the last vote was at 7 p.m. If it was at 10 p.m. it was a hard drive in terms of tiredness but it was usually a little quicker as the roads were clear and I could go faster, sometimes cutting five hours down to four something. One night early in 1992, just the other side of Doncaster on the A1, I pulled over just after 2 a.m. for a rest as I was getting tired. I was just closing my eyes as the passenger door opened and a large hunky Scot got in, saying he was amazed I'd seen him hitching on the side of the road. I quickly gathered my thoughts, didn't have time to be scared, and decided it would be more dodgy to try and get him out, so I started the engine. He was a cook off the boats, going home to Glasgow. He chatted happily all the way to Darlington, where I dropped him.

Back in Redcar, I decided to invite folk up to my house there because it was much bigger than my flat, as well as by the sea, although it has to be said it was a long way from London. It had the advantage of picnics on the beach and barbecues in the garden, which meant very limited cooking. I invited a whole host of folk, including Jon and his wife Geraldine and their children. I had eaten at their house before to meet potential donors to the party, and for help with policy research in preparing for government. Little did I know that when Jon and his family accepted it was the last weekend when he and his wife would appear in public as a couple. In fact they had already split up and had decided to get divorced. Jon had specifically asked his wife to come as he felt it would be awkward if he came to visit me as a separated man.

As the weekend approached, Geraldine found she could not make the Friday night anyway, but promised to come on the Saturday morning. Jon arrived with the kids on Friday night, having got lost in Leeds on the way up and therefore not arriving until almost midnight. The kids went exhausted to bed. He and

I sat and talked over a whiskey. As the conversation progressed he explained what was happening with his marriage. The weekend was a strange one, but we all got through it. I still have the bizarre image in my head of us all sitting on the beach using saucepans and large spoons as buckets and spades.

After that weekend in Redcar, Jon and I had dinner a couple of times, and were getting on very well now. But the election was imminent and things were put on hold as I spent my time travelling all over the country. It was inevitably a chaotic time. After the election was over, and lost to John Major, Jon just arrived at my Black Prince Road flat and never seemed to leave. There was a period just before that which I call the 'green bag' phase. He used to arrive after work with a little green bag with all his goodies, a change of underwear and socks and family bills he had just picked up, and slowly more and more items involved with cooking, books and specialized bits that my kitchen had never experienced. When he had first arrived, the only contents of the fridge had been Lean Cuisine's frozen food, needing only a microwave to warm it up. Now all that changed.

I was not kitted out to accommodate two young children. Little did I realize then what changes were ahead. I had never made a conscious decision not to have children. Earlier in my life, I had travelled a lot and changed jobs two or three times and the option of settling down had not been on the cards. I didn't regret it then and don't now. In many ways I feel that I have had the best of both worlds, no pain of childbirth, no full-time responsibility for children, but a great deal of pleasure and excitement in sharing in their growing up. The enjoyment is still with me. It is great, for instance, to hear eighteen-year-olds saying what they think on different topics like drugs or wars. It keeps us from becoming too set in our ways or our views.

We had very happy, but at times not easy, years up to the 1997 election. We had a year in Black Prince Road before moving to a two-bedroom flat in Dolphin Square in Pimlico, just up the road from Westminster. While at Black Prince Road, we had to put the kids in our bed together, so that we could sit and work or watch TV in the sitting room. We then unfolded the settee, transferred the kids to that and went to bed. We had them with us every other day and every other weekend. It was a bit chaotic, but we all mucked in and made it fun rather than a chore. It was a great relief to move to two bedrooms in Dolphin Square.

We also did some entertaining in the new flat. It was wee but I can remember one dinner party with Tony Blair and Howard Davies, who was then head of the CBI. There was a long economic discussion with Tony and Howard having different views and Jon disagreeing with both. We were a bit short on furniture and the Blairs offered us their old kitchen table. It fitted perfectly into the flat and is still going strong in the kitchen in Redcar.

Coping with the lack of space in London was helped by making the journey to Redcar at weekends. We survived the long journey by having picnic meals in the car to keep everyone going, and by having two sleeping bags on the back seat to maximize sleeping time for the kids. When we go up now without the kids Jon breathes a sigh of relief that we don't have to play I-Spy or the Word Game – capitals, rivers, countries – or sing Beatles or ABBA songs. We were stopped by the police once because we had the children in the back in sleeping bags without seat belts and because I had been driving with a sausage in one hand conducting and singing away. Luckily I got away with a warning. Actually, unlike Jon, I quite enjoyed the games because it broke up the tedium of the long journey. Despite the hassles, it was a very happy time. Occasionally now when Jon and I drive back and forth to Redcar, which we do in the middle of the week to minimize traffic hassles, I sing some of the old songs, beautifully in my tone-deaf voice. He drowns me out with the radio.

During my time in opposition I learnt a lot that would be useful to me later in the jobs I did when I was in cabinet. Doing just over a year (1989–90) as a shadow Minister in N. Ireland was invaluable. I picked up a lot from Kevin McNamara and his assistant Jim Marshall that I couldn't have got from books or the news, like the crucial importance of the whole issue of human rights – that it's not just about equality and fundamental rights for every human being, but is an important litmus test to the Catholic population showing that you are willing to address issues that are important to them and to take their problems seriously. I also began to understand the mindsets of the two sides: why they feel as they do and why they find compromise so difficult.

So my first stint in N. Ireland gave me a good grounding on the issues for when I returned as shadow N. Ireland Secretary in 1994. In the intervening years, I kept an eye on developments in the peace process – not because I imagined I would return, but because once you have engaged in the problems of N. Ireland it is very difficult to let go. Once in post as shadow Secretary of State, I and the other shadow Ministers used what spare time there was to think and work out our longer-term strategy as well as responding to day-to-day issues as they arose. In policy terms we concentrated on matters like human rights and fairness, policing and parades, and the economic questions we would have to address in government. We were helped by academics like Conor Gearty at the University of London, Brendan O'Leary at the London School of Economics and Chris McCrudden at Oxford. But I learnt most of all from going across to N. Ireland almost every week to talk to people, to listen and make contact. This had the advantage not only of expanding my knowledge, but also of giving me a much better understanding of who, if we were elected, I would be working with.

Other areas I worked on in opposition helped too to equip me better for the challenges I would face in government. My job as shadow Minister on City Affairs was of less direct use, but was very helpful. Personally it taught me confidence and an understanding of risk, from folk who spend their lives making risk assessments. It taught me what can be done with a little

knowledge and a lot of confidence, and it gave me a large number of contacts, many of whom were useful when trying to encourage people to think about investing in N. Ireland.

I learnt a great deal about the importance of working with – and not just for – a group of people from my time as spokesperson on women's issues: if you are inclusive from the beginning, then change is easier to deliver. With women all issues are women's issues, and just trying to get them tagged on to policy announcements doesn't really help anybody. I concluded that to have a separate women's ministry is good window dressing, good to build the morale of women, but doesn't help get women any closer to power. I think the best model to fight for equality is to have a team of people or a unit in No. 10 so that every time the Prime Minister breathes on a policy issue the unit is there, to get decent legislation in place including a delivery mechanism to ensure that a policy like equal pay is actually happening – not to mention a mechanism to take men with you. Until attitudes begin to shift, equality will continue to be elusive.

To take men with you is important if women are to achieve real change. I think this could happen if we tackle some of the inequalities in law which are now hitting men, say on divorce and access to their children. But nothing will make quicker progress than having a committed person at the top.

When I did it, the Women's Ministry was tagged on to the position of shadow Minister for the Cabinet Office, a job that gave me an opportunity to offer encouragement and support to people in public service, who often get such a bad press. I understood then the drive that was going on to modernize the structures and systems of government and the civil service, but it was also clear to me that it had to be at least a ten-year cross-party plan if it was going to be successful. The urgency of modernization became clear to me eight years later when, as Cabinet Office Minister, I met a number of visiting Ministers from Britain's ex-colonies who were very keen to learn how we were coping trying to update our government and civil service structures – just the sort of structures we had left them with.

Dealing with National Heritage issues (1993–4) introduced me to the joys of the new technologies like the 'information superhighway' (the Internet) and the impact of the digital revolution. I learnt a lot and could see great opportunities in terms of employment and in terms of growth in new and exciting technology. I also discovered that government is not the only institution slow to deliver and bureaucratic to the point of inactivity: welcome to the BBC. ITV by its very nature was more flexible, but the backbiting in both organizations made politicians look cuddly. I also met a good number of media people, journalists at the chalk face, but also the top management – useful people to know. The work I did on the sports front gave me a much better understanding of the importance of sport in holding communities together and giving people a sense of belonging. Its value in building people's confidence was wonderful to see. I learnt a lot too about the cultural industries

– music, art, sculpture, theatre, film. I worked with shadow Culture Minister Mark Fisher on all these areas, putting together our policy programme for the next election. I wanted to make sure libraries didn't miss out, and the smaller community theatres, but I have to admit to a bias against the opera and ballet. I think as a result of that job I became a more rounded person, finding artworks and sculptures I loved. We also ended up with some good policies, thanks to the knowledge of people like Mark and my desire to talk to and include as many folk as possible with expertise in all these fields.

After the radiotherapy in early 1997, I was put on a course of steroids. These are terrible things because they make you very rapidly put on weight. In fact the weight gain was so fast I did not realize how fat I was becoming. By the time the election came I had got a lot bigger, and began to need to buy a lot of new clothes. I have always been awful at choosing clothes and have always hated doing it. My sister or friends used to do it for me. My old friend Betty Boothroyd, who was then the Speaker of the House of Commons, was a great help. She put me in touch with her favourite clothes shop, La Chasse, run by Mr Crown with his wonderful staff. I was a little reticent at first as I thought the shop's stock was too old for me, but whenever I went I found something I liked and the price was less than where I had shopped before. And the best thing, particularly in view of my weird size, was that they altered free of charge dresses that I bought so that they would fit me.

Mr Crown will probably not thank me for the mention, because I always manage not to look smart, and seem to have a reputation for being a little dishevelled. Anthony used to despair when I had hair, and does again now when I have a little, that I look so unsmart on television that he always hopes people don't know he is my hairdresser. (After the general election in 1997 I was also greatly helped by Adam, one of my close team of protection officers, who remained with me until my protection was removed in early 2000. Over the years we built up a firm friendship and he also had an excellent clothes sense, so whenever I needed something I went with Adam, as I could almost always rely on his choice.)

As Speaker of the House of Commons, Betty had a very grand residence in the Palace of Westminster. Part of it is for official functions, but there also goes with it a very comfortable flat, located in the tower nearest to Westminster Bridge – the one that does not have Big Ben in it. I have always been close to Betty, and we had holidayed together in the past. One day she met me in the Commons and insisted that I go and see her in private. She knew something was wrong and wheedled it out of me. Once I had told her she insisted I use her flat to sleep in during the day. She is what friends are all about. She responded to a very practical need that I had – sleep. She did it without fuss and didn't talk to me apart from a 'Hi' if I passed her on the way to my sleep. Her housekeeper Roseanne was an absolute wonder. She would wake me with a cup of tea and marmite toast (heaven) and get me on my way feeling human again. It meant I could do time in the House of Commons and be seen there, before leaving for campaigning or home. It meant I could keep on trucking.

During my treatment what I needed most of all was just to put my head down and keep going. I took each day at a time, getting all the support and help I needed from Jon, H and Fred, Kate and Nigel who worked so closely with me, my doctor and friends like Betty. I think what I went through then made me more accepting of life. I am of the view that you are dealt cards in your life and you live with what you are given. I think the experience made me a little wiser and calmer about life and more able to focus on what's important.

I got the all-clear in July 1997. I had a couple of six-monthly check-ups and since then I have been on yearly check-ups. People often ask how I'm feeling. I try to say 'Very well, thank you,' because I know they care. But my answer is always a little wary, since there have been people asking me to see if they can get a story: that I am not well enough or capable enough to carry on working as I do. I feel fine and count myself very lucky to be as well as I am.

2

Geordie Trucker

PREPARING FOR GOVERNMENT AND SOME HISTORY

In the run-up to the 1997 election I slept a lot. I kept to my daily diary of commitments, most of which were meetings on policy with people who wanted to influence what Labour would do if we got into government. But there were other more particularly memorable occasions too.

One was dinner with Ken Livingstone and his partner Kate. I had been dreading this because at night I was far from my best, and I thought we would get involved in heavy discussions. Fortunately there were only two other guests: the old bastard from the TV sitcom *Drop the Dead Donkey*, David Swift, and his wife Paula, life-long Labour supporters. Before we ate, Ken had us roaming his garden peering into his pond with a torch to observe his mating toads. This was not very exciting, as they lay in the shallows in a static embrace – an activity that takes a very long time. Indeed it can take anything up to three days for an orgasm to happen. I wondered if their sex is more satisfying than ours. We also had a long discussion on the life cycle of newts. I managed to avoid heavy political discussion and just observed Ken and Jon talking and agreeing on most issues. It was a pleasure and a relief to talk newts and not much else.

Another daunting evening do was a dinner at Belfast City Hall – a large gathering, I'd guess about 350 people. I was the after-dinner speaker and eventually stood up at about 11.30 p.m. As usual when I'm on my feet talking away I enjoyed it and the audience found my jokes funnier than usual and listened attentively to what I said. It took every bit of energy I had left. I vowed that night, and have stuck to it ever since, that when speaking at dinners I do so either before the meal or between the first and second courses. You can't as a politician with something serious to say, however limited, speak at the end – you are often tired, and the audience are usually too pissed to listen. I remember on a later occasion talking to the then President of Ireland Mary Robinson about this problem and found that she, like me, no longer speaks at the end of meals. A trend to be encouraged.

I also remember a visit to Prince Charles at Highgrove to discuss N. Ireland. Nigel drove me down there and we joked about needing to keep my dodgy arm still so I didn't spill my tea on the Highgrove carpet. In the end it was a good visit and I didn't shake at all. On arrival we had a quick look at the organic farm and a pleasant, relaxed chat about N. Ireland and life in general. My feelings on the monarchy – which I can't believe he didn't know about – were not on the agenda. I quite liked him. Every year since, I've sent him a Christmas card, in later years a joint one to him and Camilla. The cards I had back were signed by him alone.

As a result of the steroids, my appearance was changing dramatically. But with everyone's minds so focused on the election, I don't think anyone really noticed; or perhaps they were too polite to remark that I'd had a series of rather odd haircuts and put on a lot of weight in the past few weeks. When I say this to friends they say they had noticed but didn't want to comment. I was concerned most of all that one of my friends, such as Adam Ingram, might try to ruffle my hair and discover that it was a wig. So I kept more than my usual distance whenever I thought I might bump into him or other friends in the House of Commons Lobbies.

At that time, I saw quite a lot of the then Tory N. Ireland Secretary, Paddy Mayhew. He was having a bad time. John Major's majority in the Commons was dwindling to nothing, with the threat that he would soon be reliant on the votes of the nine Ulster Unionist MPs to keep him in power. So Paddy's desire to make progress ahead of the election (at which he was standing down) was hamstrung by his party's closeness to one side of the community in N. Ireland. He was so frustrated.

Paddy was a bizarre figure, tall and huge in an old colonial sort of way. People described him as patrician, but he also had a warm and humorous side. Once when we were both leaving a funeral we had attended together, I saw some advantages to his height. We were being harangued by a ferocious woman unionist. She was shouting at Paddy, but he was so tall that I took it in the face. I looked up at him and he was staring straight ahead and quietly muttering, 'Bollocks, bollocks, bollocks,' under his breath until she went away. I think Paddy was grateful for my support and reasonably happy to take me into his confidence. At times, looking over his shoulder at his own back-benchers, he must have thought I was one of the few supporters he had left.

Bipartisanship was important then. It was important for us in the Labour party, because it meant the Tories couldn't use N. Ireland as an issue to attack us on in the run-up to the general election. But, much more important than that, it kept the issue of the peace process above normal party politics, which is where it should be. That didn't mean I couldn't criticize the government when they were getting it wrong, like over the Orange parades or the failed anti-terrorist legislation, but it did mean that on the core issues of the peace process they could rely on Labour's support. It also meant that no party in N. Ireland had any reason to delay making progress in the hope of getting a better deal out of a Labour government than they were getting out of the Tories. It was an important thing to say to stop progress being unnecessarily held up by the election.

Both Labour and the Tories had come a long way in relation to N. Ireland by the time of the 1997 election. The whole peace process had. Relations between the British and Irish governments and the communities in N. Ireland were slowly changing in ways that would have far-reaching consequences in years to come. It was a battle, to start with, to try to understand how people had got to where they were and why such a long and apparently insoluble conflict had arisen. You really have to look back into the history, something I was always wary of – I wanted to look forward to start from where we were and move on. But without an understanding of the history that would always be impossible. I had taught British politics at Newcastle University and so had read my way into the N. Ireland situation back then. My periods in opposition, reading, listening and talking, gave me much more – but I'd be the first to admit that my knowledge is far from encyclopaedic.

The history of division and conflict between Britain and Ireland goes back centuries. Some people trace it back to the twelfth century and beyond, to the Norman invasion of Britain and Ireland and the subsequent wars between rivals for the English throne and their French and Spanish counterparts. Some go back still further into the mists of time. My own understanding is that you should start looking for the roots of the conflict in the Irish wars fought by medieval English kings like Richard II. The religious dimension came to the fore after the Reformation of Henry VIII and his daughter Elizabeth. Fears about the power of the Catholic Church and the potential for Catholic adversaries from France or Spain to use Ireland as a springboard to attack the English throne led to repression of dissent in Ireland and attempts to settle key parts of the island with individuals loyal to the English Crown. This established a pattern for centuries ahead.

The flight from Ireland of the Catholic Irish earls in the early part of the seventeenth century and the settlement in the northern part of Ireland by Protestants, especially from Scotland, began to shape the island's religious and geographical divisions. It also became a war of words with towns like Derry becoming Londonderry when it was settled by Protestants supported from the City of London – a name the Catholic Irish have never accepted and would never use. I remember in 1993 I was speaking to a select committee of MPs in the House of Commons and was corrected by nationalist Seamus Mallon to say Derry, whereupon unionist Ken Maginnis jumped up and said it was Londonderry. They were playing games and laughing a lot, but the language point was reinforced for me. A thought I have had repeatedly is that there is probably a lot more shared now between the Catholics and Protestants of N. Ireland than with the English. For different reasons – as the history indicates – they both see us as the cause of the problems.

The seventeenth-century campaign of persecution by Oliver Cromwell against Catholics in England was shipped over to Ireland with cruel and devastating effect. Later, when the short-lived reign of Catholic King James II came to an end, he fled to France and then to Ireland in the hope of mounting an expedition from there to recapture his throne. The battles between James II and the newly invited King, William of Orange, are crucial and living parts of the memory of Ulster and Ireland. With the help of the French, James tried to rally Ireland against the English but was thwarted in northern cities like Derry, County Londonderry, where the town's Protestants withstood a three-month siege that sapped the strength of James's forces. (Hence the commemoration of the 1689 siege of Derry by Protestant parades in August each year.) William's pursuit of James across Ireland came to a head at the Battle of the Boyne in 1690, where James was defeated. (The 12 July Orange Order marches across N. Ireland commemorate this battle.) Protestant authority was therefore established, with a Parliament in Dublin subordinate to London, and laws passed to restrict the rights of Catholics to own land and property – and hence their political rights: Catholics didn't get the vote in Ireland until 1793, and then most of them fell foul of a property qualification.

The Act of Union of 1801 was meant to bring Britain and Ireland together, but it took another twenty-nine years for Catholics to be granted the right to stand for Parliament in London. The first half of the nineteenth century was a period of growth in Ireland – especially population growth. But a combination of widespread poverty, poor farming and poor weather led to a terrible famine in the 1840s which left about a million people dead, and a million more fled the country – many for America. As Tony Blair acknowledged in 1997, 'Those who governed in London at the time failed their people.'

For much of the nineteenth century, thought was given on both sides of the Irish Sea to establishing home rule in Ireland. Efforts by English Prime Ministers such as the Liberal Gladstone to pass new home-rule laws were thwarted by the House of Lords and by opposition from Protestant members from Ireland. Early in the twentieth century that opposition – led at the time by the founder of the Ulster Unionist party, Edward Carson – continued, contrary to the will of the House of Commons, in the form of a campaign against a new bill granting limited home rule, which was eventually suspended at the onset of the First World War. Seizing their moment in 1916, the campaigners for Irish independence staged a short-lived rebellion in Dublin (commemorated at Easter each year by Irish nationalists with the wearing of lilies, in honour of the leaders of the rebellion who were subsequently executed by English soldiers).

After the First World War, and the failure of the 1916 rebellion, the conflict between British and Irish forces escalated through 1920, when the Liberal Prime Minister Lloyd George passed the Government of Ireland Act offering two Parliaments to Ireland, one in the south and one in the north. In 1921 the leaders of Irish republicanism including Michael Collins signed a treaty in London accepting the establishment of the two Parliaments and the effective division of Ireland into two parts – with twenty-six of Ireland's counties forming the Free State in the south and the remaining six counties forming N. Ireland in the north. The signing of the treaty led to a civil war in the south of Ireland during much of the 1920s between the pro- and anti-treaty factions – who later became the two main political parties in Ireland today, Fianna Fail and Fine Gael.

N. Ireland was established with a Protestant majority of nearly three to one, ruled from Stormont, which became, as the First Prime Minister of N. Ireland and unionist leader Lord Craigavon put it, a 'Protestant Parliament for a Protestant people'. Meanwhile the Free State was declared a republic in 1949; earlier the country's nationalist leader Eamon De Valera had laid down a constitution that claimed by right the territory of N. Ireland as part of that republic.

Opposition to the government in N. Ireland – with its inbuilt Protestant majority and its treatment of the Catholic minority, which is widely acknowledged as having been unfair (or as David Trimble put it in his 1998 Nobel Prize lecture, N. Ireland was a 'cold house for Catholics') – built up in the late 1950s and 1960s into a campaign for civil rights. Alongside the peaceful protests led by men such as John Hume, there was a resurgence of paramilitary violence from the IRA and their loyalist counterparts. Events like Bloody Sunday in 1972, a policy of imprisonment without trial and IRA atrocities all fanned the flames of conflict in the early 1970s. Attempts at resolution – like the Sunningdale settlement of 1973 – were brought down by widespread unionist opposition.

Successive British governments tried and failed to get talks going so that the parties could reach agreement. Attempts at restoring local democracy, like the Assembly of the early 1980s, foundered when one side or the other objected to the pace of change – either too slow for the nationalists or too fast for the unionists. Reforms of institutions like the RUC were proposed and then shelved amid a rising tide of paramilitary violence. British governments tried openly and then secretly to negotiate with the paramilitary groups and their representatives. IRA violence reinforced the siege mentality among Ulster Protestants, while loyalist violence and intimidation reinforced the sense of fear and grievance among N. Irish Catholics.

The first real glimmers of hope came when the British and Irish governments began to work closely together. The 1985

Anglo-Irish Agreement signed by British and Irish Prime Ministers Margaret Thatcher and Garret FitzGerald was a major milestone, accepting for the first time the shared responsibility that both countries had towards the interests of all the people of N. Ireland. In 1993 British and Irish Prime Ministers came together again to sign the Downing Street Declaration in which both governments acknowledged the right of the people of Ireland to self-determination based on consent freely and concurrently given in both N. Ireland and the Irish Republic. More detailed proposals, known as the Framework Documents, were agreed in 1995 between John Major and the new Irish Prime Minister (or Taoiseach), John Bruton, offering a new set of political institutions in N. Ireland which, for the first time, set out how the relationships within N. Ireland, between N. Ireland and the Irish Republic and between Britain and Ireland could be better managed in an atmosphere of peace and growing mutual trust and confidence.

And so the story comes to the more recent past: the progress from agreement between the two governments to talks and agreement between the N. Ireland parties, to referendums of the people north and south, and to all the problems and successes of implementing that agreement and making it stick. Throughout this long and tortuous history, conflicts over land and power have predominated. Throw in a large dose of religion, bigotry and intolerance and an even larger dose of mismanagement and incompetence by generations of rulers and politicians and you begin to get the picture.

Slowly and carefully over the months and years both Labour and Tory policies towards N. Ireland had shifted towards the centre. Throughout the 1980s Labour had argued for a policy of Irish 'unity by consent'. This meant that we would work towards Irish unity but only with the consent of the people of N. Ireland. In reality it was a compromise drawn together in the early 1980s by people like Clive Soley MP (later to become Chair of the Parliamentary Labour party) between those in the party who argued that Britain should withdraw from N. Ireland altogether and those who argued that N. Ireland should stay British unless a majority living there wanted to change.

It was an unhappy position from my point of view because it was never clear to me what we would actually do if elected. Would we try to persuade N. Ireland's unionists that a united Ireland was in their best interests? It was hard to imagine anything more provocative. I had a lot of meetings before the 1997 election with Labour backbenchers interested in N. Ireland and some of the academics that had helped us, as well as with the small but vocal pro-unionist group within the party. Slowly, and doing my best to keep everyone on board, the policy shifted from 'unity by consent' to 'reconciliation between the peoples of Ireland' to 'reconciliation between the two traditions in N. Ireland and to a new political settlement which can command the support of both'. In effect this new formula, outlined in the 1997 election manifesto, put us in a much more neutral position in government to mediate between the two sides and work for agreement between them. We were now fully in line with the latest British–Irish agreements and in a position to offer both continuity and renewed momentum in the peace process.

N. Ireland policy was one of many areas where the Labour party had moved on dramatically beyond the difficulties and divisions of the 1980s – progress made possible as a result of a huge programme of change instigated by Neil Kinnock. I was (and remain) a great supporter of Neil Kinnock. I worked hard in the campaign to get him elected after Michael Foot's resignation when we lost the 1983 election. I will never forget Neil's speech at the People's Theatre in Newcastle as part of his campaign. Hilary Armstrong and I had helped to organize it. It was a speech about the vision for the future that he had for the people of this country, about the poverty and inequalities he despised and what he believed a Labour government could do. There is talk today in politics about a lack of vision for the future. Neil's speech that night was of a vision I shared. It was an amazing performance. I remember watching him speak. Every part of his body was committed to what he was saying; his shirt was wet with the emotion and passion he was putting into it. What I liked best when he spoke was his ability to go from abstract ideas to everyday examples, and with enough humour to keep people engaged. I think it was one of the best political speeches that I have heard, because of the degree of emotional commitment in it. It made me think it must be how another inspiration of mine, Ellen Wilkinson, had sounded in her speeches when she led the Jarrow marchers down to London in 1936. Afterwards I drove Neil across the Pennines to his next speaking engagement. He talked all the way; his energy was amazing. I can remember only being brought down to earth by the sound of discarded beer cans left in the back of my car hitting Hilary's feet as I turned corners.

After Neil became Labour leader I was one of a number of party members who believed the party was going to have to change if we were to ever have a chance of being elected. I don't know how many times in the following years I have said that I am not about changing our beliefs and our values, but I do want us to appeal to a larger section of the public and I do want us to look at how we achieve our aims in the society we live in, which has changed a lot since many of the party policies were written.

I wrote in conclusion to an article in the *Fabian Review* in 1993:

Until the Labour party can mentally make the leap that says aspiring to be middle class is positive, the public will always have trouble believing that we want to represent them or want to help anyone less fortunate. People want more money, a decent house, a good car, and so do people in the Labour party. The changes introduced by the Labour party fifty years ago in health, education and housing gave the post-war baby-boom generation a decent home, free health care and a comprehensive education which made university a possibility.

Some of us who benefited are now middle-class MPs and should work to provide the same economic and social freedoms for the next generation.

In today's political climate, this seems common sense, but at the time it caused a stir. We've come a long way in the intervening years.

I wanted by this article to encourage discussion in the party about the realities of what we needed to face up to if we were to get elected. For example, there was once an acid test in the party to prove your working-class credentials. If you didn't come from a poor background and your parents weren't in manual jobs, then in some way you were less of a socialist. The stupidity of this argument was later made fun of when in conversation about who had had an outside loo or who had shared their bedroom with their siblings someone would end up saying – in *Monty Python* style – 'I was born in a brown paper bag in the middle of the motorway.' It took many years for this 'I'm more working class than you' mentality to die away. There is a difference between respecting the experiences of people who have had to struggle to get on in life and saying that just because others have not struggled in the same way or to the same degree they can't be proper socialists. My husband Jon is a good example of this. He was ridiculed and one night physically threatened in his branch in Dalston Labour party in the 1980s because he has a posh accent and worked in the City. This didn't happen across the party, but it wasn't an isolated incident either. People who were different from what some existing party members thought a Labour member should be were not welcomed and often did not bother to return after the first meeting. For this and many other reasons, change was necessary.

That process of change was started and inspired by Neil. The first necessary step was to deal with the Militant Tendency, which had infiltrated the Labour party in many parts of the country. The Militant Tendency's disregard for Parliamentary democracy resulted in many MPs being undermined in their own constituency parties and drove out newcomers who weren't Militant supporters. The best-known example of this mindset – and its consequences – was in Liverpool, where the Leader of Liverpool Council, Derek Hatton, was a Militant.

Neil had the guts to give leadership and stand up to the Militant Tendency. At the Labour party conference in 1985 he gave a speech that was very brave and passionate and that was, I think, the beginning of the process that made it possible for us to be elected in 1997. In his speech, he slaughtered the Militant Tendency, lambasting the 'grotesque chaos of a Labour council . . . hiring taxis to travel round the city handing out redundancy notices to its own workers'. Hatton, followed by many of his supporters and much noise, walked out of the conference. But the vast majority in the audience cheered. The fight-back had begun to regain control of the party. Neil immediately set about putting a structure in place to support local parties and to deal with the militants. I was asked if I would go to Liverpool as a party worker. While I was thinking about it the party came back and said that Peter Kilfoyle and Jane Kennedy, members of the Unison trade union (then three unions NALGO, COHSE and NUPE) in Liverpool, were going to do the job. Both later became Labour MPs and government Ministers.

The reform process continued through the election defeat of 1992 and the transition from Neil Kinnock to John Smith to Tony Blair. My relations with Neil Kinnock were good. I'd supported him in the leadership campaign and we got on well. When Neil resigned and John Smith took over the leadership after the 1992 defeat, I remained on the front bench. But though John and I rubbed along we were not natural soulmates. After his tragic death I worked for Tony to become leader in 1994. I had got to know him over the years as another MP from the North-east, often meeting up on the train or plane going south to the House of Commons.

As a member of Labour's National Executive Committee I

took part in a major reform project called 'Party into Power'. Seminars were held at Cranfield Business School, for members of the National Executive Committee to discuss our proposals. The task force I convened looked at the relationship between the party and a Labour government, with all the stresses and strains that would be involved. We looked at how previous Labour governments had fared, examined how sister parties in Europe were structured and consulted widely in the party and the trade unions on potential changes. We made some progress overall, for example on helping reverse the marked decline in Labour party membership during the 1980s and early 1990s. We also paid a lot of attention to reform of policy making, which was essential. Before the reforms, Labour policy was debated and decided on at the annual party conference. This had some bizarre results. For instance, one year we debated and decided Labour's whole strategy on N. Ireland in just eight minutes! There was simply not time in a five-day conference to discuss and agree all the key parts of what would make up Labour's policies for the next election. So, as part of the reform process, a National Policy Forum was established, with Regional Policy Forums in each part of the country to enable more party members to have an input into policy all year round, not just one week each October. The forums worked well, but they came in for a fair amount of criticism because they took away some of the aggro at party conferences between the unions, the delegates and the party leadership. There is no doubt that the reforms were necessary to prepare us for government, but equally there is no doubt that they have resulted in a greater centralization of power within the Labour party.

On our approach to N. Ireland we were in pretty good shape by the time of the 1997 election, with a clear and defensible policy established and no one side or the other of the party having been lost along the way. This was not so much because of my skills as because many diehard supporters of Irish unity in the party realized that working with me rather than against me was likely to give them some influence rather than none. Inevitably there were some in the Parliamentary Labour party – who were more loyalist or more republican than the people I would negotiate with in N. Ireland – who didn't agree, but decided to stay quiet.

We concentrated on trying to put together a clear strategy on possible talks: the big picture. But to make progress there were many smaller issues that could not be forgotten. The problems people faced in N. Ireland went across the board and we had to have measures worked out to address them. Unemployment, for example, was then running at 16 per cent, the highest for any part of the UK, and in some places it was as high as 50 per cent. In these areas there were generations that had been out of work and young people, especially young men, who had no hope for the future. To these people the temptations of a life of status and excitement through belonging to one of the paramilitary organizations were very strong. Of course there were lots of other reasons why some people got involved in violence and others didn't, but having no hope of a job or a chance to make your way up in the world was often part of it.

Putting together a workable strategy for jobs and prosperity was an important part of what we did ahead of the election. It had the advantage too of opening doors for discussion with people across the political spectrum without always getting stuck on the big political problems every time. I and the rest of the shadow team, Tony Worthington, Jim Dowd, Eric Illsley and (Lord) Gareth Williams, got over to N. Ireland as often as we could to consult with people on what we were discussing and planning. The Irish Congress of Trade Unions was helpful, especially Inez McCormack from Unison. Many people who worked hard on the ground to make a difference to people's lives, like Brendan Mackin of the Belfast centre for the unemployed, gave a lot of help too.

We also talked to business people, like the head of Ulster Bank, George Quigley, the chief executive of Shorts, Roy

McNulty, and Chris Gibson of the CBI. They wanted to talk about jobs and the economy and how to get more investment into N. Ireland. I made some very good contacts through those discussions with people who would later do a lot more publicity to win support for the peace process. Other so-called 'bread and butter' issues like health and education needed tackling too. I was happy to leave most of the work on these to Tony Worthington and others in the team, and then to discuss them at our weekly meetings. This approach gave Tony and the other shadow Ministers a chance to build up their own reputations and contacts in N. Ireland.

In addition there were lots of other issues like human rights, policing, equality in employment and anti-terrorism that were important to the political parties in N. Ireland and on which we had to have a view and a policy for the future. Again we talked across the board and called in experts and practitioners in the field in London and Belfast. Some folk, like the Quilleys, a Quaker couple in Belfast who allowed their house to be used for meetings, would be a great support throughout my time in N. Ireland. As we formed our opinions ahead of the election they and others like Conor Gearty, Chris McCrudden, Paul Bew (Queen's University Belfast), Paul Arthur (University of Ulster), Robin Wilson (the Democratic Dialogue think tank) and Quintin Oliver (Northern Ireland Council for Voluntary Action) would all be trustworthy and crucial sounding boards for ideas and advice. In discussion forums at colleges in London we thrashed out ideas and discussed ways forward. On occasion, Jonathan Powell and Pat McFadden from Tony Blair's office would attend, people who would continue to be closely involved in the future.

By the time of the election we had quite detailed papers drawn up in all the major policy areas – papers we handed over to senior civil servants who are allowed to meet the Opposition before an election and who begin to prepare their own documents and briefings in case there is a change of government. It was a very useful exercise and, after the election, looking at the package of proposals they put to us (in big documents that all new Ministers get called First-Day Briefs) it was clear they had taken our ideas seriously and made a real attempt to pull together what they called our 'Integrated Approach'.

Many other important relationships were formed in those years in opposition, not least with members of the Irish government and Irish diplomats and key people in the US like Senator George Mitchell and the Clintons. We could not have done as much as quickly as we did in government in N. Ireland without all the preparation that went into nearly two and a half years in opposition. It was an immensely valuable time, helped no doubt by the widespread expectation that Labour would be the next government and I would be N. Ireland Secretary – neither of which could be taken for granted as we got towards the beginning of the general election campaign proper. After eighteen years in opposition, and especially after the devastating defeat of 1992 when many people had expected us to win, none of us was being complacent this time round.

As February 1997 rolled into March, I was still having almost daily radiotherapy treatment, and coping with it was getting harder and harder. I was on automatic pilot, but I just kept on going. I can remember one weekend I was in Redcar with the family. They were enjoying themselves walking along the beach, while I as usual was sleeping. Our house in Redcar is on the front and overlooks the sea – out of the door, across the road and you are on the beach. It is rather beautiful. Sitting up in bed and watching the sea is one of the best ways of relaxing: however difficult or tough times were in Westminster, that always put life into perspective. The sea is constant and strong and makes other things look petty. The view to the right of the house is sea and more sea, and often there is a queue of tankers waiting to enter Teesside harbour. By contrast, to the left there is a good view of the Corus Steel Works, the biggest blast furnace in Europe, and, across the Tees estuary, Hartlepool nuclear power station.

As I was sitting on the bed admiring the view, I noticed the

CCTV camera, which is on the beach front to watch the antics of tourists and to protect the caravan park further up the coast. The camera now was pointing directly into our bedroom. Yet we had an agreement with the police that the camera would not be used to look into our bedroom. I had even been up to the police station when it was put in to find out what they could see if they pointed the camera at our house. I had campaigned to get CCTV put in, but I got more and more angry as I watched the camera pointing directly at my bed. However, I let it be, knowing that there would be many other things in the future to frustrate me. We had already had Security Branch from the Home Office in London looking at what changes might be needed in London if I became Secretary of State, and this electronic intrusion into our privacy was the beginning of the security in Redcar.

On 17 March 1997 John Major finally called the election, to be held on 1 May. He had limped on as long as he could, but the Tories by that stage were a spent force in Parliament. It was a huge relief, as we could now all get on with the campaigning. I had kept up my constituency commitments from the start of the radiotherapy. I held my regular surgeries, and campaigned to try and save the swimming pool in Redcar from closure. Right up to the election I had done my usual visits: to Aveco shipyard to mark the building of a new trawler; speaking at a youth rally in Darlington; and welcoming the boundary changes which enlarged my constituency to include Marske and New Marske (areas which contained mainly Tory voters taken from the marginal constituency of Langbaurgh, to the south of mine). So during the general election I campaigned very sparingly in my own constituency. It was the party's strategy to get out and help in the marginal constituencies where the fight between Labour and the Tories was much closer than in Redcar, and we were determined to get back constituencies like Langbaurgh, lost to the Tories in 1992. And we did.

Kate or Nigel were with me all the time during the election

campaign, keeping visits as short as was decent, making it possible to sleep a great deal without interruptions. We did what we were asked to do around the country. For example, I can remember visits to Bradford, High Peake, and one where I had to walk up on to Offa's Dyke on the England–Wales border for a photo-opportunity. It was a windy day and both Kate and Nigel were neurotic that my wig might get blown off, so a scarf was produced and I ended up looking very *Horse and Hound* in the photos. Most of the time I was kept going by means of lots of chocolate and careful planning.

I was out and about visiting constituencies for most of the campaign, and was only very rarely back at the Millbank media centre in London where the daily press conferences were held. The big boys dominated those. The occasion when I did stay in London for the manifesto launch was a defining moment for me. All the shadow cabinet were there by instruction, although only Tony and Gordon spoke. But the attention in some of the press the next day was less on the detail of the manifesto and more on what I looked like. 'What has happened to Mo Mowlam?' they asked with a circle around my head in the cabinet picture. One columnist, Lynda Lee-Potter, writing in the *Daily Mail*, said I bore 'an undeniable resemblance to an only slightly effeminate Geordie trucker'. The pressures on me to go public about my illness got very intense. One paper printed side-by-side photographs of me before and after radiotherapy. It was clear that something was wrong with me and the press weren't going to give up until they knew what.

It was Sod's Law that whenever anything dramatic happened Jon was away on business. He had been in Jordan when my hair fell out, and now he was in Bahrain. I rang him and we discussed what we should do. The treatment was nearly over, Tony Blair had been kept informed, and there was an election on. First I told my mother and my sister Jean. My mother particularly was very upset that I had not told her, but my sister understood. I issued a short statement to the media: 'It has become clear that my appearance and health have become a matter of some speculation in the press and I would like to set the record straight.' I went on to say that after a health check in January it had been found that I had a tumour. 'I had a worrying week while further tests were carried out but was relieved when it was found to be non-cancerous . . . I am grateful to the NHS for the treatment and care I received. The course of the radiation treatment is now over and I feel fit and well.'

The press went into overdrive. Those that hadn't commented on how fat I looked were very smug. I didn't blame people like Lynda Lee-Potter; she wasn't to know. I tried to make light of her article in an interview, saying that I 'quite liked Geordie truckers'. I later discovered that I had become a Geordie trucker pin-up, with my photograph adorning many of their cabs. I got a lot of coverage over the next few days without having to say very much. Simon Hoggart from the *Observer* came up to the constituency on my next visit there and walked round with a photographer and me. It was an emotional day with a lot of people I knew coming up to me in the streets and being very kind and wishing me well. In the *Observer* that Sunday, above a nice photo of me hugging a woman friend in the street, they put a big headline, 'Queen of Redcar'.

The tremendous support I was getting, all the letters and phone calls, made April a good month for me. I continued campaigning throughout the month. I owe a lot to Kate, who was always there to steer me to sleep and wake me when I needed to be pointed in the right direction. Without Kate and Jon I don't think I could have kept going. If Jon was not with me he would call regularly just to be supportive. He was always good because he was not fussy, just practical – I couldn't have coped with too much attention. It was physically tough to keep going, but the relief at the end of April when the results of the radiotherapy came through was fantastic. Dr Glaser could not believe how well the treatment had gone. Kate, who had nursed me so well, was as relieved as I was. We gave each other a big hug to celebrate. I miss so many people from my time in Parliament, but Kate is the one I miss most.

There wasn't much N. Ireland news during the election campaign. The IRA made a number of hoax calls claiming that bombs had been placed under various motorway bridges, all of which made getting around the country harder. It was a tactic for maximizing their publicity while not risking any loss of life, which might have jeopardized Sinn Fein's chances in the election in N. Ireland. They managed to get the Grand National at Aintree cancelled with one of these hoax calls, which pissed everybody off.

One comment I made during the campaign about N. Ireland was considered by some in the press and party as unhelpful, to say the least, but since it struck me as common sense I didn't think there was any problem in saying it. The comment was about the time period that should elapse between the IRA calling a ceasefire and Sinn Fein being invited to join the other parties in the talks. John Major's government had realized that to bring Sinn Fein back into the process meant setting such a time limit. How else would we know if Sinn Fein were serious about the ceasefire? It was only by setting a date that anyone would find out. If it was set for a very long time or left open, the people on ceasefire would not see the benefit from it and therefore it was more likely to fail – as the previous one had done in 1996, with catastrophic results, including the bombing of Canary Wharf which left two people dead and caused millions of pounds' worth of damage.

We had been discussing a suggestion for a period of some six weeks. But it was always going to be difficult to announce that 'a period of so many weeks or months of probation' would be enough to convince us of the republicans' commitment to lasting peace. Many Tories and unionists wanted a very long period or preferably no time scale at all; nationalists expected it to be short and specific. As is my wont, I said in a media interview in April that what we were thinking about was 'some six weeks'. People thought I was trying to jump the gun on the discussion under way. I may have been. We had had a long time to discuss it and in my view there comes a time when not to decide can become counterproductive and make a decision harder.

Reactions to my comment were predictable. Some in the media thought it was realistic, others thought it was an insult and far too short. The political parties divided as expected. I knew it was what the Tories had been thinking but had not been in a position to say. I ignored the criticism because I found it paid to be as honest as circumstances allowed, and it often turned out to be the right thing to say and helped to move the process another inch forward. But it was clearly not a popular statement to make in some quarters. Nigel, who was based most of the time at Millbank, bumped into Peter Mandelson at the time who said to him, 'That's enough Northern Ireland, thank you' – ironic as it turned out.

As the election campaign drew to a close, the Tories got more and more desperate and it became clear that Labour would not only win, but win big. Only one poll during the campaign had suggested otherwise and that was regarded as a rogue one. On polling day itself I was in Redcar with Jon. Ulster TV was filming us and there were lots of photographers around. It was the beginning of the end of our privacy.

Jon, with a full-time job as well as looking after me and the kids, hadn't been out and about in Redcar very much. When I was out doing surgeries and visits he would be looking after H and Fred. The only time the press got a photograph of him was when we were married. We had not planned to get married but a number of factors suggested to us it would be a good idea. We thought it was a clear positive signal of stability to the kids. There were no signs that the divorce had caused them any deep-seated problems, and all concerned had done everything they could to avoid tensions. But we hoped it also indicated how important they and their dad were to me. I hoped it made them feel more secure – especially as I was so rarely home.

There is also a degree of hassle in not being married, not only with paperwork and bureaucracy, but also with silly things like invitations. For instance, Betty Boothroyd only invited married partners to formal events. We thought that if it bothered her, and she was a close friend, in government it might lead to many other difficulties both for us and for the system.

We got married on 24 June 1995 at the registry office in Middlesbrough, a very simple, quick event with a small group of people in attendance: both mums, Jon's dad, my sister Jean and her husband Roger, my brother Jim and his wife Jill, and various friends from Redcar and London – Adam and Maureen Ingram from Scotland, Jill and Steve from Chesterfield and Aileen and Jim from Leeds. Not a great number. After the ceremony and the inevitable photographs, taken in spite of the swirling fret (what we in the North-east call a sea mist), we all went back to our house for a lunch of curry (Jon had spent the day before in the kitchen) and champagne. Adam had also brought a wonderful smoked salmon.

As with all weddings we were eager to see how the two families would get on. They had only had a passing acquaintance before, so this was an important day – especially when combined with all the tensions of a wedding. Lunch went well with lots of champagne (courtesy of Ken and Barbara Follett, who had arrived with a case of enormous bottles). We had decided to move the reception to the Redcar racecourse for the afternoon. We thought it would be a bit different and would give folk something to do after all the small talk and waiting around earlier. More champagne was waiting for us in a box on arrival courtesy of Mark, the owner of the racecourse, otherwise known as the Marquess of Zetland – a wonderful man who has been very supportive of me both as a person and as the MP for Redcar. He cares about Redcar and the people who live there, but is a Tory through and through. The racing and the champagne made for a very successful day. I knew it was going to be all right when I saw Jon's mother Liz and my brother Jim depart arm in arm to place a bet.

The photos for the wedding were taken by a photographer from one of the local papers, Doug Moodie, who was later to become a good friend. We did a deal that if he would take them he could release those of just the two of us to the national press. A fair smattering appeared in the Sunday papers the following day. But those with the children were private. They have never appeared in a press photo with me. We felt very strongly that they would be better off being in the background – not least because, important though it is for stepmums to do their bit and be loving and attentive, children only have one mum and one dad and that should not be messed about with or made confusing in the child's mind.

Back to the election, where photographs of me sticking my ballot paper into the box were being taken from every conceivable angle. Immediately after voting I went back to bed to maximize energy for the count and the expected party in the evening. I felt knackered and numb rather than excited. It was a very hot day, so Jon and H wandered up the road for a Lemon Top, which is a Redcar speciality of vanilla ice-cream in a cone covered with a very lemony ice-cream on top, vivid in both taste and colour. Part of me wanted to go with them but tiredness won out and I went to bed, thinking of the days I hoped for in the future when I too would feel up to walking up the front for a Lemon Top.

Early evening I got up to go over and help with the knocking out (going round to people who've said they'll vote Labour, to encourage them to go and vote) in Langbaurgh, where Ashok Kumar was fighting to win back the seat he had lost at the previous election. It was only a short visit to raise spirits and to encourage people to keep working right to the end. I needn't have worried though about the spirits; there was an air of anticipation, an air of real excitement everywhere we went. I won't easily forget the kids climbing up the lampposts as we walked down streets singing at the tops of their voices the Labour party song for the election, 'Things can only get better.' It reminded me of the accounts I've read of elections in the 1920s and 1930s when without the media attention campaigning on the streets had been a real party event.

After this visit I went back to bed, as I knew from my experience of campaigning over the last few weeks that every moment of rest helped and that election night was one where I had to stay the course and be lively for party workers and the press. I struggled out of bed as I heard Dot and John Pallister arrive to go with me to the count. They are my closest friends in Redcar: John is a retired steelworker and Dot cleaned in the local bank. They really adopted me when I first stood for Redcar in 1987. Their house was always a second home for me. In a rush I could pop in to be fed, have a shirt ironed and leave a dirty blouse to pick up cleaned and ironed the next day. They are very astute politically and, along with another very good friend, Vilma Collins, they were my eyes and ears in the constituency when I was in London. I remember once dropping Dot and John off at the square in Eston to go to the local club when a man got in the back of my car and asked to be taken to the Redcar Workies (Working Men's Club). My car being a big Ford Granada, he'd just assumed it must be a taxi.

The result for Redcar was not announced till two o'clock, which was later than usual. My majority jumped from 13,000 to over 22,000. It was a great result, amazing. That vote gave me new strength – people were voting for the work I had put in. I did a round of the media and then we all went off to the celebratory party. Alastair Stewart (from Sunday breakfast television) forgave me for standing behind the television camera when he was speaking to it pulling faces and making rude gestures to try and put him off. I failed. At the party, I thanked all the folk who had worked so hard over the years and especially Vilma. The spirit of the party kept me going. When we got home I watched television for five minutes to see the fantastic results across the country, then it was straight off to bed without waiting up to see the rest. Jon stayed up and watched well into the early hours and told me in the morning the story of the stunning national victory we had won.

The next morning I did a bit more media and then drove round the constituency thanking people for voting. However tired I felt I knew that the thank-you trip had to be done. I had done it after every previous election and I think it is the least an MP can do when people have gone to the bother of voting. Afterwards Jon, Kate, H and I got the train down to London. There were a lot of congratulations on the way, staff at Darlington station very pleased to see me and shake my hands. In opposition I had got to know the platform staff well. I often cut it very tight to catch trains and often had too many plastic bags. I would be running to get on the train and the platform supervisor would be racing behind me picking up what I dropped, and then he would literally throw it into the train as the door was closed. When I travelled as a cabinet Minister later, they used to sit and talk to me about me and trains and how it had been before I had all these security staff to help me get on and off.

On the train down to London, I slept. Got home, slept again. I can remember as I went off to bed feeling very grateful for all Kate, H and Jon had done. It meant that I was not in bad shape at all, and was ready to see what government post was offered, and prepared to face the press.

3

'Sodomites' at Stormont

INTO GOVERNMENT

Arriving in N. Ireland as Secretary of State was a weird experience. I left London straight after seeing Tony at No. 10, so as to be in Belfast city centre by the afternoon. The process of being appointed to the job was brief and unceremonious, quickly into No. 10, very businesslike, and then quickly out. Time for Tony to say you have the job of Secretary of State for N. Ireland, and for me to say thank you. But I remember driving out of the gates at No. 10 (gates, in my view, no longer necessary) feeling very excited. I was now leaving No. 10 Downing Street as a cabinet Minister in a smart, expensive car. Unlike most of the male Ministers of the cabinet who were keen to know where their car ranked in order of size and cost, and therefore status, I just knew it was big and comfortable. This was an attitude that would later frustrate my new driver Ken, who pushed for a stretched Jaguar, with little support from me. He was too nice to ever say so, because as long as it moved and didn't break down, I really didn't care what kind of car we were in.

Ninety-nine per cent of the time when I flew to Belfast it was from RAF Northolt, an airfield about three-quarters of an hour's drive west out of London on the A40. It was even quicker when there were police motorcycle outriders to escort you there. We sometimes had them, especially if we were going across with Tony Blair, and, while it was slightly embarrassing, it did make a difference. I have experienced motorcycle outriders now in about half a dozen countries, and I have to say that the best are the Irish police, the Gardai. They put on a real show, all dressed in black leather, fiercely holding up the traffic with outstretched hands and making a lot of noise. Once, on the way into Dublin from the airport, all the traffic was stopped at a crossroads to let us through, but as we drove up to the lights with the outriders leading the way, half of them went one way and the other half the other. They soon regrouped, but it was funny at the time, especially seeing the Irish officials travelling with me trying not to laugh.

It quickly became clear to me that you could very soon become full of yourself in this job. You were flown about in a small private jet, car doors were opened for you, you were saluted, and occasionally people called you 'Ma'am'. If the plane was not completely ready when you got to the airfield you were escorted to a plush waiting room (and saluted again as you entered) to read the newspapers until you could leave. I was invited to attend RAF Northolt's annual dinner as speaker, but I was too busy to do it, which was disappointing because I am sure it would have been a good evening.

On that first day I walked to the plane, being saluted a couple of times before getting there, and then I was greeted by the crew. It was a small aircraft, hired from the singer Chris de Burgh, and it was great. I got to know the three-person crew well; the one who looked after the passengers was Jay. She was lovely and took care of us so well I never wanted to get off. In the plane on my first journey I met folk from what was to be my private office. Ken Lindsay, my new private secretary, whom I had already met, pointed out that there was one more salute before we took off, which I ought to acknowledge. I did, but over time I developed what I called my regal wave – which, even though I say so myself, is pretty good compared with the Queen's.

I knew from the outset that Ken and I would get on, as his manner was one that I would not get annoyed by and I saw that I would be able to learn from him.

Private planes spoil you: on–off, no checking in, no baggage problems, no queues. Luckily, by the time I left N. Ireland, I was so tired of all the security and being steered along everywhere I went that I was happy to be a normal punter again. To be honest, though, I am still often not a completely normal passenger. The airline staff, particularly the many Irish ones, spot me and put me in a lounge before they come and get me and put me on the plane. I had a funny security moment once at Gatwick airport when I was going off on a short break to Morocco. I was put on the plane by a machine-gun-toting security man. The passengers, already on the plane, saw him and some thought (so the air hostess told me) that they had a terrorist coming on board and feared for their lives. My security disappeared a few months after I left N. Ireland, but when in the next couple of months I travelled to Portugal and Spain I got on the plane with no security and got off to be greeted by a phalanx of armed guards who hurried me to a waiting vehicle. It reminded me of when, before getting into government, I went for a short holiday to Sri Lanka, joining Betty Boothroyd, who was already staying out there. She was so well respected there that, as her friend and as an MP, I was greeted by a driver with an enormous car. I had wondered, as I got off the plane, which passenger was so important as to warrant such a big car. Then while I was standing in the queue for passport control in my jeans and tee-shirt and carrying my holiday gear, I became aware of a number of earnest-looking officials searching the crowd. At last one of them recognized me and pounced: 'Your car is waiting.' It takes some getting used to.

On arriving in Belfast we drove immediately, with Keith and John, my two new protection officers, to Royal Avenue, a big pedestrianized shopping street in the centre of town. I had said before the election that this would be the first thing I would do if we won and I got the job. I wanted the first pictures after my arrival in Belfast to be of me talking to people on the streets rather than sitting behind a desk or meeting people on official business. It worked and it was a good early image of my time in N. Ireland, which was repeated a lot on the TV and stayed with me. I wanted to say as clearly as I could to the people of

N. Ireland that they were what was going to be important to me in this job.

It was also the first time I really felt the frustration of being surrounded by an entourage, a frustration which has been with me ever since. It is very difficult to say hello or have a brief conversation with someone on the street if you are followed by a phalanx of people – special advisers, civil servants, press, police and, at a slight distance but still adding to the phalanx, Special Branch. I used to be able to recognize Special Branch before I got to know them and even when they weren't talking up their cuffs (where they kept their not-very-secret microphones). It was their stance, their relatively smart dress and the swivel eyes. I developed a technique of moving quickly from one side of the street to the other so that I could at least start a conversation with someone before we were surrounded. I never learnt to live comfortably with this entourage problem. During the 2001 election campaign I used to prevent everyone but the local candidate and myself from approaching members of the public; otherwise they get scared off. Both in N. Ireland doing the job and while campaigning in elections, all we often achieve when a great phalanx marches through is to piss the public off in a shopping mall or high street or annoy the stall holders in a market.

I didn't hear any personal abuse that first afternoon on Royal Avenue – only one shout of 'Brits go home!' Later when people shouted at me, I often wanted to stop and tackle them, but a confrontation in front of the media was not considered a good idea, and I could see why. I just wanted to say to them that there are many Brits across the water in mainland Britain that would like it if our boys went home, but they and the shouters had to think about the bloodbath that would follow if that's what we did.

Having met the people, I had to fly back to London to see the Queen. Because I was in the cabinet, and also because I would have to be allowed to see sensitive security material, I needed to be made a Privy Councillor. This is an ancient position and refers to the first real cabinet in England. It was the council of the monarch's closest advisers and in theory still is. Once a Privy Councillor, you hold the position for life, and can call yourself Right Honourable, if that's what you like. To become a Privy Councillor you have to attend a ceremony at Buckingham Palace. I went as part of a package deal of five Ministers. We were led into the Queen's room and stood in a line. In turn we knelt before her, words were said and that was it. We then returned to the line and she walked along having a brief conversation with each of us. It was very formal and felt a little bit daft. I then flew back again to N. Ireland with H, to explore our new home and meet with my own set of advisers. Jon and Fred arrived later that weekend, Fred's singing rehearsals for a concert at the local church having delayed them.

Over the weekend I read most of my First-Day Briefs. They gave a lot of background on the peace process and the talks as well as setting out plans based on our strategy. But I couldn't get out of my head the impressions from my first afternoon in Belfast and what people had said to me in the short time they had to talk. The overwhelming view was: please help to stop the violence; the Brits have never sent us a woman before – perhaps you can help. I took strength from the fact that men and women on the streets regarded the fact that I was a woman as a good thing. It continued to give me strength as the months went by and I was abused as a politician and because I was a woman. The other thing I remembered from my first official encounter with the people of Belfast was how friendly they and the RUC (Royal Ulster Constabulary) were. Some of the reading I had done had led me to think there would be more opposition. In reality it was a welcome tempered by wariness about what I was going to be like – a quite understandable response. Was this one going to be any different from the others?

It was a Bank holiday weekend, although hardly one for me, and Jon and the kids went back to London on Monday night. The kids were still in an excitable mood having spent the weekend exploring the Castle and its extensive grounds. Hillsborough Castle is not actually a castle but an impressive eighteenth-century mansion built by the Hill family in the village of Hillsborough, a few miles outside Belfast. Officially it is the Queen's residence in N. Ireland, but it also has a flat for the Secretary of State and numerous other apartments for Ministers and officials to stay in. It was to be a home for me for the next two and a half years. When Jon and the children left, I spent my first night alone at the Castle – which, contrary to my expectations, I enjoyed. Some previous Secretaries of State have stayed in the accommodation provided for Ministers and senior civil servants down at Stormont House, which was the residence of the Speaker of the Stormont Parliament until the early 1970s and is set in the grounds of the Stormont Estate on the outskirts of Belfast. I had already decided to use Hillsborough because I knew I needed time by myself to think, and living right above the shop would be a mistake.

My actual office in the early days was in a wing of Stormont Castle, another building on the Estate, which again wasn't really a castle but a big grey house with turrets on the roof. It was divided into offices, though it wasn't really supposed to be an office building. Some of the rooms were quite poky, but mine was very palatial, with a connecting door to my private office. That Tuesday I had my first meeting with the rest of my private office staff and, although we were all wary to begin with, we got on well and, by the time I left the job, John, Arlene and Ken were good friends. We still keep in touch. At that meeting we plotted the next couple of weeks' engagements.

Stormont Castle was a temporary home and felt like one. The builders were coming in a few months and things were beginning to be packed up and got ready to move. In the first few days I tried to get round and meet all the staff, but I failed. I only managed to talk to those in the immediate vicinity and those in the Social Security department, which was just down the road. The N. Ireland Office (NIO) is just one part of the bureaucracy that ran things in 1997. There were also big departments mirroring departments of state in Whitehall and covering areas like agriculture, education, health and environment. They had a lot to do, partly because local government and local democracy in N. Ireland did very little, another source of grievance and a legacy of a difficult past where sectarianism had made local government unworkable. Everyone I met at the beginning was very friendly and I hoped to get round all these other departments very quickly. But meetings started to fill my daily diary and the speed of work picked up, so I never made it.

The old Stormont Parliament building was only a short distance away and it wasn't long before I made my first trek up to see it. Well, trek is a bit of an exaggeration, as I was driven everywhere for security reasons. This results in two things. The first was the 'Ulster stone', fourteen pounds of extra tummy that seems to come with the territory, which, along with my extra weight from the steroids, has meant that it has taken a long while for my Teletubby shape to disappear. Being waited on hand and foot with large amounts of good grub meant that dieting was difficult. I used to tell myself that I was building up my strength for the months ahead. The second problem was that it was very hard to talk to staff or anyone on a casual basis, because of the formality of my position. It became a little bit more possible when I went to Stormont House to have breakfast with my fellow Ministers or officials. I often stopped in the kitchen to chat to the cook or the staff or to Michael on the door to find out what they were up to and see if they said anything that would help me to understand what was going on. I always thought it was best to listen to whoever talked to me to get a full understanding of what was happening around me.

Stormont House was not just ministerial accommodation; it also housed the intelligence and security branches of the NIO, and was used for briefing meetings. I have to say I found these formal meetings of little use. I always sensed I was not getting a full picture but a sanitized one, meant for politicians. Looking back at the general security situation in N. Ireland, it felt perfectly safe there the vast majority of the time. I think the army and the police did a good job in difficult and at times almost impossible situations. I had a lot of time for the RUC Chief Constable, Ronnie Flanagan – more than for his predecessor, Hugh Annesley. Annesley was a decent enough bloke but his attitude to policing, particularly of the Catholic community, had proved pretty nearly disastrous on occasion. Two years of chaos and near civil breakdown over Drumcree spring to mind, although admittedly the politicians were as much at fault as he was.

Ronnie Flanagan had a good understanding of what was happening on the ground and a determination to do the best by his men who were risking their lives on a daily basis. He was always a constructive voice in discussions. Even though I sometimes fundamentally disagreed with him, we never fell out. Similarly with the army chiefs, General Sir Rupert Smith and his successor Lieutenant General Sir Hew Pike. We had good discussions and I found Rupert Smith an impressive, rounded (in personality not body) individual. It gave me more faith in the folk that were leading our armed forces. This sadly did not always translate into behaviour on the ground. Allegations of collusion with paramilitaries and of direct responsibility for deaths or tolerance of violence have dogged the police and the army in N. Ireland for many years. These were all difficult issues that would have to be confronted if we were serious about our search for lasting peace and reconciliation. Police and army officers were always very amiable, answering all my questions, but there was always a formality, which meant that the information was of limited value. I learnt as much, if not more, talking to John Steele, my head of security, because I then got the facts plus an interpretation of them through his very capable mind. On top of that, I trusted him, and therefore valued our talks and his views.

Going up to the Parliament itself, I enjoyed looking round. The chamber was then being renovated but was still beautiful, and some of the rooms very impressive. The view from the long gallery out across Belfast is amazing. I had seen the building from the air the first time I ever flew in to Belfast. You can't miss Stormont – up on the hill looking down across the city. It is a very imposing building, in every sense a symbol of power. The statues in the building and in the grounds make it a symbol of *unionist* power. I could quite understand why it was not easy for nationalist or republican politicians to enter it. I, over the months, tried to find ways to turn it into a more neutral environment. That was difficult, thanks to the enormous statue of Sir Edward Carson, father of Ulster Unionism, that greets everyone as they walk up the long drive through the lovely grounds.

I managed to achieve two things in my attempt to humanize and neutralize Stormont. Obviously it was impossible to alter the building or the statues. It is a wonderful building, an important part of history, and any attempt at change would rightly have been seen as an insult to unionism. So I looked for ways round the problem, including opening the grounds up more for public use and attracting more people to them. One idea I had was to hold an open-air concert. I enlisted the help of concert promoter Jim Aiken to organize it for me. The perceived difficulties were enormous, but I and those of my civil servants who thought it was a great idea to have live music at Stormont beavered away. I asked Elton John to play. He did not need persuading about the importance of the event. He understood quickly that, not only would it bring the young of all communities together as other musical events did, but it would also be the first step in redefining the Stormont Estate as somewhere that people from all over N. Ireland could use and enjoy. Reaction to the announcement that Elton was playing did not go down well universally. Ian Paisley was quoted as saying despairingly, 'And now she's bringing "sodomites" to Stormont.' It took a lot of hard work but, as more and more of the young staff in the N. Ireland civil service bought into it, the organization became easier. As the large vans started arriving to build the stage, you could feel the excitement among the people working in the offices.

On the day of the concert, Elton John was fantastic. Standing on the stage to introduce him to the large crowd in the grounds of Stormont was a great experience. As I looked out into the sea of faces, it was obvious there were all ages there set on having a good time. There was no trouble. I went back to Elton's room after the performance to thank him. He was housed in a bright yellow tent with a long rack of clothes, a table covered in different-coloured belts and a large settee. We sat and talked. He wanted to know about the situation in N. Ireland – he wanted the detail on what was happening. He already knew a lot. It was a tremendous experience for me and for the people there. The concerts continued after I left N. Ireland, with Pavarotti and the Eagles. People have visited Stormont who had never been before and I hope began to see it in a new light, for the beautiful space it is. Elton is now a friend and, despite all his fame and the hassles that brings, he is a genuinely decent man.

Another attempt I made to humanize the Stormont Estate was to try and get some neutral sculptures in the grounds. I had one success: a gorgeous sculpture called *Reconciliation* by Josefina de Vasconcellos. I also had plans to use part of the grounds as a playground for children so that again there was a bit of Stormont that could be used and enjoyed by everyone, whatever tradition they came from. It worked. I understand that it is now regularly used by the local community and the children of civil servants and politicians that work at Stormont. Looking back these are little changes. But small steps bring movement that can amount to big changes in attitudes, without people having to do it consciously.

After my first day in the office I drove out to Hillsborough. As we turned into the gates, I thought, 'This can never really be home,' and it wasn't. It was good fun and very impressive, but it never felt like home. Keith and John, my protection officers, whom I got to know very well, were still treating me very formally. It was 'Secretary of State this' and 'Secretary of State that', telling me about the beautiful gardens and how good the staff were. When I saw the butler ready to greet me at the door I said something like 'Bloody hell'. Keith said, 'That's just the start. The rest of the staff will be waiting to see you inside.' Keith quickly understood me and often saved me, if not from disaster, then from great embarrassment by giving me some idea of what a visit or meeting with someone would entail. His little briefings were very helpful on visits to Church folk, for example, when I knew little about them or about how I was expected to behave.

The butler, David, knew a lot, as I now understand proper butlers do. I think I was a bit of a shock for him, as he was for me. But, as with all good butlers, you couldn't tell, and I tried to be on my best behaviour. We rubbed along, and relations got easier – particularly after my mother visited and he felt his proper role had been understood. I had a dinner in the middle of September 2001 at the Natural History Museum to meet the sales team for this book. The catering was good. When I went to the kitchen at the end to say thank you to the catering staff, I was introduced to the man in charge – David the butler from Hillsborough. While I was saying what a small world it is, I was thinking thank goodness I had not been rude or humorous about David or Hillsborough in my speech.

On entering Hillsborough, I was introduced to the rest of the staff. It was all so formal. It felt like a Dickens novel where the master arrives back at his country house from London and the staff is there to greet him. After a while, I got to know the women working there – Olwyn, two Margarets, Sandra, Brenda, Shirley and Myra. We used to have a good chat in the kitchen at weekends before the guests arrived that I had coming to stay and they told me that they found it as difficult as I did not to giggle sometimes. They were all obviously well trained to cater for ladies and gentlemen of high rank, and the Forces do's that they served at, but with us they soon learnt that everything was pretty relaxed with the people that came to stay.

I was so amazed to be living in Hillsborough. I had never stayed in such posh surroundings by myself before. The entrance hall is tall and wide, the size of two good rooms, with a stag's head above the main door. There is a discreet little door to one side where we kept the bits and pieces for badminton, tennis, croquet (darling), and Fred's go-kart and football. The rooms on the ground floor were state rooms, for state visits and for hiring out for other important events. There were two incredible dining rooms, one 'small' that could seat twelve people and one large that could seat forty, and sometimes a few more. The larger of the two led into the kitchens at one end with two screens behind which the staff entered and exited, all with perfect timing. I don't know why, but for me it had overtones of *Fawlty Towers*, and I kept expecting Manuel to enter the dining room and trip.

Olwyn, the housekeeper, basically looked after me. She was wonderful. I would leave her a wee note as to when to wake me. If I came in tired and just dropped my clothes on the floor where I stood and jumped into bed, they miraculously found their way to the wardrobe and washed and ironed themselves, if they needed it. Olwyn and Keith talked frequently. As a result, with my wake-up call and cup of tea, Olwyn would often say, 'You remember the Chief Constable will be here for breakfast in twenty minutes?' It gave me enough time to dress and think about what I wanted to talk to him about.

I haven't told you about the bedroom yet. It was an enormous room with a dressing room off it, where I stored all my bits of rubbish, and a bathroom. Given the size of it all, it felt like a hike when I went to the loo in the middle of the night. And the bed was the largest I've ever slept in, before or since. It was enormous. When Jon was over it was a major effort to travel the distance to find each other. Because Hillsborough is a royal residence, there are bedrooms for both the Queen and Prince Philip. The Queen's bed is also enormous, even bigger than mine. One weekend when we had a lot of visitors and I was doing the guided tour of the Castle, we decided to see if we could all get on the bed. All eighteen of us did, and there is the picture to prove it.

Other state rooms included the throne room, which has two thrones (really – they are there for investitures) set at one end of a very long room designed for receiving guests. It is very beautiful, with gorgeous curtains and carpet and with less gorgeous pictures of former florid-faced governors on the walls. When in use for an official function, it did look stately. But when the family and friends were there at weekends I had to make sure that whatever games children were playing there they did not involve footballs. More often than not I would walk in to see knights fighting or some other kind of royal pageant being enacted.

The main sitting room was the largest room in the house. If you think of a school classroom and multiply it by about five you will get some idea of the size. It had doors opening out into a rather formal part of the garden. It was furnished with loads of settees and an ottoman (I had not come across one of these before) and much other beautiful period furniture. I always think it is amazing that, in a house that was not used to children or our rowdy visitors, nothing valuable got broken. Some friends on entering the room used to just gasp at the size. The artwork was traditional, eighteenth-century gentlemen on horses, views of Windsor Castle in every light and the occasional strange oriental *objet d'art*. Either side of the entrance doors were large portraits of the Queen and Prince Philip, not the best I've seen, but I'm no expert. The room was soon humanized. During the autumn conker season we had tournaments among the guests and the prize-winning specimen was kept in a priceless piece of china on loan from the V&A known as the conker jar. The overall winner was our close friend Waheed Ali.

The other great feature of the room was a good-sized piano, which inevitably led to some raucous sing-songs, with our friend Richard Coles at the piano. Perhaps the most memorable was the night we invited back to Hillsborough the entire cast of the *Rocky Horror Show*, who had been performing in Belfast. I think they had all expected a dry sherry and a stuffy atmosphere, but we soon got the musical director playing the piano and we and the cast danced and sang the night away. I still have this wonderful image as we waved goodbye to them all. The sun was just beginning to rise as two enormous white stretch-limos, with arms and legs sticking out of the windows, swept out of the gates at Hillsborough Castle, under the rather suspicious gaze of the RUC guards on the gate.

The top of the piano and the side tables were covered with pictures of the Royals and Prime Ministers, as was the table in the entrance hall, where the visitors' book was. We always had a rough idea if anyone important was coming to stay, because the photos would change before they arrived. We used to have fun guessing who was coming to stay by which pictures were set out by David the butler. The appearance or non-appearance of Princess Diana was always a particular clue!

The final room was a lovely normal-sized sitting room known as Lady Grey's Room. It was comfortable and almost cosy if it hadn't been for the tales of it being haunted. Once the story of the ghost was known, sightings were inevitable. There is no doubt that there were very noticeable temperature changes in the room, and Jon, an individual not known for seeing ghosts, saw with two of his friends, admittedly late at night, a dark shadow move slowly across the room.

Finally, there were the grounds, which are incredible. At about 110 acres they are large enough to go for a proper walk in. They were wonderful for Jon and me, the one place where we could walk together without protection people shadowing us. There were a large number of cameras to catch people entering the grounds, which it was very difficult not to make rude faces at. You could take a long stroll through the trees and around the lake, and there was a wonderful moss-covered walk to a garden house covered by lovely arched trees. Sitting in the garden house it was almost possible to be at peace looking across a lake up towards the house. As we ambled around the grounds we used to try to guess whether squirrels or foxes were responsible when we came across the feathery remains of a happening or some digging in the moss.

As you will be able to tell from reading this, I never thought I would live somewhere like Hillsborough. It was an extraordinary place to spend part of your life. The only real time I managed to enjoy it was at weekends when the family and friends came to stay. For this reason it was very important to me. It was where Jon and the children came to see me, and it meant that Jon and I kept up some semblance of a relationship, and the kids had a ball. It was obviously big enough to have friends to stay. This was also important to help me to relax. Relaxation was so crucial if I was to keep the peace process in perspective. At work the time in N. Ireland for me was one of total determination to make progress; but weekends of family and friends kept me going.

They also made me see the advantages that many Tory MPs have with their country homes. It always used to amuse me when I used the excellent service provided by the telephonists at No. 10 Downing Street in locating someone for you. It is one of the real perks of being in government, as they are so good at tracking someone down. But what amused me was the way they referred to an MP's constituency phone number as the one for their country residence. For some MPs, a reality; for most Labour MPs, a giggle. But these big country homes really are a chance to get away from folk and politics and rest up. Not so for the vast majority of Labour MPs, who live in the town they represent, and as a result their job as an MP is much more demanding.

The opportunity to live in a castle that is the Queen's official residence was a great experience and one that I will never forget. As a family we enjoyed the space. We had barbecues in the rough bit of the grounds and played stately-home games like badminton and croquet. I will never again be surrounded by the beauty of such a house or gardens. Funny though it may sound, leaving it was not as hard as I had expected, because in the end it was not home. Now that I have returned to somewhere I can say is my home, I can look back at the enormous pleasure of living at Hillsborough as a wonderful experience, but I have no great desire to repeat it.

I was very keen to share the comforts of Hillsborough with the people of N. Ireland. But as it was the Queen's residence, and a working house, it was too difficult to open it to the public. Security was an issue that had to be addressed in both the house and the gardens. When I arrived, the gardens were open only half a day a week and there had to be a pre-booking. I managed to get the gardens open for a little bit more.

There is at one end of the grounds a walled area, which had once been an enormous market garden supplying the house with fresh fruit and vegetables. When I arrived it was just grassed over with the fruit trees running wild and the greenhouses and potting sheds falling down. I had a hope that this could become a garden again, and be economically self-sufficient by selling produce from a stall near to one of the back security gates on the other side of the estate. It was, I thought, an ideal project for people with disabilities because it would be a safe and pleasant area for them to work in at their own speed. I wrote to Prince Charles to see if he would be interested in giving it his seal of approval, as I was hoping the Prince's Trust would be able to help. As I was about to leave the job we made some progress, so now it is a walled garden producing organic fruit and veg and worked by people with a disability under the supervision of Action Mental Health.

My most successful effort to open up Hillsborough was the Queen's Garden Party. It was her party but we organized it. I missed the first year in 1997, but the next year I wanted to have it just for children – though that was not for me alone to decide. The civil servants talked to the Palace and they agreed. We called it 'The Party in the Garden'. Two children were invited from every school in N. Ireland, Protestant, Catholic and mixed. I was told later by John McKervill in my private office that what I had set in train was a logistical operation akin to the Normandy landings. Every school was invited to select two pupils between the ages of seven and sixteen. In the end over 2000 children attended. Organizing the transport was a nightmare, but the work was done and on the day it ran like clockwork, with colour coding and staggered arrival and departure times. Food was not so difficult as barbecues, soft drinks and ice-creams were provided around the grounds.

A stage was set up for bands to play on, and the show was compèred by comedian Patrick Kielty, who was brilliant. Acts included Gary Barlow, Brian Kennedy, Next of Kin and Rab C. Nesbitt. There were clowns, fire brigade displays, a hot-air balloon, sumo wrestling and a bouncy castle. Also there were the boxer Barry McGuigan and local presenters Pamela Balantyne and Frank Miller, along with all the *Blue Peter* presenters, who devoted half of one of their programmes to the party. The footballer David Ginola was disappointed not to come and sent a signed number 14 shirt as a prize. Prince Andrew came on behalf of the Royals and seemed to thoroughly enjoy himself, as did the kids. The party ended with Patrick Kielty and I leading the celebrities, officials who had worked on the project and 2000-plus kids in a specially written rap.

Overall my social time in N. Ireland was limited, so I was not a great entertainer of the folk that used to come for fancy dinners at Hillsborough. I was told delicately that there were a number of people who used to come to Hillsborough who had not yet been invited. I decided not to do any dinners. I am sure I offended a few of the Anglo-Irish elite, the Ulster *Tatler* crowd, among whom were some great people whom I met at official functions. But my time priorities did not extend to such dinners.

Looking back, my first day at work was not as nerve-racking for me as some of my cabinet colleagues told me theirs had been. My private secretary Ken Lindsay made life easier. I was glad I had had the chance to meet him with Paddy Mayhew before the election. On first impression Ken has a very conservative demeanour, but his sense of humour and mine meant that we got a good working relationship together. He is very competent and I realized early on that his was a judgement I could trust. I would not always agree with him, but I learnt that he was straight and gave me advice that he thought was in my best interests. He did not give opinions lightly, but when I asked he told me exactly what he thought. Along with John McKervill, my deputy private secretary, and Arlene McCreight, my diary secretary, we worked well as a team with the admin folk in what was called my outer office. We laughed a lot, which helped keep us all sane. I think I drove them quite hard, demanding results more quickly than the civil service machine could deliver. I had a similar team of people in London, who I liked but increasingly saw a lot less of.

As well as getting to know people, my early days in the office were spent being briefed on key issues including security matters by John Steele, as well as on the situation in the prisons by Alan Shannon. I had useful briefs on previous talks and the political parties. I received a lot of detailed material on the bread-and-butter issues of health and education, which were important, as there are major differences between our systems in England and those in N. Ireland, particularly in education. I received piles of reports and briefs on human rights, though a lot of the material was duplicated in different reports. The work I had done in opposition made all the paper relatively easy to cope with as I had already seen or read a lot of what I was given. The only difference was it had not been written by the civil service.

It took a day or two to find out who the other Ministers on the team would be. The civil servants were as anxious as I to know who they were. They had already met Nigel, who had seemingly been easily accepted. I found out later that the women in the office thought he was good news as he was handsome, and they all seemed pleased that he was willing to listen and express views, and did not seem to be a difficult, doctrinaire man. Anna Healy, my newly appointed special adviser in London, was also making a good first impression.

When the Ministers were announced I was delighted. I was very happy to get Adam Ingram and Paul Murphy. Both were already close friends, particularly Adam (the kids love him and his wife Maureen). Paul, like Adam, has a great sense of humour. We made a good team, Adam on the security side plus economic development, and Paul on the talks process and finance. Paul's gentle Welsh manner would prove invaluable in the talks.

The two others on the team were Tony Worthington and (Lord) Alf Dubs. We all got stuck in, and made an impact as Ministers prepared to work with the people of N. Ireland. Tony was only in the job a year, as he was moved aside in the 1998 reshuffle to make room for George Mudie to come out of the whips' office. As it turned out, George refused the job and went to the Department of Trade and Industry instead. So Tony, who was doing so well, was pushed aside very unfairly. He was replaced by John McFall, a hard-working man, competent and good at detail.

Apart from numerous introductions, the major event of the first week was the opening of the new Waterfront Hall down by the River Lagan in Belfast. A tremendous, imaginative modern concert hall, the Waterfront was part of the huge Laganside development and a symbol of the new confidence in Belfast. It means a lot to the city, and the opening was special with a concert starring Kiri Te Kanawa, with Prince Charles as the principal guest. Both Kiri and Charles came back to Hillsborough for dinner afterwards, which was a strange introduction to my new job, to say the least. Actually it was an enjoyable and relaxed dinner. They had met before and we all three chatted about everything under the sun.

The next day I returned to London for the first of many, many meetings at No. 10. Paul Murphy and I were joined by the permanent secretary at the NIO Sir John Chilcot for the meeting. John was an excellent civil servant, very able and astute. They don't make them like him any more. He could say no in style. He and John Holmes, his counterpart in the private secretaries' office at No. 10, had been the guiding hands on the British government's N. Ireland policy for a number of years. Because of their experience they knew the pitfalls and, unlike some in the civil service, would warn their politicians so they could avoid them. I remember one incident, during a problem over a prisoner transfer from Scotland to N. Ireland, which was getting very awkward, and someone on the telephone was recommending that we use the advice we had had from a government law officer to publicly defend a difficult decision we were having to take. John Chilcot, who was listening to the conversation on the phone – as civil servants always do – literally ran into the room to warn us that it would be disastrous to quote publicly any such official advice. I thought that when a permanent secretary comes running it's time to take notice.

I was also in London for my first N. Ireland Questions in the House of Commons. This was why I missed my first royal garden party at Hillsborough. You do not miss your monthly Question Time, unless something really dire is happening. It's the one occasion Ministers are held formally to account in Parliament. But it was difficult: I didn't want to offend the Queen, but neither did I want to offend the Commons. So in the end I met the Queen off her plane at the airport in Belfast and introduced her there to Alf Dubs, who took over as her escort for the day. I think he enjoyed it, in spite of himself. I then immediately got on my plane and flew across to London for Questions in the Commons.

It was the first time I had stood at the despatch box on the government's side of the House – answering questions rather than asking them. The Prime Minister has the hardest time, as he doesn't know what he is going to be asked. At least we as Ministers know what half of each question is going to be because

MPs have to put in (or 'table') their questions two weeks before. So in answering you know what the first one is, but have no idea what the follow-up will be, or any subsequent ones. The best you can do is guess what they might be, and then work out an answer in each case. We did this each time, and usually we weren't far off because the Tories weren't that imaginative. But questions from the N. Ireland parties, and from some on my own side, were often more difficult to predict.

For most cabinet ministers, Question Time is a nerve-racking experience. For me it was a scary time right up to the last one I did. It was the formality of it all, which for me made it harder. The least scary ones were in the middle of the talks when most of my concentration was on making sure my brain was working, as I was so focused on the talks. It never gets any easier because every four weeks it is a chance to show that you either are or are not on top of your brief, to the most critical audience possible, your enemies – the Tories on the opposition side and your enemies within the party behind you. A mistake or a weak answer has an immediate and devastating effect, silence behind you and howls of false laughter in front of you. I always tried to answer the question, which was not the best way to handle the House. It was most effective if you took scant notice of the question, said something about what you were doing and then just hammered the Tories. Honesty made it harder, but I grew to really dislike the shouting and howling event that Question Time has become.

Prime Minister's Question Time in particular has become an unruly scrum. I found it more and more difficult doing my best to look interested in what was being said. I tried to look supportive, but actually all the time I was thinking, 'This is appalling.' We were just like animals in a circus being watched by the press and the public in the galleries above and by a section of the public on the TV. It is a ghastly but necessary part of democratic accountability. People at home watching TV don't get the full effect of the enclosed bear-pit feeling when the House is full. It is both exhilarating and oppressive. My Questions always fell on the same day as the Prime Minister's, so I was guaranteed a full House. However scary that was, it was not as bad as speaking to just twenty or thirty MPs, which can sometimes happen on other Question Time days. I never stopped being a little bit scared before Question Time or (even now) before I make a speech, however small the audience.

I can still remember that at my first Question Time I answered questions on the talks process and on the parades issue. Everyone began their questions with the usual courtesies welcoming me to the job and then went for the jugular. Michael Ancram was then interim Tory spokesman as he had been Paddy Mayhew's second in command, but he was soon replaced by, in my opinion, the less decent and much less experienced Andrew MacKay. I had met Andrew on holiday the year before on the Greek island of Ithaca. You could only reach Ithaca by flying to Cephalonia, crossing that island by bus and then getting a boat to our destination. I watched Andrew and Julie Kirkbride, then a journalist on the *Telegraph* but soon to be an MP and Andrew's wife, and a friend of hers, get off the plane and on to the bus. When they and we and hardly anyone else got on to the little boat, I thought, 'There goes a peaceful non-political holiday.' But we were all very British, chatted amicably, and ascertained that our accommodation was on opposite sides of the island, and didn't see each other until the return journey.

It became clear at N. Ireland Questions after MacKay was appointed that the Tories were going to be nowhere near as supportive of us under William Hague as we had been of them under John Major. MacKay came across to me as the worst kind of Tory, snide and arrogant. He was never that pleasant and became progressively worse as time went on. Why did I expect anything different from a Tory, you might ask? Well, under John Major, with Paddy Mayhew as Secretary of State and me as his opposite number, bipartisanship had worked well. The contrast between Mayhew and MacKay was like chalk and cheese. MacKay kept professing support, but when the situation got tough, so did he. He was pressured by hostile editorials in the staunchly unionist *Daily Telegraph* (which once described John Hume as the 'arch appeaser', which he is not). It was never easy and Paddy Mayhew knew that on certain issues I would be critical, but when it got tough we would talk in private together, so we could all work towards success in the peace process.

On the evening of the first Question Time in the House there was a reception at the newly opened Unionist Information Office in London. I was invited by David Burnside, who was always in the background in unionist politics and eventually became an Ulster Unionist MP in 2001. He was considered by many, including me, an unhelpful influence in the peace process because of his strident views. He was close to David Trimble and therefore crucial to talk to. At the reception both Davids were there. I worked the room. Some folk were genuinely pleased to see me, others were clearly less so.

In these early days my relationship with many prominent unionists was good. I had worked hard in opposition to talk to everyone. When I was first appointed shadow N. Ireland secretary, I as warmly welcomed by the unionists (primarily I think because I wasn't Kevin McNamara, who was seen as too pronationalist). On my many visits to N. Ireland in opposition I visited Ken Maginnis at home, David Burnside at home and delivered a speech to a packed room at the Garvagh British Legion Hall in Willie Ross's constituency – and I stayed the night with Willie and his wife Christine, who were friendly and hospitable. By the time of my last year in N. Ireland, Willie Ross was barely speaking to me. Mind you, by then he barely spoke to Ulster Unionist leader David Trimble either.

The rest of May was a whirlwind of activity. I was back and forth across the water from Belfast to London. You can tell how busy it was: I really had to concentrate when I got up to go to the loo in the night – I had to think, 'Is this the long trek across my enormous bedroom in Belfast or two feet in London?'

The most important meetings at that stage, in my view, were with the Irish government. If we could work closely together, I believed we could make most progress. The quality of relations depended in part on personalities, but there was also a long history of distrust on both sides to get over. Could we trust them? Were they being devious and playing Sinn Fein's cards? The Irish questioned our degree of serious commitment: were we prepared to drive the process along or were we going to play the delaying game with the unionists? Improvements had been made over the years. For example, a degree of trust had been built up between the officials in London and their opposite numbers in Dublin.

In opposition our relations with the Irish embassy in London were good. The arrival of Ted Barrington as the Irish Ambassador in 1995 had been excellent news. I got on well with Ted and his wife Clare. At first Ted was a bit wary of us. Secretaries of State came and went, and I got the feeling that he tolerated the British government, but would have been quite happy to see us leave his beloved Ireland. Nevertheless, we worked well together, building a degree of trust, which over time was a definite plus to the peace process overall. Nigel had also built up a relationship with Ted's number two, Philip McDonagh, who had arrived at a similar time as Ted with his wife Ana. Philip is a lovely man with a fine mind; we had some great evenings together. His almost weekly breakfasts with Nigel helped relations a lot. I don't know how much politics was discussed, but both grew a lot fatter. When we got into government our relations were much more formal, but our more relaxed time in opposition was a useful foundation to work from.

Also in opposition I talked a lot to two of the main Irish journalists in the Lobby. (Lobby correspondents are Westminster-based journalists who have the privilege of being able to talk to MPs at any time in Parliament's corridors and lobbies.) I used in opposition to phone Des McCartan on the *Belfast Telegraph* and Frank Millar on the *Irish Times* (usually from my car when stuck in the London traffic) to find out what was happening and talk it through with them. Not only were they both knowledgeable but, more importantly, their ability to evaluate and judge situations (based on years of experience) was impressive. They told me I wouldn't call them when I was in government. I said of course I would and was keen to keep in touch. But they were right. When you are in government and you are in the process of making decisions the last people you want to talk to are the press. So I stopped doing it and felt a heel for cutting them dead when they had been important in my understanding of what was happening across the water in opposition.

A potential problem reared its head with the June elections in the Irish Republic – no specific problems with the Irish, but elections could potentially be destabilizing to the talks. I can remember worrying about it because from a personal point of view I did not want to lose the then Foreign Minister Dick Spring or his deputy Ruari Quinn. I felt I had a terrific relationship with them both, which had developed over the years between us. I had built up a good understanding with John Bruton, then Taioseach and his Fine Gael party too. Of the two biggest parties in southern Ireland, they are the least sympathetic to the republican view. I felt they would put more pressure on Sinn Fein to deliver, and John Bruton had certainly worked hard to warm up relationships with the N. Ireland unionists. My personal relationship with him was fine. I had seen him in opposition (as I did all party leaders, north and south) and we had gone to Navan, in his County Meath constituency, where warm relations had been sealed with a pint in his local.

But the outcome of the election was that Labour and Fine Gael lost power and a new coalition of Fianna Fail, the Progressive Democrats and a few independent Members of Parliament (known as TDs) formed the new Irish government. I always thought that Fianna Fail would be 'greener' (more pro-nationalist), and they clearly are, but in the end that proved to be more of a help than a handicap. Because they were trusted more by Sinn Fein, they could take a tougher line, and hold public opinion in the Republic at the same time – just like when Margaret Thatcher signed the Anglo-Irish Agreement in 1985. No one thought she was pro-nationalist, even though the Agreement went further than any had before in giving the Irish government rights to be consulted on issues in N. Ireland, like political development, security, legal matters and improving cross-border co-operation. So when it came, the criticism, though fierce from the Ulster Unionists, was much less from the public. And this had allowed her to take things further forward.

I got on very well with the new Irish Prime Minister, Bertie Ahern, and his officials. I think it would be fair to say that both sets of officials found the changes tough, although nothing was ever said. I certainly felt more like a Brit than I had before. References were made often in humour about the British establishment and 'Perfidious Albion' (a phrase describing the alleged wickedness of the British, widely used since the Napoleonic Wars). There was a part of me that understood the Irish wariness. They had been brought up on their Irish history and what role the British had played in it – for example, putting down the 1916 nationalist rebellion. On the British side there were folk who said to me, 'Watch out. They can be very cunning – be sure you are not taken for a ride.' The British belief was that the Irish would only tell us half of what they were up to. Our approach was no different. I'm sure we didn't tell them all our intelligence material – come to that, I'm sure I was not told it all either!

The relationship was never as open and positive as I would have liked. It is possible that my sense of nationhood is weaker than other people's, although if you'd seen me playing hockey you wouldn't think that. I think it is because to me, as a priority in any situation, it is the people that count, especially when it is saving lives – that's when you put people before nationhood. We met frequently with the Irish government, either in London or in Dublin, or wherever there were enough of us gathered together. I also continued my meetings with the parties in Belfast. I had meetings galore every day right up until the time I left N. Ireland. From the outset in 1997 I had meetings on the issue of the summer marches, but more of these later. Others were with groups and Ministers on bread-and-butter issues of education, health and housing and with Adam Ingram on questions of security or army or police matters.

Life in a bizarre sort of way carried on as normal in N. Ireland. I thought it was important to support those people who kept normality going, thus providing some hope for the future. As a result, when I could I went out and joined in many community activities such as addressing the AGM of the N. Ireland boys' and girls' clubs at the Waterfront Hall, and doing the honours at the Lurgan Junior High School prize-giving.

There were also certain meetings I couldn't miss in London, such as cabinet on a Thursday and ministerial meetings on finance and other issues, which were clearly important to N. Ireland. After a while, I gave up many of these and sent a deputy because, to be honest, depending on the subject it was usually either Gordon Brown or Derry Irvine in the chair telling us what was going to happen. There was the odd comment from the other Ministers, and that was it. Comments from others around the table did not seem to have any value. There was a distinct sense that decisions had already been taken. I just felt that it was easier and more efficient to read the minutes. But I tried to get to all the cabinet meetings. At the very first one, a photograph was taken for the press. Over time (as these were taken whenever there was a major change or an event requiring us all to be on show together) I began to learn that in certain photos of the cabinet where you sat indicated what the pecking order was. I started on the front row, but by the second-year photo I was on the second row. When the Prime Minister launched the government's annual report in the garden of No. 10 a year later, I was a bit further back still. I assumed they had decided I was getting too big for my boots.

Most of my time and the focus of my thoughts were on the future of the talks. I did a lot of meetings and talking with the parties then at the table. John Major's government had successfully launched a talks process a year earlier with all the parties of N. Ireland apart from Sinn Fein. There had been a lot of procedural wrangling and argument, but, I think it's fair to say, little progress of substance. The big question continued to be how to get Sinn Fein on board. Whatever you think about it, it was a fact of life that without Sinn Fein there at the table, along with the representatives of loyalist paramilitaries, the talks were never going to resolve all the issues in a way that would bring lasting peace.

The waiting period of 'some six weeks' was now settled, but there was still an enormous amount of suspicion around whether or not Sinn Fein would be invited into the talks even if there were an IRA ceasefire. In discussions with Tony Blair and civil servants, the question was how to communicate to Sinn Fein what they could do to get their seats at the talks table in a way that was possible for them to accept and others to live with. The team of officials working on the talks were itching to make progress. Of course under civil service rules they couldn't say so, but the frustrations of the previous months of delay had been getting to them, especially the N. Ireland Office political director, Quentin Thomas. If there was an architect of the George Mitchell-led peace process it was, from our side, Quentin. He had worked with other officials from N. Ireland, the Republic and Britain to bring Sinn Fein in from the cold after the 1994 IRA ceasefire. He worked especially closely with the Irish First Secretary Seán ÓhUiginn. Sean and Quentin crossed swords many times, but they did help produce the first ceasefire in 1994 and the 1995 Framework Document. No one had a better grasp of the issues involved in the peace process than Quentin, nor a better brain.

Long before the 1994 IRA ceasefire, 'lines of communication' had been opened with the IRA. In plain speaking, this means people were talking to the IRA in the government's name. This is a normal way for talks to start. I remembered Paddy Mayhew coming into the Commons in November 1993 to confess embarrassedly to years of secret talks with the republicans. I didn't want to be put in that position, and neither did Tony Blair.

So on 16 May Tony came to N. Ireland and made a groundbreaking speech. It was cleverly crafted with statements that both the unionist and nationalist communities wanted to hear. He said that he valued the union and, in a remark that echoed the words of Dick Spring earlier in the year, 'None of us in this hall today, even the youngest, is likely to see Northern Ireland as anything but part of the United Kingdom.' At the same time he announced that NIO officials would be allowed to meet with Sinn Fein and make clear to them face to face what the government's policy was on their entry into the talks. It seems an unremarkable thing to say now, but at the time it was a first to have open contact with the republicans without the IRA being on ceasefire. The speech was listened to almost in silence with only one or two hecklers, which was amazing in view of what Tony said to a predominantly unionist audience.

The speech was delivered in a hall at the annual Agricultural Show on Belfast's Balmoral Show Ground. Memories of that day will always be with me. The security was intense, and the tension inside the circle of government folk there was palpable. This was a speech of seminal importance in our attempt to build an inclusive talks process, being delivered in an environment which might not be expected to be friendly. My other memory of the day was walking alongside enormous cattle with vast bottoms. I have, to this day, never seen buttocks like them.

Two meetings between Sinn Fein and our officials followed. The discussions were tentative but positive, and resulted in Tony sending a written note to Sinn Fein setting out the government's position regarding their entry into the talks. Officials called it an 'aide-mémoire' so as to avoid the charge that we were negotiating. This had to be done to keep things moving. My view was we had to take risks to get the talks going. If folk are constantly waiting for someone to make a move, you can wait till the violence starts up again.

The response was swift and depressing. On 16 June the IRA murdered two RUC officers, Roland John Graham and David Johnston, in Lurgan, County Armagh. It was the first fatal attack on the RUC in N. Ireland since the ending of the IRA ceasefire in 1996. It was clear that the IRA were not going to stop the violence immediately. It felt on one level that these murders threatened to halt our initiative before it had really got started. Inside my head I knew if I started thinking that this meant we might not make progress, it was very likely we would not. I had made up my mind that we had to get everyone into the talks if we were going to get anywhere. I kept going by saying to myself 'Remember Canary Wharf', and how John Major and Paddy Mayhew had had to climb over that appalling atrocity with two people dead and millions of pounds' worth of damage to come back to the table and to try again.

I also said to myself that the history of violence in N. Ireland often had an element of tit-for-tat between the two sides. In the short time I had been in the job we had seen the murder by republicans of RUC officer Darren Bradshaw when he was having a drink in a Belfast bar, of another RUC officer, Gregory Taylor, beaten to death by loyalists outside a pub in Antrim, of Robert Bates – himself a killer – killed in a twenty-year-old act of vengeance, and of an official of the GAA (the Gaelic Athletic Association, who do Irish sports), Sean Brown, killed by the LVF (Loyalist Volunteer Force). All vicious murders that caused untold pain to the families of those killed. I also still had on my mind the death of Robert Hamill, just six days after I took office. He had been attacked and savagely beaten by a group of loyalist thugs in Portadown and died twelve days later. His family and many others said that, if the RUC officers sitting in a nearby Land Rover who witnessed the beating had acted, Robert would have lived. The police said it was too dangerous to interfere, they

Our wedding 1995

Redcar fishermen – my constituents

Speaking at Ulster Unionist conference, Portrush, 1995

'Geordie Trucker Pin-Up'

Mo Mowlam pays in pounds for giving up her cigarettes

By
**VICKY
WARD**

IT is a problem which faces everyone trying to quit smoking. And poor Mo Mowlam has to confront it in the glare of the spotlight.

As she wins the war of the weed, she is losing the battle of the bulge.

When she sat next to Jack Straw at the Labour Party's manifesto launch on Thursday, some speculated that Mr Blair had found himself a new frontbencher. With her striking new bob hairstyle and dramatic weight gain, some observers needed a second look to confirm she was indeed the party's vivacious 44-year-old Northern Ireland spokesman.

Yesterday it emerged that Miss Mowlam's new appearance stems from a New Year's resolution to give up cigarettes.

In the three months since kicking her 20 Silk Cut-a-day habit, her weight has ballooned from 12 stone to 14.

Comfort eating — she has admitted to cravings for Smarties, sausage rolls, scotch eggs and jelly babies

‘I'm eating too much junk food’

— sparked by nicotine withdrawal pangs is blamed for the initial increase. In recent weeks, she has piled on thepounds even faster as the frantic pace of the election campaign left her virtually existing on fast food.

Miss Mowlam is struggling with the double pressure of life without cigarettes and the stress of electioneering.

‘I'm eating too much junk food and it's got to stop,’ she told friends this week.

The MP for Redcar began smoking at 15. After giving up briefly when she was made her school's head girl, she returned to smoking a pack a day despite health warnings from colleagues and the embarrassment of taking so long to finish a half-marathon that the winner, who was waiting for her to present the trophy, got fed up and went home.

Miss Mowlam has always been fond of food and drink but only started to become slightly overweight five years ago when she moved in with banker Jon Norton, whom she

married in 1995. It is Mr Norton, a Delia Smith devotee, who does the shopping and cooking at home.

His wife has complained that, while his breakfast fry-ups and delicious dinners help her to unwind, they don't do much for her waistline.

Experts put the blame for her present shape on both her frenetic lifestyle and the vulnerable state of mind experienced by many fledgling ex-smokers.

‘If she has gone and put on all that weight so quickly, the chances are it means that she has not yet managed the final stage which is to quit *the desire to smoke*,’ said psycho

‘Better to be fat than to smoke’

therapist Robin Hayley, managing director of Allen Carr's EasyWay, an international chain of smoking therapy clinics.

Maureen Moore, chief executive of the anti-tobacco group ASH (Action on Smoking and Health), said some ex-smokers replace cigarettes with the wrong kind of food.

She added, however: ‘It is far worse for your health to smoke than to be fat.

‘When Miss Mowlam feels more in control of the smokecraving, she can address the weight problem.’

Old Labour: Mo Mowlam as she used to be

New Labour: Out electioneering yesterday

Before and after

Queen of Redcar, Election, May 1997

The Stormont Parliament Building in all its majesty

First day in the job, May 1997

Orange Order marching, Garvaghy Road residents protesting, July 1997

Drumcree Church, Orange Order on the hill surrounded by razor wire,
July 1999

Graffiti on the Ormeau Road being put to good use

My favourite graffiti

Relaxing on the Queen's bed; *left clockwise from me*:
Jeremy Paxman and daughter, his partner Elizabeth Clough, John Grieve, H,
Tessa (her friend), Freddie, Jon, Chris Smith, Jill Grieve, my mum Tina
and John Humphrys, taken by Dorian Jabri (Chris's partner)

Relaxing at Hillsborough, in the main dining room

were outnumbered and a riot would have followed, putting their lives and others' at risk. Because of the circumstances, the controversy around this murder continues. For my part, I was learning very quickly that, while it was possible to make progress, you had to live through an awful lot to get there.

The move to get talks going had started in earnest. Tony's speech set out the British position. The Irish and we were working well together. One of our first and repeated difficulties was Sinn Fein's blanket insistence on being regarded as separate from the IRA. Nobody believed them, but they insisted on it anyway. Wherever we got into a day's talks it always ended with Sinn Fein saying, 'We'll have to take that to the IRA to see what response they can give.' This charade was frustrating, but then I thought perhaps it is their way of making sure they carry the whole organization with them, so it made sense to wait a couple of days to see where they were at. This carry-on made a number of my colleagues very tetchy and frustrated. I put the best possible interpretation on Sinn Fein's activities, as I did for all participants in the talks, lived with the frustration and kept on going. If you took the statements folk made at face value it meant that the process was less likely to be delayed because they then had to come back next time with an answer. I had always to make the judgement that the other side could live with frustration, and my credibility could take being seen as a bit naive. I always thought if the outcome was to make progress, then living with a bit of personal criticism was worth it.

Events continued to move forward. Good news followed bad followed good, day after day. In June the first ever SDLP (nationalist) mayor of Belfast was elected. Alban Maginnis, a lovely man, and his wife Carmel did a terrific job. They represented so many people on either side of the divide that had kept going through the difficult times to make progress. And it was a positive sign of political maturity that Jim Rogers of the UUP (unionist), another good man, became deputy mayor.

On the downside I was forced to take steps to proscribe

(legally ban) two paramilitary groups, the Loyalist Volunteer Force and the republican Continuity Army Council. Both were opposed to the peace process. I always thought that proscribing organizations was more of a symbolic act than an effective step, more a reflection of society's disapproval than anything designed to make a real difference on the ground. What it does is allow the police to arrest someone for being a member of a group, but it's very hard to prove. Groups like the CAC and the LVF don't keep membership lists and minutes of their meetings.

Senator George Mitchell was back in town to take up where he had left off before the election, chairing the talks process. He was a generous, warm, determined and above all patient man whose presence in Belfast made all the difference. His very status as an international figure brought greater stability to the process, and participants in the talks were not rude to George as he was an outsider who had come to help. He was respected as an international lawyer, a former leader of the US Senate and a close friend of Bill Clinton.

All the time, the media were never far away. Sometimes I thought how great it would be if they weren't there at all, particularly in the middle of difficult negotiations. But that wasn't possible. The media were always an important dimension to consider, at times seeming almost like another participant at the talks table. Slowly I began to realize that the majority of people working in the press and TV news felt they had a serious job to do, and they weren't out to upset the peace process. In fact many of them, particularly the ones based in Ireland, north and south, were as keen as we were to see progress made. They, like others, had spent their careers reporting on the violence and misery of the troubled years in N. Ireland and would have loved to return to safer stories about health, education and normal crime.

As the process moved on, the editors of the main papers in Belfast got more and more involved in trying to shape opinions about what was happening. On occasion, over particular issues like the Drumcree parades or at times in the peace talks, the two main papers for each community, the more nationalist *Irish News* and the more unionist *Newsletter*, even ran joint editorials to try and move the process forward. But in the end we had to accept that the people we were dealing with were journalists, and there is something in their genes that means if they get a good story they have to run it.

I also realized early on that compared, for example, to Sinn Fein we were crap at handling the media. Monitoring the media we saw just how good Sinn Fein were in talking to their different audiences about what they were up to. Their message after an event in the talks or after an atrocity was out quickly, not just in N. Ireland and Britain, but also in the Republic, the USA and Europe, often with a different slant for each market. At the beginning especially, we had an uphill struggle with the press, particularly in the Irish Republic and the US. Some elements of the press that wrote about N. Ireland, mainly in the US, had very fixed ideas about what the Brits had been up to over the years. To put it succinctly, we had played a colonial role supporting the unionists and oppressing the Catholics – and to many in the US, including parts of Congress, we were still doing it: discriminating against Catholics and abusing the human rights of IRA 'freedom fighters'. Admittedly this is an extreme view and many had a lot more sophisticated understanding of both sides of the issues. But underneath there were still many with serious doubts about Britain's and my intentions. I used to think some Americans were more Irish than the Irish themselves.

I made a real effort to talk to foreign journalists and convince them that we were working in the interests of all the people in N. Ireland. I met with groups of journalists in London and particularly focused on the correspondents from the US. They were a great bunch. Talking to them was just like having a chat with a group of bright folk who were interested in N. Ireland. The fact that I'd spent some time in America did much to break down barriers and help us get along. It was such a difference from a pack of Brit journalists. The level of aggression was just not there. When talking with foreign journalists one hot afternoon early that summer, in my London office, I forgot myself and took my wig off. It was an incident that some have written about ever since – it has been seen as some clever ploy to unnerve them. Sadly, it was not. I had begun not to wear my wig at work and my private office staff did not look askance any more. On that day, it was hot, these were sensible folk and I thought, being predominantly American, they would be more tolerant than many other nationalities.

On my quite frequent visits to the US I made a special effort with the editorial staff of papers like the *New York Times* and the correspondents of the *Washington Post* to be sure that folk got our side of the story about what was happening in N. Ireland, and to try and persuade journalists to get in touch with us when they were thinking about writing on N. Ireland issues. I think we had some effect. I also worked hard on the Irish American community, which is extensive in major cities on the US east coast, especially Boston, New York and Washington. By speaking at lunches and dinners I got to know the Irish American lawyers in Boston, the business people in New York and the politicians in Washington. We made a lot of progress in showing there were two sides to the conflict, and that the Labour government was serious about working for fairness and equality for all and for peace.

Politically we worked individuals and committees on Capitol Hill. I made good progress with some influential individuals. People like the Kennedy clan, Senator Chris Dodds among the Democrats and the Republican (in the US sense) Peter King, who was a strong supporter of Sinn Fein. I saw several UK ambassadors to Washington come and go. The two most important in my time were John Kerr (who returned to become permanent secretary at the Foreign Office) and Chris Meyer (a former press secretary to John Major – but I didn't hold that against him). Chris, who was there longer, did a great job in getting

Britain's point of view across and building people's trust in him. He had worked on the problem for John Major and knew the issues well.

One of the toughest folk to get through to was the Republican Peter King. On my second meeting with him, I was told he was going to be late, as he was held up on the Hill at a meeting. I waited a respectable twenty minutes at his office and then left. Walking out of his office and across to the White House, I passed him on the other side of the road walking up the hill surrounded by a pack of journalists and talking, as he walked, to Sinn Fein's Gerry Adams. I quite understood the attraction of a meeting with Gerry Adams, but I wasn't going to let him get away with it. I got him on the phone later and asked him how his meeting with Gerry had gone. He was suitably contrite and to make up for it he invited me to go upstate to a university in his New York constituency and speak to a group of people interested in Ireland. I have no doubt he thought I might get a rough ride. I readily accepted the invite and had a forceful debate with some very sceptical individuals. As I had made the effort to journey to see them I got a good hearing and a good response. It changed my relationship with Peter King. He was still a strong Sinn Fein supporter, but he would now talk, joke and listen to me. He introduced me to the students and staff at the university saying, 'These are words I never thought I'd say, but it is a pleasure to introduce the British Secretary for Northern Ireland.'

The other tough nut to crack was Ben Gilman, chair of the House Foreign Relations Committee. He and most of his group on the committee didn't change their views but they took us seriously and when we made progress acknowledged it. As well as giving us a hearing when we were in Washington, they asked a whole host of questions and were genuinely interested in what we had to say. We slowly moved forward in the US by illustrating the complexity of the conflict in N. Ireland, showing that there was more than one point of view, and that we were working in an even-handed way.

To help with the media in Belfast, we beefed up the press office and started to make a concerted effort to do better. Things improved, especially after ex-BBC man Tom Kelly and ex-*Mirror* journalist Sheree Dodd were brought in to run the Belfast press office. As director of the Information Service overall and my press secretary, Tom in particular was an invaluable support and extremely good at getting the message out quickly and with enough sense of the dynamics of the process to make it effective. He knew when to say nothing as well as when to say a lot, and that mattered.

Restructuring the press office was one of the few times that I sought to make big changes to the way the civil service operated. To be honest, I had mixed feelings from the beginning about the civil service. As individuals, I found the vast majority good, bright and fun to work with. Most of them were public servants, in the real sense of those words, and we worked together well. A few I found difficult, unhelpful and people I could only really get frustrated and annoyed with. Ken Lindsay soon worked out who fitted into the latter category and handled the situation very well. He used to come in and say so-and-so is on his (it was usually a him) way up to talk to me and do his job, so try and be nice. He then gave one of his rare broad grins. It usually worked. Ken did not stay with me all my time in N. Ireland, but was replaced towards the end of my stay by Nick Perry, a completely different character but one who fitted well into the team.

I had extreme difficulty with only one official. He had worked for Paddy Mayhew before me and once, when I was in opposition attending an event at the same time as Paddy, he had sidled up to me and started slagging Paddy off and telling me how the Labour party was going to win the next election and how he was looking forward to working with me. It had the reverse effect. I soon found when I got into office that I couldn't work with him – he had been disloyal to Paddy and therefore was equally capable of being the same to me. Eventually, the civil service moved him out of my line of vision, but as always they looked after their own and, despite the fact that he was no longer in the NIO, when I left animosity was still there.

My main problem with the civil service was what I saw as their lack of proactiveness, the slowness of the system when I wanted to move quickly. I noticed this most acutely as time went on over questions like opening inquiries into events like Bloody Sunday or particularly difficult killings like that of Robert Hamill. My first months in both offices, London and Belfast, were not easy. I used to get very frustrated. I suppose I had been used to opposition, when with a very small team we had worked well and quickly together to get things done. But fighting as a team to get into government, where you all share the same objective and are all easily motivated, is different from being part of government, where many people feel they are just part of a great machine and cannot influence much by what they do.

I think the difficulties arose from attitudes on both sides and the structure we were working within. I wanted action yesterday. I just couldn't understand why things took so long. Only when I learnt that I was no longer steering a yacht that I could tack and move very quickly, but rather an oil tanker which turned a couple of degrees in an hour, did life get easier for the civil servants working closest to me, although I still went on pushing because the pace at which we produced work was not as fast as I wanted. I think this is where I got my name for being a warm human being, but often tough to please. I remember John McKervill, my deputy private secretary, saying at the end of a long day, with a grin, that they were working on Bloody Sunday, police reform, EU money, the Odyssey Centre and Springvale College, and opening Hillsborough and Stormont, but that they couldn't do it all in a day.

I was frustrated by the civil service culture of only telling you what you asked about. They always seemed to know better what was going on than you did. I think the civil servants do a better job at networking and joining up government than we as politicians ever managed. I was also frustrated by the whole culture of the civil service being so risk averse, which meant that to do anything a bit out of the ordinary could be regarded as distinctly dodgy ('an interesting idea' as they would say). Since leaving government I have wondered at Ken's ready willingness to say yes to my proposal to visit the Maze Prison (see Chapter 7) when I went to talk to convicted loyalist and republican prisoners.

Over time the system and I did find a way of working together that suited us both. I slowly began to understand that their training as civil servants was to service the Minister by delivering information. This was fine, but information was for me the first stage. When we had looked at the information, the analysis, I wanted delivery. Civil service training is not as good as it should be on delivery. I was not expecting people to take party political positions, which everyone understood they could not. But I did want more than lots of papers saying, 'There are the following options available in this area: (1) a review; (2) need to seek legal advice; (3) need to consult other departments.' That being said, the fact that the structure of the civil service does not focus on delivery should not really surprise anyone because neither does the pay structure. But I didn't learn that until much later. The longer I was in government the easier it got because I could make a judgement about what was worth fighting to achieve and what was going to be a non-starter.

4

Mo Must Go

There is never a good time to make progress in N. Ireland. We didn't have a choice, I knew, but trying to move forward in the peace process as the summer marching season approached was only going to add to our difficulties.

Whole histories have been written on the tradition of the marches and parades in N. Ireland. Depending on whose version you read they are either a 'joyful celebration of culture and heritage' or a symbol of historic dominance and oppression. Each community uses parades to mark their important anniversaries, like the republicans' commemorations at Easter or the unionists' 12 July Parades. As well as these main occasions there are many other smaller parades across N. Ireland during the spring and summer every year – some 3000 in all. The vast majority of these are unionist- or loyalist-organized by groups such as the Royal Black Perceptory or the Apprentice Boys of Derry or, by far the largest number, by the Orange Order, named after William of Orange.

The vast majority also are peaceful. But there never was a golden age in Ireland when every one of these parades was celebrated and equally enjoyed by both communities. Inevitably Protestant parades in mainly Protestant areas pass without trouble and are more akin to street festivals. But in other parts of N. Ireland the parades are a short fuse to violence. This is not helped by the behaviour of some marchers, like those who marched down the Ormeau Road in Belfast holding five fingers up outside the bookies' where loyalists killed five Catholics in 1992 – to be greeted by the residents lining the route chanting, 'Orange bastards!'

The most famous march is the Drumcree church parade through the town of Portadown. This takes place every year on the Sunday before 12 July. It is organized by the local District Orange Lodge and is well attended by lodges from the surrounding areas. Over the years of the Troubles in N. Ireland, certain towns have become increasingly segregated. When you drive across N. Ireland you can tell in some villages when the community changes by the flags flying, or in some Protestant communities by the way the kerbstones are painted red, white and blue. If the flags were not in evidence my security, Keith and John, could answer a question as to which community we were travelling through without hesitation. Sadly it was only occasionally that their answer was, 'This is a mixed community.' In some areas, especially in parts of Belfast, high concrete and steel walls (called, believe it or not, 'peace walls') have been built to keep the two communities apart.

But the situation is far from static. Over the years in Portadown, for instance, roads have changed from Protestant to Catholic and from Catholic to Protestant. This has meant that routes which the Drumcree parades took in the past which were Protestant are now Catholic. These people movements have made parades a growing problem. The Catholics do not want parades down their road, which they see as Protestants showing their power and their dislike of the Catholics. Likewise the Protestants ask why should they have to re-route their march when they are only on the road for a limited time – it's their road too. The police over the years have changed routes to minimize the risk of violence. But they have ended up caught in the middle. Being abused by both sides is tough, particularly when some of the taunts are 'We know where you live. We know where your wife and kids are.'

On the day of the march the Orangemen – all decked out with bowler hats, white gloves, umbrellas and bright orange 'collarettes' around their necks – march out from Portadown town centre up to Drumcree Parish Church for a service and then back down into the town again. By 1994 the route back to town was along the main Garvaghy Road, a length of which runs alongside a nationalist housing estate. It is along this bit of the Garvaghy Road where most of the trouble takes place. In 1995 and 1996, the violence reached a peak. In both years police attempts to re-route the parade away from the road, in the interests of public safety, were overwhelmed by the numbers of people marching. 1966 was very tense. There was a stand-off between the marchers and the police for several days. Then the world's media saw the police defeated and the Orangemen march in triumph down the road with the RUC going ahead using batons to clear protesters sitting in the road. This event gave out one very clear and simple message to the world: the British government were unable or unwilling to protect the interests and rights of the Catholics in N. Ireland in the face of a Prot-estant show of force.

As always, the reality was more complicated; both sides have rights. The Protestants have the right to march, the right to free assembly, and the Catholics have the right to live free of fear and intimidation. Both felt they were in the right, and neither side was willing to budge. I felt for the police caught in the middle and their families sitting at home watching the pictures on the television wondering if they would still be a family when all the violence had stopped.

After 1996 my predecessor, Paddy Mayhew, had established a Parades Commission of independent people to try and find an accommodation between the two sides. I supported the idea of the Parades Commission. I thought it might help, particularly by stopping the police being put in an impossible situation, and by taking most of the decisions over parade routes out of political hands and putting them into the control of a neutral, indepen-dent body. Ronnie Flanagan, the Chief Constable of the RUC, supported it too. But the unionists hated it. They thought it was just designed to stop the parades and suppress their culture.

The Commission was a good idea, but Paddy had had to

fudge it when it was introduced in the House of Commons. The Major government, by that time, were increasingly dependent on the support of the Ulster Unionists and on a staunchly pro-unionist group within the Tory party to get their legislation through the Commons. They could count on our support for the Parades Commission and over the peace process, but to keep going in other areas they needed these people on side. As a result Paddy formally established the Parades Commission but gave it no real powers, so as not to alienate those in his own party to the point where they would oppose it.

As the 1997 marching season approached, there was no time to increase the powers of the Commission, so I decided I would need to work alongside it. And since any final decision would rest with me, I felt I should engage from the beginning. So I met with all sides and had talk after talk. I went to the Garvaghy Road to talk to the residents. Going to them, rather than having them come to my office, was a good first step. I brought with me my takeaway Chinese dinner and we sat and talked. The women and a local priest were tough but were willing to chat. I am pretty sure we could have found a way forward with them. However, there was one member of the group, Breandan MacCionnaith, who had a pretty tight control of the group and was clearly not for moving. When I tried to honour my promise to visit just before the decision on the march was announced and tell them in person what it was, I was unable to do so. The build-up of the police made a visit unsafe. I tried to phone to apologize for not coming, but Breandan answered the phone and said if I wasn't there, that was it, I had deserted them. Not helpful, but I learnt a lot.

I made a similar effort with the Orangemen. I met them at their lodge outside of Portadown. It was isolated in the country-side and the local RUC took me there. The Orange Hall was festooned with banners and had a log fire burning. It was like a film set from an old movie. The Orangemen were very polite and explained what they thought and why. Only one guy got a little irate, but he calmed down. I made absolutely no progress, but I was glad I had been and talked to them face to face. The RUC dropped me back at the hotel I was staying at in Portadown and I thanked them and the escort car for taking me. One of them said in a chatty manner that was okay, but he was now going back to the hall to pick up his brother. I had no doubt about the commitment of the RUC as a force but could understand why there were sometimes doubts about an individual's impartiality.

I had meetings with two Orangemen, William Bingham and Denis Watson, who were more prepared than most to push on and try and find some accommodation. The talks were handicapped by the Orange Order policy of refusing to meet with the residents face to face. My problem was that the residents' group was the only group that had support from the folk on the Garvaghy Estate. I was told by some residents on the estate that other groups had tried to form but they were told in no uncertain terms that there was only one residents' group on the Garvaghy. Either way it was not for me to start dictating the make-up of the group on either side and, without the two groups talking directly, progress would be slow and difficult.

The problems at this time were not just in Portadown. Another main road in Belfast itself, the Lower Ormeau Road, had become a flashpoint too. The situation was never as bad there as at Portadown – partly, I think, because some people from each community were talking on the ground. They were helped by a safe and neutral house in the community occupied by my two Quaker friends, Janet and Alan Quilley. I met at their house representatives of the Lower Ormeau Concerned Residents Group, and individuals from the local Ballynafeigh Orange Lodge. These meetings were useful but did not produce any startling results. I have no doubt that the generosity and understanding that Alan and Janet had showed to all sides helped tremendously with relations between individuals on either side of the divide. Also, on the Lower Ormeau the media did not play quite as big a role in putting any problems up in lights as always seemed to be the case in Portadown.

As efforts to find a compromise over Drumcree continued, the tension could be felt. Everyone was feeling the strain. At the beginning of June, I spoke at the Police Federation's annual conference in Newcastle, County Down. I was billed to talk about some of the proposals for police reform that were in our election manifesto. I tried to do it pragmatically and cautiously, but I was heckled and some men walked out. Obviously some of the higher ranks thought this behaviour was not on, that the police should not behave like that. I was not new to heckling and did what I always did, which was to engage the heckler. He coped, but many in the hall found it difficult.

As the date of the march got nearer there seemed to be no let-up. But then came a glimmer of good news when the two local papers, the *Newsletter* and the *Irish News*, printed joint editorials calling for a deal ahead of Drumcree. It was something they would do more of as time went on. They proposed a two-year deal: the march would go ahead one year and not the next. The reaction sadly was predictable. Agreement was impossible because for each side it depended which year came first – the year of no march had to be first for the nationalists and the year of a march had to be first for the unionists.

Towards the end of June the talks were again being described as being at crisis point. I didn't feel they had ever been out of crisis. On the last Friday in June I had both sides in different rooms in Hillsborough trying once more to make progress. These were called proximity talks and were the closest we came to the two sides talking. We still had to go from room to room to see if anything could be achieved, to try and find some common ground.

On the following Sunday the police re-routed an Orange parade from the Lower Ormeau Road. There was a stand-off at the bridge at the top of the road. But there were no real problems. Everyone was waiting for the big one at Drumcree.

The next day the new Irish government team lead by Bertie Ahern flew into Belfast to discuss Drumcree. I had got on well with Bruton, Bertie's predecessor, and got on as well if not better with Bertie. He understood the situation well. He was a working-class boy from North Dublin with a canny political nous. He and his officials made a good team.

The Irish government met both sides. The Garvaghy Road residents had announced plans for a street festival at the same time and in the same street the Orange were planning to march down. Of course they knew it would not happen, but it was good publicity for them. The Orange Order had become slightly more conciliatory but still argued that in their view the residents' group was an IRA front, whipped up to stop decent church-going Protestants from celebrating their culture. This statement is hard to reconcile with the announcement the same day from the LVF, that they would mount terrorist attacks in the Republic if the march were re-routed. Some among the Orange Order were visibly embarrassed. The lack of a willingness to talk with the residents gave them an easy line with the press: 'No talking, no walking.' The residents said they would meet anyone any-where – knowing that the nature of their group was the problem for the unionists, not the meeting itself.

The lobbying on all sides grew increasingly desperate. Because everyone thought that ultimately it was my decision, they all thought pressuring me was the best thing to do. In fact it wasn't. My hands were tied much more than they, or I at the time, knew. I had everyone, Irish, British and Americans, queuing at my door. A special US delegation, including two wealthy businessmen well committed to Ireland called Bill Flynn and Tom Moran from New York, came to see me with Sister Mary Turley to say how badly a decision to allow the parade to go ahead would be seen in the States. I listened to them, particularly as I knew they had all been committed over many years to working for peace in N. Ireland.

But time was running out. More meetings with both sides

were getting nowhere. If anything the positions were hardening. Robert Saulters, Grand Master of the Orange Order, brought a delegation. Former Ulster Unionist leader (Lord) Jim Molyneaux had lunch with Adam and me. In a last-ditch appeal to the Portadown Orange, Adam and I made a late-night visit to their Orange Hall. We walked into the hall completely full of men in their orange collarettes waiting to hear from us. They weren't the easiest audience to talk to – mainly a sea of steely-looking faces. Adam was brilliant. As a Proddy lad brought up in a sectarian Glasgow, he knew the mindset of the people we were dealing with. But even he couldn't get through.

I think it would be true to say that we did try harder with the Orange side. We were facing a grim reality. If the police decided to stop the parade at the top of the Garvaghy Road, as they had in 1995 and 1996, the Orange were in a position to pull together all their might and overcome them. It was as crude as that. No one wanted a repeat of the social 'meltdown' of 1996. But at the same time we couldn't, with any sense of fairness, just back down from the outset and give into the threat of force. So appealing to the Orange Order was the best we could do.

Jon, H and Fred were over staying at Hillsborough. It was a warm and sunny weekend. Nigel and his partner Kate were there as was Adam's wife Maureen. They were all anxious, H I think most of all. She understood a lot more then than I think we gave her credit for at the time.

Saturday, 5 July was decision day. I drove to Stormont Castle, where my office was, to meet Ronnie Flanagan and General Rupert Smith. We all knew it was Ronnie's call. He had all the security information and a better idea of who was planning what the next day than any of us – information he didn't share even with me in any great detail. Under the law as it stood then, the judgement was crude and straightforward: a balance of what was in the best interests of public safety. If the Orange looked the bigger threat then the march would go ahead; if the republicans mounted a bigger threat it would be stopped. It was appalling.

It had to change. And change it would, but not in time to help us in 1997.

That Saturday morning the information was conflicting. There were dangers on both sides. I think it would be fair to say that Ronnie genuinely didn't know which way to call it. So we had to cover all eventualities. I had to go through the proper legal process, see all the necessary people, in case anyone decided to seek judicial review of the final decisions, which was quite likely. I also think the longer it took him to make the decision the less time the side that lost had to dig in. This was about 4 p.m. There was still no clear decision about what to do. But preparations had to be made. If the parade was to be stopped, the army couldn't wait any longer. They began to roll razor wire out across the road. It looked as though the parade would be stopped.

A few hours later, I think it was around 10 p.m., I was informed of the final decision. The decision was to let the parade go ahead. It was based on the view that the threat from the Orange was too great. There were plans to mobilize, not only at Portadown, but also across N. Ireland, as they had done in 1996. If the stand-off went on too long, the police would be overwhelmed. The risk to life was too great. So the decision had been taken on the basis of the lesser risk to let the Orange march.

I felt cornered by the system, which required the chief constable to make the final decision on purely public order considerations rather than broader political issues. I hadn't got the information that Ronnie had, so it was difficult to argue with him. I had the legal right to overrule him, but I felt I was left with no choice other than to let the parade go ahead. I could not choose an option for reasons of fairness and politics while I was being told there was a likely risk to the lives of police officers. I left for Hillsborough in an angry mood. I felt I had let myself be cornered. As with my return visit to the Garvaghy Road, folk must have known I was leaving it too late and I

Drumcree

wouldn't be able to go down there and tell people the decision myself, as I wanted to. As we drove down the M1 near Lisburn a column of RUC armoured Land Rovers sped along beside us. One after the other, there must have been fifty at least. It looked like an army going into battle.

Some time around midnight the army rolled back the razor wire. Word spread quickly among the residents, and they tried to get on to the road and mount their sit-down protest. They were caught on the hop, not really prepared and so even angrier. From then on I sat with Jon, H and Fred in my flat and watched it all live on the TV. There was nothing else to do. Violence between the residents and the police grew as police Land Rovers moved in to block off streets and houses alongside the road. Anna Healy, who had let the press in London know when the decision was taken, called to say that Breandan MacCionnaith was live on CNN, looking like he was in the midst of a pitched battle. We turned over to see him yelling at the cameras that I had betrayed them and broken my promise. He knew the importance of the US interest in all this. He said exactly what his audience wanted to hear. Against the backdrop of people, especially women, being hauled off the road by black-garbed RUC men in full riot gear it was a propaganda triumph for the republicans.

I didn't sleep much. At noon on Sunday 6 July the Orange March went ahead. Protesters lined the road on either side waving banners and shouting. The marchers were silently triumphant, their polished shoes gleaming. In their wake, the riots began, in Portadown, in West Belfast, in Lurgan. The pattern was familiar, as the police knew it would be – rioting contained in the nationalist areas. 'Controllable'.

A train was burnt out in Lurgan. Shots were fired at police in North Belfast. Plastic bullets were fired in return. We arranged a press conference on the steps of Stormont Castle. It was a beautiful sunny morning, the press pack was assembled. The civil servants had been working with Nigel on a statement for me to give, which I had changed several times. It was never my favourite way to operate – reading out a prepared statement, not answering many questions. But when a situation is really tight you have to weigh your words carefully and stick to them. I wanted to be straight. Yes, it was a difficult decision. It was made, as it had to be, in the interests of public safety alone. The law said that nothing else was to be taken into account. But I went further. I said I believed the law was wrong. It gave both sides an incentive to be intransigent and to threaten violence. It sent a signal that 'might was right'. I said might was never right. Right was right. And before the marching season came round again in 1998, I would see that the law was changed for good. Ronnie Flanagan gave a press conference down near Portadown. He was straight-talking too. He spoke of the decision being the lesser of 'two evils'.

Monday saw further rioting in nationalist areas of N. Ireland. Loyalism was gearing up for a fight too. A member of the loyalist Ulster Defence Association (UDA) called Brian Morton was blown up by his own bomb. Just when I thought things couldn't get any worse, they did. One of the confidential documents prepared by officials in the weeks before was leaked to a journalist. In itself it was an innocuous enough briefing paper, setting out the options. But its tone was unfortunate. It hinted that the most likely outcome was that the parade would be allowed to go ahead. The language was very unhelpful, talking about 'Orange feet on the Garvaghy Road'. The interpretation given by the media to the contents of the leaked document was that I had made up my mind what to do long before the final decision was made.

Of course I hadn't, but to a suspicious community of nationalists the message was clear. I had 'deceived' them. Two new wall murals went up immediately. One showed me as Pontius Pilate washing my hands, while people were trampled by police. Another said simply, 'New Labour, Same Old Shite. Dr Mo must go.' You could tell it was by a republican because there was a squiggly Irish accent (fadh in Irish) written above the letter i. Driving out to Hillsborough that evening, I looked back and saw the smoke from burning cars in West Belfast rising up into the cool, clear summer sky.

Drumcree 1997 saw over 1500 petrol bombs and sixty RUC and fifty-six civilian injuries in just four days. Fortunately the 12 July weekend itself passed off more peacefully, thanks largely to the continued efforts of people like Ronnie Flanagan, John Steele and others working furiously with the Orange leadership to minimize the threat of violence. With the nationalist community at boiling point, the situation was already dangerous and unpredictable. At the last minute, the Orange Order leadership announced that parades would be voluntarily re-routed away from nationalist areas including the Lower Ormeau Road. There was a tremendous sense of relief. Perhaps, I thought, the growing sense among some in the Orange Order that they desperately needed to improve their image was beginning to have an impact.

It was an impossible situation. Nationalists including John Hume were furious about the way the security forces were deployed in nationalist areas after an open admission that we had backed down in the face of the greater evil at Drumcree. Unionists, including David Trimble, were furious with the attitude the Chief Constable and I had taken, admitting that we had only acted as we did because of the threat of violence from loyalists. Friends like the Quilleys and experts on parades like Neil Jarman and Dominic Bryan, from the University of Ulster (who had helped us put our policy together in opposition), were angry too, as I expected them to be. But they were also practical and wanted assurances from me that things would be different next year – assurances I gave and was determined to keep.

Giving the Parades Commission its proper powers was never going to be easy in a fragile political situation. Given the stance the Ulster Unionists and the Orange Order had taken in advance, it was always going to be seen as an anti-unionist move. Of course it wasn't. Any new rules would have to apply equally to both Protestant and Catholic parades, and the overriding concern was with relationships between the communities. But what it would inevitably mean was that decisions would be made objectively, and people would not automatically always get what they wanted – something I am afraid some in the Orange Order were just not prepared to accept.

The last Orange parade of 1997 was in Belfast on Sunday, 26 October. It was blocked by the RUC from entering the Lower Ormeau Road but passed off peacefully. But the work had to start then to prepare the way for next year and I was keen to get moving on the parades bill as soon as we could. I announced the new laws on 17 October that year, to a barrage of criticism from both sides. But I knew in my heart that what we were doing was both principled and right. In the end neither side could take a great deal of comfort from the legislation alone. The real test was what could be done in practice to bring about dialogue and accommodation between residents and marchers and, failing that, what decisions would be taken about individual parades. I had faith in the former chief exec of Leeds Training and Enterprise Council, trade union leader Alistair Graham, who was chair of the Commission, and in the balance of people working alongside him.

I continued to meet people throughout the next ten months to talk about parades. I was determined not to let the issue drop off the agenda just because it was off the headlines. That had been a mistake in previous years: it was forgotten about until the marching season started again, and by then it was too late.

The new powers for the Parades Commission came in February 1998 along with four new members, two identified with the Protestant community, Tommy Cheevers and Glen Barr, and two identified with the Catholic community, Aiden Canavan and Rose Anne McCormick, to keep the balance right.

Despite lengthy consultations in Parliament, the Commission was still bitterly opposed by many on the unionist side. And it was clear then that the members of the Commission were going to come in for a lot of stick whatever decisions they took once the marching season started. Having taken their decisions, the people we were appointing would then have to go back and live in their local communities, unlike people like me who could disappear into our castles or across the water to London. I admired the people who came forward from N. Ireland. There is a huge number of very vocal critics of the politicians and the public servants there, but they were the ones who stuck their necks out to make a difference. And even if you were not under any particular threat, in such a febrile atmosphere it was always possible that somebody could just decide to have a go at you or your family. I have a lot of admiration for people who are prepared to do their public duty and serve on bodies like the Parades Commission.

The Commission made their first proper legal judgement on Saturday, 4 April 1998, saying that a planned parade by the Apprentice Boys could not go down Belfast's Lower Ormeau Road. The Apprentice Boys threatened to challenge the decision in court. I was already being taken to court by the Lower

Ormeau nationalist residents' group (LOCC) for the alleged 'unrepresentative' composition of the Commission. Needless to say, the LOCC spokesman was less than full hearted in his praise for the Commission's first decision, despite the fact that it had gone the way he had wanted.

But no sooner had the Commission members got their feet under the table and begun to exercise their proper powers than trouble struck. The Commission planned to publish some sort of overview of the decisions they were going to make on a number of marches at once, ahead of the summer marching season. The idea, a good one, was to show that the overall picture was fair and balanced and that decisions were not being skewed against either the nationalist or the loyalist groups.

The problem came when Alistair Graham and his colleagues planned to publish their overall view right in the middle of the referendum campaign for the Good Friday Agreement in April 1998. In the fevered atmosphere of the time it was bound to be very divisive, and a distraction from the main issues. Whatever was said, especially, for example, about Drumcree, would be seized upon by one side or the other. Tony Blair was very nervous about it. He thought publication should be delayed, or better still cancelled altogether. The main concern was that if the decision on Drumcree went against the Orange Order, it would only help to give more support for those on the unionist side who were campaigning against the Agreement. 'Aha,' they would say, 'this is just the beginning of what the Agreement means – decisions going against the unionist people and their culture' etc., etc.

I have to say that at the time I didn't really agree. I was worried about undermining the credibility of the Commission if there was any delay. And anyway people were going to have to deal with the Commission's decisions sooner or later and if they could be seen to be fair overall to both sides then I thought that might be a plus. But, at the same time, the Drumcree decision was so incendiary. It was a tough call.

Tony was not for taking any chances at that stage. He tried privately to persuade Alistair Graham to delay publication of the report. Alistair, wary of accusations that he had been secretly 'got at', said he would consider it only if Tony wrote and explicitly asked him to delay. Then he and the other members of the Parades Commission would think about it. Tony's letter was the cover he needed. The next day the Commission announced their decision to delay publication. Alistair said that they 'wanted the people of Northern Ireland to take decisions about the peace process without the emotional consequences which may have arisen from a review of parades'. He published Tony's letter to show that there were no secret deals.

The press were having none of it. They said that the Commission's independence had been 'severely compromised'. We stressed that the PM's intervention had only been in relation to the timing of the report and not its content, but it was pretty thin stuff. I only hoped the Commission would survive with at least some of its credibility left to do the job we would desperately need them to do later in the summer.

But there were two immediate casualties. Glen Barr and Tommy Cheevers both resigned from the Commission. They didn't blame 'government interference' directly, but everybody assumed that that was the main reason for them going. I think, in fact, neither had been very happy with the attitude the Commission was shaping up to take towards Drumcree and may well, in my opinion, have been glad of an excuse to get out. I tried to put a brave face on it and went out saying we intended to 'bring the body up to strength as soon as possible'. But I knew we had dealt Alistair Graham a blow, and I felt bad about it because he was good and very committed to doing a difficult job as best he could.

On 29 June, the Parades Commission announced their decision on Drumcree 1998. It was that, without local agreement, the Orange Order would not be able to hold the return part of their parade route into Portadown along the Garvaghy Road.

The decision was a surprise to no one. The Orange Order was furious. So was David Trimble. As newly appointed First Minister of N. Ireland, he met Tony Blair in Belfast a day or so after the decision and there was little on show of his brand-new mandate to serve the interests of all the people of N. Ireland. Portadown was after all in his Parliamentary constituency and he knew that the decision to stop the parade would affect his personal standing there very badly. It was his part in the 'triumph' of Drumcree '95 that had established his position within the Ulster Unionists and led to his victory in the leadership election that year. So it was personally very important to him. Tony stressed, as I had done, that the decision was conditional on there being no agreement between the two local groups themselves to resolve the issue and that he, David Trimble, should continue to do all he could to encourage the Orange Order to find an agreement.

Tony offered to send Jonathan Powell, his chief of staff, up to Hillsborough to meet the parties concerned and see if, even at this late stage, some sort of accommodation could be found. Denis Watson and William Bingham and others came to Hillsborough late that night to see Jonathan. Tony Blair stayed over too and met David Trimble very late when he turned up in his dinner suit. We all admitted that the chances of finding accommodation looked very slim.

In the run-up to the Drumcree Sunday I had many more meetings, including with Ronnie Flanagan who, it has to be said, seemed a relieved man not to have to shoulder the burden of decision-making that year. He and his team were in intensive talks too, but they failed to produce a breakthrough. So on Sunday, 5 June the stand-off began in the now familiar way. After their church service, the parade was halted at the top of the Garvaghy Road and the Orangemen gathered on the grassy hill near to the Drumcree church.

Wary that the numbers might threaten to overwhelm the police again, a major effort had been made to block the

Orangemen's path. Huge containers of concrete were placed across the road and a deep trench dug at the bottom of the field where the marchers gathered. And hundreds of yards of razor wire was stretched out each side of the barrier. Alongside these fortifications an extra thousand troops had been drafted in from the UK. Tom Kelly had ensured that action shots of the troops arriving and training were broadcast on the news for several nights. We had to let people know we were serious. Lives depended on it.

As the day wore on the mood at Drumcree worsened and in many parts of N. Ireland street protests began, roads were blocked and a few cars set on fire. A number of Catholic homes were also attacked in North Belfast. My job was to get out there and explain to people what we were doing and why we were doing it. We had to appeal to moderate unionists not to join in. This was not the beginning of the end for their culture and traditions. There could be Orange parades in Portadown in future. But the important thing this year was to uphold the rule of law. I did a round of the Sunday-morning political pro-grammes from the TV studios in Belfast. While going round I noticed that Andrew MacKay was doing the same thing and, thankfully, sending out the same message.

By Monday around 10,000 people had gathered at Drumcree. Showing that their decisions were not all one way, the Parades Commission issued rulings on a number of 12 July parades that day, including an Orange Order parade along the Ormeau Road in Belfast, which they said could proceed. There was anger among the nationalist residents there that they were being 'sacri-ficed' to soften the blow of the Drumcree decision, but it had little impact on the views of the Orange Order. Roadblocks and sporadic violence continued in many parts of N. Ireland. People remembered the loyalist workers' strike in 1974 which had brought N. Ireland to its knees and destroyed the Sunningdale power-sharing agreement which gave nationalists a seat in N. Ireland's government for the first time.

Helpful as ever, Ian Paisley addressed a rally in Portadown, declaring apocalyptically that 12 July would be 'the settling day'. Making inflammatory speeches may not be the same as actually taking part in acts of violence, but it's not a long way off. And Ian is a master at it. The situation at Drumcree itself continued to deteriorate, with sustained violent attacks on the RUC and British Army barricades. As night fell there were repeated attempts to cross the barriers, and members of the security forces came under attack from guns and blast bombs. They replied with plastic bullets.

Away from the front line, meetings continued to try to find a way through. I saw Gerry Adams, Seamus Mallon and David Trimble, as well as visiting the RUC Headquarters and the army HQ at the Mahon Road Barracks. The leaders of the Orange Order, including Robert Saulters, met Tony Blair at No. 10. We had a special operations (Ops) room set up at Stormont House to monitor events on the ground across N. Ireland. Staffed twenty-four hours a day by security staff and occasionally attended by the police and soldiers, it was our eyes and ears. There was a live feed from the police radio channel and we were in constant communication. It was like a war room, with a big map on the wall with pins stuck in it showing where sporadic incidents had occurred, including roads blocked and attacks on Catholic homes and businesses. Stormont was also where we gathered with Ronnie Flanagan, Rupert Smith and their advisers to assess the situation and let me know what their next moves would be.

Still the talking went on. As late as Saturday the 11th proximity talks were held in Armagh with representatives of the Orange Order and the Garvaghy Road Residents' Coalition involving Jonathan Powell. Throughout, the Orange Order maintained its position that it would not engage in face-to-face talks with the residents – there was no agreement between the two sides.

Sunday, 12 July 1998 was perhaps one of my darkest days in N. Ireland. Tensions continued to mount on the hill at

Drumcree. Overnight news of cars being stopped, shop windows smashed and sporadic violence came in from across N. Ireland. Then the worst happened. A petrol bomb, thrown through the window of a home in Ballymoney, County Antrim took the lives of three young boys, Richard (aged ten), Mark (nine) and Jason (eight) Quinn, as they slept in their beds. Christine Quinn (a Catholic), the boys' mother, and her partner Raymond Craig (a Protestant) escaped from the house. But they and their neighbours were unable to get back in to reach the three boys. Lee Quinn (thirteen), the eldest son, was staying with his grandmother when the incident occurred.

Ronnie Flanagan immediately came out and said it was a sectarian attack carried out by loyalists. It was a tragedy waiting to happen. Anti-Catholic violence, fuelled by the emotions being whipped up at Drumcree, was random and unthinking. Maybe the Quinns' house was targeted because they were a mixed Protestant and Catholic couple? Maybe it wasn't even as calculating as that, just a random, unthinking act that destroyed a family. I was devastated. The people being attacked were precisely the sort of people whose rights I thought I was standing up for – decent people, who shouldn't have to be bowed by threats and bullying. The political ramifications were immediate.

William Bingham (then still Deputy Grand Chaplain of the Orange Order) called for the Drumcree protest to be ended. He said that the fifteen-minute march down the Garvaghy Road would be 'a hollow victory' as it would be taking place in the shadows of three little white coffins. It was a brave and important speech, made in the face of heckling and abuse from among the crowd at Drumcree. David Trimble and the Church of Ireland Primate Robin Eames joined the calls for an end to the protest. To their shame the local Orange lodge rejected these and all similar calls. But in reality the spell was broken. The head of steam that had been ominously building up behind the Orange protests ahead of the main July parades quickly evaporated.

I sat round the conference table at Stormont with Rupert Smith and his entourage all in camouflage, with Ronnie Flanagan, unusually still in uniform, and my team of officials, some in their Sunday shirtsleeves. No one knew quite what to say. To admit that this provided us with the breakthrough we needed would have been callous in the extreme and no one did. We told ourselves that the momentum behind the protest had been slipping away anyway. But I'm not sure that was true.

On Monday the 13th the main Orange parades were held across N. Ireland. In Belfast on the Lower Ormeau Road (where a local Orange parade had been authorized by the Parades Commission), Catholic residents held a black-flag protest against this parade. It poured with rain. The local Orangemen were grim-faced and silent. Water dripped off their bowler hats. Water dripped from the black flags. There were a lot of tears. The number of people at Drumcree decreased sharply to a few diehards, who vowed to go on and refused to accept any responsibility for what had happened in Ballymoney. But their support, their crucial oxygen supply, had been cut off and their voices of protest went unheard.

On Tuesday the funeral took place of the three Quinn children in Rasharkin, County Antrim. There was a huge turnout. From Washington Bill Clinton made a pledge to young Lee Quinn to do all he could to help bring peace to N. Ireland. Later that week, I paid a private visit to the Quinns. The grief was overwhelming. It was very difficult to think of anything that could be said. I just sat with them and shared their grief. What struck me most was that they were a totally normal family, which had been destroyed by the violence.

On Friday that week (17 July) the Portadown Orange Lodge conceded that it would not be able to force its way down the Garvaghy Road this year, but they maintained they would be back next. And so they were. And the next year, and the next. But it would never be the same again. In 1999 the mediation efforts of the Parades Commission were supplemented by

Scottish ACAS (Advisory, Conciliation and Arbitration Service) director, Frank Blair, at Tony Blair's request. We thought we could get around the fact that the Orange Order would not talk to the residents or the Parades Commission by sending in independent arbitration. But despite Frank's valiant efforts, and those of the two governments, over many months the deadlock could not be broken. David Trimble risked incurring the wrath of Orangemen in his constituency by meeting face to face with the residents, including Breandan MacCionnaith. Tony Blair met personally with representatives from both sides in Downing Street on a number of occasions. A survey showed that 80 per cent of N. Ireland residents thought the Portadown Orangemen should talk to the Parades Commission. Plans were made for major economic expansion in the area if an accommodation could be found and community relations improved. But all to no avail.

Once again, in the summer of 1999, the Parades Commission was left to make the tough choice. And since the Orange Order still refused to talk to them or directly to the residents and since, if anything, community relations had got worse instead of better, the Commission decided again that the parade would not go down the Garvaghy Road. All the now familiar preparations were made. The advantage of making a decision a week or so ahead of time was that it allowed the security forces to prepare the ground properly. This year, as well as the extra troops, the massive containers of concrete to block the road, and the razor wire, the army dug a deep flooded moat at the bottom of the hill. We also borrowed two mobile water cannon from the Belgian government, just in case. All these extra measures got the Tom Kelly treatment, with prominent footage on the BBC and UTV local news each evening.

The Orange Order was now bitterly divided, especially between the Grand Lodge leadership and the local Portadown district. After his crucial intervention in 1998, William Bingham resigned from the Orange Order's parades committee, citing the pressures of work. Grand Master Robert Saulters (who had once said that Tony Blair, by marrying Cherie, had 'sold his birthright by marrying a Romanist ... and would sell his soul to the devil himself') called for the local lodge to talk to the Parades Commission. As a consequence, the protest at Drumcree in 1999, while disruptive and very expensive, remained largely peaceful and only a small group of hardliners, including men like Harold Gracey and David Jones, stuck it out on the hill. And there they remained in lonely vigil for months afterwards.

Since I left N. Ireland, Drumcree has continued to provide an annual headache for all concerned. The marching season is still a time when many unconnected with either parade or protest take their holidays to get away from it all. Will it ever be resolved? In some places, where there is dialogue with the Commission and between the two sides, there has been progress. On the Lower Ormeau Road in Belfast and in Derry in August, parades do go ahead with limited antagonism and violence. But there is still a long way to go, and the interminable battle of Drumcree is far from over.

But I think the principles are now firmly established: that arbitration is the right way forward; that local communities should try to resolve these issues between themselves through dialogue and accommodation; and that if accommodation can't be found then decisions about where a parade may or may not go should be made by an independent body fairly, on objective criteria, and never again on the basis that might is right, or the 'lesser of two evils'. That, at least, is progress.

5
Hi Gerry, Hi Martin

SINN FEIN INTO TALKS

Back in 1997, the restraint shown by the Orange Order in voluntarily re-routing some of their 12 July parades brought a big change to the atmosphere in Belfast. It almost felt that there was a sense of reasonableness around. I questioned myself on my feelings. As always I decided if there was a glimmer of hope it was important for me to be confident. Someone had to be. So in my next couple of interviews, with John Lloyd for the *New Statesman* and Barry Hildendbrand for *Time* magazine, I talked up how hopeful I was of a breakthrough.

Lines of communication between British and Irish governments and Sinn Fein had been strained since the murders of RUC constables Graham and Johnston in June, and there had been no further meetings between the republicans and British officials. Nevertheless we had been careful not to react in a knee-jerk way to the killings, and our position on Sinn Fein coming into the talks had not changed. In making a statement to the House of Commons at the end of June (on the 25th), Tony Blair had included an effective deadline for completing the negotiations by May 1998. This was going to be a tough commitment to keep, but it showed the republicans that, along with setting a timetable for them to come into the talks, we were serious and wouldn't allow the talks to be strung out indefinitely. Weapons decommissioning was to be dealt with alongside the talks as George Mitchell had originally proposed in 1996 when he first came over to N. Ireland, with the Canadian General John de Chastelain and former Finnish Prime Minister Hari Holkeri to provide independent insight into the decommissioning issue.

Even though everyone now knew what was on the table, both we and Sinn Fein were still in our minds questioning whether the other was serious. But it was clear to me that both sides had to take a risk if any kind of progress was to be made at all. In fact, I think Sinn Fein was feeling quite strong at this point. At the election in 1997 both Gerry Adams and Martin McGuinness had gained seats in the Westminster Parliament. The June local elections saw an increase in the Sinn Fein vote which many analysts thought was nationalists trying to encourage the IRA to go for a ceasefire.

Just when I felt as if we were beginning to make some progress, on 15 July a Catholic teenager, Bernadette Martin, was shot dead in her (Protestant) boyfriend's house. Renegade loyalist terrorists were suspected. It was murders like this, innocent young lovers acting naturally, ignoring the social divisions between them, that really turned my stomach. But it also made me angry and even more determined to keep going so that other families in Belfast didn't have to suffer as Bernadette's family were. To me then it felt like being in the old American South where gangs of white boys would attack another white boy for having a black girlfriend. In N. Ireland one or other side could attack you, depending on where you lived and for having a partner from a different religion. It was sectarian bigotry at its worst.

Hints through our earlier contacts with Sinn Fein showed that the position we had set out in May was attractive to them. They regarded the six-week break between the new ceasefire and joining the talks as an insult. But behind the scenes they knew that, with the August holiday providing a natural break in the talks, it was a good offer and time to make a move. Their key worry was, could they trust Tony and me? We were the ones, after all, that would make the judgement after the six weeks was up on whether or not to invite Sinn Fein in. I wasn't sure, after Drumcree (where the nationalist community felt wronged yet again), that some of the trust I had built up hadn't been eroded – a feeling that made me less sure about which way Sinn Fein would jump. But the truth was that they had their eyes on the bigger picture and while Drumcree was an important battle to fight, the war and the peace involved much more than that.

On Friday, 18 July we held one of the regular British–Irish Inter-Governmental Conferences in London. These were big, formal meetings with Ministers and lots of officials from both governments in attendance. It was the first one that the new Irish Foreign Minister, Ray Burke, had attended. I liked Ray – he was a straight-talker who I felt we could do business with. The meeting barely got off the ground. It was full of rumours. The Irish were so jumpy it was difficult for them to sit still. About halfway through, big news broke, when one of our officials came hurrying into the room in the basement of the NIO office on London's Millbank to announce that John Hume and Gerry Adams had issued a joint statement giving their view that 'the peace process can be restored' and welcoming the efforts made by the two governments towards removing the 'obstacles' to an inclusive talks process. The last time the two had made such a positive statement had been ahead of the 1994 IRA ceasefire.

The process was tortuous but familiar to us. Gerry Adams would not speak for the IRA, but would call on them to do something and they would respond. I think this was to give them time to get their boys in order. Having made the announcement provisionally, it gave them some leverage in persuading those who might be doubtful that this was the right course of action. I also think it was important that John Hume was part of the statement because it made Gerry Adams look like he was speaking as part of the broader nationalist community, which made him stronger. I didn't mind what they had to do to make progress. What was making me very excited was the thought that the IRA ceasefire was about to be restored. I was beginning to understand the hurdles people like Gerry Adams and Martin

McGuinness had to keep climbing over to make progress. But at the same time such a positive statement would not have come unless they knew it would provoke a positive response from within the IRA.

The British–Irish meeting broke up pretty quickly. I congratulated Ray on his appointment and told him I looked forward to working together closely etc., etc., then we headed out to the waiting press to give our reaction. As I walked out I thought of all that Gerry and John had done to achieve this. John Hume was working so hard to get progress he was making himself ill. I remember controlling my excitement that Sinn Fein had taken a step, because we still had to wait to see the response of David Trimble and the Ulster Unionists. In what I said I thought it safest to repeat the terms that he had set out for Sinn Fein's entry into talks, to show unionists that we hadn't made any fresh concessions and to show the IRA that we hadn't reneged on any either. I know that some civil servants and my special advisers always worried that I would say too much and make a mistake. But I was getting better at reading situations and knowing, as with my response to this announcement, when to stick to the words I had been given and when it was okay to ad-lib and take some wee risks.

I hurried away from the press, which I didn't like to do. I would have liked to talk to some of the press to see what their reaction was – people like Ken Reid or Brian O'Connell, who always had interesting perspectives. But on that Friday I was off to my fortnightly visit to my constituency. I still felt very strongly that I was doing the job I was doing because the people of Redcar had put me there. As the pressure in Belfast increased I didn't always manage to get to my constituency every fortnight – it became more like once a month. But when I had a surgery in Finnegan Hall the folk were wonderful. They would come in to see me with their problems and apologize for taking up my time when I was so busy in Ireland. The detailed knowledge of the geography and politics was not there with many folk. I can remember one guy asking if I had 'bumped into his brother who lived in Cork yet'. What was lovely was that they felt involved in the efforts I was making across the water. My problems or achievements were theirs too, as I was their MP. It made me feel less guilty for not spending much time on them. I had a good staff and so I didn't need to worry. I had worked hard to represent the people of Redcar for ten years. I found it difficult to let go, to know less of what was happening with different people's problems, but I had to because it was not possible to do everything. I did manage to keep control of what went out in my name by trying to sign everything that the office issued. This worked about 95 per cent of the time.

The IRA response to the Hume–Adams statement came quickly. The next day (Saturday, 19 July) they issued a statement saying they were calling a 'complete and unequivocal' ceasefire from noon the following day. It was signed P. O'Neill, the codename for all authentic IRA statements at that time. But my good feelings that progress had been made were still tempered by the need to wait for the response of the unionists. I remember trying to think why the IRA chose to call their ceasefire when they did. Some folk in the office thought that all the warm noises that had been made about the Orange Order acting reasonably on 12 July had spurred them to act quickly to regain the propaganda offensive. Nigel's (weirder) theory was that the period of breakdown from 9 February 1996 to 20 July 1997 was almost exactly the same as the nineteen-month duration of the 1994–6 ceasefire. So it was a sort of anniversary. (But then he always reads everyone's horoscopes in the morning.) I stuck to my belief that they were serious about making progress, and I would continue to do so unless violence returned and I was proved wrong.

Later on the same day, Ian Paisley's Democratic Unionist party (DUP) and Robert McCartney's United Kingdom Ulster party (UK UP) announced they were going to pull out of the talks. This had always been on the cards. It would clearly make things worse for David Trimble and the Ulster Unionist party. He would be facing Sinn Fein without a united front of unionism and, whatever he did, Ian and Bob would snipe at him viciously. Bob is one of the nastiest politicians I have met. Both were uncompromising in anything they said, which is life, and fine. Everyone is entitled to his or her point of view. Ian was always tough in what he said. He used to drive me mad because when he was not making a speech he could be more than polite, even pleasant. Whenever he saw my husband at a reception he used to say how sorry he felt for him married to someone who supped the 'devil's buttermilk' (meaning me drinking whiskey). It didn't seem to bother him that at a reception Jon would have a glass in his hand of the very same devil's buttermilk. It was almost as if Ian wanted to give a friendly greeting and that what he said in a jokey fashion with one of his enormous laughs was all he could manage before he remembered how much we disagreed about.

Bob McCartney on the other hand was vicious. I tried but could find nothing nice to say about him. His hatred of what I was doing was scary. When he had a rant I used to leave the room, and then he would carry on about how I had no manners and was a very rude woman. He seemed to ignore the bile that was coming from his mouth. When the talks were up and running I always secretly thought what a relief it was that Bob McCartney was not there. We had enough difficulties without having to suffer unadulterated doses of Bob McCartney wasting everybody's time.

Meanwhile I was on tenterhooks waiting to see what the Ulster Unionist response was going to be. Twenty-four hours after the IRA ceasefire came into being, we were in No. 10 with David Trimble explaining why he could not support the way we were proposing to handle taking the talks forward and particularly the parallel approach to decommissioning. We knew that David was in a very difficult position. He wanted more specifics on decommissioning, like a timetable. But we could hardly go back to the republicans and say, 'Thanks for the ceasefire, now we've changed the rules.' That would have put us straight back to square one or worse. David was going to have to decide which way to jump. I think he wanted to be part of the process, but he knew that many in his party would not support entry into the talks process without a start to weapons decommissioning by the IRA. This was an argument that had raged since the first IRA ceasefire in 1994. It had died down because without an IRA ceasefire there was no way Sinn Fein could be at the talks table. But now the ceasefire had been restored, the argument, which the Mitchell proposals on decommissioning had been designed to resolve, threatened to overwhelm the process once again.

When I first began work on N. Ireland, I had met and liked David Trimble and his wife Daphne. My early concern was that I didn't think he had the courage and determination to lead the Ulster Unionists in the difficult times ahead. I thought Jeffrey Donaldson would be a better bet: younger, more media friendly and, from what he said back then, more flexible. How wrong I was. In my opinion, Donaldson went back to the dark ages as the months passed and things got tougher, and David showed an iron will to keep going with, at times, very little support. He was very impressive.

That day, in Tony Blair's small, informal sitting room in No. 10 we set out our position once again, which was agreed with the Irish government and based on the 1996 Mitchell report. This was the first of many make-or-break moments which we were to experience in the months and years ahead. The Major government had been unable to stand apart from mainstream unionism on decommissioning or parades or on many other issues. We could. We had a clear, principled position and we stuck to it. We were in a position to take a lead. I often sympathized with Major or Mayhew during Prime Minister's or N. Ireland Questions in the House of Commons when they were desperate to make progress, going through questions, giving answers designed not to offend the unionists in the House or the nationalists either in the House or across the water. At times we had to do much the same, but never to the same extent as John Major and Paddy. We were able to make statements and progress in a way that had just not been possible for them. The responsibility was now with unionism to decide what to do next.

Debates within N. Ireland are usually loud and tetchy, conducted at megaphone level. But there is also an insidious background of whispers and mutterings about plots and conspiracies. And when bad stories emerged in the press it was hard to tell who was responsible. So when a story appeared in the Irish *Sunday Tribune* newspaper the next weekend claiming that 'security sources' were saying that the IRA ceasefire was time-limited to four months, the atmosphere changed dramatically. Was the story true? Were the IRA just playing people along and not really serious about the talks? Or were those opposed to the peace process, perhaps even among the security forces in N. Ireland, trying to undermine confidence in it by spreading these rumours?

My view was this: doubtless there were some folk on both sides with interests in undermining the process, but I learnt very quickly not to join the chorus of doubters and play the guessing game. I believed the best way was to deal with what you knew. I found that when there was a lot on, and some of it involved difficult decisions I was going to have to take, I could fill a couple of hours worrying about who was saying something damaging to the process or saying something scurrilous about somebody else. I made every effort to close my mind to all that and just focus on the important decisions. Alongside the talks we still had the parades issue to cope with and we had to think about domestic issues, jobs, education, talking to people and keeping the press onside. I knew I could rely on Nigel or Anna Healy or Ken, my private secretary, or John McKervill in my private office to tell me if there was something being said that I should know about. I did have a good network of folk from all sides who kept in touch, which gave me, I think, quite a balanced view of what was happening on the ground in N. Ireland.

With David Trimble agonizing over his decision, Sinn Fein lost no time moving their computers and faxes into the talks building at Stormont. Ian Paisley and Bob McCartney packed and left the same day. A double win for Sinn Fein – good press for their being eager to get going and a harder time for David Trimble and the UUs (as we called the UUP for short). The Shinners always manage (it's a great skill) to turn the knife just that little bit further each time. On this occasion they did it to David Trimble, by inviting him to join them in the talks building, and to me, who had yet to decide whether they were formally to have a place at the negotiating table. When I pointed this out to Sinn Fein, they would be very innocent and say they were just getting ready and they were entitled to be there anyway because of their democratic mandate. But they were too sharp not to be aware of how they soaked every event to get press coverage that showed them to have the advantage or placed them in the best possible light.

Just before the whole talks circus shut down for the summer, the UUP formally vetoed the British and Irish governments' suggestions for getting the talks going in earnest in September. But David Trimble was too astute to leave it at that. He managed to keep the door open. Now he was leading; he decided to reach out to the wider unionist community, beyond the hardliners among his own party activists. I believe he talked this over with Tony Blair beforehand, knowing it was a strategy Tony had undertaken in developing new Labour.

The broad unionist community that David turned to contained a lot of Protestant business people, trade unionists, Church and civic leaders, members of N. Ireland's civil society – the non-combatants. Some more cruelly described them as the non-engaged. But they were there, quietly getting on with their lives, worrying about jobs and the economy, the health service and education – the sorts of things that everyone cares about.

And mostly just wishing the Troubles would go away. They might to some be disengaged from the politics on a daily basis, but to me they were the hope for the future. Despite all the violence they had stuck it out in N. Ireland. As long as they were supporting the peace process it would, to my mind, have a very good chance of survival. That is why, on many occasions in the months ahead when the press were issuing dire warnings about the collapse of the process, I kept the faith because the people of N. Ireland were still going strong.

David Trimble, I think, had the same understanding as me. From his point of view the business community were a key source of support. Their politics was mixed but practical and realistic. They were not as rabidly anti-republican as many of the more active unionists were. And, as later polling was to show, for many people, especially the women, talking to Sinn Fein was not such anathema if it meant that progress could be made.

I think David, as much as is possible, knew the outcome of his consultation before he started out. But it was a tough time nonetheless. We did what we could to help, not I hope too obviously – because if there is one thing people dislike it is being told by government what to do, whether it is N. Ireland or anywhere else in the world. I continued with my meetings and visits around N. Ireland, managing where possible to talk about the politics of what was going on in Belfast. For example, I was booked to talk to a group called the G7, which included many of the business interests that David was consulting, along with trade unionists and the voluntary sector. The people there knew what I was doing when I emphasized in my speech the importance of making a success of the talks process to help to create jobs, a stable economy and a secure environment for business to flourish. It was a case of covering as many bases as you could.

A nasty undercurrent of violence continued despite the relative calm at the start of the August holiday period. A small parcel bomb was sent to Bob McCartney's office, but there was no disaster. Bob was on holiday and the staff at the offices where it was sent were very alert and spotted the crude package. The body of a sixteen-year-old Catholic lad, James Morgan, was found on a farm near Annsborough, County Down. He had been tortured and murdered. A twenty-one-year-old, Gerard Marley, hanged himself from railings outside his house, after having his legs broken in what the press described as an IRA 'punishment beating'. All these were cruel, outrageous and devastating events for all of us, particularly the families concerned. Each one made me more determined to make progress, so that not another life was lost.

One death, through natural causes, at this time in N. Ireland was very hard for me personally to cope with. It was the death of a very good friend of Jon's and mine, Vincent Hanna. He was a fine journalist and broadcaster, a bright, humorous man with an incredible understanding of the politics of N. Ireland and a real love of life. We had spent many an enjoyable night eating and drinking well and discussing Irish politics, culture, literature, music, in fact most aspects of Ireland imaginable. We, as many others do, miss him badly. I can see him now at the front door, food or drink in hand, looking forward, with a big grin on his face, to a good evening.

One thing about Irish politics that some folk find strange is that, alongside the difficult times of the marches and the talks, most of the time life in N. Ireland continues much as anywhere else. I think it is a tribute to the strength of character of the people there that despite the violence they make the best of what they can in their lives. Ironically it is also true of the politicians. At the end of Parliament's summer term there are always lots of receptions and events. One of the best is held at the Irish embassy in Grosvenor Place near London's Hyde Park Corner. Ted and Clare Barrington, the Irish Ambassador and his wife, hosted events at Christmas, around St Patrick's Day (17 March) and again before the long summer break. The parties were crowded, full of MPs, peers, journalists and notable and not so notable London Irish. It is always great fun; folk turn up to meet, chat and consume large quantities of whiskey and Guinness. Usually you will see a good spread of N. Irish politicians of all persuasions. Some though are missing, depending what is happening across the water. I haven't seen Ian Paisley and Bob McCartney at them, but Ian and Bob will go to the American embassy where they mix on similar terms with the other political parties from N. Ireland. The embassy splashes out in true American style. I can remember a party under Ambassador Crowe where there was jazz, boogie, great food including Ben and Jerry's ice-cream and a good spread of all the N. Ireland parties represented.

But the celebrations on this side of the Atlantic are modest compared to the great jamborees that go on in the United States on St Patrick's Day. I remember several celebrations when Bill and Hillary Clinton were in the White House that were spectacular events. Great numbers of Irish Americans and planeloads from Ireland north and south turn up. It is one of those things that I could never prove, but I think these social events brought N. Ireland politicians together in ways that formal talks never could. It didn't mean they had great conversations about the peace process, but it did mean they mixed together and socialized with people of many different political persuasions. It can only have been a plus.

Social events had limited pleasure for me. Lots of people understandably asked questions about how we were getting on, and as usual it was better to say nothing very specific so it could not be interpreted negatively. Any comment with any meaning would be rehashed in the press the next day. So I avoided engaging with folk, which was not my style at all. I got bored doing this, and so must the people listening to me. I really felt sorry for my old mates from the Lobby like Des and Frank who could have expected something and got nothing. The other group, the majority of whom were well meaning, always came up and asked how I was feeling: I was 'looking a little off-colour' or 'a little

tired', or was I 'fully back to health'? I had to keep saying, 'Oh
no, I'm fine, everything is hunky-dory.' It was difficult because
most of the questioners were kindly motivated, but some were
not. Any chink of tiredness or bad temper and it would be
evidence for the malicious to say I was not well and therefore
not up to the job. Nigel, who was usually at my side on these
occasions, understood this dilemma and often towards the end
of an evening, when it was clear that I was tired and ready to
sleep, would say we had to get off, we had to get a paper agreed
for the morning or some similar excuse. And we left to prepare
for the next day or bed or, even worse, to finish one of the red
boxes which followed me everywhere and which all Ministers
get given most evenings and weekends, packed with papers to
read and sign.

Everyone was desperately trying to make progress. John
Hume in Dublin, soon after the ceasefire, recognized that a
settlement would only be possible 'with the participation of the
unionist people'. Bertie Ahern too was trying to be helpful to
David Trimble. Fortunately Bertie and David got on fairly well.
It was one of the most important relationships that developed
in the talks. They learnt to talk and even trust each other, which
was unheard of between an Ulster Unionist and an Irish Prime
Minister before. It took some of the pressure off us to act as a
sort of filter of unionist views, which had always been necessary
in the past if the unionists and the Irish government couldn't
engage with each other. Once the talks formally adjourned for
the summer, all that could be done was to wait and see what
would happen in September. I remember sitting in my office
thinking what could be done in preparation for when we
returned. I decided there was not much, and it was best to wait
and see what the state of play would be.

More than in any other part of the UK things just shut down
in N. Ireland in August. Had I thought about it more I should
have gone away too. Both the head of the army and the head
of the RUC went away at the beginning of August. That should

have told me it was the time to have a break. But I stayed around, deciding to go late August, early September, because I was concerned that the IRA had announced a ceasefire but there was no real progress following it and I didn't want to lose it. After the ceasefire it was agreed that there would be a ministerial-level meeting with Sinn Fein on 6 August. It was my first with them in government, although we had met during the last cease-fire when I had been in opposition. It wasn't a very long or formal meeting. I think it was more for the press and to show to others that they were now meeting with the Secretary of State. It was a very important event in the slow progress towards peace. It did not seem so at the time. It went something like:

'Hi Gerry, hi Martin, this is Quentin Thomas and Jonathan Stephens.'

'Hi Mo.'

Question from Gerry: 'When are we going to be able to take the seat at the talks table we are entitled to?'

Brief discussion followed, ending with me saying, 'That's a decision in six weeks when we see that the ceasefire is holding.'

It was a very straightforward, friendly meeting. The impor-tance of the event was reinforced when we looked out of the window to see the battery of cameras waiting for interviews afterwards. Over the months we had numerous meetings with Gerry and Martin. It took a long while for them to relax – if they ever did. They were always serious and clear as to what their position was. They never shouted or lost their tempers, although that is not to say we didn't have some heated dis-cussions. They struck me as two very serious, committed human beings. Occasionally we would, at the end of a session, joke over something else on the news, Martin more than Gerry. Martin is a more open person than Gerry, and we talked of our respective families. When my mother was ill, Gerry was one of the few party leaders to ask how she was.

Most of the rest of August was spent out and about seeing people and doing visits. I visited one of the army barracks at

Ebrington. I feared it would not be a warm reception. The army were very wary of what the new government might be up to. I saw as many army folk as I could. I always asked to see at least one of each rank at the base in circumstances where we could talk informally. Such meetings, army or police, always started very formally but relaxed into questions or statements that indicated what they really were thinking. The meetings were not always easy, especially when I answered questions directly and they didn't like the answer. I always regret not having had the time to do more. But slowly word got around the rest of the battalion and more widely among the forces, and I hope it showed that I cared enough and respected them enough to go and listen and talk in an informal setting. On most of the visits I did, I listened to the folk to see how my views either differed or coincided with theirs.

Another visit, in complete contrast, was to Altnagelvin hospital in Derry. The staff were mainly nationalist. Usefully, it reinforced my view of the importance of not ignoring mainstream nationalism, as well as Sinn Fein. It was essential to bring mainstream nationalism with us whatever we did. I sensed a real willingness to compromise if we were even-handed in how we acted. I sensed also that we could be tough on Sinn Fein and not lose the nationalist community as long as we acted fairly. Much of what you read in this book is about Sinn Fein or what the unionists got up to, but you should not ignore, as I couldn't in the talks, the vast majority of nationalists who wanted, like the vast majority of unionists, a peaceful life with the possibility of jobs, decent health, education and hope for the future.

The last big hurdle of the summer marching season we had to climb over was the Apprentice Boys' march in Derry, County Londonderry, marking the lifting of the siege of Derry in 1689 and the part played in that by the town's young Protestant 'Apprentice Boys'. Discussions between marchers and the residents' group in Derry had been quite productive at first. Both sides were more conciliatory, especially the Apprentice Boys' leader, Alistair Simpson. But as the parade day, 9 August, neared (the parade is always held on the Saturday before 12 August), positions hardened on both sides. And on the day clashes between marchers and protesters quickly overwhelmed the town centre.

The riots in the centre of Derry were bad. It was very depressing to see the damage to the shops and the burnt-out cars, made worse by the fact that Derry had done so well to develop shops and businesses with the help of John Hume and a very good City Council, good councillors and a proactive chief executive in John Keanie. Looking at the damage I felt so sad and angry for the people who had struggled to build up a business, only to see all their efforts burnt or destroyed beyond salvation. Again I resolved to make progress over the marches in the autumn and winter and not just to forget about them until the next summer as previous governments had done.

Some of the extra time I had that August I devoted to the press. Most of the year it was easier not to engage with them, because while talks were going on I was never very keen to give them anything. It usually resulted in a spin by the paper, to get the headline to sell more copies, but was not often a plus for the peace process. Yet there were times when we needed them to get a message across, so there had to be a certain amount of give and take. I did a lot of phone-ins, radio shows, breakfast shows and national newspapers like the *Observer*. I gave (finally) a long-promised interview to Des McCartan for the *Belfast Telegraph*. He, as usual, was tough but fair-minded in his reporting. It was also useful to talk to him. He wouldn't necessarily give me information or advice, he would just pose a couple of questions I should be thinking about, which was always a help. The downside of talking to the media in the month of August is that it is known as the 'silly season'. With Parliament shut and people on holiday there's not much news about, so it is easy to get into the paper or on news programmes, and giving a slightly dodgy answer can result in a big story. That's what happened to me in the summer of 1997. I did an interview with BBC2's *Newsnight* about the talks and referred to the discussions being held about the principle of consent.

Sorting out the principle of consent was, in my view, the way to find an answer to the fundamental problem that was at the root of all the problems in N. Ireland. Put very crudely, N. Ireland's difficulties stem from the fact that nationalists, who are mainly Catholics, want the north and south of Ireland united under one government, while unionists, who are mainly Protestant, want N. Ireland to remain part of the UK. Many nationalists, represented by people like John Hume and Seamus Mallon, wanted unity of the island of Ireland by exclusively peaceful means. More militant nationalists or republicans, represented by Sinn Fein, wanted unity and felt that the violence that had been used against their community in the past justified the use, by groups who saw themselves as freedom fighters like the IRA, of whatever means necessary to achieve their goal. The unionist community on the other hand felt excluded from the Irish Republic in the south (which had been originally set up as a strongly Catholic country), had lived in N. Ireland, or 'Ulster' as they call it, created businesses, brought up families and wanted to retain their link to the British mainland, to their queen and the rest of their country.

In short there are two legitimate demands and no easy compromise. One side wanted more than the other side would offer. What the principle of consent gave us in the negotiations was a way through. Put simply, it meant that if there was to be a change in the status of N. Ireland in the future then it would be decided by the people in a referendum. But the first question then to ask is who are 'the people'? If you just ask people in the north, where the unionists are a majority, then you get one answer; but if you ask all the people on the whole island, where nationalists would be a majority, then you get a completely different answer. The solution put forward by the British and Irish governments, in the 1993 Downing Street Declaration, was to ask both. Or as the document put it, consent must be 'freely and concurrently given, north and south'. This ensured that any future change in the status of N. Ireland would be decided both by all the people living on the island, as nationalists wanted, and by the people of N. Ireland themselves, as unionists wanted.

This is what the two governments proposed and what the parties were to sit down and negotiate in the talks. But what was not discussed was how this would work in practice. Would it really be the case that a majority of just one person, say, living in N. Ireland, would be enough to change the whole status of the place from part of the UK to part of the Irish Republic? It's a question no one asked and few people tried to answer. But I was asked straight out on *Newsnight* and gave a straight answer – that it wasn't a settled issue. It was an honest answer, but it only made it worse. Gary McMichael and his unionist party, the UDP (Ulster Democratic party), were threatening to walk out of the talks unless I clarified my definition of consent. It was a sticky moment. It eventually blew over but it taught me not to try and answer hypothetical questions in detail. And that sometimes a little bit of fudge can be a good thing – although I still hated doing it.

At the end of August there were formal procedures to go through. Firstly the British and the Irish had to sign an agreement setting up (and agree to jointly pay for) the new Decommissioning Commission. It was to be headed by General John de Chastelain, a military man in most of his mannerisms, but also a quiet man who has patiently given many years of his life to help make progress in N. Ireland. This Commission, as John, George Mitchell and Hari Holkeri had set out in their 1996 report, was to oversee the decommissioning process alongside progress being made in the talks. The second announcement was a formal invitation to Sinn Fein to join the talks process. This I issued exactly six weeks after the IRA ceasefire had been restored. I knew that the reaction from the unionists to this statement was crucial. I knew it would be a difficult time for

David Trimble, and that there were already voices in his party criticizing publicly what he was doing. I decided the best thing I could do was to give him the space to work at it without having me around.

The day after the announcement, I packed my bags for Spain. The other Ministers were now back and I was going with Jon to stay in a villa in Spain with a pool. It was stuck in the middle of nowhere. It was so isolated it took us a long time to find it. As Jon's kids weren't with us we did nothing but sleep, eat, drink and read. When we had the energy we played backgammon or another board game called rummicub, or just talked.

One of the main things on both of our minds then was our living arrangements. After the election, we had to make big changes to accommodate the need for greater security in both London and Redcar. In Redcar it was done very efficiently, although it involved quite extensive alterations to the house. We had a plod on duty at the front of the house when we were there. Great though the view is out on to the North Sea, it did present problems for the plod out front standing in the chilly winds. As a result they built a porch. Great for us, the postman and any other poor sod visiting and standing at the door. They also took over the garage, or a third of it, so what was left was too small for a car. They had cameras around the outside of the house with TV monitors in the garage, along with a sink and all mod cons. It was right cosy. I only had one difficulty with the system, but I ignored it as I was running out of energy to complain, which was that every couple of hours the guy at the front of the house was replaced by another from the garage at the back. This involved two plods marching round the block in bullet-proof jackets, carrying machine guns, one of them taking over as they passed the front of the house. The neighbours got used to it and saw it as their very own neighbourhood crime watch. I always used to worry what the tourists thought, having come to sunny Redcar for the day, promenading along the front to take in the sea air and being greeted by two machine-gun-toting policemen.

But this was not all. It is quite extraordinary what goes into making a house secure. Some things I expected, like cameras and lights around the house – indeed I had even been prepared for bullet-proof glass. Interestingly I was told that this is not really bullet proof. All it does is divert the direction of the bullet, so that if someone aims and fires at you they will miss. But it does give you time to take cover. Less encouragingly I was told that professional hitmen would shoot two rounds very quickly, hoping to take advantage of the initial hole made in the glass.

But as well as these changes it was the number of wires that really intrigued me. For these a large trench was dug from the garage to the house, and then a whole set of wires were spread around the house itself. They told us it was to be able to sense who was moving round the house and where exactly they were at any one time – very important if terrorists managed to get in and hold us hostage (an unlikely event, I always felt). But then what about all those other wires and the very large box they attached to my phone that made very strange whirring sounds?

The security in London was even more complicated. At first we moved out of Jon's comfortable family home in Islington and went to live in a 'safe house' in Belgravia. Michael Howard, the Tory ex-Home Secretary, had lived there. When a government changes, ex-Ministers are meant to move out promptly – hence all the stories of the removal van being outside No. 10 on election day. Michael Howard obviously was not a subscriber to such fast moving, and he took ages to vacate that house. That first night after we had initially got in I must admit feeling very odd sleeping in the bed that he had occupied and thinking of Ann Widdecombe's remark that there was something of the night about him.

The house was indeed very safe, having been built for this purpose. It is the traditional home of the Home Secretary, although Jack Straw, who must have seen it before, declined the invitation, preferring to remain in his own house in London. Although quite large it had poky rooms and institutional furniture. The windows were hermetically sealed, bomb proof and shrouded in net curtains. Much to Jon's annoyance it also had a very non-user-friendly kitchen. The house was overlooked by a large residential block for police officers. But the most disconcerting aspect was the police post in the basement. Here a policeman would sit, when I was in residence, looking at a bank of security screens. We had to pass by him whenever we came or went.

Living in the safe house was difficult. Whenever there was a noise or movement in the roof two or three plods stampeded up the stairs. As this usually took place in the middle of the night, by the time it was confirmed to be birds, mostly pigeons, all of us were well awake. Early on too the police were very good at locking Jon out. The thing that really used to annoy him was that he never had a full set of keys, and so different police would choose different combinations of keys to use when leaving, requiring Jon to call up the local police station to be let in.

As I was in Belfast most of the time, with probably only one night a week in Belgravia, I didn't experience the worst of these horrors. Inevitably it didn't happen on the one night of the week that I was there. But on one visit back to the house I was faced by a friendly rebellion. The family did not like living in the house. They had had enough of the police, there was nowhere to play or walk outside, the area was sterile and unfriendly, and it was a long way from where the kids spent the rest of their time with their mother in Hackney. Jon was quiet, but I could tell from his body language that he had had enough too.

Next step we told the security services about our problem and they agreed to let us move back to the old house in Cleveland Road in Islington. But there were more problems. We had originally moved to the safe house because it was going to involve a lot of work to make our house secure, and they were already pulling apart our house in Redcar. It was thought to be cheaper and easier for all of us to move to Belgravia. I must give the security services their due. Once they knew our minds were made up, they quickly set about making our old house safe.

Soon we were back in Cleveland Road. The security arrangements meant a whole lot of new wires, security alarms, shatter-proofing of windows (it seemed that the security rating had fallen, and we no longer needed bullet-proofing), and a bomb-proof shed in the front garden for the police. This, to begin with, worked fine. Just like in Redcar, the neighbours were very happy, with our very own neighbourhood bobby to call on located on the street. The only problem was that the policeman or woman on duty was not allowed to leave the shed. Car thefts they could help with from the shed, by calling up the local police station to deal with it. One of these stolen cars was Jon's, taken from immediately outside the house, much to the chagrin of the plod on duty. Domestic harassment was a different matter altogether. One afternoon a woman came down the street to the shed to complain about her husband. Her voice was raised in anger and booze. She was determined that the policeman would go back with her to her flat and sort her husband out. She was scared to go back and would not leave the shed until he went with her. The policeman was trying to explain that he was phoning for help but couldn't move. He was saved by the visit of two motorbike cops to see if everything was okay. They went off with her to sort out the problem.

The motorbike cops turned up every two hours. They were a bit noisy, particularly in the middle of the night, but we got used to it. I found it quite useful the odd day I was home. I would be lying in bed in the morning working out what I was going to do that day, and the motorbikes turning up were a useful time check. Two visits from them out at the front of the house and it was time for me to leave.

We had a number of difficulties in London ranging from the minor to the serious. The minor for us, however, was serious for the kids. They were stopped, by some police, from going into their own house, despite the fact there were pictures of them up in the shed. The problem stopped when H got bolshie. She used to arrive at the shed, announce it was her home and walk in. After a while, neither she nor Fred had any more trouble. Another problem was with the alarm system going off in the night. I hoped that the neighbours thought that a police presence was worth such disturbances. Only one night did it get difficult, when the policeman in the shed could not get the alarm to stop. After five minutes the motorbikes arrived and they had a go at the alarm, but with no more success. Soon after them the local police from Islington tried, still no luck. By now the noise was getting unbearable and had been going on for a long time. So to escape it, and because it was a warm evening, Jon and I took a walk down the road. We must have looked a sight because when the noise started we put on our thobes (these are the long white flowing robes worn by men from the Arabian Gulf – Jon had taken to wearing them when he had lived out there, and they were very comfortable indoor wear in the summer). So we were walking down the street looking like a pair of Arabs. But no one seemed concerned on the evening of the alarm about how we were dressed, nor that we had just wandered off. The police were far more interested in stopping the alarm. Eventually they just switched it off at the mains and left it at that. No one actually ever searched the house to see what had set it off. It was events like this that limited my faith in security.

But the event that finished me off with the London security happened to Jon one morning when I was in Belfast. When I was not there, there was no police presence in the security shed in the front garden. Jon was woken up at seven o'clock by a lot of noise and shouting outside the front of the house. He looked out of the window and saw a policeman in bullet-proof jacket pointing a revolver at the house, with police cars closing off the street. As he waited he heard people entering the house through the basement door. It was clear the police were mounting an armed raid and it would not be long before they burst into the bedroom. He had nothing on and wondered whether to get back into bed and wait for them or put his trousers on and see what was going on. He put his trousers on and got to the half-landing when he saw six or seven police in full armed-response gear with shields and automatic rifles pointing at him.

He told me afterwards that the panic and fear he felt at that moment was not necessarily that they were going to kill him on purpose, but that they were so psyched up that one of them could have fired by mistake. They demanded to know who he was and he unhelpfully gave them his real name, Jon Norton. This did nothing for them as they knew that I lived there as Mowlam, but he had said it as a perverse way of showing his anger at this intrusion. The next question was 'What are you doing here?' Jon responded, 'I live here.' A not unlikely answer as he had quite clearly just got out of bed, and was only wearing a pair of jeans. They then demanded proof. Luckily he had just got back from a trip abroad and his jacket with his passport in the pocket was hanging over the bottom of the stairs. He told them to look there. They looked and the atmosphere calmed down. He asked why they had come, and they replied that the alarm had gone off in Scotland Yard. They pointedly asked if they could search the house, just to be sure it had been a false alarm.

Coming close together these two events did not make me a happy person. I was asked, after the first incident with the alarm, to address the very vocal complaints I was making to the head of the security unit at the Home Office. No thank you, I thought, that will only result in keeping it within the unit. Getting to the office, I phoned Metropolitan Police Commissioner Sir Paul Condon, and told him about it. There is no doubt that afterwards relations with the security bosses at the Home Office were a little tense.

To my mind, they had their revenge when they attempted to remove my security the day after I left the NIO, an attempt in which they were to succeed after only a few months. It was them saying, 'We are in control.' When I questioned the speed at which my security disappeared, the letter I was sent said that my security risk was low because I was at no risk from republican terrorists on the mainland. I asked about loyalist terrorists and was told they did not operate in mainland Britain. I asked if any other Secretary of State for N. Ireland had ever had security removed. Only Jim Prior, was the reply. By the time I left N. Ireland, there were still active republican groups operating on the mainland, like the so-called Real IRA, who were not stupid. They understood that what I had potentially done was split the republican movement, not a big positive from their point of view. Anyway, by the time I left, I hadn't got the energy or desire to argue. It just galled me when I saw virtually every other Secretary of State right back to Roy Mason from the 1970s still receiving full protection.

There is no getting away from it, the comforts of security and a driver are considerable. More sleep in the morning because you are picked up and driven to your first meeting. Ken was my driver for almost all the time in London. He was never late for a meeting and always knew where we were going having either checked it out the day before or looked carefully at the map. He spoilt me. Often I would come out of the house in a bit of a hurry, but always making sure I had the dreaded red box or boxes. After a while Ken kept a comb, mirror and lipstick in the car so there was no panic if I was only halfway ready. I spent more time with Ken than I did my husband. By the time I left government we were like an old married couple. We knew when to talk and when not, we knew how the other had their coffee, and Ken understood that I preferred weak tea in the morning, and we had established what kind of chocolate or flapjacks (if we were trying to diet) we should have in the car to keep us going at that sleepy time of four or five in the afternoon on a long journey. He would drop the dry-cleaning off if I was in a rush, wait for me on the rare occasion I went to the supermarket if I was trying to help out at home with domestic chores when Jon was pushed, and deposit me outside the shops and wait for me if I was doing a bit of retail therapy. From Ken I know more about scuba diving than I ever thought possible and about Mauritius, where his partner Agnes comes from. He knew what Fred and H were up to and in great detail how Jon's paintings were going.

For personal protection (done by Special Branch) in London I had a great team that changed over time. To begin with I had Robin, who had a very dry sense of humour and had a lot of the mickey taken out of him as he stuck religiously to the rulebook. I remember one sticky moment he had with me when I was speaking at the Labour conference in Brighton in 1998. There was, as usual, a Socialist Workers' demonstration outside the conference hall and there was a problem getting me in. Robin tucked me under his shoulder and with a policeman either side got me into the hall. The protesters not being able to see me thought that Robin's hair, which was similar to mine, was me and went for that. Thankfully he was okay. I had other folk who weren't with me that long, a lovely big Scot, Dave, and Sally and Alex.

And then finally there was Adam. He stayed with me the longest, and he and Ken the driver are the ones I miss. Adam had all Ken's skills plus one: as I've said, he is great at choosing clothes. Before I discovered Mr Crown and La Chasse, I was living in two suits I'd bought on a visit to the US. Because there are, to say the least, a number of large women in the US, they have in some of the superstores a big section catering for 'the larger woman'. I felt good trying on clothes there – I was so much thinner than the other women, even though I was fifteen stone. The other place Adam and I had explored was Harrods, on the grounds that wealthy people and (again) Americans ate a lot of rich food and so they must cater in some way for women the size of me. We were right: it was not as brazen as in America, but we found a little corner for the larger woman. For speed Adam used to choose the clothes and I would stay in the changing rooms while the assistants brought them in. Once in Harrods,

I must have been becoming quite well known by then, news of my presence in the store had found its way to the boss, Mohammed Al Fayed. He offered a discount on the clothes I was getting and Adam gently said, 'No, thank you.' This took place while I was in the changing room! I've always felt a bit sorry for Al Fayed. Even though he is in England, giving discounts to individuals he wants to return to the shop is how business is done in the part of the world he is from. And in a sense that's no different from inviting a lot of famous people to an opening to make it an important event and ply them with food and champagne. I also have never been able to understand why he has not been given a passport.

While I was in Belfast my driver and protection team remained the same two guys, Keith and big John. I got as attached to them as I did to Ken and Adam in London. On the way to our destination I used to be able to do my hair and put my make-up on, by which I mean lipstick. That is all the make-up I ever wore, except when I was going on television and I was made up by a professional. Then people used to notice the difference and say how good I looked. It still didn't mean I bothered with the stuff if left to my own devices. It was more important in the mornings to read the papers for the second meeting of the day. I always made sure the night before that I was ready for the first meeting. So travel time became crucial to prepare for the subsequent meeting as the day went on. On the daily journey from Hillsborough to Belfast, Keith also brought (in his head) a run-down on the events of the night. I often would not have seen the news the night before as I would be sitting in bed doing my red box and I didn't have a television in the bedroom.

Reading this you might conclude that I loved my security. I grew to love the individuals, but never the institution. It seriously restricted my freedom. If I wanted to take a walk or do something after work or at weekends I usually had to give at least an hour's notice or pre-plan it, so it was never spontaneous. Also the boys had families and a life. They worked long hours and weekends. If I said I wasn't doing anything they would make plans to arrange a rare occasion with family and friends. They always said I should not think about that, but I did and that was it. Once they had become friends I couldn't just take my interests into account. I tried running away a couple of times, once in Hillsborough, down the hill from the residence to the local pub with Jon. Keith and big John soon found out about our little visit.

It was the same with Adam when we were up in Redcar. One morning I made a run for the local shops, a bid for freedom, a bid to do something normal. They were all very understanding about why I had done it, but just said very delicately that they would be the ones that would be in trouble if anything happened to me. I remember them being particularly unnerved to discover one day that a man regularly came to my Redcar surgery with a machete! It was clear that if I was going to have a decent relationship with them I was going to have to guarantee to play by the rules. The main reason why I found protection such a waste of time was that if someone really was intent on getting me it was so easy to do, on my walks at Hillsborough, for instance, where the grounds are overlooked by many houses in the town.

I also had to deal with police protection when I went south of the border to the Irish Republic. When I went south as an official person the Gardai were always out in force, but they were much more relaxed if we went south for a holiday. They were still with us, as were the N. Ireland RUC boys. And they all knew their way round Glandore where we used to go and stay. All the police knew it because Margaret Jay's dad, Jim Callaghan, holidays there in the family house. The house is beautiful with an incredible terrace looking over the inlet. The nearest pub is just behind the house and Mary and her family who run it look after everyone. Often we would drink up there at night with the Gardai (off duty, of course) just as Jim did. From whence comes an (apocryphal) story in which a member of the Gardai is asked, with a whiskey in one hand and a cigar in the other, what he would do now to save his principal (me or someone else being protected) if they were attacked. He replies, 'I would make sure I got the guy that got him.'

Jon and I went one weekend to explore the west coast down from Connemara through to Rosspoint in Sligo where we all settled for a night in the pub. It was a great night singing and dancing on the tables. We sang lots of songs including 'Kevin Barry' and 'The Sash', and everyone joined in. A good time was had by all. Jon sang and I did nothing. I knew no poetry by heart and I can't sing for the life of me. As a result of that evening I have mastered ten lines of a poem, so next time I can join in. Our last night was at Clifden in County Galway when we changed to darts and poker. I think we won at both poker and darts, but I'm not sure the Gardai boys would agree.

While I was away in Spain on holiday, thinking as usual where we had got to in the peace process, Adam Ingram and Paul Murphy, my two Ministers, managed the situation in Belfast so I didn't get hassled. They didn't disturb me even though there was quite a serious problem in the prisons, in particular a riot by the LVF prisoners in the Maze. The LVF argued that their status as an organization had not been recognized, as was tacitly the case with existing inmates in the IRA, INLA (Irish National Liberation Army), UVF (Ulster Volunteer Force) and UDA (Ulster Defence Association). The riots in the prison were accompanied by tensions and trouble outside. There were attacks on prison officers' homes, for which the LVF were blamed. The other loyalist grouping, the UVF, smashed up the Golden Hind bar in Portadown that was frequented by LVF supporters. The tension on the streets played back into the talks process. A prominent PUP (Progressive Unionist party) member, Billy Hutchinson, said he thought the talks process had nothing to offer his party and he would vote against their participation. It was a tense time within loyalism and unionism in general, with a lot of nervousness about what the IRA ceasefire would mean and a lot of scepticism about finally sitting around the table with Sinn Fein.

The only call I had from the office was to tell me that Princess Diana had died, and did I want to come back for the funeral? I thought about it and phoned back and said no. Sad though I was, I decided I would be of more use to people if I slept a little more and got my strength up for whatever was ahead.

6

The Hand of History

TALKS PROGRESSING

After a long hot summer I approached the beginning of the talks with mixed emotions. There was in me an overwhelming wish to get moving. I was convinced if we hung around and didn't move things on, life would get tougher for everyone. I also knew inside myself that it wasn't going to be easy. But I hadn't understood just how tough it was going to get; there was as yet no realization that every day would have to be approached positively, whatever my real emotions were. I knew then, and had to keep reminding myself as the days and months passed, that however much I thought so and so was an arrogant prick, or so and so was not worth listening to, or how sick I was with the lack of progress, I just had to stay in control and keep focused on what we were working towards. Occasionally, I went and vented my frustration on Adam and Paul. They sympathized, gave me a cuddle and sent me on my way. Ken, my private secretary, also took a lot of my frustration but just seemed to understand and soak it up.

The talks formally started on 9 September 1997. The sight of the Sinn Fein negotiators and back-up staff formally entering the talks building through the large iron gates was very welcome. Those same gates had so often in the past been closed to keep the Shinners out, each time granting them another PR triumph. On 9 September, they walked through the gates, across the small car park and in through the mirrored-glass doors of the talks building with their heads held high, all in the glare of an enormous number of cameras. Politicians and civil servants watched behind the net curtains in the windows above, more hopeful than anything else. One civil servant turned to me and said, 'Let's hope this is for real.'

Castle Buildings is an ugly, squat, 1960s block, three storeys high. Each floor contains a single square corridor circuiting a large central room. All the parties had rooms off the corridors on the first and second floors. My offices, and George Mitchell's, were on the top floor, the main room at the centre of which was used for plenary sessions of the talks. It is a building with a very clinical feel and many of the rooms on the different floors look exactly the same. It reminded me of hospital corridors, so easy to mistake one for another. The sameness of some of the rooms proved to be a good thing when all the parties in the talks were allocated theirs because it meant that it was possible to give the same treatment to folk who did not want anyone else to be more important than them. Nevertheless it took some time until everyone was satisfied that their space was as good as the other parties'. I had the same sized room as the leader of the Irish delegation. John Hume and David Trimble had the same sized rooms, other parties got smaller rooms, but more of them wanted a bigger one. The only party that did not complain about their accommodation, however, were the Women's Coalition, who just wanted to get on with the talks.

To get their seat at the table, each party had to sign up to the six principles of democracy and non-violence drawn up by George Mitchell and his team. These, known as the Mitchell Principles, asked all parties taking part to make these absolute commitments:

to democratic and exclusively peaceful means of resolving political issues;

to the total disarmament of all paramilitary organizations;

to agree that such disarmament must be verifiable to the satisfaction of an independent commission;

to renounce for themselves, and to oppose any effort by others, to use force, or threaten to use force, to influence the course or the outcome of all-party negotiations;

to agree to abide by the terms of any agreement reached in all-party negotiations and to resort to democratic and exclusively peaceful methods in trying to alter any aspect of that outcome with which they may disagree; and

to urge that 'punishment' killings and beatings stop and to take effective steps to prevent such actions.

It was obvious that for Sinn Fein to sign up to all of these was going to be an important step forward. But at the same time I could not see how hardline republicans were going to accept agreeing to use only peaceful means to achieve their end of a united Ireland, when they had fought for so long, and lost so many of their comrades, trying to drive the British out of Ireland.

It only took two days for my question to be answered. On 11 September an IRA spokesperson said the IRA would have 'problems' with some sections of the Mitchell Principles but that what Sinn Fein did was a matter for them. This statement was just what Ian Paisley had hoped for. He was out immediately saying, 'I told you so.' David Trimble, as so often would be the case, was in an almost impossible position. He wanted to make progress, if possible, but he had said he was not prepared to go into negotiations with a gun at his head. He called his party executive (of the UUP) together on the 13th to decide whether or not to go into the talks. No clear decision was reached; it was put off till their next meeting on the 15th.

In the meantime, I met with the smaller loyalist parties (the UDP and the PUP) to gauge their reactions. They were angry at what they saw as Sinn Fein trying to get into the talks while the IRA kept their options open about a return to violence in the future – although, it has to be said, there was precious little enthusiasm for disarmament among loyalist paramilitary groups too. But, more worryingly, neither of the loyalist political leaders was particularly confident that David Trimble would be able to bring his larger unionist party back to the table.

I thought long and hard about the Sinn Fein statement. I always tried to put myself in the position of the person making the decision, be it David Trimble or Gerry Adams. It could, I thought, be as the loyalists had said: republicans wanting to have their cake and eat it. Or it could be that there were divisions within the Sinn Fein–IRA camp, as our 'sources' told us, and that while some wanted to go in, other IRA members distrusted the process and wanted to stick with the violence. One of republicanism's founding principles has always been to stay together, stay united. So, faced with this division, a decision that said the IRA cannot accept some sections of the Mitchell Principles but that what Sinn Fein do is up to them was a unifying compromise. I was not alone in my views. Some civil servants who had been at the negotiating game with the Shinners thought the same. My view was we had to give them the benefit of the doubt. There was the risk that if I was wrong, then it might prolong the talks and make it even more difficult to reach an agreement, but my bottom line remained throughout that while they were talking, they were not killing. And if the killing did start again, then the Mitchell Principles gave everyone the clear assurance that they would be out.

The next morning as I was lying in bed at Hillsborough, mulling over the IRA's statement, the phone went. I remember thinking, 'Who is phoning so early? Jon can't be awake yet.' It was Ken, my private secretary, to tell me a 400lb bomb had exploded in the town of Markethill, in County Armagh. As yet there were no reported casualties, but the town was devastated. My immediate thought was, 'Is this the IRA saying no to the talks?' Or was it an indication from other republicans, more hardline, that even if the IRA called a ceasefire and Sinn Fein joined the talks, they were not interested in peace? Later in the morning it was confirmed that there had been no casualties, and that the renegade Continuity IRA, that opposed the talks process, had claimed responsibility.

I was worried that the bomb would destabilize the little progress we had made. But as we were to see with other atrocities during the talks process, the press and public reaction showed there had been a mood shift among the people in N. Ireland. The bombers were now people opposed to the talks and it made the talks process look right: it was the only alternative to bombing, which was clearly wrong. It gave more strength to the process, rather than weakening it.

The UUP leadership backed David Trimble and decided to come into the talks. But on their terms, just like Sinn Fein. This is how they would face down Paisley: they would not 'run away' as they said he had, but stay in there and defend the union. At the same time they would seek to expose the republicans and try and get them expelled from the process. On 17 September a phalanx of unionists and loyalists entered Castle Buildings. David Trimble was surrounded by his UUP colleagues, along with Gary McMichael, leader of the Ulster Democratic Party, and David Ervine, leader of the Progressive Unionist Party, with their own teams of delegates. It was a welcome sight. It now felt like there were two opposing teams entering the ring to start battle. But as always in N. Ireland, you have to distinguish between what is done for the benefit of the media and the watching world, and what is said inside the building.

Immediately a hurdle had to be climbed over before talks could start. Because of the IRA statement about the Mitchell Principles, the UUs called for Sinn Fein to be expelled. The test the two governments had to apply was whether or not a party had 'demonstrably dishonoured' any of the principles. I listened carefully to all views from the parties and to the civil servants and decided with the Irish that Sinn Fein should stay in the talks. But in saying they should stay we made an important statement that we expected the republican movement 'as a whole' to honour the commitments Sinn Fein had given. That would mean that if the IRA did commit any acts of violence during the talks we would hold Sinn Fein responsible. It was an important principle to uphold, but it was to cause us major headaches in the months ahead. With the exclusion of Sinn Fein rejected, there was nothing to stop the negotiations proper from starting – some eighteen months late.

Now, for the first time ever, representatives of all four main groups in N. Ireland, unionist, nationalist, loyalist and republican, were at the negotiating table together. Yes, some people just glared at each other, some spoke through the chair, they exchanged insults and tried to goad each other. No one was going to lose face and be pleasant. But I began to sense for the first time that the peace process was getting its own momentum, which was very positive because it meant that no one party would want to be seen to be the one to bring that process to a halt.

In order to avoid arguments over who sat next to whom, the parties were arranged round the table in alphabetical order. Each was limited to three seats at the table and five supporters sitting scribbling away behind. Each delegation had a little microphone in front of them with an on–off button and a red light to show when it was working. The acoustics were awful in the room and it was sometimes hard to hear folk well – the more quietly spoken ones anyway. Some were plenty loud enough. The image, looking round the table of determined faces, and the backdrop of the room in dull, neutral pinks with plastic plants stuck on shelves in the corners and a raised sky-lit roof above us, will stay with me for ever.

In the alphabetical order, the non-sectarian Alliance Party were first, to the left of the Irish government delegation (the Irish government sat on the left and we sat on the right of the talks chairs). The Alliance leader, John Alderdice, I found amiable. He was bright and probably one of the more articulate party leaders around. Much to his party's disgust he left it to become speaker of the new Assembly in July 1998. He was a good leader for a non-aligned, moral-high-ground sort of party. John is a psychiatrist by trade, which certainly gives him a very well-developed sense of self. I'm not one to criticize that – his self-confidence was a plus in a process where the battle involved such titanic egos as Ian Paisley's. You needed to be tough to get a word in edgeways, and John always managed.

One of the quirks in the way N. Ireland's peace talks were constructed meant that parties got a seat at the table even though they weren't direct protagonists in the conflict. In an attempt to please the unionists and prise in Sinn Fein in 1996, John Major set the talks up by a process of election. Ten parties were duly elected to take part (reduced to eight when the DUP and the UK UP walked out). Among them was a loose non-sectarian coalition calling themselves the Labour party. They hadn't really been a party before the talks, and throughout the process they were forever falling out with each other. NIO officials kept bringing me legal documents to study to judge who was and who wasn't properly the Labour party. I was even threatened with court action by one group who had fallen out with another. But all of the time it was Councillor Malachi Curren and Hugh Casey. On the whole they were a sensible and stabilizing influence, though not very exciting.

Sitting next round the table to Labour were the N. Ireland Women's Coalition. Like Labour they formed as a party to fight the talks elections, and from the outset they operated in a determinedly collective manner: their strength was their solidarity. They were derisively called 'the women' from the outset, especially by some of the older male politicians. They would not have a leader – they decided things collectively and democratically. They shared out the spoils, like the trips to America, and the jobs the talks entailed. But two in particular, Monica McWilliams and Pearl Sagar, became the most prominent spokespeople. They were an unlikely couple. Monica came from a Catholic nationalist background and was a senior lecturer at the University of Ulster. Pearl was from Belfast's Protestant Shankhill Road, and first and foremost a community activist. They were supported by a capable and determined bunch that included May Blood, a legend from Protestant Belfast (now Baroness Blood – a well-deserved peerage); Ulster People's College academic Bronagh Hinds; the former head of the European Commission office in N. Ireland, Jane Morrice; and Kate Fearon, a student at the start of the talks.

One of my very first visits to Belfast in opposition was to the Blackmountain housing estate for a cup of tea with May Blood. When I entered her house, I was a little bit scared as she was so formidable – she reminded me of my Girl Guide leader! As we talked, I relaxed and listened. I grew to respect women like May for their strength and determination to stick by what they believed in and survive in a very male-dominated environment. She was not alone. There were other women showing her strength and determination across N. Ireland – many I didn't know, others like Avila Kilmurray I did. Monica and Pearl were not the kind of feminists to be habitually anti-male. They were aware of the inadequacies and insecurities of the men around them, and could be sympathetic to them when it helped. They acted together and very impressively. Their balance, their ability to understand and bring people along and, in the end, their willingness to talk to the paramilitary-related parties gave those parties a lot of support when they needed it.

One of these was the Progressive Unionist party – the PUP. They were the political representatives of the loyalist paramilitary group the Ulster Volunteer Force (UVF), led by David Ervine and Billy Hutchinson. Both had served time on the loyalist paramilitary wing of Belfast's Maze Prison. Both had learnt their politics there, especially under the influence of one of the Maze's longest-serving inmates Gusty Spence. I had a great deal of time for Gusty Spence – self-educated in prison, a fine mind and a good leader of men. I learnt a lot from him about loyalism and what loyalists thought of N. Ireland. He had been instrumental in bringing about the combined loyalist ceasefire and seeing it maintained since 1994.

I couldn't help liking David Ervine as a person. He reminded me of so many of the men in the Labour party back in the North-east of England, who believed and cared passionately. He remains a good socialist politician. And, while he can get as gloomy and grumpy as the best of them, he has a great sense of humour and love of life. He also has a bright, amiable wife, Jeanette, who backs him all the way. I hope he will be an important player in the future of N. Ireland. I bumped into David and Jeanette in the very early days of involvement in N. Ireland, at Heathrow airport. For a split second while I placed him I thought they were a couple from Redcar who had come to see me with a problem at my surgery – something to do with an operation that had gone wrong. Luckily I placed David before I asked how his tummy was.

Billy Hutchinson, who served fifteen years of a life sentence, is more difficult to pin down. There's a lot of energy there – I believe he still runs up to ten miles every day. I think he was more focused than David and, while less good in public, he was more influential within the loyalist camp. Occasionally these two fell out, and then Hughie Smyth, another loyalist, would sort it out with his ever present humour. Hughie had been Mayor of Belfast in 1994. He had a wise head, and most in the talks liked and were amused by him. These three were supported by men like William 'Plum' Smith – so called, he once said, after the American Indian in the *Beano*, Little Plum. Then there were other more shadowy characters around them. One of them, Winky Dodds, looked very scary but was always very polite when I bumped into him in the corridor.

Next to the PUP were the Social Democratic and Labour Party, the SDLP. Their leader, John Hume, had been there at the start. He had led the civil-rights marches in Derry in the late 1960s, and been a leader in the N. Ireland Civil Rights Association. He was fond of quoting Martin Luther King, a man who had been an inspiration to him in those dark days thirty years before. The important start to the peace process, talking with Sinn Fein, was achieved by John. He took a lot of criticism for it, but it was his work and his vision which made the later progress possible. I think his contribution to the peace process will never be forgotten. It would be true to say he gave his life to finding peace. Some complained about his use of 'Hume-speak', his propensity to use the same words and expressions over and over again, but to me this was his way of describing his nationalism, which was ultimately unthreatening and inclusive. When he retired as leader of the SDLP in 2001, I fervently hoped he would find more time for himself and take care of his health.

Alongside every great man there is usually an equally great woman. Pat Hume is such a woman. She has worked tirelessly beside John, she has looked after the local party and she has brought up a family. The prominence of John made it difficult for others in the SDLP to get the experience and attention they deserved. Mark Durkan worked alongside him in Derry. He was John's natural successor as the SDLP leader, bright, even-tempered, humorous and, without a doubt, part of the future in N. Ireland. He was elected leader when John Hume stood down in mid-November 2001. The other man at the head of the SDLP was Seamus Mallon. He remains, in my opinion, the most outstanding politician in N. Ireland. Like John Hume, he was a veteran of the civil-rights movement and had been an active campaigner for peace and justice for more than thirty years, and deputy leader of the SDLP since 1979. Where John Hume was necessary to bring Sinn Fein in, it would be Seamus Mallon with all his political skill who would be needed both to work with David Trimble and to keep the republicans and nationalists onside. In the talks he worked hard out of the public eye, making progress. I have a great deal of respect for Seamus as a human being who sticks by his principles, such as human rights and equality, and will keep going as long as it is necessary. He also stood down in mid-November 2001 and was replaced by Brid Rodgers, a strong, competent woman and the first woman to be elected to an important mainstream job. Two others in the SDLP group, Sean Farren and Denis Haughey, were also prominent members of the team who would be important for the future.

Seeing the SDLP politicians there, sandwiched between representatives of loyalist and republican paramilitarism, it always struck me how much more tolerant they were than their unionist counterparts. They were just as fierce in their opposition to violence as, say, the UUP, and yet they were prepared from the outset to engage with loyalist ex-prisoners and ex-paramilitaries – one of whom, the UDP's John White, had been convicted of the brutal murder in 1973 of an SDLP Senator, Paddy Wilson, and a friend of his, Irene Andrews. That being said, the UUs always had to consider far less tolerant and far less forgiving critics over their shoulders in the shape of Ian Paisley and Bob McCartney.

Then came the new Sinn Fein delegation. From the outset the Shinners exercised their internal democracy by rotating the personalities sitting in the front row at the table. Gerry Adams and Martin McGuinness were usually both there, but the third seat was occupied at different times by Gerry Kelly, Alex Maskey, Mitchel McLaughlin, Bairbre De Brún and others. Unlike most of the other parties, the organization of Sinn Fein was specifically designed to share the workload, to bring on new people, or encourage others to take a higher profile whenever it was useful. On one particular occasion I asked, I can't remember if it was Gerry or Martin, why it was that they were letting Pat Doherty do all the media interviews. The answer, which came with a smile, was that Pat was likely to be one of the new candidates to become a Member of Parliament at the next general election and they wanted to 'bring him on a bit' and raise his profile. Doherty was duly elected in 2001 in West Tyrone, narrowly beating Brid Rodgers to the Westminster seat.

Next to Sinn Fein was the Ulster Democratic Party representing the political leadership of loyalist paramilitary groups the Ulster Defence Association (UDA) and the Ulster Freedom Fighters (UFF). The UDP were led by Gary McMichael, a young man in his twenties when the talks started. His father, John

McMichael, had been a leading loyalist killed by the IRA in 1987. I think Gary always felt he had a lot to live up to. He was clever, serious, determined, but lacked the support mechanisms of the PUP. Davey Adams, his deputy, was a bright guy and politically savvy.

The UUP team, the eighth delegation, completed the circle around the table sitting just to our right. David Trimble led a young team. The older heads among the UUs kept a wary distance, only occasionally taking one of the party's allotted three seats at the talks table. Ken Maginnis was there, but up and down emotionally. It was said he was not well and it was this that made him even more volatile than usual. Nevertheless Ken was central because he was one of the few that was prepared to stand his corner and stick with David Trimble. John Taylor, the deputy leader, was there occasionally and was rarely positive. Taylor was regarded as a barometer for mainstream unionists. Through his supporters he kept his finger on the pulse of the heartlands. His detractors said he simply swung whichever way the wind blew. I found him difficult especially when he was critical of David Trimble behind the scenes, which didn't help David's leadership.

David himself remained a little apart from his party. He got used to working with Prime Ministers, Senators and Presidents. Jeffrey Donaldson was a very valuable member of the UUP team at the time. He was bright, affable and worked well with the moderate SDLPers. Others around of note were Reg Empey, a capable and, I believe, genuinely nice man, and Dermot Nesbitt, a likeable and experienced politician, who grew in stature and became more and more positive as the process went on. Both men are good politicians and part of N. Ireland's future.

Then we move on to the chair of the talks process. As chair and co-ordinator, George Mitchell was much more cunning and more politically adept than people gave him credit for. They thought it was just good old George, nice George, patient George, tolerant George. But he carefully thought out moves, sought out what was happening and managed the process much more than anybody ever realized. He was quite a loner. Even with his tireless aide Martha Pope – who did a lot of chivvying behind the scenes, a lot of networking, a lot of supporting, and created some good moves – he was not that close. Martha is very capable and, like me, got frustrated occasionally at being excluded. I think George was very clear and very controlled all along about the strategy he was following.

George was joined at the talks table by the former Finnish Prime Minister Hari Holkeri, who is a fine example of how patient and tolerant people could be towards N. Ireland. His English was poor, his Irish worse, yet he stuck with it – he was a bright man. He forced people to be thoughtful, to explain things and work with him. I think he gave a positive contrast to George's style. Canadian General John de Chastelain was the third chair. I think he is everything a general always should be: tight and controlled. He didn't bring much flexibility of thought to the process, but he helped make the triumvirate as a whole a good team. I think there was a certain degree of tension because George didn't always include the other two in everything he did, but amazingly for three such powerful men from different walks of life, they worked well together.

The only other faces round the table were those of the two governments. For the Brits there was me and Paul and at times Adam. From the Irish government, Ray Burke began with what I thought were all the right instincts: pragmatic, looking for the deal. Unfortunately he was lost to the process after only a few months when he resigned from the Irish government over a political financial scandal. David Andrews replaced him. Alongside both men sat Progressive Democrat (Fianna Fail's major coalition partner in the Irish government) TD, Liz O'Donnell. Liz was great. She put up with a lot of shit, because she was bright and attractive and female. But she stuck in there and played the boys at their own game. She outlasted both her bosses at the Irish Foreign Ministry.

All of these people I came to know a lot better as the weeks and months passed. But right from the start I was able to build on relationships with them which I had forged in opposition. Paul Murphy did the same. We felt good then, felt like we had made a really promising start. N. Ireland was up there at the top of the national agenda only a short while after the general election, before many other policy areas had really had a chance to get started, let alone deliver any real change.

The structure for the talks was inevitably not simple. There were too many issues to discuss. So the talks were divided into three strands, with different chairs for each. The first strand was to deal with new arrangements for government and other issues within N. Ireland itself. Strand Two would look at the new arrangements for better co-operation between N. Ireland and the Irish Republic. And Strand Three would focus on new arrangements for working together among all the different parts of these islands, British and Irish. In addition there were other issues which had to be sorted out – policing, human rights, criminal justice, equality, security, prisoners and, of course, weapons decommissioning.

An Independent Decommissioning Commission had been established to help move the talks forward without losing sight of the weapons issue. It had a central role to play if progress was to be made. We asked John de Chastelain to chair it and he was joined by two other foreign nationals, US Ambassador Don Johnson and Brigadier Tauno Nieminen of Finland. Once again, when an independent voice was sought on a key issue, other countries were willing to step in and help by finding good people to come over and take part. Their task was enormous. As decommissioning was voluntary, we hoped the international status of the Commission members would help to bring a wider perspective and moral pressure to bear.

Looking back I, like many, wish that decommissioning had not succeeded in becoming the main dividing issue between the two sides. I now firmly believe that knowing the importance of parity to both sides in the process we should have made efforts to make the dividing line something other than weapons. It had been there since the earlier IRA ceasefire in 1994 and always looked to me like one of those enormous obstacles that the two sides were just never going to agree upon and, if we let it, could prevent progress for ever. Everybody knew really that, even if all the arms were decommissioned, the republicans (and the loyalists) could soon get new ones if they wanted to. And, anyway, the bombs that were most often used and did most damage, as at Canary Wharf, were made mostly from basic ingredients you could get down at the DIY store. But on the other side there was always the argument that if the IRA are really committed to peace why not destroy the weapons?

Both sets of paramilitaries on one side and the UUP on the other were very unwilling to move on the issue. In fairness, David Trimble and the Ulster Unionists did (under some duress) moderate their position to give Sinn Fein room to move. But for Sinn Fein the focus was on the wrong thing, and they felt unable to act unless the loyalists were doing the same and unless reform of the police and security was under way. From their point of view, they were an army on one side in a conflict and the RUC, the British Army and the loyalist paramilitaries were on the other. So why should they disarm if none of these was expected to do so at the same time? But as more and more moves were made to reduce the security presence and reform the police, the arguments for not decommissioning got stretched ever thinner.

The only solution I could think of, at the beginning of the talks, was to try to keep moving on every front at the same time in the hope that enough would get done on different issues to keep everyone in the process. We had already lost Ian Paisley and Bob McCartney, but as they were so implacably opposed to Sinn Fein's involvement it was probably easier without them. But we couldn't afford to lose anyone else. If there is a big obstacle in your path, you have two choices: to butt up against it again and again in the hope, however vain, that it will move, or to look on one side and then on the other to see if you can find a way to go round it. When it's a matter of making progress and building momentum and, in the end, saving lives, I have always favoured the second of these two courses of action. So we had the decommissioning body working away alongside the three strands and then various committees looking at 'confidence-building issues', like policing and justice and prisoners.

The talks took place three or four days a week, and each day groups would meet to discuss issues under the different headings. George Mitchell called regular plenary meetings at the beginning to bring everyone together in the same room to review progress. It has to be said that for the first few months there was very little progress to review. With a degree of frustration at one point I said that if the parties were willing, we could have an agreement 'by Christmas'. My comments were thought a little ambitious (to say the least) by some people, but the truth was that we all knew what the issues were and could have resolved them earlier. What predictably happened was that very little progress was made until we got much nearer the Easter deadline for the end of the talks, which was very frustrating for everyone. But at the same time we did have (as I repeated at the time till I was blue in the face) all the main players in the same room for the first time ever, against a background, again for the first time, of ceasefires from both sides. And that, in itself, was remarkable progress.

Day to day, Paul Murphy chaired the talks on Strand One. He spent most of his time holding one-to-one (called bilateral) meetings with each party which all were carefully noted by our officials to see whether any common ground was emerging. George and his team did the same on Strand Two and I worked with the Irish on Strand Three, also striving at the same time to make sure the three strands were moving in unison. In addition I oversaw all the other areas looking out for problems and potential sticking points. When they inevitably arose, I would have a meeting with de Chastelain, with George, Hari, Paul and the Irish Ministers, David Andrews and Liz O'Donnell. Frequently everyone would be there, all in my office, with people perched on tables and chairs and me trying to stop too many people speaking at once, and a whole bunch of civil servants trying to see what could be done.

I also met regularly with each of the talks participants. These meetings were useful for the parties to let off steam about something in the process they weren't happy with and also for me to get an overall picture of how we were doing. But the meetings were very tiring, because it was often difficult to make progress, and because they saved positive points for the talks with George and Paul, but needed to offload their problems in front of me. I wasn't going to question what Paul or George were up to, so I just listened and took the shit. I often used to get up and serve the tea at these meetings because it helped people to relax and talk.

I also worked with the folk who were trying to make progress on human rights, policing, criminal justice, equality and security issues. My obsession with lists, as Nigel and Ken would agree, became invaluable as there was so much to keep track of. I needed to keep checking on each issue as we could not have any area falling behind, because if it did it would create trouble in the future.

My first main task was to work on the prisoner issue, something that I expected would cause more problems among British public opinion than in N. Ireland itself. The mainland population were not aware of the way that the prisons were managed in N. Ireland. As in many prisons, the staff had to find an agreed way of working with the prisoners: if the regime is too harsh the prison becomes unmanageable and officers' lives are put at risk. The additional threat from the different groups within the prisons to prison officers' families on the outside was a real one and could not be ignored. The very high sickness rate among the prison officers is partly accounted for by these threats.

Because the prisoners in N. Ireland jails, principally in the notorious Maze Prison, were organized along political lines, the different political groupings had to be kept segregated from each other for everyone's safety. That is where all the images you saw on telly of the IRA or UVF wings came from. Within these wings, or separate parts of the prison, inmates were allowed a lot of freedom of movement as well as being able to wear their own clothes. Alongside this more relaxed regime there were more generous leave arrangements and parole terms, all of which was much harder to justify in the British press than it was across the water. People in N. Ireland knew that you had to deal with the world as it was and not how you would wish it to be.

Despite concerns about public opinion in Britain, we were making progress. Prisoner transfers or repatriations were a case in point. Special procedures for repatriating prisoners from gaols in Britain to N. Ireland or the Irish Republic had been in place for some time. I was pushing hard to speed them up, to reduce the potential for grievances on either side to cause problems in the talks. Jack Straw, the then Home Secretary, despite his 'hard man' image, was very helpful. He wanted to accelerate the process, but also understood, like me, that if you put prisoners in gaol nearer their families, the families don't suffer as much and the prospects for rehabilitating a person when they get out of prison are greater. In fact, this arrangement was going quite well. As we were all agreed to do it, I saw no harm in tackling the bureaucracy to make it happen more quickly. But some of the transfers were proving very difficult for my colleagues at home, particularly in terms of public opinion.

A good example was the case of Jason Campbell. He was convicted in Glasgow of a particularly nasty murder involving football and religion. The person he killed, with a knife in broad daylight outside a Glasgow pub, was a Catholic – a fact Campbell deduced simply because his victim was wearing a Celtic football scarf. Campbell's case had been raised with us by the

PUP as a suitable one for transfer to N. Ireland. But as soon as the Scottish press got wind of it all hell broke loose. Poor Adam Ingram got the brunt of it, for being Security Minister in Belfast and for being a Glaswegian Prod at home. It was vicious. It was sorted out late at night over a pizza in Donald Dewar's office (Donald was then Secretary of State for Scotland), with Tony on the phone from France. Campbell's application for transfer was refused when the 'family' he was supposed to have in N. Ireland never materialized.

All this time life seemed to go on around me. In September my sister came to stay and we did an interview on being sisters for the *Observer* magazine. I continued to do visits out and about in N. Ireland, like to the Sperrinview Special School in County Tyrone. These kinds of events helped to keep me sane, along with all the kindness and support from others in the community. I also began discussions with broadcasters in N. Ireland who wanted to help and asked my views on what they could do. I met and talked to BBC N. Ireland controller Pat Loughrey and his team about one idea, which was for the BBC to initiate and sponsor a special 'Making a Difference' award ceremony to honour people from across N. Ireland who helped improve the lives of others. It was just the kind of feel-good event that people needed to see broadcast, so that at difficult times we could all be reminded of what people can do to support one another and to overcome their differences despite all the problems.

Jon and I were also beginning to use Hillsborough Castle as a place where I could relax. I've mentioned already that because of its size and extensive grounds it meant that I could have friends to stay at weekends, and we would not be hassled by having to have security with us all the time. It was also big enough for us not to get under each other's feet. People could walk, take the boat out on the lake, play tennis or just catch up on much-needed sleep. Over time these weekends became quite famous – or infamous. People came and had fun and let their hair down. I think this was for two reasons: firstly, most people never get to stay in a country house and, given the backdrop of what was happening in N. Ireland, the place had an other-worldly feel; and secondly, these places were built for entertaining. There is space to be private, to exercise and to have fun. Also when the night has finished you just crawl up to bed instead of having to go home.

One of the cornerstones of most weekends was the games we played after dinner. For these we all filed into the large sitting room, which was still not really full when we had twenty-five or more people staying, quite often the case with kids as well. We usually started relatively sedately with a game called Chinese Whispers Charades, and as the drink flowed moved on to the Animal Game and finally, if we had a pianist in the group, indulged in a sing-song round the piano. Only a very few people refused to join in. I will not embarrass them by naming names.

Chinese Whispers Charades is a great game, and combines the acting of charades with the misunderstandings of Chinese whispers. We used to divide the guests into two teams. One team had to go into the haunted room (Lady Grey's) next door, and those that remained had to think up a recent event or subject that could be acted out. An example would be one of Richard Branson's abortive attempts to balloon round the world, or Monica Lewinsky and Bill Clinton. What would then happen is that one member of the team would be nominated to act out the meaning of this, with all the mimed actions agreed by the team. No words were allowed. Then the first person was brought in from the other room, and the mimes were acted out in front of them. They then had to remember all the actions so they could act it out in front of the next one of their team who was brought through. The last person had to guess what was being acted out. You can imagine that, as the drink flowed and the giggling intensified, everyone had a great time. My best memory is of a slightly drunk ambassador's wife doing a wonderful interpretation of the Millennium Bug.

I won't go into the complexities of the Animal Game.

The following Sunday morning was usually a more subdued affair, as people drifted into the kitchen in our flat, to cook themselves bacon and eggs, or sit quietly in the corner with black coffee. Sometimes people were remarkably lively though. I remember one weekend which had a particularly Welsh flavour, with the Kinnocks, the Folletts and the Howells staying. I don't know who started it but suddenly we had a full male Welsh choir singing 'Men of Harlech' in the kitchen.

Autumn is the time of year for the political party conferences. I could not physically manage to go to all the party conferences in N. Ireland as well as Labour's own. And, as Secretary of State, if I had gone to one I would have had to go to them all. With, by that time, at least ten political parties in N. Ireland that was impossible. But Labour's conference was a must. It was in Brighton that year. I had been going as a visitor and then as an MP for many years, had made lots of friends around the country and used to have a good time, talking to folk and attending fringe meetings. It is also a very good indicator of how the leadership is doing – in government or out. It also means loads of work for party workers but is important because it gives us all a sense of belonging to the party, to something we are proud of, and something that will guide us when in government.

After I became a member of the cabinet, party conferences were never the same. My schedule, like that of other Ministers, was planned with military precision from dawn to dusk and beyond, with little chance of a relaxed coffee or drink with a friend or journalist. If I managed to have one it was only because a casual moment was programmed into the daily schedule alongside: addressing a fringe meeting; opening or chairing at least one other meeting; and visiting the conference stands to thank all the hundred or so exhibitors for being there.

As more and more companies, besides the charities and trade unions, got interested in Labour as a potential and then actual government, the number of exhibition stands got larger and larger. Getting round them all in the two hours I had allocated – with everyone wanting photos – meant doing it at break-neck speed. Someone from the party would keep one stand ahead of me to get them ready. I would bowl up, when we had decided if it was a shake, a snog or just a smile; the photo would be taken and then on to the next stand. One of my assistants followed me with a carrier bag so that at every stand I could collect the freebies, usually pens or paper hats, and give them to the kids on my return. It saved having to find time to buy them something, and they had fun sorting out who got what. Every year we made it in the time allowed, but it was like a marathon.

Each evening there were receptions that were almost obligatory to attend, including those hosted by the British and foreign press, then there were the Ambassadors' parties, Irish Night, Northern Night, Welsh Night, Scots Night, the party workers' night, the sponsors' party, and events hosted by trade unions and business people attending the conference. The only other social occasion was the one I organized for local delegates in my hotel room on the Sunday night.

But the main reason for going to conference was to speak on the policy area I was responsible for. I updated conference on where we were in N. Ireland. I always found it harder speaking at conference than almost anywhere else. The party officers used to like us to use an autocue (those little glass screens that stick up either side of a speaking podium that the audience can see through, so it seems like the politician is looking at them, but that have the words of the speech projected on the other side for politicians to read), so we did not make any awful errors in front of an important audience of party members, the world's media and overseas visitors. I hated it. I used to practice and rewrite again and again right up to the end, making it hard for the poor people organizing the autocue.

My speech in 1997 went down well. I was determinedly upbeat

about the peace process, highlighting what I saw as being accomplished so far: 'The IRA ceasefire has been restored and the loyalists' ceasefire maintained, a peaceful 12 July weekend during the marching season despite the failure to reach accommodation at Drumcree, and now, most important of all, the launch of talks designed to bring a new agreement among the parties for all the people of Northern Ireland.' I talked about us being ready to 'listen, consult and respond to change'. As always it was a case of saying that we were confident there could be a better future for N. Ireland, and there were things we as a government could do to advance that, but at the same time we wanted to take the people with us. There was always a bit of tension within the Labour party between those who wanted everything to rest on the peace talks and those who wanted to see change driven through anyway.

This would have been even more difficult without the changes in overall party policy made in the previous couple of years. As members of a party with a long tradition of fighting for justice and a fairer society, a lot of people in the Labour party had been close supporters of the civil-rights movement in N. Ireland in the 1960s and 1970s, which translated for many into support for Irish nationalism. But we were no longer a campaigning opposition. We now had a clear position, standing, in my shorthand, for 'neutrality, with fairness, justice and equality'. That meant we could do things as a government to further those crucial values, while at the same time maintaining our neutrality in the talks.

After the conference, negotiations began again in earnest in N. Ireland. This involved an even-handed approach to all sides. While doing all we could to help the unionists we couldn't ignore Sinn Fein, nor the need to keep up momentum in the process. On 13 October Tony Blair came across to Belfast. He met all the parties in Castle Buildings, including Sinn Fein. It was the first time a British Prime Minister had ever met Gerry Adams – the first meeting of a British Prime Minister and an Irish republican leader for over seventy years. There was no handshake for the cameras – the meeting was held in private. But afterwards, when asked if he had shaken hands, Tony just said he had treated Gerry Adams as he would 'any human being'. There is no doubt that it was a breakthrough and a crucial step to take, as Tony was taking so many crucial steps throughout the process. He was ready to risk a lot more with public opinion then than a lot of people gave him credit for. I always felt that, if only he could have talked with me more and been inclusive of others as time went on, I would not have got so angry so often and we might have worked better together.

Later on in the day, we went walkabout in a shopping centre in East Belfast to show that Tony was prepared to meet people from all backgrounds and all political views. The choice of Coniswater Shopping Centre was made, hoping he would be exposed to a broad mix of people. But this was not to be. The shopping centre was in Peter Robinson's constituency and his party, the DUP, came out in force. I think the closest Tony got to meeting people was a group of women throwing plastic gloves at him and shouting that he should wear them when he met Gerry Adams to keep the blood off his hands. It was one of the worst jostles I had encountered in N. Ireland. The police steered us through the mall to the manager's office and we exited through the back door. Tony was very calm. If he was angry about what had happened he did not show it.

Despite the jostling, Tony's visit had been a success. We had met with all parties. All parties were now engaged. The issue of one party or another being excluded had been put to rest. It was a huge psychological hurdle to have climbed over. That we got there just six months after the election is a terrific tribute to the determination of everyone involved. Now we had to get the talks going in earnest. There were many very difficult issues to resolve. Thinking ahead I began to worry that we would not make the deadline in six months' time. The only way we had a chance was to start immediately working as hard as we could. That's what we did.

The British government's role in the talks was an odd one. As Secretaries of State have said over the years, N. Ireland is a balancing act. It felt like walking a tightrope, weighing the interests of one side against another and trying not to lose anyone. On some issues I didn't have a view on what the outcome should be. As long as both sides of the community in N. Ireland could agree to it, in my view that was fine. But to say we had no interest in the shape of the outcome would not be the truth. We had our own agenda based on fairness and equality of opportunity. We could hardly ignore Britain's role in Ireland and N. Ireland. But, whatever had happened in the past, now the British government had to be, in my mind, a referee, especially when it was important to the process to keep shoring up the moderate leadership on both sides against the hardliners on the fringes. We had to make progress and try to reward either side for moving as we went along, so that they could say to their followers they weren't moving first or they weren't moving for nothing. It was essential to keep David Trimble and Gerry Adams in place, because without them it would have been much harder to sustain the peace process.

Each side had their lists of demands, right from the start of the talks. Sinn Fein, for example, would come in for a bilateral meeting, with me and a group of officials, on a Monday morning with a list of demands they said had to be met. In truth, many of the issues I had some sympathy with. But making progress on the issues was only part of what their having lists was about. The lists were bargaining chips in the negotiations, to try and get the best deal they could before allowing progress to be made.

You had to be careful and think tactically in dealing with the lists. As soon as one item on the list was achieved, another took its place. Over the months I had to make judgements about which were genuine grievances and which were try-ons, while at the same time always gauging where other parties were on the issue. Equally it was important not to give all the credit for progress on issues on the nationalist agenda to Sinn Fein. The SDLP had played an important role in getting the talks going and had fought long and hard within the democratic system on many of the issues on the Sinn Fein agenda. On the other hand, I had to give the republicans some of the credit because they were using the issues to get support among their followers. So they could say, 'Look, it is worth being in the talks, we are making more progress than we ever did by violence.' And at the same time I was always watching where the unionists were. It was no good holding the Shinners in if, in the process, we lost the UUs.

As the talks progressed we began to put into action other commitments we had made before the election for change, including improvements in human rights, changes in policing structures and tackling discrimination in employment. We also made progress on the parades. I desperately wanted to avoid another Drumcree, like the one we had just experienced. I knew that what I was planning to do on parades would please neither side. That was inevitable, since compromise and accommodation were the only realistic ways forward.

At the time Sinn Fein also began pressing hard for an inquiry into the death of Patrick Finucane, a Belfast solicitor who had died at the hands of loyalist gunmen in February 1989. There had been allegations that the security forces, either the army or the police, had colluded in his murder by passing to loyalist killers information about his whereabouts. I had looked at this case in opposition and thought then that an inquiry was necessary. In government I intended to call one, but while there was still the possibility of a criminal prosecution it was out of the question. I knew that whatever I did would be too little for Sinn Fein, and too much for the police or the army. For the moment, I just listened intently to what they were saying and bided my time till I could act.

There were repeated calls by the republicans for a scaling down of the British military presence in N. Ireland. They weren't alone on this issue. The SDLP pushed hard for it too, particularly Seamus Mallon. This was always a chicken-and-egg problem for me. They wanted us to move before the paramilitaries did. But we could only move in response to a reduced security threat, which meant there would have to be some action by the paramilitaries. Ronnie Flanagan and Rupert Smith were willing to co-operate. They didn't want to keep their forces on full alert a moment longer than was necessary. There was always an unspoken pressure on the army to get the boys home as soon as it was safe. But equally neither was going to risk the lives of their men or women.

The IRA ceasefire did bring about a marked reduction in the security threat and the security forces knew they had to respond. But years of attacks from the IRA made movement very difficult for them. How could they be sure the ceasefire was for real? The heads of both the army and the police did not want to risk further deaths on their hands by moving too quickly. I kept on talking to them at our weekly security meetings and by the end of November the security forces judged, on an operational basis, that daytime patrols by the army in West Belfast could come to an end. This was an important step forward towards what we would come to call 'normalization' and a very welcome one, because people on the streets of West Belfast would actually feel some progress. Of course it was far too little for the republicans.

Another issue on the nationalists' shopping list was the ending of the anti-terrorist legislation. Labour had argued in opposition that it should be reformed and I had already announced (causing a flurry of unnecessary excitement among the press at Labour's conference) that internment would end at the first chance I got to make the necessary change to the law. Internment was the power to put people in prison without first having a fair trial in court. It had been used in the early 1970s to lock up for as long as two years people whom the police suspected of terrorism. It was the best recruiting sergeant the IRA ever had. It was and is fundamentally contrary to basic human rights. Ending internment was just part of a package of reforms we would introduce to bring the UK's anti-terrorism laws up to date. I, like many others in the Labour party and in government, was not opposed to anti-terrorist legislation as such, but I wanted it reformed so it didn't just target people from N. Ireland but applied equally across the UK, respected basic human rights and was effective against the changing nature of international terrorism. With new types of terrorism exploiting all the advantages of the Internet and modern communications, we had to get up to date with our response. And that meant ending some of the old-fashioned methods, like excluding people from travelling from one part of the UK (N. Ireland) to another (mainland Britain). It did not work, it made us look like we were discriminating against people, and that autumn Jack Straw brought the practice to an end by scrapping the remaining exclusion orders that were in operation against twelve individuals.

A major difficulty we had throughout the talks was that it was easier to move on some of the nationalists' issues – because they were often about making N. Ireland a fairer and more equal place to live for everyone – than on unionist demands. Take, for example, the introduction of the Human Rights Act. When we introduced the change it was not enough for Sinn Fein and too much for the unionists. We learnt very quickly that nothing would ever be quite enough for Sinn Fein, but the main difficulty we were having was finding sufficient measures to build up confidence on the unionists' side. This was made all the more difficult because most of their demands were about not changing things. So while changes to the police or to the security presence on the streets or to the anti-discrimination laws were not all opposed by more moderate unionists, it was never easy.

I had a meeting with Jeffrey Donaldson towards the end of October to talk about the lack of what we called 'confidence-building measures' for unionists. Some small steps we did take included giving John Taylor a job in Europe, reconstituting the

N. Ireland Grand Committee at Westminster, which was designed to give local MPs more power of scrutiny over laws passed applying to N. Ireland, and, one of my personal missions, making the operation of the Anglo-Irish Secretariat at Maryfield more open and transparent.

Maryfield was a word most unionists said as if they were spitting. It is a boring enough set of buildings in rather nice grounds, just outside Belfast, but it is what went on there that upset the unionists the most. It was established under the Anglo-Irish Agreement that Mrs Thatcher's government signed in 1985, to deal with all the administration that arose from that Agreement. The buildings housed a group of British and Irish officials working more or less permanently together. The idea was for them to discuss ideas and prepare the agendas for the regular formal meetings between British and Irish Ministers. Depending on how you looked at it, it was either a useful aid to a good working relationship between the British and Irish governments or, as the DUP put it, an 'Irish serpent within the bosom of Ulster'.

I wanted to keep Irish and British civil servants talking but I did not see the need for all the secrecy which just aroused unfounded suspicions or for a special building with all the additional costs that entailed. I started to work for change, but the meetings with my civil servants were mostly like the ones portrayed on the TV series *Yes, Minister*. There was a 'problem' with any suggestion that I made, and it soon became clear that I was going to have to work for months to get progress. I continued to push in a half-hearted way, but eventually needed all my focus on the main body of the talks. In the end, Tony Blair got rid of Maryfield in an instant, as a concession to David Trimble in the last stages of the talks. Actually, after that only the location changed, and the daily exchanges continued, I believe more effectively, in another building. Once Maryfield was abandoned I tried to get it turned into something useful, and I think it ended up as a police training centre and home for a charity for the disabled.

Another minor boost for unionism was a beefed-up role for the House of Commons N. Ireland Affairs Committee. This was originally strongly opposed by nationalists, as it was seen as a strengthening of the link between N. Ireland and Westminster. We extended its members' ability to travel to N. Ireland and I gave evidence once when they came to Belfast. As with most committees, I was not that convinced of its value. It was also expensive to transport every member to Belfast and feed them. But it seemed to please the committee and at least allowed us to say we were responding to something on the unionist list, so it had its value.

By now the political conference season was well under way in N. Ireland. The UUP conference threatened to be a rocky ride for David Trimble. In fact, apart from a rallying cry from Willie Ross to pull out of the talks, David came away relatively unscathed. Adam Ingram went down to Newcastle (County Down) where it was being held, and became the first British Minister ever to speak at it. I had spoken at it in opposition and remember going round the few stalls there to make money for the party, looking for something to buy and deciding on marmalade. It was very good but so orange in colour (it obviously contained food dye) that the children refused to eat it. Adam was a very good N. Ireland Minister at many things, including not shying away from difficult tasks. He does not take any prisoners when he speaks, which, contrary to what many people might think, works well in N. Ireland. His standing with unionism went up and down over the years he was in Belfast – he was the longest-serving member of the Labour government to be a N. Ireland Minister. At this point his rating was up. He was able, without hassle, in a Scottish sort of way to talk to them about the need for police reform and come away in one piece. As Security Minister he did a lot behind the scenes to work the very difficult politics, which helped the peace process considerably.

A telephone poll in the Belfast *Newsletter* the day after the

UUP conference appeared worrying. It showed only 24 per cent of callers supporting Trimble's position in the talks compared to 47 per cent supporting Paisley. It made a glum start to the day. But it emerged late morning that the phone line had been swamped by DUP callers. It made me think, never put your faith in telephone polls, however depressing or positive the results are, as they can be easily biased.

While I couldn't go to all the party conferences, there were many other conference-type events which were a very useful way for me to talk to many people and hear many different views about what was happening in N. Ireland. For example I spoke to the Trades Union Congress General Council in Bournemouth, to a Generation 2000 conference for young people at the Waterfront Hall in Belfast, and I can even remember one weekend going up to Redcar for a regular visit on the Friday and then over to a conference with Hillary Clinton at the Waterfront Hall in Belfast that night and then back again to Teesside for my surgery on the Saturday. Mad.

At one conference at Belfast's Queen's University, I talked to a group of students about the increase in racist attacks in N. Ireland, mainly against the small ethnic Chinese community. It was of concern to me as I remembered reading at University that if in a conflict the violence decreases or ceases between the main groups there is a tendency for another group to be picked on and a level of violence to continue in a different form. I wanted to be sure that, if there was a decrease in violence between Catholics and Protestants and a subsequent increase in violence towards ethnic minorities or domestic violence or sexual violence, we would be watching for it and had some plans in place with the police to respond.

We also had to watch carefully for relatively small disputes that had the potential to blow up out of all proportion and cause problems in the process. We had an example of this at the Coates Viyella factory in Derry in November. It was a sad development as industrial relations in N. Ireland had generally been good and had managed to avoid being dragged into the Troubles. Usually the work places have been managed through the unions, which had done a good job in holding sectarian divides out of the factories. They were also very helpful in the peace process. To be honest, a lot of the factories, because of their locations, are mostly one religion or the other, so the problem rarely arose. But in somewhere like Coates Viyella in Derry, which is mixed, there are difficult issues, especially around the commemoration of important dates to one side or the other. Remembrance Day in the UK is one such event. The issues are complicated, but, briefly, a combination of the Irish Republic's neutrality during the Second World War and opposition to British imperialism, and its effect on Ireland during the First World War, gives the wearing of poppies a different significance to nationalists than it would have for unionists and the rest of the people of the UK.

To try to defuse any potential tensions, the trade unions and the management at Coates Viyella reached an agreement that poppies could be worn for up to ten days before Remembrance Day (11 November), but no more. But this year a number of workers decided to wear poppies before the agreed dates. It's hard to see how this could be anything but a provocative gesture, as there was an agreement in place. But when Coates Viyella suspended the three or four men involved, it was taken up by the UK press as an issue of freedom of expression. It's difficult to think of an issue more likely to cause a wave of national anger in the UK than someone being punished for wearing a poppy, a national symbol of remembrance for our war dead – especially when whipped up by the press. I felt sorry for the management at Coates Viyella. They ran a good factory, and they were operating within the law and on the basis of a negotiated agreement. They took a lot of abuse particularly from the bright sparks at the *Daily Telegraph*. In the end the whole thing fizzled out when the ten days' suspension ended and the men returned to work, each wearing as big a poppy as they could find.

That year Jon and I attended the Remembrance Day service at Belfast City Hall. It wasn't something I was accustomed to doing. But we had spent a lot of time talking about the needs of the families who had lost loved ones in more recent decades and it felt right to acknowledge the pain still felt by those bereaved through the many wars of the twentieth century.

As the talks continued, despite the presence of George, John and Hari as independent chairs, there was still an awful lot of knocking on my and Tony Blair's doors. Both sides, unionist and nationalist, still looked very much to the British government to sort things out. They basically believed that we would play an important role in making the running. After twenty-five years of direct rule during which the N. Ireland parties had lobbied the British government for everything, they just continued to do so. It would have been ideal if we could just say, 'Talk to George, he is in the chair,' but they did have a right to talk to us and all hell would have broken out if we had refused to talk with parties that came knocking on the door for a meeting.

No. 10 were pulled into a lot of meetings, especially when the party leaders were in London. Tony would set days aside to meet them – as he did in the middle of November – seeing most of the parties. Talks like these, running parallel to what George was doing in Belfast, were not a problem at this point. But it became tougher as deadlines approached. Tony and Bertie Ahern were determined to make progress, and in the end any package to put to the parties had to be agreed by them too, so it made sense for them to talk as much as their busy schedules permitted. However, I know it worried George that he might not be getting the whole picture, which put him in a difficult position.

All the N. Ireland parties went through times when they had trouble holding their followers onside. The unionist divisions became better known as they were often played out in the media, but because Sinn Fein were more secretive it was sometimes difficult to tell with them. When twelve Sinn Fein members resigned in November from Dundalk over the Mitchell Principles it was clear there was discontent within the ranks. We all knew that a split within the republican movement was not in their interests or ours. But we always had to judge how serious the threat of a split was and how much it was a ploy to maximize their negotiating position.

As Christmas loomed the atmosphere in the talks became more and more tense. It was like living in a slow-heating pressure cooker. Many within the unionist community were getting very agitated at the direction they feared the talks were taking. In an effort to boost morale among some unionists, Lord Cranborne, a Tory unionist and member of the shadow cabinet, launched a new Friends of the Union group with a weekend meeting at his country house in Hertfordshire at the end of November. As it excluded the loyalists it was unhelpful, and became another irritant I had to deal with from our bipartisan 'friends' in the Tory party. Worries within unionism meant that Ian Paisley was on top form. He had a meeting with Tony Blair in London, also at the end of November, and went out afterwards and denounced the whole process to the press as a sham and a farce. So he had his meeting with the PM, got his headline, and that was his contribution to building peace.

At the end of a tense and difficult period I went to the United States for a couple of days just to be sure that on the other side of the Atlantic they were up to speed with what was happening and we were both still working closely together. However short the meeting, compared with the length of the flights involved, I always found it best to talk face to face with the relevant people in the White House, Senate and Congress. They were all very keen to help but had trouble understanding why progress was so slow. I spoke to the US journalists to make sure that what was happening from our perspective was clear to them. I said in one interview that I wanted an inquiry into the events of Bloody Sunday in 1972. It caused a fair bit of neurosis among the press back home, and in parts of the government too. I believed it was essential. It is unthinkable to have fourteen unarmed people killed and not have an inquiry, and the one that had been conducted at the time satisfied nobody. I stressed that no formal decision had been made, but my call for a new inquiry ran hard in the press.

In the first week in December we held Christmas drinks in my office at Millbank for Irish journalists based in London and the commentators on N. Ireland from the British press. Frank Millar and Des McCartan were there, as was Aiden Hennigan and Bernard Purcell from the *Irish Independent*. A collection of the Westminster Lobby came too, as they occasionally had to think and write about N. Ireland affairs when they came up in the normal run of politics. I enjoyed seeing folk I had not seen for some time – many like Tony Bevins had become close friends over the years. (His unexpected death was a great sadness to me.) It was like so many other evenings: put Irish politics and booze together and you get good hard discussions and great humour.

The key issue at that stage in the talks process was how to narrow the agenda and pin down the main issues to focus on. It had all been a bit diffuse so far and, after eighteen months, George Mitchell in particular was keen to get on with it. He wanted to get something down on paper, a page or two of key issues, or headings to discuss. He thought this should be attainable before the Christmas break, and worried that people would begin to lose heart if it was not. I was with him on that, conscious of the need to keep up the momentum. There had been big steps: the IRA ceasefire, the start of talks proper with all sides at the table. But we were still struggling to get beyond process and into real substance. On 2 December George launched a new initiative, which involved setting up a core working group of party leaders to try to make progress. It was a smaller format than in the main talks, which George hoped would help people relax a bit and work more pragmatically together.

Meanwhile the steady drift towards normality (by which I mean normal human relations) continued. New Irish President Mary McAleese visited N. Ireland for the first time as President. That she came from N. Ireland made this a lot easier and she went on to travel back and forth almost without comment. Bertie Ahern attended the talks for the first time (on 8 December) and had what was described as a 'friendly' meeting with UUP leaders.

On 11 December a Sinn Fein delegation went to Downing Street for a meeting. It was the first time such a group had been there since Michael Collins came to negotiate the Anglo-Irish Treaty in 1921. Afterwards, Tony Blair said that finding a lasting settlement was 'worth every risk'. Having pictures of Gerry Adams and Martin McGuinness splashed on every newspaper's front page (and the rest of this big delegation, Lucilita Bhreatneach, Siobhan O'Hanlon, Michele Gildernew, Martin Ferris and Richard McAuley) standing outside No. 10 beside a big twinkly Christmas tree was certainly a risk for a British government to take at that time. But we felt we'd come a long way and public opinion would wear it, which it did. I jokingly suggested to Gerry that he should use it as his official Christmas card that year. He wrinkled his eyes, said he'd already got one, and then smiled.

Sinn Fein's tireless lobbying was not all bearing fruit. The two MPs, Gerry and Martin, were pushing to get offices at the House of Commons – despite not taking up their Westminster seats because they would not swear the oath of allegiance to the Queen. But when they went to see Betty Boothroyd (the Speaker) they got a polite but firm no. 'You don't want to sit in the House and do all the work of an MP. You don't deserve the privileges.' Betty, as usual, was spot on – more progress was needed first.

But a number of more hardline republicans were finding all this 'cosying up to the Brits' hard to stomach. After reports of meetings in Dublin the weekend before, on 8 December

Bernadette Sands McKevitt, the sister of Bobby Sands who died on hunger strike in 1981, was one of a group of republicans who launched the Thirty-Two County Sovereignty Committee opposed to aspects of the Sinn Fein policy towards the talks. So the extremes on both sides were getting nervous – as they always will when there is a faint whiff of compromise in the air. That's something you have to watch and cater for in any peace process. The ranting and hardline speeches at the UK UP's first annual conference on 6 December were par for the course, but worrying all the same.

Despite some outward signs of progress, advances in the talks were still proving very hard to come by. On 15 December the talks broke up for Christmas. The new working group had failed to produce any agreement even on what the key issues were. It was depressing. Even George Mitchell was gloomy. Despite all the progress of the last few months, we were still no further forward in terms of resolving all the important and difficult issues we had to discuss. In fairness to party leaders, they were knackered – we all were. The pressure of constant carping from outside the talks process was taking its toll. Ironically the best defence we had against them was progress, and that is precisely what was lacking. But still, a brave face was put on for the press. 'Yes, I was disappointed, but every one was engaged, everyone was serious and everyone was there round the table,' I said. It was not much consolation, but people needed hope. There were plenty of cards stacked up on the other side – with further killings that month by groups opposed to the peace process, riots in Derry after the Apprentice Boys' last parade of the year, and brutal so-called 'punishment beatings' going on in some of the most difficult loyalist and republican areas.

My job then was to keep talking about how far the parties had come, keep reinforcing the positive messages until I was blue in the face. That was not just about the politics of making it look good, as some said, nor did I want to look like some modern-day Pollyanna. But it was important to keep the public in N. Ireland interested and supportive of the process overall. That, in turn, was crucial to keep the politicians engaged – what my civil servants called a 'benign dynamic': a sort of upward spiral of hope and confidence that creates more hope and more confidence and so on.

The talks were at an end until after the New Year. But the old year had far from faded. There were grumblings of trouble in the prisons. On 10 December an IRA lifer, Liam Averill, had escaped from the Maze dressed as a woman. At first it made me laugh, like Mr Toad escaping from the dungeon as a washerwoman. But it made the prison officers look foolish, and it focused attention again on security at the Maze (whether it was because it was Christmas time and things were slightly lax, I don't know). There was certainly a lot more toing and froing at that time of year. Prisoners were let out on Christmas parole, which was more generous in N. Ireland than in Britain because of the history. And because of the discipline, they invariably all came back. But it stuck in the craw of a lot of prison officers.

The Irish government had its agenda, which on 17 December involved releasing, permanently, six IRA prisoners from Port-laoise Prison, near Dublin. It was the same day that Tony Blair made his pre-Christmas visit to Belfast. We were not told about the Irish plans beforehand, which annoyed me because (a) Tony should have been forewarned by the Taoiseach and (b) the Irish always created hell if we did not tell them what we were planning to do.

Loyalists like the PUP were furious. None of their prisoners was being released. They were all held in N. Ireland under UK control and we didn't have an early-release scheme until the Good Friday Agreement was signed. We could only continue our transfer policy, as with Jack Straw's announcement a week or so later of the transfer of seven IRA prisoners to the Republic. But even that, as the Jason Campbell row had shown, was difficult to operate to the benefit of loyalists. We could make sure both sides were let out for Christmas, and we did. But the Irish just released people anyway. They saw it as helping the process along, which it undoubtedly did on the republican side. But, for loyalism, this was a step too far.

The PUP threatened to walk from the talks in protest. And someone who was then considered pretty much on board, Jeffrey Donaldson, began (on 18 December) to complain bitterly about too many concessions being made to the republicans. On the 22nd the UUP and the PUP came to Stormont to 'discuss' their concerns. They vented a lot of anger, which was partly put on, but also partly a result of the pressures of the previous months. The UDP went further and said, that same day, that they were reassessing their whole attitude towards the peace process. Four Unionist MPs – Willie Ross, Roy Beggs, Willie Thompson and Clifford Forsythe – wrote to Trimble urging him to withdraw from the talks process. It was a foretaste of much worse to come for the UUs leadership.

Christmas was finally upon us. On 23 December I was presented with an extraordinary chess-set made by a local sculptor called Anton. It was beautiful. Its pieces were little caricatures of all the politicians in the peace process, including me with wig and big round glasses, and little IRA and RUC men as the pawns. I kept it in my office and it amused everyone. Anton was not really a businessman, more an ageing 1960s hippie, and when I tried to get him organized to apply for a government grant to start a business it wasn't what he was interested in. For a while I became his unpaid salesman, even getting US Senator Ted Kennedy (brother of JFK) and Richard Branson to buy a set.

On 24 December, Jon, Freddie and H arrived. We collected a Christmas tree from a farm near Hillsborough. In fact we had two – a big one in the entrance to the hall at Hillsborough Castle, which was the Queen's and which had been up for weeks, and our smaller one in our sitting room upstairs. We managed to make it all quite Christmassy. Jon cooked, we drank a lot and walked a lot in the gardens. We played games and settled into Christmas fun.

7

More Tea, Mad Dog?

GOING INTO THE MAZE AND FINALLY REACHING
CONCLUSION ON GOOD FRIDAY AGREEMENT

Two days after Christmas 1997 we had arranged to go and have lunch with Henry and Iona Mountcharles at a beautiful house called Beau Parc near Slane in southern Ireland. I had met Henry when still in opposition, and both Jon and I had stayed a couple of times before. Henry is actually the Marquess of Slane and is of an Anglo-Irish family going back many years. He is now most famous for organizing pop concerts at his family home of Slane Castle, although he has a keen interest in the politics of Ireland. Jon and I have enjoyed watching Robbie Williams in a great performance there, as well as U2.

Going to the Republic when you have security is not that easy. We were driven as usual by my two RUC bodyguards Keith and John, in a people carrier as H and Fred were travelling with us. Then at the border we picked up two Irish Gardai cars that escorted us to Slane. We were looking forward to a relaxed day with friends. It was not to be. It was as we drove down the Republic that we first heard of the murder of LVF leader Billy Wright, one of the most efficient and ruthless killers on the loyalist side. He had been shot dead inside the Maze Prison by two INLA inmates. It was an audacious act. The INLA men made no attempt to escape. They immediately gave themselves up to a prison chaplain in triumph. We decided to carry on with our visit, although we knew it would have to be cut short and that I would have to get back to Belfast to handle the situation. So when we arrived at Beau Parc we told the Gardai we would have a quick lunch and then we would have to dash back north.

By two o'clock we said our farewells and got back into the people carrier. Our entourage had increased and there was now a police Range Rover as well as the two other cars. John suggested that we put our seat belts on, as we were going to be taken at our word – we were going to have a quick dash to the border. He was not wrong. It must have been one of the most scary rides I have ever had. With a blue light flashing and siren going, we sped off, only slowing down in Dundalk, when we were travelling at ninety miles at hour. We even, for some reason, went round a roundabout the wrong way. We all kept looking at each other in disbelief. When we reached the border, having lost the Gardai, we slowed down considerably and were still well in time for the press conference.

Wright's death sent shockwaves across N. Ireland. With feelings on the loyalist side already running high, it threatened to kill off the already fragile peace. Not that most sensible loyalists liked or supported Wright. They didn't. They hated him. But he was one of their own, their side, and he had been killed by 'the other' – which meant war. Some of the self-appointed 'democratic' politicians waded in hard, keen to exploit the tensions. The DUP MP the Revd Willie McCrea shouted about 'state-sponsored murder'. He claimed to have a dossier showing there was a conspiracy involved in the murder of Billy Wright. Now this was a DUP tactic we saw time and time again. Whether the information existed we did not know. They up the ante and make the situation much harder to cope with for everyone. Slowly over time you don't even bother to register the outrages that either extreme is putting into the press. But the slow drip-drip of bile and insinuation undermines the process. It makes people more uncertain and fearful, shakes their belief that progress can be made. Of course McCrea's allegations were nonsense, but it was dangerous nonsense, which fed into an already fearful and paranoid community. Some of whom were highly armed and very dangerous.

Within a few days, Billy Wright's supporters were out each night randomly shooting and killing Catholics (like hotel doorman Seamus Dillon, and Eddie Treanor over his pint in North

Belfast's Clifton Tavern). Soon the republican INLA were doing the same on the other side. So the situation could hardly get worse.

Some 5000 people attended Wright's funeral. Considering that his paramilitary mob had refused to call a ceasefire and opposed the peace process, it was a startling and unsettling show of support. When I met David Trimble just afterwards, he was clearly seriously worried, like all of us in the talks, and he blamed me. I had let security go lax in the Maze; I had encouraged the Irish to release republicans at a time when loyalism was already on the edge. We argued. But this was him performing his duty and, by listening and keeping my temper, I was performing mine. On Sunday, 4 January 1998, the loyalist UDA–UFF prisoners in the Maze held a vote. Would they continue to support the peace process? Sixty per cent said no. Their political representative, Gary McMichael, tried to reassure everyone that their 'ceasefire was not over'. They maintained a 'no first strike' policy. (But, as we later learnt, they were not averse to a little 'retaliatory' killing.)

On Monday the *Daily Telegraph* called for my resignation. During difficult interviews on the Sunday political programmes I was pressed hard and said I wouldn't resign. Calling for my resignation became a popular pastime. Ian Paisley sought me out just before I left N. Ireland in October 1999 to say proudly, 'Don't you forget, young lady, I was the one who called for your resignation first.' The N. Ireland Secretary has always been, and probably always will be, everyone's scapegoat when things get tough. Sometimes it's deserved. We all make mistakes. But on this occasion it was not.

Early in the week I met with all the parties at Castle Buildings in Belfast. Everyone was a little jumpy, particularly the Irish. Then David Trimble made an important move. He went down to the Maze to meet with the UVF and UDA prisoners. It is something no mainstream unionist leader had done before him. He was under a lot of pressure, but he needed to keep the smaller loyalist parties in the talks, so that he could say he still had the support of a majority of unionist voters. Without the loyalist parties he couldn't deliver his side of any eventual bargain.

By Wednesday I was back in London, but Gary McMichael and a couple of his UDP members took the unusual step of flying over to meet me in my office on Millbank. They were always short of money, so they could not come over as often as others. But this could not wait. They wanted to see me alone, with no civil servants. We sat at the board-room table in my office. I listened to their hushed voices, looked at their nervous faces. Gary McMichael's confidence was clearly shaken by what was happening around him. His face was straight, but the eyes gave it away. His people thought the process was all going one way, towards the republicans. His people thought no more of Billy Wright than anybody else, but the enemy had killed him and that made all the difference.

We spoke for a while. Gary made it clear that he was in trouble. He told me we were losing it. He needed my help, and he asked me to go into the Maze and talk straight to the prisoners. My gut immediately told me this was the right thing to do, but I wanted first, before agreeing to it, to run it past my civil servants. I asked my office. Ken Lindsay, my private secretary, a good man and always honest with me, thought it worth a try. I also spoke to my permanent secretary, and he also was in agreement. Interestingly Ken Lindsay later told me that by that time he was no longer surprised by anything I did. He had taken the view that I ran the politics, not him. And this was as political as you could get. So I returned to the meeting and told Gary I would go. By mid-afternoon Gary had spoken to the press and announced that I would be visiting the Maze in the next few days. It seemed to me – both at the time and now – the only course of action for me to take. That afternoon I spoke to my mother. Always a good litmus test, she was then in her seventies and lived in the suburbs of Coventry. Her view was that there was no alternative.

On the next day, the Thursday, I saw Tony Blair and Jack Straw in Downing Street. They were not as negative as I had feared. What I had thought of as a reasonable course of action was certainly exercising the press. I think the fact that David Trimble had already done it swung the argument for me. It wasn't as if this was completely unthinkable; it was just unprecedented. But most of what was happening then was unprecedented. They could both see that. And they could see I was sure that, without a gesture like this from the government, the process could well be lost. Jack was already getting grief from the *Daily Telegraph* for transferring republican prisoners from British to Irish gaols. Gerry Adams called it repatriation; to the *Daily Telegraph* it was 'appeasement'. By way of contrast, and as an illustration of how life goes on in spite of the dramas of politics, my husband Jon and I had dinner that evening with the founder of Habitat, Terence Conran, and his partner Victoria at his restaurant Bibendum. I know this because it is recorded in my official diary. What we said has long past gone. I suspect I was not very good company.

I woke on the Friday morning of 9 January, as I often did in my house in Islington, to the sound of the police talking as they changed the guard. It was six o'clock, dark and cold with the noises of the city beginning, cars starting and people's footsteps on the pavement outside. I had slept well. I had been tired, but also I felt that today I was going to do the right thing. Today, I told myself, I was going to visit the prisoners in the Maze to try to restart the peace process. People had kept asking me how I felt. I felt completely fine: to me it was just another step in that process. I dressed in trousers and neutral colours. In N. Ireland clothes and colours are important. I was conscious I was going into an all-male environment and that trousers would be best; as ever I avoided orange or green. I was still wearing my wig as my hair had not grown back. I hated it. Jon gave me a big hug and wished me luck. As usual my bullet-proof car was waiting outside to take me to RAF Northolt to fly me to Belfast.

I sat in the back behind my police bodyguard, as I always had to, as we drove through the dark streets of London. It was wet and it was cold. We swept through the gates of the airfield and drove up to the plane. As usual an RAF officer was standing to attention saluting as my car drove up. The officer then welcomed me. As we took off, he saluted again. The same ritual, whatever the weather. Like every other day I waved to him.

I breakfasted on the plane and as usual managed to dribble food down my clothes. This is a constant problem I have, but one that was particularly unwelcome on that Friday. We landed in Belfast at the airstrip behind the Shorts factory down by the harbour, one of two or three landing options depending on where in N. Ireland I was heading for on the day. I was met by Ken Lindsay and we were driven directly to the Maze Prison by Keith and John. And that was what in many ways was so odd. This meeting had taken the media and the world by surprise, it was being billed as the biggest political gamble of my career, and all I could see it as was the obvious next step in a process where you could never predict what would happen next. I did not feel particularly nervous. Everything was so normal. I did not at this stage fully realize what a media circus I had created.

We arrived at the prison. Like all prisons it was a process of locked doors and checks that had to be gone through to get in – a grim ritual before meeting those who were incarcerated there. It was not unfamiliar to me. I had visited the Maze while in opposition, so I already knew of its smell: disinfectant, not smelly socks and maleness that I had once expected. I had seen the great political murals. I had walked along the corridors of the H blocks, seeing men's legs peep from under the doors of wash-rooms, and felt the intense heat of the place, which keeps most inmates in tee-shirts and shorts. I had experienced before the studied formality between the prison officers and the inmates when in my presence, but as with all institutions there was an understanding between the prisoners and the staff. After all, they had to live together.

I was met by Martin Mogg, the Governor of the prison. I always called him Moggy. I had a great deal of time for his good sense and humanity. I knew with him that we were both working to find peace in Ireland, through our very different and equally difficult roles. We discussed who I was going to see and what would be the procedure. We headed off to the H blocks for the first meeting. I had decided to see not only Gary's lot but also the others with representatives in the talks, including the IRA. As I walked towards H block 7 to meet the first group, I felt no fear. I had met some of them before. Some were murderers, but I knew they had no interest in alienating me. If any progress in bringing peace was going to be made, then I was their best chance, because I talked to them. I knew there could be no question afterwards that I had negotiated or made concessions to the prisoners while I was there. But I had to try to convince them that the peace process was worth sticking with.

We drew up a fourteen-point note that I would speak to, leave with them and give to the press afterwards. Most of it was a reiteration of established positions, reassurances that any peace deal would have to have explicit support across both communities in N. Ireland, a restatement of our commitment to a fair, just and inclusive process for all. But point 13 was controversial. It said, 'We are prepared to work on an account of what would happen in respect of prisoner releases in the context of a peaceful and lasting settlement being agreed.' But it added that 'There would be no significant changes to release arrangements in any other context or for prisoners associated with a paramilitary organization actively engaged in terrorist activity.' It was a portent of what was to come in the Good Friday Agreement, and it was a position I never moved from. But at that stage it was new. The language was as guarded as ever, but the signal was clear. We all knew that an eventual agreement would be impossible without something for the prisoners on both sides. But I hadn't said it so overtly before. That was the real gamble we took that day.

Meeting with loyalist prisoners in the Maze, including Johnny Adair, who the press nick-named 'Mad Dog' Adair.

The meeting with the UDA–UFF prisoners was not run formally. It was like any meeting of people – we introduced ourselves; we shook hands. I noticed that some of them had changed from the casual prison uniform of shorts and had put on long trousers. It was a symbolic act that gave me great comfort that I had done the right thing. It is very important that everyone is given dignity if you expect them to take you seriously. As the meeting went on we all became more relaxed and an element of humour even emerged. This meeting was very important to all of us, a point that was not brought out by the media. These men knew the peace process was fundamental to their futures and the future of their country. They took what they were doing very seriously indeed, and that was why it had been crucial to go and see them. By the very act of visiting these men they knew that I was taking them seriously. It was really of very little importance what was said – it was the act itself that held the meaning for them.

They had someone to start the discussion and then others spoke up. Their main concern was that they thought I was going to pull out of the union and leave them high and dry. I did my best to convince them that that was not the case and that, if we were going to make it, everyone was going to have to swallow hard and make some tough decisions, including very much Sinn Fein and the IRA. I did not work to a script. I never do unless it is forced on me. What I had to do was establish a degree of understanding. I knew that trust, that elusive element in N. Ireland, would have been too much to hope for. To keep the peace alive, the honest bottom line was that I had taken the risk to go and see them.

Despite the apparent normality of the encounter I could feel much more. There was a clear intensity in their eyes, a restlessness caused by the responsibility they were being asked to take. There was in all of them an up-front honesty – they were not going to take any shit. They were straightforward and intense rather than aggressive. There was a clarity and intelligence that was slightly bizarre given the location of the meeting. I never felt nervous, and can remember feeling some comfort from having Ken, my private secretary, next to me. His suit in contrast to the attire of the prisoners was a bit of normality. I stopped myself thinking of the murders that they had committed and focused on winning their confidence, as that was crucial for them to change their minds and give the process for peace a chance.

I was meeting the UDA–UFF prisoners in the corner of what I assume was a room for visitors. It was like a run-down waiting room anywhere, apart from the bars on the windows and the cleanliness, and the complete lack of graffiti. Then I met the PUP's associates, the UVF, in another wing. After about forty-five minutes I left them. I went to another of the blocks to meet the IRA prisoners. They knew this was more for balance than because it mattered. But there was a marked contrast in style. The IRA were polite as ever, but more political, never missing a chance to make a political point. For example, they gave me the posh chair with the arms, and then mentioned it. Their support for the process was still solid. One thing about the republicans is that they were always more of a hierarchy. The loyalists were a looser alliance, and less predictable for it. All three meetings ended without ceremony and without conclusion. One of the loyalist prisoners said something like, 'You have allayed many of our concerns.' I didn't know what their final decision would be, but it felt like it had gone well and I could go out and face the media convinced that the visit had been the right decision.

Had I been manipulated? Were the loyalist politicians using me to shore up their position among their own side? Yes, I think that's probably true, and we knew it at the time. But it didn't matter. If that's what it took, that's what needed to be done. But I'm sure there was more to it than that. These people crave recognition, on both sides. They wanted to be taken seriously and be listened to. We worked throughout the peace process to include everyone; it was essential. Being listened to, which afforded status on a par with others, was crucial, particularly for the representatives of paramilitary groups. I'm sure that's what people like Ian Paisley hated so much – that others were being listened to and he was not. It was not something he was used to. But then he chose to walk out of the talks. No one forced him to leave.

Any relief I might have felt on leaving the prison wings disappeared when I entered the gymnasium to speak to the press. There were a lot of extraneous people hanging about. I suppose they wanted to witness this 'historic occasion'. A small table was set out with three chairs behind it, one for me, one for Ken and one for Moggy. (I'm told I called him Moggy during the press conference, but I can't remember.) I had never before faced such ranks of cameras, flashes and microphones. All I could see was a wall of faces and lenses, all blinding lights above, with knees and feet and ladders beneath them. The full importance of the meetings then suddenly hit me. I had never created such media attention before and it was somehow shocking. It was really only then that I realized how people, and particularly the press, felt that this was a political high-wire act.

I could not be sure at that stage what the groups I had met would eventually say. So there was no note of triumph to hide. I read the statement flatly. I said I had met prisoners on both sides. The questions were brief and my answers even briefer. I think I said, 'We will all have to wait and see,' which came out more nonchalantly than I wanted to sound. But I meant it. A few hours later the UDA and UFF prisoners took another vote. This time they decided to reinstate their support for the peace process.

That night I visited a victims' group called WAVE at their centre at the Elmwood Hall in Belfast. I had apologized to the victims of violence on both sides when I came out of the Maze, but here I expected a rough time. As ever, the reactions were mixed. I got some cold shoulders and open criticism. But also some resigned voices: 'We don't like what you've done, but if it keeps this peace process going, if it stops other families going through what we have, then for God's sake keep going.' It's a message I had heard before and would hear many times again. It was a voice that kept me going.

But the degree to which I had offended those proud of their democratic credentials was summed up by Lord Alderdice, leader of the non-sectarian Alliance party. He accused me of sacrificing the democratic principles of the talks. But he also said that the talks must continue. Others said I was pandering to terrorism. I think it was shock rather than disgust, although probably both were felt. I think that, if the loyalists had not reacted as positively as they did, the criticism I would have faced could possibly have driven me from the job. But when I did it, it didn't really seem to me such a bizarre thing to do. They needed talking to. I was talking to ex-terrorists outside of gaol and whether there was prison wall between us or not didn't seem to me to make a great deal of difference.

First Labour cabinet, May 1997

Speaking at the despatch box, House of Commons

Returning to the talks; David Trimble and members of the UUP, David Ervine and members of the PUP, Gary McMichael and members of the UDP, September 1997

Gerry Adams and Sinn Fein entering the talks at Castle Buildings, September 1997

SDLP talks team outside Castle Buildings: Eddie McGrady, John Hume, Seamus Mallon and Brid Rodgers

Talking with the Women's Coalition

Press conference in gym at Maze Prison, January 1998

Seamus Mallon and David Trimble at Poyntzpass, following the murders of Philip Allen and Damien Trainor (one Catholic, one Protestant), March 1998. They are being shown around by the brother of the owner of the pub where the men were shot.

After the expulsion of Sinn Fein, with David Andrews and Paul Murphy

With Bertie Ahern at the talks at Stormont

With Tony, where next in the talks?

Bertie Ahern and Tony Blair with Senator George Mitchell,
after signing the Good Friday Agreement, 10 April 1998

David Trimble meets
unionist opposition to the
Good Friday Agreement

Right: 'Yes' poster campaign
unveiled by Richard
Needham, ex-Tory Minister
who served in N. Ireland
and helped in the 'Yes'
campaign

Below: The 'Yes' Concert
with David Trimble, Bono
of U2 and John Hume

Reacting to standing ovation during Tony's speech at Brighton, 1998

Introducing Elton John at the first ever pop concert in the grounds of Stormont, summer 1998

My action was described by some as giving the loyalist prisoners a victory. The Secretary of State had gone in to see them. Because I don't care very much about status, people said I would begin to lose respect. I disagreed and think I was proved right. I think here, particularly on the unionist–loyalist side, they believe in respect for people in authority. Because I was prepared to see them it showed that they were important in their own right – in terms of the peace process the prisoners clearly are and they cannot be ignored. I think the acknowledgement of the centrality of prisoners in the process is one of the things that made it possible for progress to be made and possible for Sinn Fein and the loyalists to understand that they had a chance now of moving things forward.

One of the factors that is not often mentioned, which explains why progress was made then, is that many of the people that had been involved in terrorism for the previous thirty years had started it when they were in their late teens or early twenties. Thirty years on they are in their late forties or fifties, their children are growing up and they are getting too old and fed up to continue on a personal basis. John Hume's work over the previous fifteen years was to convince Gerry Adams and Martin McGuinness that there was another way forward, and with the Labour government he proved that there was. Paddy Mayhew and John Major, to be fair, tried against the odds, with a very sensitive situation at Westminster where their party found it difficult even to contemplate talking to terrorists. But they didn't have a big enough majority to push things through. If you were prepared to take risks and acknowledge that you had to talk to people to get change, then it was possible. I think the leaders of the paramilitary groups, for the main part, but not most of those I met in prison who were much younger, were ready to consider making a move.

The next day, Saturday, the press showed all its schizophrenia on N. Ireland – all its passion and its uncertainty. The pro-nationalist *Irish News* lauded my efforts: 'Full credit to Mo

Mowlam.' The pro-unionist *Newsletter* said, 'Prison Histrionics Must End Now'. They fell short of openly criticizing me. Their call was a sensible one, for the loyalist paramilitaries to get back on board. They insisted that this visit had to be a one-off. They were right. On the mainland the British press were full of stark contradictions in their reactions, even within different parts of the same newspaper. The story on the front news pages of the *Sun* said, 'Brave Mo Mowlam shored up the ailing peace process by pulling off the biggest gamble of her life.' Yet in its editorial it declared, 'The terrorists have scored a victory.' I think that summed up for me the contradictions in my own position. I was supported because of who I was – and, if I'm honest, because of what people thought I'd been through personally with the tumour. But what was going on in the peace process was still hard for many people to stomach.

Other papers like the *Guardian* and the *Independent* were, and remained pretty much throughout, openly supportive. The *Daily Telegraph* was not. They hadn't yet got to the point of calling for my resignation week in, week out, but it was getting close. It was silly really. They said I was incompetent and could never deliver, yet called for my resignation at the same time. Surely if the peace process was as bad as they said it was, keeping someone as incompetent as me in there was in their best interests. I never understood their position. I don't think they understood it themselves. They just didn't like what was happening. But, like the opponents of the process within N. Ireland, they never once suggested an alternative – at least, not one that had the remotest chance of gaining support across the community there, without which nothing could ever work.

But it wasn't support in the press that kept me going or kept my confidence up. Throughout my time in N. Ireland it was the messages of support from the people that made all the difference. During that difficult January, I had many letters. I thank everyone who wrote to support the process then, when it might have been easier to criticize or just say nothing. They are letters I have kept and cherish, like Mark's letter from Warwick saying:

I hope you are aware at this very difficult stage in the peace process of how much respect and affection there is for you and your colleagues among ordinary folk such as ourselves as you try to make meaningful progress. Your courage and honesty, displayed in so many ways over recent years, are greatly admired and valued and we will continue to pray for your safety and success in this most difficult of jobs.

Or this from Mrs Lynden of Buckinghamshire: 'For what it is worth, I wish to send you my support for your efforts in the Northern Ireland peace process. I have not written to an MP before, let alone a Minister, but in this particular instance, seeing how easy it is for people to criticize your actions, I feel that I would like to help redress the balance.' Or from Madelaine in Belfast: 'You are right to speak with everyone if it brings peace. Like most people I have suffered and have lots of hurts since the troubles started, some of my friends have been murdered. I still believe dialogue and reaching out to each other are the only real way to make progress.' So do I. Tony Blair put it simply. It's about treating people as human beings. Even if they've said or done terrible things, you can only reach them if you treat them as human beings. It's hard, it's tough. It makes you question your own morality and wonder whether you have become hardened yourself. But when the object is building peace, there really is no other way.

That same Saturday a relative of Gerry Adams, Terry Enright, was murdered by the LVF, while working as doorman outside the Space nightclub in Belfast. I expressed my condolences to Gerry and his family too. They're human beings.

Life slowly returned to normal, as normal as life ever was in the talks. George Mitchell on 12 January presented the parties with a paper drawn up by the British and Irish governments called 'Propositions on Heads of Agreement'. It was our first shot at the bare bones of a possible agreement. George's tactic before Christmas had been to try to get the parties to come up with a paper like this between themselves. When that proved impossible, it was up to the two governments. In reality, the parties were much happier working from something produced by the two governments. It meant that none of them had to be seen to make the first move or surrender the first compromise.

Propositions included a devolved government for N. Ireland and a north–south ministerial council. These were not new – they had been floated in the Framework Documents three years earlier. One new and significant proposal was included for a Council of the Isles, to look at issues that concerned all the parts of the UK and Ireland. With new devolved institutions in Scotland and Wales and one proposed for N. Ireland, this made sense. But it was symbolically very important too. It gave N. Ireland status alongside Scotland and Wales and brought the Irish Republic back into a formal set-up with all the different parts of the UK. In a sense it was the counterbalance to the strengthening of the relationship between N. Ireland and the Republic through the North–South Council. For the unionists it meant they could say that the east–west link was just as important. This was a key part of their politics, to rebut the criticism from the outside that they were letting N. Ireland be sucked into a united Irish state by stealth. David Trimble liked it. Fortunately for John Hume and Gerry Adams it was at best neutral and at worst an irrelevance. So it worked.

'Propositions' also included proposals for a balanced change in the constitutions of the Republic of Ireland and the UK. This was another touchstone issue for unionists, who resented the claim in the Republic's constitution to control over the northern part of the island of Ireland. A throwback to earlier times, it would be replaced by a more modern statement recognizing that whether N. Ireland was part of the UK or the Republic was up to the people who lived in N. Ireland to decide – i.e. the principle of consent. 'Propositions' also suggested further work on human rights, civil rights and political, social, economic and cultural issues to safeguard the interests of both communities in N. Ireland.

Sinn Fein was the only party to react badly to it. They weren't ready to sign up to the principle of consent or to devolved government in N. Ireland. They continued to say that the only outcome they would consider from the negotiations was a united Ireland. Of course, people like Gerry Adams and Martin McGuinness knew that wasn't going to happen: that the eventual outcome would have to be a compromise from their hardline position. But they weren't going to concede that with months of negotiation still to go. Their supporters would destroy them. They needed to say that the idea of a united Ireland was still seriously on the table. And anyway, the Sinn Fein leaders would never agree to anything until everybody else was onside and they'd had time to go round and convince their people that it was worth doing. That way they had maximum room for manoeuvre for later on. But in some people's minds, at the time, Sinn Fein's rejection of 'Propositions' raised questions about how seriously they were committed to realistic negotiations. Nevertheless, I began to feel that, with the talks edging forward, we were really getting somewhere.

But the killing was continuing, on both sides: 19 January was a particularly bad day with two murders, one Protestant and one Catholic. Jim Guiney, a prominent loyalist, was shot by the republican INLA, who were not on ceasefire. A Catholic taxi driver, Larry Brennan, was also killed. At that point, we didn't know who he was killed by. Then on Friday, 23 January, the UFF issued a statement saying that 'The current phase of republican aggression initiated by INLA made a measured military response unavoidable. That response has concluded.' It was short and to the point. The UFF had temporarily breached their ceasefire but had now restored it. I knew then we had no choice but to take action against the party close to the UFF in the talks: Gary McMichael's UDP.

Monday, 26 January was the beginning of the London end of

the talks. All the parties had agreed to one session in London and one in Dublin. We booked Lancaster House just off Pall Mall as our venue. It is a building of great stature with a vast entrance hall and soaring gilded ceilings, very grand and imperial. It was where the talks over the future of Rhodesia (now Zimbabwe) took place in 1979 and so had historical significance as a place where important world events occur. I wanted to make the parties feel important and to understand that the eyes of the world were upon them. We treated the press pack lavishly too, kept them warm and well fed. Many remarked what a contrast it was to the tented misery of their usual camp outside Castle Buildings.

The plan was to be in London for two and a half days and concentrate on trying to flesh out the bones of the 'Propositions' paper in relation to Strands Two and Three. But the UFF statement focused all the attention on the UDP and the accusation that they had breached the Mitchell Principles. No one wanted to force the issue. So it was up to the governments to call for action against the UDP. It was a lengthy process with lots of deliberation between the governments and the talks' chairs. It was a joint decision for the two governments to make together, but there was no serious dispute between us. The case was clear-cut.

Exactly what to do about it was the real problem. There were rules governing a breach of the principles but no rules on what sanction to take. Permanent expulsion? That would be disastrous for all, and unfair considering the timetable Sinn Fein had been given after the restoration of the IRA ceasefire in the summer. Suspension? For how long? It had to be long enough so as not to trivialize what the UFF had done, but not so long as to effectively rule out UDP involvement for the remainder of the talks. We decided to say that the UDP would be suspended for 'a period of weeks' until we were sure the ceasefire was properly restored. This avoided suggestions that we were not taking the UFF actions seriously enough by specifying only a few weeks' suspension. But in reality we had in mind about four weeks, and privately McMichael knew that. Via Nigel and Mitchell's assistant Martha Pope, I encouraged McMichael to walk out of the talks before his party was formally suspended – which he did, and with dignity.

But all of this had taken over the first two days of the talks. I was very concerned not to waste the whole of the London leg. We had hastily drafted papers on new north–south and east–west structures. These were basically a statement of general principles with a list of something like fourteen questions attached for the parties to answer to aid the preparation of more detailed documents later. It wasn't much, but it was something to salvage from all the aggro, time and expense that hosting the talks in London had caused. Jeffrey Donaldson stole the show at the end by saying that the proposals on Strands Two and Three now meant that the 1995 Framework Documents, which unionists hated, had been laid to rest. To reinforce his point he tore up a copy in front of the cameras. It was a scene-stealing gesture and, by the look on David Trimble's face, I'm not sure he quite expected it.

Having lost the best part of London, our next hope of progress was when the talks moved to Dublin on 16 February. We particularly wanted to make progress on the difficult north–south issues, which were currently going nowhere. Dublin would not be the ideal place to do it because the unionists wouldn't want to be accused by their opponents of having done a deal down south. Nevertheless we set about in earnest working on more detailed topics for discussion in the hope that progress would be made. It was a hope that was dashed, while the preparations for Dublin were still being made, with the murder of Brendan Campbell on 9 February. It was not a random shooting: it was an execution. The finger of suspicion was pointed at an IRA front organization called Direct Action Against Drugs.

No one claimed responsibility for Campbell's killing. Sinn Fein members insisted that the IRA ceasefire was still intact.

The problem was that their definition of a ceasefire was not quite the same as for the rest of us. Republicans saw their 'cessation of military activities' as just that: an end to military action against the 'enemy': the police, the army, loyalists. But 'disciplining' or controlling their own side was, by their definition, okay. So even if the IRA did kill Campbell it didn't count as a ceasefire breakdown because he was one of 'theirs'. This put all of us in the talks in a very difficult position. The day after Campbell's death a prominent loyalist, Robert Dougan, was murdered. Again the finger pointed at the IRA. They must have been feeling the heat because on 12 February IRA leaders issued a rare statement (with the familiar codename signature of P. O'Neill) saying 'contrary to speculation surrounding the killings in Belfast, the IRA cessation of military operations remains intact'. This statement, of course, still left room for 'disciplinary' attacks.

On a more positive note, that night was the first of the BBC's 'Making a Difference' concerts which had finally come together in Belfast. Pat Kielty was the MC. He became a good friend to me and is one of the few people I know who can tell good jokes against both communities in N. Ireland without people taking offence. For example, he stops people clapping to a piece of music and says, 'Will all the Protestants stop clapping, and then when the music starts try and copy the nearest Catholic to you.' He changes 'Catholic' and 'Protestant' around, at different venues. 'Making a Difference' was the kind of variety show that would seem a bit old-fashioned outside N. Ireland. But, perfectly set in the Grand Opera House in Belfast, which is like an old community hall, it was a great night. At the end I leant over the top of the balcony where I was sitting, thanked everybody and said a few words in support of the peace process. The reaction from the crowd was very supportive.

It was a tremendous occasion, but in the real world I was really on the spot. Although in theory a decision on whether or not to act against any party in the talks was for both governments, it was my call based on all the information, including secret intelligence material, that I had available to me. It would be wrong for me to write about all the things I was told at the time and who said what. But suffice to say that the views of my various security advisers were clear: the IRA was responsible for the deaths of both Brendan Campbell and Robert Dougan.

All of which made for a very sour atmosphere when talks opened in the grand surroundings of Dublin Castle on the 16th. The parties were jostling to see who would call first for Sinn Fein to be excluded, though no one wanted to take the blame for creating problems in the talks. In the end I think it was the Alliance who formally made an allegation based on the material I had made available in the talks. Had the Mitchell Principles of non-violence been breached? Once again the two governments had to decide. Sinn Fein immediately started legal action in the Dublin High Court against both governments and the team of talks' chairs. George Mitchell thought this was amusing. I think it was the first time he had had a writ served against him. In government you get used to it.

The legal action gave the talks a surreal quality. George Mitchell, an ex-Senate majority leader and a lawyer, knew his stuff. He said from the outset that the decision on exclusion was a political and not a legal one, so no court could say whether it was right or wrong. He was correct of course. But we had to go through the motions, which included having lawyers in the talks room, recording what everybody said. We got a government lawyer flown over to Dublin, who was excellent and a human being, unlike most lawyers I've known.

The atmosphere around the table got very hot and heavy. I was under a lot of pressure. I had been clear at the outset that, whatever happened, if we were going to throw Sinn Fein out of the talks we'd better have a damn good case to make for doing so. But my hands were tied. I couldn't even say what the evidence was, because it was all secret. All I could keep saying like a parrot was that both Tony Blair and I 'accepted and agreed with the [RUC] Chief Constable's assessment that the IRA authorized and were responsible for the murders'. At first the Irish were wobbly. If this was bad for me, it was even worse for them. Fortunately the information they were getting from their security people was the same as mine, and in the end we issued a joint statement concluding, 'The IRA was involved.'

The wrangling over Sinn Fein and the court action poured buckets of cold water over the prospects of getting any real work done. On the Tuesday night, US Ambassador Jean Kennedy Smith, John F. Kennedy's sister, hosted a reception at her splendid house near the Irish President's even more splendid house in Dublin's Phoenix Park. Jean had put on a great spread and had even booked a jazz band in a marquee. But it was not much fun. I did feel a bit sorry for her as she went around trying to cheer everybody up. She worked especially hard on Sinn Fein, to whom she was close. I think her presence in the Republic helped to keep Sinn Fein engaged. She was a positive force in the process.

By the Wednesday the decision to expel Sinn Fein had been taken. The lack of publicly usable evidence embarrassed me, but I knew we had to act for the talks to continue to have any credibility. There was a lot of pompous talk about the 'integrity' of the process. But it did matter. Sinn Fein lost their court case the next day. But there was a twist. We couldn't just expel Sinn Fein. Like the UDP we had to decide on a length of time for them to be thrown out. And with the Easter deadline for the talks fast approaching, it would have been disastrous to put them out for so long that no business got done and we ran out of time. So we had to be practical and say they could come back in after just two and a half weeks: out on 20 February; back on 9 March, provided there were no further breaches in the cease-fire. This was, of course, a gift to unionist hardliners: 'Seventeen days for a life,' they said. We kept our nerve and pressed on. In the end, I think the Shinners expected their expulsion and were relieved that it was for only a couple of weeks. They would never say it to your face. Even in private with me Gerry Adams and Martin McGuinness stuck to their 'We are Sinn Fein, they are the IRA, so don't ask us about them' line. But when they left the talks in Dublin, though their voices were angry, their body language was much more relaxed.

The talks went into a lull in Sinn Fein's absence. I worried that such a setback and the lack of progress by the politicians would set the killings off again. I didn't have long to wait. Wednesday, 3 March started like any other day. I had back-to-back meetings and didn't notice the hours passing. But early in the evening we got news of an awful killing in County Armagh. At first the details were patchy. Gunmen had walked into a pub called the Railway Bar in the village of Poyntzpass and started shooting. As the details came in, the story got worse and worse. People had been forced to lie on the floor and had simply been shot in the head. Two people were dead, others injured. Then the story began to unfold in full. The two dead men were Damien Trainor and Philip Allen – one a Catholic, the other a Protestant. They were lifelong friends. Philip was planning his wedding and had just asked Damien to be his best man. The village of Poyntzpass was a close community, without sectarian divisions. The men had been singled out to die by loyalist gunmen who were opposed to the peace process and opposed to the very idea that Catholics and Protestants should be friends.

The killings seemed to sum up for people everything that we were working to try to leave behind. It was nothing else but naked bigotry and sectarian hatred. The next day local MPs for the area, Seamus Mallon and David Trimble, arrived in Poyntzpass together to visit the families. In what was a hugely symbolic moment, the two senior figures of the unionist and nationalist traditions walked up the main street together, sharing the grief of the village and doing what they could to comfort the families. The image was shown around the world. Despite all the problems we were having in the talks, it seemed to sum up the strength that was there to unite people from both sides of the community against the violence and sectarianism that had plagued N. Ireland for so long.

The vacuum in the talks didn't last long. On 12 March, the Sinn Fein leadership came to London for a meeting at No. 10. This was their way of getting back into the system, on their terms. They told the press pack permanently stationed outside that famous black door that they should never have been suspended from the talks and they were here to tell Tony Blair what a mistake he had made. Blair handled the meeting (as he always did) by being quite honest and quite direct, which is helpful. But when the crunch came it ended, as usual, with Sinn Fein stating their position and the Prime Minister stating his and nobody reaching a conclusion. Tony would say a few warm words, which could be interpreted in a number of different ways, as Sinn Fein always did. I gave up being frustrated at inconclusive meetings at that stage. We all knew this was going to the wire, and no one was going to reveal their bottom lines until we got a lot closer to it. More importantly it meant they were back in the talks. We had an inclusive process once again. The Irish government and the SDLP could stop sitting on their hands. We could get on with business.

But not until we had all spent a week in the USA. Not until we all, Brits and Irish, nationalist and unionist, loyalist and republican, had travelled 3000 miles to enjoy each other's company and hospitality and celebrate together the international day of Ireland's patron saint. The great jamboree for St Patrick's Day in Washington became all important under President Clinton, part of his determination to galvanize Irish American support for the peace process. By 1998 it was the event-you-couldn't-afford-not-to-be-at for all the players in the N. Ireland peace process. Sinn Fein had been going to the US for years and were well known. John Hume had done a lot in the US to get support for peaceful methods to achieve progress and to encourage industry to invest, because jobs would make a great difference to the chances of finding peace. We and the UUs hadn't done enough and had suffered as a result in getting our views heard.

I knew America from my student and teaching days. I had lived there for five years. I liked the people and the place, I liked the 'can do' feel of it. So right from the start of my time in the job I felt we were missing a trick in letting one side of the argument make all the running there. Clinton was interested in N. Ireland for both domestic and foreign policy reasons. He had given up his great friend and sparring partner George Mitchell to the process. I worked hard when I was shadow Secretary of State to make sure our side of the arguments was understood. I went across and talked to whichever officials at the State Department and whichever members of the Congress and Senate would talk to me.

Access got easier when it got closer to the British general election of 1997 and we had a chance of forming the next government. It meant that before getting into the job I had met Hillary and Bill Clinton, formed a positive relationship with Hillary's assistant Melanne Verveer, who is now a firm friend, with White House staffers and national security advisers such as Nancy Soderberg, Jim Steinberg and Sandy Berger, as well as with Secretary of State Madeleine Albright and Tom Pickering at the State Department. I think it is always a neat idea to take a small gift for people you are seeing who have busy schedules, as well as for staff like the drivers and the security that look after you. I hadn't (neither had the Department) got the money for the most common gifts: coffee-table-size books, or the Irish option of Tyrone crystal. So I took what we called shakies from the tourist shop in Whitehall. For a couple of pounds our host would get a gift that when they shook it gave them a snow scene over the House of Commons or Big Ben. I never found one person we visited or who came to my office who was not amused by these things. I was slightly worried with ambassadors from Latin America or the Middle East like Iran. But they all saw the joke. When I gave a tin plate, costing ninety-nine pence, with a picture of the Changing of the Guard on it, to Bill Clinton he laughed and said it was a great gift. Because of the formalities when

'Shucks, Miss Mowlam. I think the President's intention was just to shake your hand.'

dignitaries visit another country, a bit of humour can make a difference. I think with a mixture of determination and humour I got our message across in the US.

Now, at an important moment in the talks process, the British, Irish and US governments stood together, shoulder to shoulder on the road to peace in N. Ireland. I am not saying it was just me – the personal chemistry between Bertie, Tony and Bill was important, as was the work of others, but I think I helped.

The St Patrick's celebrations were very lavish. The queues to get into the White House were always very long but the excitement of being there kept everyone in a good mood. I'm not sure any real business was done, but you never know; any peace process needs its social side too. Everyone mingled, and there was a good amount of food, drink and entertainment as well as a shake of the hand with Bill and Hillary – again a need to queue. There was always singing. It was all really politicking in the broadest sense, making people feel important. It wasn't just the White House that entertained everyone. The Speaker of the House gave a more exclusive party; one or two from each group in N. Ireland were invited. Clinton gave a speech at this event and the food was amazing.

Not to be missed out, the Irish embassy gave an evening drinks party which everyone went to and where we all drank too much. I can remember one year loyalists were standing round the door singing republican songs and demanding that we had to sing to gain entry. It was always a great party. We were more sedate at the British embassy: full dinner, white-gloved waiters, the full Monty. Everyone left the British embassy and headed for the Irish embassy after dinner was over. A clearer contrast between the two cultures was not possible, though the British embassy was slowly losing its over-the-top Britishness, thanks in no small part to Ambassador Chris Meyer and his wife Catherine. They were very good news and a real bonus to the British government's cause in the US – open and progressive, with a good sense of the politics and of Britishness. I liked them both.

As usual, my time in the US was hectic. Like talking to the parties in the talks, visiting certain events and not others was seen as rude and an affront by the British government; sensitivities are always there, but during the talks it was potentially dangerous to ignore someone. More to the point with Irish America is that you never know when you will need them. My trip started in Boston. A quick visit to a couple of events in Irish pubs, a couple of breakfasts and a word with some of the key players on the Irish American scene, like the Costello brothers, Joe O'Leary, Bob Connolly, John Cullinane, Kingsley Aikins, the Dunfey family and the Kennedys, Ted, Jean and their nephew Joe. There were others like Chuck Feeney who were less vocal but long-standing and valuable supporters of the process. St Patrick's Day gave me the chance to talk to all of them. They all started off by calling me Madam Secretary but I soon had them calling me Mo.

From Boston it was down to New York – sadly not for the big parade, which always clashed with events in Washington, but to see other players like Loretta Glucksman, Tom Moran and Bill Flynn, lovely people who have used their common sense and understanding and their wealth to help bring peace to the island of Ireland. They have been players for years through good and bad times. A quick interview with Adrian Flannelly on the most popular New York Irish radio station and I was off. It was such a pleasure to be interviewed by someone who understood the issues, did not ask soft questions but was not aggressive.

After New York it was straight down to Washington and up for breakfast with the press, most of them from Ireland north and south, a lot from the BBC. Staying in Washington with Chris and Catherine was a pleasant breather, time for a swim and a chance to talk with someone rather than be talked at before all the evening events. Next morning I was up early and with a sense of relief getting on the plane. No more hectic socializing – just back to Belfast and down to work again.

The talks resumed with a vengeance after the week in the US. Sinn Fein formally returned to the process after expulsion. It was barely commented on, which made me think that people did want to make progress.

The Easter deadline for the end of negotiations was approaching fast, only eighteen days to go to Good Friday. The meetings with all the different parties had an edge to them, but the smaller parties were the most desperate to make sure that everything possible that could be done was being done. Sinn Fein and the UUP turned up for meetings, a little more aggressive than their normal level, but with nothing much different to say apart from repeating what their outline positions were. The ones working away frantically were the British and Irish civil servants who were writing, rewriting and revising papers every day and long into the night.

The last week in March, a pretty crucial time by anyone's reckoning, I decided to split my time between the talks and talking to the folk outside so that people didn't feel cut out of what was going on in the talks. It wasn't in anyone's interest to say anything specific about what was being said, but just to be out engaging with others I thought was important. So I met journalists, domestic and foreign, saying nothing of substance but at least if someone talked to them they had a peg to hang their report on. I talked to the Young Politicians at the British Irish Association in Oxford, talked to the N. Ireland Voluntary Trust, had a reception for Amnesty International, met the army and Ronnie Flanagan, and rather bizarrely had a very pleasant meeting to talk with Jeffrey Donaldson on the subject of the Lagan Valley Regional Park. I presume he wanted to act as if the talks were irrelevant and he was doing business as usual. I found it weird as at other times he would just stare aggressively at me, but I knew he would hit the press if I didn't meet him, so to save the hassle we had a chat about park developments.

I couldn't, as Secretary of State, just abandon all my other duties and focus on the talks, even though I wanted to. But I had more time because Paul was fully engaged and No. 10 were becoming more and more involved. I'm not good just sitting round waiting to do something helpful, so out and about I went.

I think it is very important in any negotiations to be as inclusive as possible. People understand that not everyone can be included in the talks. There is however a very important difference between inclusion and exclusion. People like to know in broad terms what is going on, particularly if they have been involved in earlier negotiations. So I worked hard talking and visiting as many interested and concerned groups in addition to the parties and the police and army. I could have hung around the centre acting important, but I felt that doing what I was doing was of more value. I think it had some effect because, however pissed off other parties were at not being included, no one broke rank.

The talks even at this late stage were still all about parties fencing round each other. No one had really moved very far from the positions they had adopted at the beginning of the year. There was much more flesh to be put on the bare bones but in reality none of the parties wanted to do it. None of them wanted to be the first to move, the first to show their hand. It was going to be up to the two governments. That's what Gerry Adams and John Hume kept saying. And while David Trimble resented the fact that it was beginning to look like a good old-fashioned British–Irish stitch-up, he wasn't going to put his head over the parapet either until there was something on the table.

George Mitchell knew this and shared my frustration. He could see the process slipping out of his hands and all being done between London and Dublin. We both knew that the Prime Ministers were essential to reaching an agreement. I didn't think we could do it without them, but it was exasperating, particularly for George, when No. 10 and the Taoiseach's office were working together, and he was not in the loop. I think that was one of the reasons why he set out the timetable when he did. He said that he wanted all the parties, including the two governments, to give him ideas on the core issues by the end of the week, Friday, 3 April.

So by Wednesday, 1 April, April Fool's Day, the civil servants began working like mad pulling bits together from old papers and putting new ideas in so that by the Friday George Mitchell would have a paper to put on the table for the parties. But it was a dangerous process. It was back to the old problem: the Irish government were basically nationalists, closer now to Sinn Fein than the SDLP, and they had to watch their own backs as they couldn't be seen to be putting anything forward that sold the Irish people short. We knew and understood the unionist position from our many discussions, and David Trimble and Tony Blair were in regular contact. But we were still effectively working as neutrals. George and I would have liked to see more involvement from all the parties in N. Ireland, but just had to accept that that was not going to happen yet. Even so, phone calls with a few ideas came through to me at this time from party members and from others who had followed the process keenly.

The main issues of dispute were still over north–south co-operation (Strand Two) and the main action was all between No. 10 and the Taoiseach's office. Tony Blair and Bertie Ahern were working better together with just the two of them, with a few officials on hand to take notes and give advice. Bertie was in London on that Wednesday. I was in London too, but not in the meetings. I had to give evidence to the N. Ireland Select Committee in the House of Commons on the future of the RUC, which was tough. I couldn't give very helpful answers because, even though we were committed to make changes, I didn't want to issue any public statement at this time as it could have upset the negotiations on broader issues, although police reform was clearly on the agenda. It was not easy, but I think the committee understood, and certainly did not want to be counterproductive.

The meeting at Downing Street wasn't going well. The Irish officials were briefing the press as Bertie went into No. 10 that the Irish government had already 'given enough' to make pro-gress. The talks went on late into the night. The main issue of disagreement was over the cross-border bodies: where were they to be located, what areas were they to cover and what powers were they to have? A host of other problems remained, including the arrangements for the new assembly in N. Ireland. But in reality this was not for the two governments to debate, as it could only be sorted out by the parties themselves.

Friday afternoon arrived. George's deadline was already look-ing shaky and he was tense. He wanted to give folk time over the last weekend before the Easter deadline to read over a first draft. But the British and Irish had still not agreed on the powers of the north–south bodies. Bertie and Tony were still struggling to agree and even though both had to attend an Asia–Europe summit that Friday their minds were on N. Ireland and they met in the margins of the summit to keep up with progress. Reports kept coming back that the two leaders were close to agreement, but not close enough.

Late on Friday we set up a three-way conference call between

George, Tony and Bertie. During the call, George agreed very reluctantly to let his deadline pass. I was at the Belfast end and saw how frustrated George was, but he had no option. To my mind George was a process man by this stage: consult and redraft, always trying to get the maximum possible buy-in from the parties involved. That's why he wanted to get a draft to the parties so they could have a look at it over the weekend and come back to him with their views and changes. This seemed to me a sensible way to proceed and I supported George. But I just wonder, with hindsight, whether giving too much of a total package too early would have just given more time for it to be unpicked, especially as there were so many issues still to be resolved.

The Saturday-morning papers in Belfast were not good. The Mitchell paper had been expected and had not appeared. All the press blamed the two governments, despite the fact that George had gone out to the press and nobly said 'he' had failed to get the paper out on time. George knew that if he was seen as failing the blame culture would not swing into action, and he was keen to minimize any further public disagreements between the two governments. The civil servants and Tony and Bertie had a busy weekend.

I was back in Hillsborough for that weekend. There were a number of other important issues I had to turn my mind to. The Parades Commission's first legal decision was out and the Apprentice Boys were challenging it in the courts. Meantime, I was being taken to court by the Lower Ormeau Road residents' group. So I had all the legal papers to read and approve. I also had two depressing papers on why it was necessary to build a new peace line in the White City area of Belfast where Catholic and Protestant communities met. I approved this unhappily, commenting that it was a necessary but disheartening development, and it showed just how far we had to go.

On the phone that night I said to No. 10 that I was concerned at the growing distance between London and Belfast. We discussed when Tony could fly over and meet all the parties in the talks. 'Whenever you think best' was, I thought at the time, the less than helpful reply.

I had just settled down for the night thinking I had finished all the work – all the red boxes had been emptied, the papers gone through and put back again – when the phone rang. It was my ever vigilant press secretary, Tom Kelly, to say that someone had leaked a memo he had written to me about mobilizing support for any agreement to help in the referendum. It listed the names of the great and the good in N. Ireland that we hoped we would be able to rely on for support. The local Sunday papers published the list in full. Coming on top of everything else it didn't make for a good night's sleep. The worst thing about the leak was that it allowed people opposed to the government to say that everyone on the list was a government patsy whose views as a result were not worth listening to. Of course that wasn't true – many of them were just names that Tom and others had drawn together as people who were independent and hopefully would support the Agreement. When I saw names like Archbishop Robin Eames on the list I knew I would have to spend a fair amount of time on the telephone that morning apologizing to people who might feel that their personal integrity had been damaged. As I suspected, Robin was both angry and hurt that his independent standing as a man of the cloth could be questioned.

It was far from being Tom's fault – he was just doing his job efficiently. But it is not really surprising that the divisive atmosphere of fear and suspicion was affecting some in the civil service in N. Ireland. After all, they were part of the community too. That atmosphere took a while to seep into the civil service, but when it did it made these kinds of leaks inevitable. With each leak, a lot of time, in my opinion, was frittered away trying to find out who had done it. I considered these 'leak inquiries' a waste of energy and just made sure the permanent secretary had someone look into it, knowing it was never likely to produce a result.

On the whole the Sunday papers were fairly positive. In what was a typical editorial the Dublin-based *Sunday Life* said, 'We can't afford to fail.' I got up early and did GMTV's Sunday-morning news programme. I knew that the most important thing I could do was to sound positive and keep talking up the prospects of success, at the same time hopefully building public expectations up and therefore making it harder for any party to let them down. I know it sounds very manipulative, but on one level it had to be – so many battles were fought in the media to win public support. I think I said on the programme something like, 'It is the people's spirit of determination that will make all the difference.' I fundamentally believed this to be the key and I put my faith in the people.

Back to Hillsborough, and Jon had cooked me a full breakfast – eggs and bacon had never tasted so good. We went for a long walk in the grounds just to relax and feel as normal as possible. Back in the house I called Tom. The leak hadn't caused too much fuss, and I think my early-morning calls had helped. I talked to No. 10 and the signs were better. George had almost threatened to go home if we didn't get him a paper on Strand Two by the end of the day. But I didn't worry as the paper was near to completion, albeit with sections where it would be clearly indicated that the two sides had not agreed. The negotiations were at last bearing fruit. By Sunday night we and the Irish were ready to send a paper to George. All the discussions now were about cross-border bodies; the issue of decommissioning would surface later.

The Mitchell paper – the first draft of an agreement – was a hybrid. Strand Two was an overlong result of a tortuous negotiation between two Prime Ministers. Most of the rest was the inspired work of George and his team based on notes and comments from the parties – more detailed in some places than others – setting out options in places where George knew the parties were a long way apart. I think it would be fair to say that the George bits left both sides enough room to manoeuvre; the Strand Two part did not.

It was late at night on Monday by the time the parties got their hands on it. In a plenary meeting, George solemnly pleaded with them to take it away and study it in detail and not to react instantly to the press. Not wanting to be seen to act in unseemly haste, the parties bided by his terms. But the next day they reacted – boy, did they react. The unionist family revolted en masse. Even the Alliance, from whom I expected a measured response, rejected out of hand the Strand Two proposals, and particularly the detailed annexes on areas the new north–south bodies would cover. John Taylor, now the catchphrase king, said he wouldn't touch it with a 'forty-foot barge pole'. The nationalist side were warmer but reserved, although Sinn Fein quickly saw their advantage and warned the Irish government not to allow the document to be subsequently 'unpicked'.

The press had held over their front pages on later editions for late-night leaks. The *Daily Telegraph* urged the parties to abandon Sinn Fein and their agenda and forge a middle-ground solution – a hoary old non-starter. The London *Times* said the text was 'saturated ... with nationalism'. In the *Independent* David McKittrick wisely queried 'whether the chairman had caused a genuine crisis for the UUP or whether its rejection amounted to a strategy intended to extract concessions in the last days of the talks'. Mitchell was no fool and McKittrick was the best journalist around on N. Ireland. This for me made a lot of sense.

Other reports in the press said that a secret IRA convention 'last week' had approved Sinn Fein's participation in the N. Ireland assembly. I didn't receive anything more concrete from my officials to substantiate this. On Tuesday night Tony Blair flew to N. Ireland, amid rumours that David Trimble had phoned and insisted he come. In a way it was right. We had done the parallel negotiating bit, with some going on in London and some in Belfast. Now the two had to come together. People had to look each other in the face, read each other's body language and drink in the atmosphere of tension and excitement that was all around us. That night Tony met David Trimble and John Hume. There were no tantrums, no walkouts, but the UUP leader was adamant – something had to shift and shift fast.

The next morning Bertie Ahern flew in to Hillsborough for breakfast and a long walk and talk with Tony in the grounds. Hillsborough came into its own then. The gardens gave people the space to think and talk in peace, one to one, without fear of taps or bugs from one side or the other! Bertie wore a black tie with his suit that morning. His mother had died recently and her funeral was at eleven o'clock, back down in Dublin. It was a very hard time for him and my heart went out to him. The loss he felt was evident, but he kept his emotions under control and kept focused on the talks. His commitment to try and find a solution at a difficult time for him personally showed a great deal of courage. The other party leaders recognized it too.

I missed the monthly N. Ireland Question Time back at Westminster, to stay at the talks. Paul stood in for me. It was a good arrangement because he could say I was at the talks and he was holding the fort in London, so he could not answer any detailed questions on what was happening in Castle Buildings. With Bertie and Tony now each locked in their own separate suite of rooms in Castle Buildings, the real hard negotiations started. The parties were all in their rooms. The press were camped outside and the long hard slog for agreement started.

Inside the building there was not a great expectation of historic progress, just the knowledge that there was a fair distance between parties and that we had our work cut out. There was for many a sense of relief that after months and years of getting the talking up and running an end was in sight. The security guards on the outside gate were a little overwhelmed by the press. Their job of many months was now being usurped by the many security men from both sides of the Irish border hanging around. There were supposed to be only limited numbers of folk in the building. It clearly didn't work. At different times I would go to the Shinners' rooms or the UUs' rooms and it looked like they had the whole of their executives there. Only the Shinners and the Women's Coalition did anything to make their surroundings hospitable.

Tony and Bertie saw the parties jointly at first. They held meetings back to back all day. The focus was all on north–south issues. The unionists refused to discuss anything else until those were solved, which meant a lot of people, with a lot of expertise on other issues, were left hanging around. I worked at engaging the parties on the confidence issues like prisoners, policing and help for victims. When not in meetings I wandered the corridors, and kept in touch with all the other folk from other parties also wandering the corridors, trying to measure the temperature, to see if there were any problems developing that we could deal with then and there. I sat down with David Andrews and Liz O'Donnell of the Irish Republic and both sets of officials to make sure we were still all batting together. In between the party leaders' meetings I would pop into Tony's room and talk to John Holmes, Jonathan Powell and Alistair Campbell and Tony himself to find out how the meetings were going and to offer advice.

The talks kept going through the day and late into the evening. Eamonn Mallie led a press protest against the lack of refreshments: hot sausage rolls and pasties and coffee were hastily despatched. Upstairs in the main conference room there was a running buffet for all the participants, with new dishes served up every few hours. On occasions when we didn't want to make even more demands on the catering staff we sent out for a Chinese takeaway or fish and chips to keep us going. There was also a bar with big windows covered by Venetian blinds where folk sat watching the TV. Every so often a news bulletin would pop up showing the cameras from the outside trained on the same big windows with their Venetian blinds. Smoke was everywhere, lots of it from Seamus Mallon's pipe.

As the evening wore on and people got tired, more and more folk came out into the corridors to try and find out if anyone knew what was going on. When it became clear that there would be no agreement that night a decision was taken to adjourn. George said it would be the last time we could adjourn till the talks were over, one way or the other. Most of the parties camped at the Stormont Hotel at the bottom of the hill. The good sign was that as the parties left Castle Buildings their comments to the press did not make the negotiations harder. The UUP referred to 'signs of movement'. 'Positive and intensive discussions' was the view of the SDLP. The Shinners were the least helpful (what's new – they had most to gain and most to lose), saying, 'There is no room for slippage.' Neither PM said anything. Alistair said, 'We are nearly there.' I, as I got into my car, said, 'There has been a fair bit of momentum today.' As usual the really negative comments were from Paisley. He held a press conference to announce that he was refusing to see Blair because Blair 'was putting the knife into the union'. Paisley always knew how to win folk over. That night he said to one woman reporter who dared to ask more than one question, 'I know that women find it hard to hold their tongues.'

We flew back to Hillsborough in helicopters. The Irish stayed at Stormont House, as Hillsborough had still too much of a colonial air for them at that time. Feeling tired and exhausted I was heading for my bed (because the next day was clearly going to be a marathon, working to a deadline of midnight) when the news came through that a Protestant man with four stepchildren had been shot in Derry. I went to bed vainly hoping that Trevor Deeney would be the last.

Thursday was D-Day. I woke up to a cold and snowy morning. I couldn't decide if the snow was a good or bad omen. I was tired but excited. I must have walked miles in my stockinged feet the day before to try and keep everyone on board. The last thing we needed was someone peeling off because they felt the talks were not inclusive enough. I knew from talking to

Tony and Bertie how hard they were finding it to discover ways through on the big issues with the main players. I felt the best I could do was to keep talking to everyone. Arriving at Castle Buildings we stopped to talk with the press, who were as tired as the rest of us, and also very cold from standing in the snow. My message was as clear and as upbeat as I could manage: 'Everyone has got to give a little. No one is going to get 100 per cent of what they want. If everybody is willing to accept some change we can do it.' It was an accurate statement of where we were at.

The honest answer throughout that Maundy Thursday was that no one could be sure whether we could reach a positive agreement. On the side of making progress, everyone there was seemingly doing what they could to find a way forward. No one wanted to be blamed by the press outside, and more importantly by the people of N. Ireland, as the party that blew it. There was also another factor in play, which is difficult to explain; everyone taking part was proud to be there, they knew they might be taking part in an historic event and so they wanted to see progress. As the talks dragged on through the day and into the night people got more and more tired and increasingly wanted to see a positive decision. There was always a feeling around that failure could be round the corner, but there was an equally strong feeling that a successful outcome was possible.

The focus in the talks on the cross-border bodies continued. Then, quite quickly, two key elements broke the deadlock. Firstly, the Irish agreed to a reduction in the annexe pages (accepting that the level of detail was too much for the unionists) from three to one. This was now a list that was called 'illustrative' of areas to be finalized at a later date, with a deadline set for 31 October 1998. The list included areas like 'animal and plant health' under 'Agriculture' and 'teacher qualifications and exchanges' under 'Education'. It was drawn up to sound as ordinary and common sense as possible, making it all the more difficult to disagree with. Secondly, a 'mutually assured destruction' clause was put in so that if any of the institutions fell the others would fall also, reassuring unionists that if an assembly in N. Ireland fell, the north–south arrangements wouldn't just continue. It gave unionists a measure of control over the north–south set-up that they needed to sell the deal.

This was real progress at last. Tony and Bertie wanted to put it in the bank and carry on. The press were told (by Alistair) that they were still hard at work and the determination was still strong, or variations on that theme. When any group was not in talking to Tony and Bertie they were convinced that something was going wrong for them. I went round constantly trying to reassure folk that, just because they hadn't seen either PM for five hours, it wasn't all going against them. I also did my best to ensure that the parties were kept fed, watered and as content as was possible with the limited information available to me to share with them. Feeding and watering, I was told later, was a menial task for a Secretary of State to do. I disagreed. Hungry people are more likely to be tetchy and negative.

The midnight deadline came and went, but none of us were prepared to stop. Tony and Bertie were driven to keep going until the final deal had been done. As the concerns on both sides about the north–south arrangements began to subside, thoughts turned to the new institutions for N. Ireland itself, Strand One. Admittedly Paul Murphy and the parties had done quite a lot of the legwork already and the atmosphere was already quite good. Basically it was down to the UUP and the SDLP. If these two could agree on the institutions, then the other parties would fall in behind them. (Sinn Fein at this stage were still refusing to really engage on what they continued to call the 'internal settlement', which for them meant a return to the bad old days before when N. Ireland was run by the unionist-dominated parliament at Stormont.)

At about midnight the UUP and the SDLP went into a huddle. The main dispute between them was over the make-up and functioning of the executive of the new government. The UUP could face being part of an elected assembly with Sinn Fein members, but they didn't want to be seen to be working with them in government. They wanted everything done by individual committees of the assembly with the chairs of the committees chosen in proportion to their electoral votes – which in practice would mean the UUP not having to be seen to work with Sinn Fein. The SDLP basically wanted a cross-community coalition government in which all the parties worked together to make decisions. It took just three hours (till 3 a.m.) to reach a compromise. The final deal involved a bit of both, with a mathematical formula (called D'Hondt after its Belgian inventor) allocating the government jobs to each party based on their electoral strength, and only a few decisions, for example the budget, requiring formal cross-community agreement, which meant all parties working together. There was a lot of concern among the smaller parties that the electoral system agreed by the two big parties would make it difficult for them to get seats in a future assembly. We pushed hard to ensure that the smaller parties got a look in – after all, they had done a great deal of work and were an important part of the political future of N. Ireland.

While these talks were going on we were trying to make progress on Strand Three and on all the other issues that would make up a comprehensive agreement. Our efforts were momentarily halted when we were told that Mitchel McLaughlin was out briefing the press that a Sinn Fein walkout was imminent and that the talks were close to collapse. We decided very quickly that this was just Sinn Fein playing hardball. They were angry at what had been conceded on north–south bodies, and felt they were being frozen out of the Strand One talks. So they were kicking up a fuss. As I said then, they always put Mitchell McLaughlin out when they wanted something saying that they might later want to row back from.

We had called on Bill Clinton a couple of times already to

use his considerable powers of persuasion. He said we could call any time in the night, which we did. At several different points he had talked to David Trimble, Gerry Adams and John Hume. This was one of the times that we used him to get Sinn Fein back on board. And they soon were back in, with the Prime Minister going through their list of demands. It was long, and much of it would be very difficult for the unionists; many of the points were what the officials called 'deal-breakers' for the unionists. The key issue though was on the fertile but difficult ground of prisoner releases. On this issue I put my views to Tony, and gave my assessment of what was under discussion. At the same time I continued to talk to the parties, to tell them the two leaders were still talking. At this point in the process it was important to avoid negative rumours. Coffee was kept on tap all night. There were sleeping bodies in odd corners. A few shady-looking young men in bomber jackets and dark glasses wandered about. The bar filled and emptied by turns.

The only light entertainment in the night came from Ian Paisley. With a group of supporters he broke through Massey Avenue Gates into the Stormont Estate and marched on Castle Buildings. He was stopped by the police and there was a rowdy stand-off. He telephoned John McKervill, in my office, to demand to know why he was being kept out while 'terrorists and murderers . . . and at least one homosexual' were allowed in! One of my most polite officials, David Hill, drew the short straw and went out to talk to him and his supporters. Sarcasm apart, Paisley could not be ignored. He was a democratically elected politician and had to be handled carefully. He was no fool and used the media with great skill. It was agreed that they would depart after a small delegation had gone into the press compound and made a statement. Paisley started to make his statement to the press but was shouted down by many of the loyalist supporters who had come out from Castle Buildings to heckle.

Inside, the discussion on how much time should elapse before prisoners should be let out went round and round. It was a tough one. As usual it was a judgement between the shortest time possible for Sinn Fein and the loyalists, what Tony Blair could live with in terms of public opinion, and what the UUP would accept. In the discussions I argued for one year, because the flak from one or two would be the same, so go for the lowest and therefore hope to make some progress on the other issues with Sinn Fein. Tony decided on two years. It became one of the most difficult issues. I was expecting us to be murdered in the press. (In the end we were badly mauled, but there was a growing understanding of what needed to be done – or a growing boredom by the press and public wanting to see more progress). But, since it was an issue that not only Sinn Fein but also the two loyalist parties insisted on, none of the other parties could reject it and hope to get agreement.

Dawn broke and there were still outstanding issues that folk wanted to be sorted, but none of them were 'deal-breakers'. One last huge effort was made and as the daylight grew it seemed we were there. At around 8 a.m. the final draft was being prepared for the parties to see. I kept awake by punching the stomach of the security guard in the corridor; seeing me coming he would tighten his stomach muscles.

We were beginning to think we had reached the end, but then as the day wore on there was a phone call from David Trimble from his rooms on the floor below. He had shown the document to his negotiating team and they had raised two key objections, on prisoners and decommissioning. Tony kept amazingly calm considering how long we had been going and just said it was too late now to make any changes to the agreement because it would mean that all the other parties would want to do the same and we could not carry on indefinitely. As a compromise, Tony offered to provide a side letter, which was drafted and given to the unionists. In it he offered to 'support changes' to the provisions for excluding parties from executive government in N. Ireland if, 'during the course of the first six months of the shadow Assembly or the Assembly itself, the provisions [in the

Agreement] have been shown to be ineffective'. It gave Trimble the cover he needed to say that if things weren't working out as he wanted and issues like decommissioning were not being properly dealt with then he had some redress through the British Prime Minister.

David Trimble called his party together and read the letter to them. In doing so, he managed to satisfy the majority of the unionist negotiating team. It was a difficult meeting but he succeeded in holding in John Taylor and Ken Maginnis, which was important. But Jeffrey Donaldson couldn't be persuaded to support the deal. He walked out of the meeting and out of the building, got into his car and drove away. Fortunately by then all the media attention was on what came to be known as the Good Friday Agreement and less on Donaldson's departure.

David Trimble then indicated, as the other party leaders had done, that he was ready to go with a final statement. George Mitchell called all the parties into a plenary session for 5 p.m. Tom Kelly arranged for a pooled television camera to be there, with pictures but no sound. But the pictures were enough. George went round the table asking solemnly if they were agreed. Everyone apart from Sinn Fein said Yes. Gerry Adams said, as expected, that their negotiating team would 'report back to the Ard Chomhairle [their party executive] of Sinn Fein who will assess the document', but he added that the Sinn Fein leadership would 'approach this development in a positive manner'. We assumed, as on previous occasions, that it was the Shinners' way of holding their followers together. But it was clear that we had made it. At the end of everyone's comments, a large cheer went up and we all started clapping.

George and his team and all the party leaders went out in turn and said a few words to the press. Tony Blair spoke of his hope that 'today the burden of history can at long last start to be lifted from our shoulders'. Bertie Ahern said the Agreement marked 'a new beginning for us all'; it was 'a day we should all treasure'. I finally went round all the delegation rooms to thank everyone for their efforts. I found a number of people who were very emotional. Many in the building had worked for years to get to where we had got. There were lots of tears, hugs and photos. Nigel came for me and said folk were ready to go home. We headed out to the airfield and it was as much as I could do to climb up into the plane. Along with Nigel, Paul, Bill and David, we all had a whiskey to toast a happy ending and promptly fell asleep.

8

It's Your Decision

I awoke on the morning of 11 April 1998 in surprisingly good shape. The pain in my shoulder, which oddly came on while swimming in the army's pool down at Thiepval Barracks at Lisburn and had plagued me throughout the previous week, had disappeared. (The first couple of times I went to the Barracks pool they ordered the troops and their families out so I could swim alone in privacy. I soon put a stop to that and swam along happily with everyone else.) That morning I lay in the bath trying to get the past week's events and the next steps into some sort of order in my head.

I could hear the fax machine buzzing away downstairs. It was the morning's press cuttings from Belfast. I had already seen the London papers, some of which were wonderfully positive. The *Independent* declared, 'Peace at Last for Ulster' in two-inch-high letters across the front page, with a big colour illustration of a bright-red new dawn rising over the cranes of the Harland and Woolf shipyard, Belfast's most famous landmark. I had sat staring at it for a while, blinking back a few tears. I am so proud of what people achieved at that time, overcoming all the sneering of the sceptics and the bitching of the cynics. It was the sort of moment when as the Irish poet Seamus Heaney put it, 'hope and history rhyme'.

But it was also a simple triumph of human will – the ordinary, hopeful, positive way that people are, wanting the best to happen, and which is so often missed by politicians and others who are too engrossed in the difficulties of a problem that they can't find the way through. It was such a big moment. I wondered how much of a part exhaustion played in getting a result.

I collected the press cuttings from the fax and curled up on the settee with a cup of tea to read them. The mood in the Belfast papers was realistic and spoke of the difficulties ahead. Already – predictably – there were reports in the *Newsletter* of people's concerns about the early release of prisoners, reports that dominated the negative coverage. There was much less concern reported among unionists about the north–south bodies. Either by accident or design the issues there had been so fully aired already and so many horror stories put about that when the real truth emerged people were much more relaxed about it. The *Newsletter* editorial summed up the sceptical reaction, saying that 'Despite the brokering of the deal among the Stormont Talks participants, major questions remain to be answered over how the proposals can be made to stick.'

This was sensible and, with hindsight, very perceptive. More worryingly, there were early rumblings from other UUP MPs that they would not support the deal. At his post-Agreement press conference David Trimble had brushed aside Jeffrey Donaldson's early departure from the talks as 'tiredness' on Jeffrey's part. But there was much more to it. The Agreement was to face its first test later that morning when the UUP executive met to vote on it. It was, by all accounts, a difficult meeting for Trimble. Six of his MPs were said to be against the deal – including Donaldson. But the final vote was more positive, with the executive voting nearly two to one in favour.

With the Good Friday Agreement in place, the referendum campaign was the next step leading up to the vote on 22 May 1998 and it now started with a vengeance. The next six weeks would have as many ups and downs as the talks had done. Both the UUP and the Shinners had immediate and big hurdles to get over in the next week. Sinn Fein had arranged a conference, or Ard Fheis, for Saturday the 18th. The whole of the 800 or so UUP council were due to meet on the same day. Both would be crucial meetings in deciding whether or not the new Agreement could indeed be 'made to stick'.

The IRA's first official reaction was issued on Sunday morning (12 April). In a statement it said it would judge the Agreement 'against its potential to deliver a just and durable peace in our country'. But in other parts of the republican movement the reaction was much more hostile. Republican Sinn Fein (which had emerged in the 1970s when the movement split and the 'Provisionals' were born) called for a no vote in the referendum. Its members were mostly based in the Irish Republic and objected strongly to the Irish government giving up their historic constitutional claim to N. Ireland. It was a small voice of dissent, but worrying nevertheless.

Messages of support had come in over the Easter weekend from all parties and across the world. Former Prime Minister John Major called the Agreement a 'beacon of hope'. The Tory leader at the time, William Hague, said it was 'a massive step forward' (shame he didn't do more to help us implement it when it got difficult later on). From the US there was talk of $100 million in extra economic support, and Bill Clinton said he would visit if it would help support the Agreement. At home, Gordon Brown's office gave details to the press of a new economic development package we had been discussing in the event of a positive result in the referendum. Sinn Fein were still being very cautious and at the republicans' traditional Easter Monday rally Martin McGuinness said they needed a 'period of consultation' with their membership before they could sign up to the Good Friday Agreement. Ian Paisley, meanwhile, formally declared that the DUP would campaign for people to reject the Agreement. The maverick UUP MP for West Tyrone, Willie Thompson, announced he would be supporting the DUP campaign.

My plans for the week largely involved relaxing with Jon. After the Agreement was reached on Friday I had joined him on Saturday at a house party at Budd's, the lovely country house of Waheed Ali and Charlie Parsons in Kent. They have a house full of old friends each Easter and we thought it would be an immediate way for me to unwind. Unfortunately I didn't get there until eleven o'clock at night, but Wahid just plonked Jon and me down with a bottle of whiskey in front of a roaring fire while he went and entertained his other guests. After two days of country air with people from worlds other than N. Ireland and complete relaxation we returned to London, although still not back fully into the fray. I found over the years that it is really important to make an effort occasionally to do nothing and to lower stress levels. Also in a way it felt right to step back and let the parties and the people in N. Ireland digest what had happened and begin to weigh their views. There was no point trying to bulldoze the people into supporting the Agreement – it would never be made to stick if we tried to do that.

On Tuesday, the Irish government released nine IRA prisoners from Portlaoise Prison, near Dublin. Once again, I don't think they told us they were going to do it. Fortunately, the prisoners quickly issued a statement pledging their 'total support' for the leadership of Sinn Fein. It helped to soften the blow a little and, I felt sure at the time, was a further sign that the Sinn Fein Ard Fheis would approve the Agreement. The timing of the release was no doubt designed to help bolster support for Gerry Adams and Martin McGuinness and encourage a positive vote at the end of the week.

Further reactions on Wednesday included the Grand Orange Lodge saying that it couldn't support the Good Friday Agreement without further clarification on a number of issues from Tony Blair, including on prisoner releases and decommissioning. I ought to nail this down now. Decommissioning was not made a precondition to either the release of prisoners or the taking up of executive office in the Good Friday Agreement. Some might wish it had been. But it wasn't. If it had been, Sinn Fein and the rest of the nationalist side would never have supported the deal. Neither would the loyalist parties. In other words there would have been no deal. So to insist – as the Tories subsequently did – that you could support the Agreement and at the same time

"SURELY SOMEONE WANTS TO CLAIM HIM?"

argue that prisoners should be kept in until decommissioning had begun was simply false and unhelpful. At least others – like the DUP and eventually the Orange Order – were more honest and simply opposed the Agreement throughout.

Thursday saw brighter news with a joint *Guardian–Irish Times* opinion poll claiming that 73 per cent of the people in N. Ireland were in favour of the Good Friday Agreement. I welcomed this when I arrived in Belfast. It was my first return to the office since the talks finished and the building was eerily empty. I thought I could just smell a faint whiff of Seamus Mallon's pipesmoke still in the air, but the chief reminder of the week before was the huge patch of dead, yellowed grass out the front of the building where the journalists' tented city had been. All gone now; the world's media had moved on.

I had returned mainly to announce that the Springvale project to build a college of further and higher education in West Belfast would go ahead at long last. It had become something of a personal mission for me as well as for Tony Worthington, who was Education Minister at the time. Most of the arguments had been over the site, but finally we managed to get agreement. The site was at a crossroads between the two communities in Belfast and we hoped it would act to help bring together young people from both sides to study. And not just the academically minded either – I wanted kids from all backgrounds to go there, even with few or no school qualifications, which is why the further-education side of it was so important to me. It was also my attempt to get something of an equivalent for West Belfast to the large amounts of money being poured into the Laganside development in the east of the city. Much of the money for Springvale was government funding, but it wouldn't have happened without the hard work of people like Maurice Hayes and Loretta Glucksman who through the America Ireland Fund made it possible. Maurice from N. Ireland and Loretta from New York did many things over the years to help the peace process, making an incredible contribution to the peace.

On Friday morning, David Trimble delivered a speech at one of the last sessions of the N. Ireland Forum. It was a speech long on reassurances for unionists, who were still undecided about whether or not to support the Agreement. On the list of 'things achieved in the Agreement for unionists' most were ticked off in the course of his speech: the ending of the Anglo-Irish Agreement (and the closure of Maryfield, which raised a cheer); changes to the Irish constitution; the accountability of the north–south structures to the N. Ireland assembly; and, crucially, the recognition in the Agreement of the principle of consent. On this basis, Trimble could say with confidence that 'the union is secure'. These were all the messages that the predominantly unionist audience at the Forum would want to hear. Trimble's rhetoric was tough against the republicans, claiming that the new Agreement was 'a disaster for Sinn Fein/IRA'. Trimble also said that as far as the bits of the Agreement he wasn't happy with were concerned – like on prisoners, policing and equality – further changes would be made as time went on and legislation was debated in Parliament.

At the same time in London Tony Blair made clear the government's position that the RUC would not be disbanded and that only those prisoners whose organizations were on ceasefire would be released, on licence, from prison. It was the opening performance for a double-act that would be crucial in helping to secure a yes vote among unionists in the referendum.

As long as the message kept within the terms of the Agreement we knew that, while many nationalists would grumble at the rhetoric, they would stay on board. I know it sounds a bit like the nationalists were being taken for granted, and to a certain extent they were. It was very quickly apparent that moderate nationalism was happier with the Agreement than moderate unionism – although why it should be assumed that they would be any happier with loyalist murderers being released than the unionists were with republicans being released is a good question.

That night I travelled over to Redcar for my monthly constituency surgery. The normality and steady pace of life in Redcar, in spite of the problems, was always a tonic.

On Saturday morning it seemed that the comments by both Trimble and Tony Blair had paid off when the UUP ruling council met and voted by 540 to 210 (72 per cent) to support the Good Friday Agreement. But six out of the ten UUP MPs were now openly opposed, including Jeffrey Donaldson, which was a serious blow to David Trimble at the time.

Meanwhile, in Dublin Gerry Adams was addressing the Sinn Fein Ard Fheis. His rhetoric was tough for unionists. He said things like 'Britain will never have any right to be in Ireland', and – in a direct reply to Trimble – that the Agreement meant that 'the union had been severely weakened'. He too was playing to his audience, trying to convince the sceptics. Fortunately the Agreement had space built in for each side to argue its merits in their own way. So for Trimble it 'secured the union' while for Adams it 'severely weakened' it. Both could point to different bits in the text to justify their views. That the Good Friday Agreement was open to multiple interpretations proved to be both a strength and a weakness – but it was the only way to get an agreement between all the different parties.

Bowing to Sinn Fein democracy, Gerry Adams didn't declare himself openly for the Agreement in his conference speech. But his language was very positive, talking about the Agreement as a 'basis for advancement'. He also addressed the republicans' policy of abstention from government in N. Ireland, saying, 'If that abstentionist policy underpins our contest in the Assembly elections then the seats on the cross-border bodies which have the power to make and implement policy on an all-Ireland basis, and which would rightly belong to our electorate, could be allocated to other parties. We need to ask ourselves if this serves our struggle.' It was a rhetorical question to which the answer was clearly no. It was the first time Gerry had said clearly that, as far as he was concerned, Sinn Fein should be 'in'. It was a crucial step, but it would be nearly a month before the Sinn Fein membership formally delivered their final view on the Agreement.

In an aside during his address, Gerry learnt of the UUP vote and informed delegates of the result. He added, 'Well done, David' – words that were, as David Trimble later said, a 'poisoned chalice' for him.

Of course life is not all politics and Jon and I were still enjoying having Hillsborough Castle as a place to entertain old friends in great comfort. In the middle of the referendum campaign we had a particularly memorable weekend when we managed to have journalists and broadcasters John Humphrys, Jonathan Dimbleby and Jeremy Paxman all to dinner on the Saturday night, a slightly surreal experience. At one particularly memorable moment during the weekend John Humphrys and Jon's son Fred went out on the small rowing boat (called the *Tom King*) we used to get around the lake. Fred understandably felt that he was in charge, as it was his boat and his lake. John surprisingly was having none of this – of course he was in charge. We watched them drift out into the centre of the lake shouting and gesticulating wildly at each other. I think Fred put up a better defence than many that have had to confront John on the *Today* programme each morning on Radio Four.

Monday morning and the vote-no campaign came out with a vengeance. Paisley, as ever, was quick off the mark – quicker than the much more politically diverse yes campaign, who were still deciding what to say and do. He held a press conference saying that his party aimed to secure a 40 per cent no vote in the forthcoming referendum on the Good Friday Agreement. His aim was clear: to be able to say afterwards that a majority of unionists had opposed the Agreement.

Parliament returned from its Easter recess on the Tuesday. I met that morning with Tories Andrew MacKay and Lord Cope at my office in Millbank. I got the feeling that McKay was not out to be helpful. He said he had some difficulties with the prisoners issue and Sinn Fein being on the executive. I replied that he had to realize that everyone had those difficulties, but the most important thing to do was to support the N. Ireland parties who had signed up to the deal and now had the difficult task of convincing their electorates. That afternoon Tony Blair made a statement in the House of Commons on the Agreement. It was a great parliamentary occasion with people who had been involved in N. Ireland politics for years all taking turns to welcome what had been achieved.

But the threat from those still opposed to the peace process re-emerged that evening when a 29-year-old Catholic man, Adrian Lamph, was shot dead by the LVF at the council yard where he worked in Portadown. It was the first sectarian killing of the conflict since the Good Friday Agreement. Others indicated their opposition to the Agreement in other ways. The DUP held the first of a series of anti-Agreement rallies in the run-up to the referendum. From the other extreme the small gang of rejectionist republicans, the Thirty-two County Sovereignty Committee, issued a statement rejecting the Agreement as 'fundamentally undemocratic, anti-republican and unacceptable'.

That night we had leaving drinks at Stormont House for Quentin Thomas. He didn't show much emotion at leaving – I'm sure that is what made him a good negotiator. I was sad to see him go and said so. I wished I had fought harder to make him permanent secretary at the N. Ireland Office. But he wasn't one of the 'in crowd' in the senior civil service and they weren't going to see him in a top job. The UK government lost a major talent when Quentin retired a year or so later. He had been a central architect in the peace process, drafting the Good Friday Agreement and other documents, along with others from the British side and with his Irish counterpart Seán ÓhUiginn and his colleagues from the Dublin civil service.

I also had a goodbye drink with Martha Pope, along with the US Consul in Belfast, Kathy Stephens – good women who had worked hard for the peace process with very little thanks or public recognition. Martha had had a particularly difficult time in N. Ireland. Not only had her job been very demanding both physically and emotionally, but she also was the victim of a particularly unpleasant smear campaign. Kathy was a great networker, especially among the women's organizations in N. Ireland. It is impossible to quantify, but the contribution of individual women and women's groups to the cause of peace in N. Ireland is immense. Across all communities, the links and relationships that women forge and the work that they do – usually away from the public gaze – has been invaluable in keeping the social fabric of N. Ireland together, especially in the most troubled times. The N. Ireland Women's Coalition was formed specifically to get more women's voices heard, but other women in other parties had also worked for years, willing to argue the case for peace and stand up to the bigotry and intolerance of some of the men around them. The women in the talks were a really positive force.

There were so many women's groups, it was impossible for me to get round them all. My parliamentary private secretary (PPS), Helen Jackson, did a great deal of this work on my behalf – and later for Peter Mandelson. Helen was not only my eyes and ears in the House of Commons, as a good PPS should be, but also spent much of her time over in N. Ireland meeting people, speaking at events I couldn't get to and keeping me up to date to make sure I didn't miss anything. She would write me regular reports on this group or that she had met and what their views were – it was crucial in keeping me up to speed with what people were thinking and saying on the ground. I was very sad to lose Helen when I left N. Ireland; she was replaced as my PPS by another capable and supportive woman MP, Margaret Moran, when I moved to the Cabinet Office.

The women's network stretched across boundaries, across the Irish sea and across the Atlantic. Hillary Clinton was an important link in giving women in N. Ireland encouragement and support. At her initiative a Vital Voices project was started, and driven forward by Melanne Verveer and another very able woman, Theresa Loar. The project, aimed at giving practical support to women in voluntary work, in business and particularly in politics, developed into a series of high-profile conferences in different countries and regions of the world. Hillary came to N. Ireland to promote the project, which brought women from across the sectarian divide together to campaign for peace. With government help an office was established and a database set up to help women's groups link up. For a few years Vital Voices became an important channel of communication between women from many different backgrounds with views, advice and experiences to share.

Bill Clinton's N. Ireland trade envoy, Jim Lyons, joined me for dinner late that night at Hillsborough. Jim was appointed after George Mitchell (who had done the job before) came to do the talks. We talked about Springvale and about when Bill Clinton should visit N. Ireland. We agreed that if the referendum result came through it would be a good time. But Bill remained throughout ready to come at any time if we thought it would help.

On Wednesday (22 April) the Irish parliament passed a bill to allow the necessary changes to their constitution to go through following the Good Friday Agreement. They would hold a referendum on 22 May to seek public ratification for the changes. Some Irish politicians talked up how difficult it was going to be to get the people's support in the referendum, but in reality it seemed the vast majority of Irish people would be happy to see the old territorial claim to N. Ireland go in exchange for peace.

The 'United' Unionists – as the no camp were now calling themselves – rallied in the Ulster Hall in Belfast on Thursday. Paisley was there along with the dissident UUP MPs – Willies Ross and Thompson and Roy Beggs, and Bob McCartney. Although they had not formally taken a position, representatives of the Orange Order were there too. While his fellow MPs looked on smiling, David Trimble was dismissed as a traitor, a 'Lundy' (after a seventeenth-century Governor of Derry who argued for surrender during the siege of the city) and, more fantastically, as an MI5 agent recruited by the Brits in the 1970s to sell out Ulster. It was no doubt a rousing event, but the turnout was a lot lower than Paisley had predicted.

I was in London for a lunch in the Westminster Press Gallery. This was quite an occasion, when all the journalists in the Lobby got together and invited a senior politician to speak to them. Jon Craig, then at the *Daily Express* and chair of the Press Gallery, introduced me with a few jokes at my expense. I did my joke about my security guards being called the 'Shirleys', because they're always saying 'Surely not, Secretary of State' – which I said in my best impression of a N. Ireland accent. It was light-hearted and I felt people were genuinely interested in what had been happening in N. Ireland.

I also took my positive message over to Brussels, where I had been invited along with members of the Irish government to address the European Parliament, to explain what we were up to and hopefully get some reinforcement from MEPs for what we were doing. The visit went well. David Andrews and I spoke at the beginning of the debate. From the Parliament floor, MEPs John Hume and Jim Nicholson from the UUP both spoke. Ian Paisley, the third member of the European Parliament from N. Ireland, sat at the back seething and saying nothing. I'd never been to the European Parliament before, but listening to the Members from across Europe, many of them women, I found the debate less aggressive and more focused and practical than debate in the British Parliament. My visit gave me faith that the European Parliament does have an important role to play now and in the future.

To my mind Europe's engagement was crucial for N. Ireland. In the short term it was a source of potential financial support: for deprived areas and through investment to help the economy. We were unlikely to see considerable results from this, but it would be good to see some. The other value of Europe was in relation to the institutions under the Good Friday Agreement. When the institutions were up and running, N. Ireland – alongside Wales, Scotland, England and the Irish Republic – could begin to learn the benefits of co-operating with each other within Europe without having necessarily to tackle all their political anxieties.

But dream on about the role of Europe and all that positive stuff. When I woke up the next day John Humphrys was on Radio Four announcing that the IRA had just issued the following statement on the Good Friday Agreement: that it 'falls short of presenting a solid basis for a lasting settlement . . . Let us make it clear that there will be no decommissioning by the IRA.' Inevitably, as is the way in N. Ireland, the next day the Orange Order called on its members to vote no in the upcoming referendum. It was not a surprise, but on the back of the IRA statement it made for an uncomfortable weekend for all of us, but particularly for David Trimble, who was engaged in maximizing his support among unionists for the Agreement. I had learnt during my time in N. Ireland – if faced with bad news, don't hurry to an answer, but let the party leaders and the public think about it for a while.

I was due back in the North-east of England at the weekend; the diary was full of engagements, but it was still a break to be out of the hothouse of Belfast. On the Friday night I was speaking at a party fund-raising dinner in Newcastle. People were genuinely delighted by the Agreement – the reception I got was incredible. Many members of the Labour party had cared about N. Ireland for a number of years. The inequalities and injustices and the appalling levels of violence were uppermost in their minds. It concerned me that there was a feeling in the room that we had made it – that lasting peace was on the way. I kept saying we had a long way to go and lots of hurdles to climb over, but people did not seem to want to hear. I was worried that people would get too buoyed up and would not find understandable the weeks and years of progress yet to be made.

I travelled back down to London after my Redcar surgery on the Saturday to spend the weekend with the kids and Jon, reaching them by teatime and leaving at teatime on the Sunday. They were all pleased to see me – no one thought to point out to me that a weekend should be more than twenty-four hours.

During those twenty-four hours we also had one visitor, the Secretary of State in the US, Madeleine Albright. We were living back in Islington by this time, and the neighbours turned out to see the cavalcade of black American cars that blocked all the streets with men in dark glasses parading up and down speaking into their sleeves. Inside it was a much more normal affair. Madeleine and I had met a number of times before and got on well. This particular afternoon we sat round with H and Jon and Fred having a cup of tea. I had just appeared in a recent opinion poll as more popular with the British people than Tony Blair. Madeleine commented that that was a dangerous position to be in. She gave us a bottle of Tibetan vodka, as she had just been in Tibet.

At an earlier meeting in her office in Washington we had sat opposite each other at the fireplace with a semi-circle of about twenty people – mostly men – listening to what we were saying. It's a really weird experience trying to have a conversation watched by an audience. We did our business and then in unison decided it would be useful to adjourn to her private office together. We stayed a good while, some of the time talking about the issues we had discussed in front of the audience, making sure that was the best way to deal with the problems, and the rest just chatting as two women in positions of power with very few people you can talk to. The suits in the room next door were not necessarily going to be supportive and the boys' club at the top of both administrations was not welcoming. There was a group of women who tried to get together and be friends. When I was in New York and time and diaries permitted we got together – sadly, I only made it once. I had a great evening with Hillary Clinton, Madeleine Albright and Donna Shalala, in charge of Health. It was amazing how much our experiences matched – a shared loneliness, a shared sense of being outside the boys' club. On another occasion Madeleine and I insisted on eating in a restaurant in Washington's laidback Georgetown, an area more used by normal people than by senior politicians. The attempts made by both her security staff and mine to be unobtrusive were hilarious. We both understood they couldn't afford to lose us but they just had no idea how to respond to the level of threat in a small restaurant in Georgetown – it was more like a comedy.

So it was good to have Madeleine at home to meet Jon and H and Fred. It was great to see her in our house. Personal friendships are important in politics. Obviously it helps to get business done, but for women it is our support network, which the boys by their very nature don't give us.

The next morning I had to be back at my desk in Belfast. The referendum was only eighteen days away and the campaign was hotting up. In some ways, as a government, we needed to be as neutral as possible in the campaign. Under the law governing referendums, for example, we had to provide equal funding to the yes and no campaigns, which I thought was mad. So while a yes vote was clearly in all our interests, there was a limit to what we could do. As Ministers, Paul, Adam, Tony, Alf and myself had agreed that we would continue with our planned engagements across N. Ireland but at the same time make sure in any interviews with the smaller local papers to take the opportunity to speak up for the Agreement. By the end of the campaign I think we had talked to a large number of the fifty or so smaller local papers. There was a lot we could and did do behind the scenes, but in the end we knew that this agreement belonged to the N. Ireland parties and unless they sold it successfully to their constituents it was never going to work in the long run. I always kept in my head the caution from my Quaker friend Alan Quilley, about how easy it is for 'people with English voices' to dream up solutions. This time it was for the people who lived there themselves to decide.

I was still very worried that the United Unionist campaign was making all the running. They launched a campaign slogan 'It's Right To Say No'. It was a good slogan because it said to people 'Don't feel guilty about not voting yes.' I began to worry about when the yes campaign was going to get off the ground. Attempts to get a cross-party campaign going for a yes vote had run into the sand early on. First the UUP and then the SDLP backed away, both believing that the suspicions in the unionist community would not be allayed by seeing their politicians lining up with the other side. Two friends from the voluntary sector, Quintin Oliver and Fiona MacMillan, prominent voices in N. Ireland, tried to get a cross-party campaign going, failed, and then forged a new alliance of non-party people to work together for a yes vote. They created some of the most memorable images of the campaign – especially their big 'Yes' banner down the front of the Europa Hotel and another huge 'We Say Yes' written in white cloth on the Divis Mountains near Belfast. It could be seen from miles around.

Where good cross-party support for the Agreement did exist was from previous Ministers in N. Ireland. This was very valuable reassurance to David Trimble and his party. They were very helpful in rebutting more negative forces in the Tory party such as Andrew Hunter and David Wilshire, as well as the leader writers on the *Daily Telegraph*. One real star from the Tory benches was former N. Ireland Minister Richard Needham. He was liked in N. Ireland, which was rare for Tory Ministers – I think because he was amiable, straight and spoke his mind. I liked him because he so obviously cared about N. Ireland and he had a sense of humour. As a Minister in N. Ireland in the Thatcher years, in a mobile phone call to his wife Sissy he had said he thought it was time 'the cow resigned'. Amazingly Mrs Thatcher did not sack him. Richard travelled across to Belfast to attend the yes campaign's first big poster launch. It was a good one, designed by Alan Bishop and his team, who work in an advertising agency and gave their services free during the referendum. The message was unmistakable: the way ahead versus a dead-end. Simple and effective. Using roadsigns was quite common in graffiti in N. Ireland. Smaller versions appeared on many lampposts – political fly-posting is still legal both north and south of the border in Ireland, though in the rest of the UK it is illegal.

On the roller-coaster ride to the referendum vote, Sinn Fein announced on 6 May their support for the Good Friday Agreement and their support for a yes vote in the referendum. At the same time there were press reports that the IRA had decided to drop the ban on members of the republican movement taking part in the assembly in Stormont. It was a step many had believed Irish republicanism would never take. It meant there was a recognition at least that N. Ireland was a legitimate political entity – although republicans were very quick to point out it was a 'transitional step' on the road to a united Ireland. The positive work of the Sinn Fein leadership was matched by what David Trimble was doing within the UUP. But he didn't have the advantages of discipline and loyalty that were there within the republican movement, and it was still unclear how much progress he was making towards increasing support for a yes vote among unionists. He was obviously going to need a lot of help and I hoped the arrival in N. Ireland on the same day of Tony Blair and the former Conservative Prime Minister John Major would boost his efforts. John Major's support was most welcome. Despite the problems at the end of his government, he was still widely regarded as a sensible and well-intentioned man, and it was helpful to us to show that the Agreement had the support of people like him from across the water in England.

Things were going reasonably well. Surely, I thought, it was about time for a setback. It came early in the morning on Thursday, 7 May with reports of a new republican paramilitary group emerging – formed from dissident and disaffected IRA members and calling themselves the Real IRA. They declared war on the British cabinet as a first act. The warlike rhetoric didn't bother me much, but the beginning of the fragmentation of republicanism did. To me this illustrated that Martin McGuinness and Gerry Adams had been telling the truth about their struggles to keep the movement together. All the information I received was that the Real IRA was a very small group who had been opposed to the Adams–McGuinness leadership for many years. But I worried that they would be able to attract more support from within the IRA. I feared that over time some of the younger members of the IRA, who had been used to the status and romantic image they had of themselves as paramilitaries, would find life dull and unrewarding when searching for peace. Badly split republicanism – i.e. a weak Gerry Adams and Martin McGuinness – would make further negotiations difficult, just as the splits in unionism that David Trimble was facing were bad for him, and raised worries about his ability to remain strong enough to negotiate for unionism. We also knew that even a small group of dissidents and hotheads could pose a significant new threat to people's lives.

We had to keep momentum going and keep our confidence, our spirits, up. But there was little I could do immediately about these problems, so I put them to the back of my mind and headed off to Westminster to brief as many folk as I could and to answer doubts and queries on the referendum. I had started with folk who I knew could cause problems over the Agreement and be the most vocal, like Tories Brian Mawhinney and Norman Tebbit. The hardest question to answer was on prisoner releases. It was not difficult to understand the opposition of people like Norman Tebbit to prisoner releases. Of course he would be opposed politically to such a policy, but there was also the pain there of the serious injuries his wife Margaret had received from the Brighton bomb in 1984.

It is very difficult to give enough support to individuals who have been injured or have lost loved ones in the Troubles. The pain they and their families go through is hard enough without having the government take actions like releasing thugs and murderers early from prison. I understood this and did my best by seeing families and groups whenever I could to listen and try and explain what we were doing. But it was never easy to explain to someone in a wheelchair or to a woman who had lost a husband or a son that their grief was listened to and respected as much as they wanted. It would not have been possible. I tried to say to them gently that I could not condone revenge rather than progress as a way forward, as that was not going to prevent other families from suffering as they were doing. However much anger and hatred exists towards killers, not talking to them will only mean they continue killing and maiming people; rather we have to try to stop any more deaths and injuries taking place.

The biggest fear among the families of victims of the Troubles was that they would be forgotten and their grief disregarded with the advent of a bright new dawn. I was determined not to let that happen and immediately thought of a monument for the victims of the Troubles. It only took a three-minute conversation with my private secretary Ken to see that there was no quick solution. Whose lives were being remembered? Police families alongside the murder of an IRA man by a loyalist or a loyalist family by the IRA? It would be a nightmare trying to decide – a general event or monument for all the dead was clearly not on for either side.

It was suggested instead that I talk to Sir Ken Bloomfield, ex-head of the civil service in N. Ireland, who had been asked before the signing of the Good Friday Agreement to chair a commission into ways to commemorate N. Ireland's many thousands of victims. Sir Ken had consulted all the victims' groups and individuals and was, in mid-May, just about to publish his findings in a report entitled *We Will Remember Them*. The introduction was a letter from him to me in which he said, 'I could only describe the task you gave me as a painful privilege: painful because I have encountered grief and human suffering on an enormous scale; a privilege, because I have encountered also such courage, such endurance and – often from those most gravely affected – such generosity of spirit.' It was a good report, containing a detailed programme of work, which was crucial for us to respond positively to.

We set aside £5 million to start making Ken's many detailed and practical proposals a reality. The amount was heavily criticized by the victims' groups, along the lines of 'Is that all you think our loved ones were worth?' It was difficult but we had to accept that whatever we did short of bringing their loved ones back was not going to be enough – what was important was that we met with groups representing victims as regularly as possible and listened to them, and gave them help, however inadequate it was thought to be.

Adam had been given the job of Minister for victims and he did it very well – especially as it was far from easy. He oversaw, among many other things, the establishment of a Family Trauma Centre in Belfast to provide therapeutic services to injured victims and their families, new education bursaries set up for young people, a memorial fund to provide grants for individuals (like people needing extra help because of disabilities) and groups (many of which were organized by victims and their families themselves). At the time, I saw those groups that insisted that a meeting with Adam was not enough. It was very difficult because they desperately needed to vent their anger and frustration at the loss of a loved one, and we as the representatives of the government were the obvious folk to see. They were not the easiest meetings I had, but they were very important. I think and hope they helped.

One example: in August 1999, I returned to the scene of the Omagh bombing for a ceremony of commemoration. When I had been there the year before, just after the bomb had gone off, when they had only just begun to clear the debris, a man had come up to me screaming abuse and waving an anti-Agreement placard at me. I remembered the event well enough, but my security recognized him when he approached again. This time he looked me straight in the eye and said calmly, 'When are you going to catch them?' His grief was still there, but he was slowly learning to live with it. I often wondered to myself, when meeting with victims, could I personally climb over the pain of the loss of Jon or one of the kids in such a way?

If I was going to have any chance, it would only be with the support of friends who had experiences to share. People like Wendy and Colin Parry, who lost their son Tim, with his best friend Johnathan, when an IRA bomb exploded in the centre of Warrington in 1993. They redirected their pain to do what they could to help bring peace. Colin and Wendy spoke where they could on why peace and reconciliation were so crucial. In March 2000 they finally opened their peace centre in Warrington after years of tireless fund-raising. The centre is now a safe place for children who come from disadvantaged backgrounds or who have experienced violence and conflict to come together and learn about the importance of peace and resolving conflicts. It also provides learning for adults and a cultural exchange programme for young people from Britain, N. Ireland and the Irish Republic.

Colin and Wendy are tremendously strong and determined. There are many others too, far too many to mention, who have dealt with their grief by trying to help others. People like Rita Restorick whose son Stephen, a lance-bombardier in the British Army, was killed in February 1997. Rita has campaigned for peace in the UK and in the US and worked to help other women who are going through the pain that she feels. Others, like Irish Senator Gordon Wilson, whose daughter Marie was killed along with ten others at a Remembrance Day service in Enniskillen in November 1987, always spoke out strongly in support of the peace effort in N. Ireland, earning tremendous respect and trust from both sides of the community. Still others, like Diana Hamilton-Fairley, whose father was killed by a bomb in London in 1975, worked hard during the referendum campaign to help to explain why it was important to vote yes. The support of people like these and many other victims of the violence from both sides in N. Ireland throughout the peace process was worth more than a hundred politicians' voices. Of course, many of those who lost loved ones had to find other ways of handling their grief differently from people like Rita or Colin. The pain of losing a loved one may be too great to do anything but try to cope with your emotions in whatever way you can.

Within N. Ireland many of the victims established or joined support groups. Some of the support groups – like WAVE – are cross-community groups, recognizing the hurt that exists on both the Catholic and Protestant sides of the community. Sadly, but perhaps understandably, that is rare. Many other groups are formed from families on one side or the other. Some of these were the most difficult to deal with and a few became deeply opposed to the Agreement, especially the part about releasing prisoners. What really depressed me, and made Adam Ingram furious, was how politicians used some of the victims' groups. The DUP, in my view, exploited their grief to try and mobilize support for the anti-Agreement position in the referendum campaign. I remember discussing with Adam what we could do about this. We concluded nothing. But we felt the balance was restored when folk like Colin and Diana and Rita began to speak out.

The middle of May, and the second half of the referendum campaign, was quite an unnerving time. As Ministers we had to make sure we were doing enough to build support for the Agreement without being too pushy and going over the top. That would lose votes. But at the same time we had to stay confident and make plans for the next steps after the referendum was over. This was hard because it meant assuming a yes vote, but we had to do it. In the middle of May that meant passing new legislation to provide for what would be unique elections in N. Ireland and the establishment of the assembly at Stormont. The plan was to hold the elections as soon as possible after the referendum campaign to keep up the momentum and, crudely, to use any lingering goodwill from a successful referendum campaign to maximize support for pro-Agreement candidates in the elections.

In London at the end of the week, I held a session to brief the international press. The US correspondents were particularly interested in what Clinton was doing to help. I gave them all I knew, which was that he was fully engaged on a day-to-day basis with parties and stood ready to come to N. Ireland any time we thought it would help. Events such as this gave me a chance to talk to journalists on the record, but not in a fully blown press conference – it was helpful, even if no printed story came out, to keep journalists up to date with what was going on and what we were doing.

The next day I drove (correction: as with any other journey, I was driven, which allowed a good four hours for work and sleep) up to Newcastle to receive an honorary degree from Newcastle University. I have since received a number of honorary degrees over the years, but Newcastle was the first. I know how important the ceremony is for the students getting their degrees, so I sit through them looking interested, but I have to say I find them deeply boring. I am just not very good at sitting still. I drive Anthony who cuts my hair mad because after the first twenty minutes I start fidgeting. The most interesting of these awards for me was going back to Iowa in the USA. I had had a good time there when I got my Ph.D. It was great to see my old tutor Professor Gerhard Loewenberg, to visit the bars I had gone to, and walk down familiar streets. I now also have honorary degrees from Coventry, Durham and my local University in Teesside – as well as being granted the freedom of the city or town in Coventry, Sheffield and Redcar.

After Newcastle that night I went to receive another award, this time in a much more relaxed environment. Every year the London-based *Irish Post* newspaper holds an awards ceremony for the Irish community in Britain and Ireland. It is a celebration of Irish culture and recognition of achievement. It is also a good drink. That night I received the Irish Post Award for my Contribution to the Peace Process in N. Ireland. It was important to me as the *Irish Post* were not always that positive about what the government was doing in N. Ireland. I can remember Kevin McNamara once telling me that getting a picture and a positive story in the *Irish Post* means more in terms of support for Labour than any number of fine words in speeches. It could not have been easy to give the award to a Brit like me with no Irish connections, which made it even more valuable to me.

I was a little hung over on the plane the next morning – the Irish certainly do know how to party. After a lot of juice, a couple of cups of coffee and fruit, I was back on course for the day. Jay the stewardess on the plane was great. She always instinctively knew when to ignore me and when to feed and water me – a great lady. On the Saturday it was just me and Jay on the plane, apart of course from the two pilots. I got down to rewriting the speech I had been given to deliver at the Women's National Conference in Belfast. I dealt with speeches in a way that was far from helpful for my staff. If there was anything special I wanted to say I would let them know with a short draft, and then I would leave it up to them. The officials would do a draft, then my special advisers would rewrite and give it to me to see if I was happy. Any changes I wanted were then made, often not extensive – a couple of examples here, or more explanation there – and that would become the official version of the speech. But only on very few occasions did I use it. What I would do the night before an engagement or what I was doing on the plane this Saturday morning was to rewrite so that it became my speech. I can't read a speech and deliver it as mine – I find it very hard. If I am to engage my audience I have to be able to look at them and preferably interact with them, which is not possible with a written speech. They never complained, but I knew it drove my special advisers crazy. They would write a clear, concise speech and I would gut it, making it wandering and illogical. But it worked, because I engaged with my audience – found a couple of receptive faces and talked to them.

I worked hard on the speech on the plane that morning. I guessed it would be a pretty blue-rinse affair, and therefore not an easy audience, and so my pro-Agreement and pro-change speech might not go down well. On sitting down after delivering the speech I said to myself I was right in my assessment of who would be in the audience but wrong on their response. I got a very warm show of support. It gave me a lot of encouragement and offset a lot of the negative things I was reading about the state of support for the Agreement among unionists.

The opinion polls were still looking good, but it was impossible to know in any detail which way the referendum vote was really going. The next day Sinn Fein had their national party conference, their Ard Fheis. They were to vote on whether they were to end their seventy-year-old opposition to taking part in the government of N. Ireland. I was not too worried about the vote. I had seen Gerry Adams and Martin McGuinness operate now and I was sure they would have their boys and girls with them in large enough numbers to win the vote. They were helped by a gesture from the Irish government, which released from prison temporarily four IRA prisoners known as the Balcombe Street Gang who were convicted in the 1970s for a string of murders in London. The gang stood together at Sinn Fein's conference on the platform to cheers and applause from Sinn Fein delegates. The pictures on the TV that night were celebratory in tone and I know they appalled many who saw them. It certainly wasn't helpful to those unionists who were campaigning for a yes vote among their community. Separately, I had agreed the temporary release of convicted IRA man Padraig Wilson so he could attend the same event. Wilson was noticeably absent from the triumphalist spectacle, as Gerry Adams had promised me he would be.

I was left in no doubt as to the effect of the pictures when I met the officers of the Police Federation the next morning. They felt, understandably, doubly aggrieved as they had lost people from among their number trying to get individuals like these behind bars in the first place. I took the protests and listened to their anger – and, at times, their heckling. But very soon we moved on to their longer-term concerns about the provisions in the Good Friday Agreement for a review of policing. Like many other people they were concerned about their pensions and redundancy payments, to guarantee them a future too.

Sinn Fein were not the only ones to have prisoners on temporary release at their conference. As a matter of course, prisoners in N. Ireland benefited from leave arrangements on compassionate grounds or, as their sentences progressed, home leave arrangements at weekends. This is all part of the rehabilitation process and is quite normal. But in the middle of a referendum campaign normal events can be explosive. Just a few days after the TV news programmes were awash with pictures of IRA men at a Sinn Fein rally, the image of the notorious loyalist killer Michael Stone out on leave at a yes rally in Belfast's Ulster Hall organized by the UDP dominated the screens. It was a gift to the anti-

Agreement unionists, who had spent much of the campaign so far talking about how all the terrorists would be released if people voted yes.

As I thought later that day about the impact of all this, I said to my private secretary that, yes, unionism was fragile and the pictures on the TV would have been far from helpful to the unionists' yes campaign. But we should never forget how far Sinn Fein and the loyalist parties have come and that they still needed an incredible amount of support to help them hold a yes position together across their supporters. With hindsight, it was also important that people realized that one of the aspects of the Agreement would be the prisoner releases. At least after the referendum was over people couldn't say that they had been misled and that the prisoners issue had not been properly discussed. But this was no consolation at the time.

The apprehensive mood of the week was only lifted for me by two events. The first was a conference I addressed of young people at the Spires Centre in Belfast. They were overwhelmingly supportive. The message I gave everywhere I went was simple: look to the future, not the past, understand your history but don't live in it; the Agreement means working together for peace; it offers fairness and respect for all. The reception I got for that message from the young folk in the hall gave me confidence for the future and lifted my spirits no end. I only wish I had had time to do more with young people. The more young people I met the clearer it became that a future generation would make greater strides than their parents had. But I did not feel too bad for not doing more because there were a number of voluntary schemes already working with young people across the divide.

We also finally agreed a package of new economic support for N. Ireland. If peace was going to hold, a boost was needed to the economy in the form of jobs. Jobs mean hope for the future – they are not just dreams but real work. When people in Gordon Brown's office had first briefed the press about a possible special package of economic support (without telling us), I was suspicious. I was hopeful that it was a really new package of new money and not existing monies repackaged. But by the time the amount was finalized it looked impressive, and I felt it would really make a difference. Gordon joined me at the Shorts aerospace factory down on Belfast Harbour and announced £350 million of additional economic help. He denied that the package was a bribe to entice voters to support the Good Friday Agreement. The package didn't come with strings attached, but the underlying message was clear. We were investing in peace and expected people to support it.

Feelings were running very high as the referendum campaign neared its close. In the final week Tony Blair came over twice and delivered two key speeches. In one, at the University of Ulster in Coleraine, he unveiled a handwritten set of pledges. As Prime Minister he was putting his credibility very much on the line, and putting things in his own handwriting was his way of showing people that he was sincere. The pledges were:

no change in the status of N. Ireland without the express consent
   of the people of N. Ireland;
power to take decisions returned to a N. Ireland assembly, with
   accountable north–south co-operation;
fairness and equality guaranteed for all;
those who use or threaten violence excluded from the government
   of N. Ireland;
and prisoners kept in unless violence is given up for good.

As reassuring as Tony was being, in that last week of the campaign, the no camp got further boosts when both Jeffrey Donaldson and former UUP leader Jim Molyneaux came out against the Agreement. At the same time, Bob McCartney threatened us with legal action unless we disclosed to him the polling information we had. Since it was mostly pretty positive, we couldn't see any problem with the request and Paul Murphy agreed to hand it over. Bob must have been pretty disappointed because he didn't use any of it as I recall.

On the more positive side, Ian Paisley let David Trimble accuse him of running away from debate (again!) when he refused to join the UUP leader on a live TV debate; the LVF announced an 'unequivocal ceasefire' in the hope of encouraging people to say yes; and we had a joint British, Irish and US government statement in support of a yes vote. One of the triumphs of the pro-Agreement campaign was an SDLP idea for making use of a major pop concert at the Waterfront Hall in Belfast on 19 May. Bono of U2 delivered a tremendously powerful, symbolic and positive message by taking the hands of both John Hume and David Trimble (who had joined him rather sheepishly on stage) and raising them in the air to acknowledge the cheers of the young crowd. The picture dominated the news broadcasts and the front pages and remains one of the most potent and hopeful images of that time.

While the local parties in N. Ireland made the headlines – which was as it should be, after all it was their agreement and they were the ones who would have to make it work – we maintained our programme of visits and did everything we could to strike a positive note wherever we went. That's not to mention my other activities: coming back to England for N. Ireland Question Time at Westminster or for my Redcar surgery; working on economic investment issues with the Americans; talking to the national press and doing interviews on programmes like BBC2's *Newsnight* and Radio Four's *Woman's Hour*; visiting schools and colleges; meeting with the smaller political parties who might be feeling excluded – like the Alliance party – and touring parts of N. Ireland with celebrity supporters of the Agreement like Richard Branson, who came over for the day. Richard was one of many high-profile people to come and lend their support. Others included the actor Kenneth Branagh, the boxer Barry McGuigan and the former Ulster and Ireland rugby star Trevor Ringland. Each time they came, the press was there and the photos were taken and another tee-shirt saying 'Vote Yes' got into the newspapers.

Eventually referendum day, 22 May, arrived. As with all elections and votes, there was a collective sigh of relief that the campaign was over and there was no more we could do, matched by the excitement and expectation as to what the outcome would be. On days like referendum day, I find it very difficult to settle to anything. I have also learnt after a number of elections that when voting is taking place politicians are superfluous. So I decided out of my long list of people wanting a visit to go and see Colin Parry in Warrington. He was working hard to raise funds for his peace centre and was struggling at the time. As I hadn't the time, nor was I allowed to actually do the fund-raising, I tried to give him the odd visit to help with publicity and at least keep spirits up.

Back in Belfast, my gut and what I had seen of polls said that it would be a strong yes vote, but you can never be sure in N. Ireland. It was the first all-Ireland poll since 1918. That night the figures for the turnout were very encouraging – 81 per cent in N. Ireland and 56 per cent in the south. I was relieved to see a good poll in the north and a majority voting in the south because it meant that no one could question the referendum itself. That was the first hurdle over.

Saturday lunchtime, 23 May, and the final ballot papers were being counted in the King's Hall in Belfast and in the Castle in Dublin; both results would be known by Saturday afternoon. The Hall was packed with supporters of the yes and no campaigns. The tension was astonishing. So much hung on the result. We were sure by that stage that it would be yes – the question was, by what margin? Unless it was sufficient to show that a majority in both communities in N. Ireland had voted yes, then the unionist yes campaigners, like David Trimble, would be seriously wounded and it would make taking the Agreement further forward all the more difficult.

In the end, after a few technical hitches like the microphone breaking down, the chief electoral officer Pat Bradley announced the result. It was good for the peace process. In N. Ireland it was Yes 71.12 per cent, No 28.88 per cent. In the Irish Republic it was Yes 94.39 per cent, no 5.61 per cent – overall, a resounding yes north and south of the border. Crucially in N. Ireland the result was just high enough for us to claim legitimately that a majority in both the unionist and nationalist communities had voted yes. Never mind that folk north of the border had voted yes by nearly three to one. As soon as the result was announced I closed my ears to the chants of 'easy, easy' being directed at a humiliated but still thundering Ian Paisley and started to phone the result round the world so that people who had an interest and had helped got a personal call. By and large they were a lot of very excited and jubilant people. Many of them knew already from the radio or TV, but I always found that a call or a letter helped people feel included. I even called Margaret Thatcher as an ex-PM with an interest. It was a straightforward conversation until the end when she closed with 'Down with the euro.' I thought, despite being strongly pro-European, that I would be wiser to give no response, as I was interested in gaining her acquiescence over the referendum in N. Ireland rather than having a debate over a referendum on the Euro.

That night I was back on the plane to London once again for a celebratory whiskey with Jon and a decent night's sleep.

9
Getting the Peace to Stick

I have no doubt that the referendum was a defining moment in the history of N. Ireland's Troubles. It was a chance for the people to say what they thought; and they spoke for peace and not for violence. This was a great step forward from the years of conflict, the years of people feeling resigned to there being no end to the war. I don't think people thought it was all over, but rather that the Agreement meant the terms for an honourable peace were now available.

In a speech to the House of Commons on 1 June, I outlined the planned next steps in making the Agreement a reality. These included: elections to a new N. Ireland assembly; the choice of a speaker; consideration of assembly rules of procedure; the election of a first and deputy first minister – one unionist, one nationalist; work to proceed on new departments of government (there were only six then, and the new government would need ten as there were to be ten ministers); and the allocation of the government posts to the successful parties in the election. To keep with the balance of the Agreement, there would need to be parallel progress on north–south issues and on the British–Irish Council too. It was a big, big programme of work, and I worried from the outset that people would not have the energy to keep it up after many exhausting months with the talks and the referendum campaign. But I knew it was crucial that we didn't ease up and lose the tide of local and international good-will that was surging with us after the Agreement.

The elections to the new Northern Ireland Assembly followed swiftly in June. The result produced a solid majority for the pro-Agreement parties, who won 73 per cent of the seats. There was a particularly strong vote for the SDLP – who overtook the Ulster Unionists in terms of votes for the first time ever – and for Sinn Fein. But despite the pro-Agreement parties out-numbering the antis by more than three to one in the Assembly, the split on the unionist side was very tight for David Trimble. Overall his twenty-eight seats had to be balanced against a loose alliance of anti-Agreement and disaffected unionists, who also had twenty-eight. Fortunately the election of two PUP candidates, David Ervine and Billy Hutchinson, kept the pro-Agreement unionists in the majority on their side – for the time being at least. On the whole I was pleased for the pro-Agreement parties (especially the SDLP), but worried about the split on the unionist side, and genuinely surprised and delighted that Monica McWilliams and Jane Morrice of the Women's Coalition had won a seat each. Less of a surprise and more of a worry was the fact that Gary McMichael's UDP had not secured any seats at all. Having no political voice was dodgy, particularly as the PUP had one.

The Assembly met for the first time on 1 July and David Trimble and Seamus Mallon were elected on a joint ticket as First and Deputy First Ministers. John Alderdice was selected as Speaker. But as work started on all the practicalities – like organizing new government departments ready for devolution – attention did not stay for long on the Assembly: the 1998 marching season was upon us. As I have already said, the emotional turmoil of that July with all the tension and violence and, following the killing of the three Quinn brothers, all the sadness and pain took a great toll on us all. At the end of it I think we were all left with a weird sense of hope mixed with fear and fore-boding about what might happen next.

I took that feeling away with me on holiday to Greece. I was utterly exhausted; everyone was. I just wanted a few days of nothing but sleep and quiet. But my holiday was to be interrupted after just seven days in the worst way imaginable.

On Saturday, 15 August, a 500lb car bomb exploded in a busy

high-street shopping area in Omagh, County Tyrone. The bomb had been planted by the Real IRA, the group of dissident republicans who opposed the peace process. In order to maximize devastation and the numbers killed, the bombers gave the police a false warning. They said the bomb was at one end of the high street, which led the police to begin evacuating the Saturday shoppers up to the other end of the street. But that's where the bomb was really planted. This piece of utter cynicism and cruelty left twenty-nine people dead and more than 200 injured. It was the worst single incident in the history of the Troubles, made all the more frightening because people were slowly beginning to hope that an end to the violence was in sight.

The TV images sent around the world were appalling. A whole street strewn with glass and bricks and bodies, blood flowing down the street in a torrent of water from a burst main. Eyewitnesses spoke of the 'horrendous' sights that greeted them when the smoke cleared: of 'people lying on pavements crying'; of dazed faces, 'blackened like workers from a coal pit'; of the sense of 'utter shock' that overwhelmed them and then of being jolted into action, grabbing 'the nearest pieces of wood or shelving to use as makeshift stretchers' to ferry the injured away from the scene.

But it was only later, as is the nature of these things, that the full horror emerged. The dead included all generations, men and women, babies and pensioners. A woman pregnant with twins; a family on whom terror had struck again after losing a first child to an earlier bombing; tourists visiting Omagh from Spain; people out shopping for wedding outfits; toddlers in buggies. And everywhere there was the fear that this could spell the end of any attempts to find peace.

When the explosion happened that Saturday, I was on holiday in Lefkes in Greece with Jon and the kids. I was rung by my office and told about it. After discussions with the family and my office I decided that I would have to break the holiday and return. I rang John Prescott, who was holding the fort as Tony

Blair was also on holiday. He was going to Omagh the following day, Sunday, and it was agreed that he would avoid the difficult questions by saying I would be arriving the following day. I contacted Tony, and I had a three-way conversation with him and Alistair (also away on holiday). It was decided that I would fly back the following day, and that Tony would not visit. I asked my office to get me a plane as the quickest way back, there being no seats on commercial flights out of that part of Greece at that time of year. By lunchtime the following day I had still heard nothing about a flight. The family and I were having lunch in a Greek taverna, beside the Mediterranean, when I got a call from Tony on my mobile. He had now decided that he should go and had taken the plane arranged for me. I was told that the N. Ireland Office would find me another. After a great deal of difficulty the NIO rang to say that no planes were available, but that I could have Tony's plane the next day.

I eventually got to Omagh on the Monday. I walked down the main street, stunned by the level of destruction and horrified by my imagining what it must have been like on a busy Saturday afternoon. Now it was desolate. Trauma was still etched on the faces of the people I spoke to: the police, rescue workers and hospital staff, not to mention the survivors and their families I visited in the Erne Hospital in Enniskillen. The following day I returned with Prince Charles. I had to stop off at M&S on the way to greet his plane as the only change of clothes I had with me were holiday ones. He too was deeply moved by the scenes he saw and the people he met.

I visited a number of times that month, the last time with Bill Clinton. What was amazing was that the incomprehensible shock, desolation and anger I felt from people on the first visit did not turn into a desire for revenge, but slowly into an amazing determination that Omagh people were not going to let the terrorists beat them. They would stick together and keep going. And I was determined that that was what we should do too. Getting on with it and implementing the Agreement was the only long-term solution to this kind of horror. However destroyed I was feeling inside, I knew we had to go on. By early September a tentative plan was emerging to allow the next phase to begin and N. Ireland's new government to be formed. But there was a real problem because a significant number of people in David Trimble's Assembly party were adamant that there had to be IRA decommissioning before any Ulster Unionist nominees could take up their ministerial places. And if there were no UUP nominees, then there was no possibility of the kind of cross-community government envisaged in the Agreement, and it would fail. Clearly this problem had to be resolved, and so began a series of negotiations that would last throughout the rest of my time in N. Ireland and beyond.

Part of the first of many plans to resolve this dilemma involved a carefully planned series of steps, which included the first face-to-face meeting between David Trimble and Gerry Adams. On 10 September the first meeting between a Sinn Fein and a unionist leader took place since the formation of N. Ireland. It was said to have been frank and businesslike and there were thankfully no recriminations afterwards. A further step would be a statement from Sinn Fein to the effect that the 'war was over', which duly came in the form of 'Sinn Fein believe the violence we have seen must be for all of us now a thing of the past, over, done with and gone.' But the prospects for a beginning to the actual process of disposing of the weapons was shattered when the IRA issued a statement declaring that they would not start decommissioning and that the unionists were trying to rewrite the Agreement. So we were stuck – with the unionists on one side saying 'no guns, no government', and Sinn Fein saying they were entitled to be in government because of their votes and there was nothing in the Agreement to say that guns had to be given up first.

Clearly we could not force the unionists to take up their positions in the N. Ireland executive, just as we could not force the IRA or any other paramilitary group to decommission. Both would have to be voluntary acts taken in the kind of atmosphere of growing trust and confidence that the Good Friday Agreement envisaged. That our first efforts failed to get it all up and running didn't worry me too much. Everybody needed time to get used to the new realities, and I felt that if we pushed too hard the whole thing might just break. A degree of flexibility was needed. And anyway, there was a great deal of work going on with other parts of the Agreement which I hoped would help encourage one side or the other to take the steps necessary to make progress. The independent commission on policing began its work, for instance, chaired by the former Tory Minister and Governor of Hong Kong, Chris Patten. The new laws on setting up the Assembly and cross-border bodies and on the early release of prisoners were passed at Westminster. Sadly, the Tory front bench opposed the latter stages of the provisions on prisoner releases, despite their avowed support for the Agreement.

The message of the progress being made was one I took with me to the new Labour government's second annual conference in Blackpool that year. But in my speeches I was very cautious, saying that implementing the Agreement would be just as hard as reaching it in the first place and that there were tough times ahead. I said that I thought people should be given 'space' to come to terms with what was required of them – a public line I was slightly nervous about. I knew we had to give people time to adjust to their new responsibilities, but at the same time we couldn't let inertia creep in and lose the huge sense of momentum and goodwill the Agreement had created. The people of N. Ireland needed to see progress being made or they would lose faith.

One of the most talked-about features of that conference was a moment in Tony Blair's main speech where he referred to the contributors to the Agreement and made reference to me. As I watched in astonishment, the audience in the hall slowly got to their feet applauding. I was more embarrassed than anything else, as it was obvious that this wasn't part of the plan for the leader's speech. Tony handled it well, with a joke, but I knew that there would be certain people among Tony's entourage who would be looking at each other with raised eyebrows at such a show of support for someone other than their man. It was a great conference for me. Everywhere I went people wanted to stop and talk and touch me. But that in itself is more exhausting than any other aspect of the job, and I began to rely more and more on the people around me to make sure I had time and space to myself during the day so I could keep amiable.

Shortly after getting back into work after conference, I was off again to America. This time, the mission was jobs and investment with a huge team of people including Adam Ingram, the Minister responsible for Trade, David Trimble and Seamus Mallon. Adam and I were determined to push the message in America that we were ready to hand over the reins of power to local people. We stressed that David Trimble and Seamus Mallon were leading this trip and we were there in a supporting role. Overall the trip was very successful, with many new business contacts being made and eleven US cities visited in all. The plan meant that in each city a dozen or so business people were brought together for dinner and David then Seamus talked about what was happening and why we were there. Hearing Seamus talk at one of them was the only time in the peace process that I cried. He looked old and tired but spoke with such emotion and commitment about why peace was crucial – it was very moving. I was there for the first leg in New York, where I was joined by Gordon Brown. The trip was a success, but already the strains between David Trimble and Seamus Mallon were beginning to show.

Those strains between Seamus and David, and between the rest of the pro-Agreement parties and the Ulster Unionist party, grew over the next few months. They spilled over into the ongoing negotiations and meant that important decisions on the new structures of government in N. Ireland and the north–south bodies were not made by the 31 October deadline set out in the Agreement. It was a blow that at the time we all tried hard to

gloss over, but I was worried that the first deadline we had set ourselves had been missed.

Fortunately we were all given a boost by the international community's continued emphasis on the positive – believing that peace was on the way – when David Trimble and John Hume were jointly awarded the Nobel Peace Prize. David was the uncomfortable peacemaker. There were still those among the unionist community who saw reaching out to your opponents as selling out or appeasement. When David referred, as we have seen, in his acceptance speech to N. Ireland in the past having been a 'cold house for Catholics', it was an admission of something that some unionists found hard to accept. So while most in N. Ireland celebrated the acknowledged achievements of the leaders of their two communities, the hardliners on the unionist side sneered at the 'Hume and Trimble show' – as they called it – and these were the people David had to deal with most. Meanwhile, I was made European Person of the Year by *Time* magazine, which I took as another signal of the international community's continuing interest and support for what was happening in N. Ireland.

December was a difficult, messy month. People were tired and looking forward to a much deserved break at Christmas, but it was not to come early. The talks over what the new departments would look like and what would be the remit of the north–

south bodies got acrimonious. At the same time David Trimble was arguing that decommissioning should take place in front of cameras so that people could believe it was happening, and the IRA general council announced unhelpfully that a decision had been reached that there would be no decommissioning of fire-arms or explosives at all. Sinn Fein's Gerry Kelly argued that the unionists were trying to push the IRA back to war. On a brighter note, Bob McCartney's anti-Agreement UK Unionist party split in a dispute over whether or not they should keep their Assembly seats if Sinn Fein got into government. Bob was all for walking out, but his colleagues were rather keener on the new jobs they had in the Assembly. I took this as a good sign, that people were beginning to get used to and enjoy some of the benefits of the Agreement and would sooner or later support taking them further.

Conscious of the need to keep people informed at all levels about what was going on and the need to talk up the positives in the Agreement, I took to the airwaves. A vacuum of no news is not helpful at difficult times and I tried to keep up an image of progress being made. I appeared on the sorts of programmes where politicians are not normally seen discussing serious issues, like Richard and Judy's *This Morning* and *Live and Kicking* (a Saturday-morning children's show). Some people considered doing this sort of thing 'lightweight' and not serious. But to me it has always been a case of talk to everyone and get your message across at every opportunity you can. I continued with other engagements, like presenting honours at the London Comedy awards and at the national 'Children of Courage' awards. The latter were very moving and impressive – it was human courage in a form I was not used to. I also launched 'Live Wire', N. Ireland's business start-up awards, which are crucial to the growth of the economy and therefore jobs – a plus in the search for peace. I ended the year on the last BBC *Question Time* before Christmas. We didn't neglect our friends in the press either and laid on the usual Christmas drinks in both London and Belfast. I also made time for a private drink with my old friend Des McCartan. Des always gave me a very balanced picture of what was going on, a useful person to listen to.

To provide something positive for people to take away with them over the Christmas holidays, we put a last-ditch effort into the ongoing talks. The negotiations had their by-now-familiar focus, with the nationalists trying to get as much done as possible on a north–south basis and the unionists as little as possible. All the time I could not get the previous Christmas out of my head when a void of political progress had been filled by the murder of Billy Wright and a killing spree which had nearly sent the peace process completely off track. So, like many others, I was anxious to make progress. And almost at the last minute, just as everyone was beginning to give up hope, an early Christmas present was delivered on 18 December in the form of a final agreement on the government departments and cross-border bodies. It would mean six north–south bodies (covering inland waterways, aquaculture and marine matters, food safety, the Irish and Ulster languages, European Union funding programmes and trade and business development) and an increase from six to ten ministers in the N. Ireland Assembly to accommodate all the parties that were eligible under the Agreement. The final push took nearly twenty hours of negotiation at Stormont, involving, once again, both Prime Ministers and a host of Irish officials and Bill Jeffrey, a very likeable Scot who replaced Quentin, and his team on our side.

On the same day this agreement was finalized, the LVF, in a highly symbolic gesture, handed over some weapons to be destroyed by the International Decommissioning Body. The LVF were the first group to voluntarily do so. The TV pictures of guns going through the grinder made a really powerful image, and felt good. At a meeting of his executive David Trimble convinced the UUP to endorse the new agreement. But there was the continuing proviso that there had to be some decommissioning of IRA weapons.

Overall the last three months of 1998 were pretty decisive in moving the peace process forward. It was a difficult time. I could never be sure that we were going to make it, but in the end everyone kept going and progress, slowly, step by step, was made. One final drama before the Christmas holiday kicked off was the sudden resignation on 23 December of Peter Mandelson as Secretary of State for Trade and Industry over the issue of a private home loan from Geoffrey Robinson (then Paymaster General), who also later resigned. Peter was someone I never really disliked, and I had a respect for his talents. In fact we had actually spent part of a holiday in Spain together, and got on very well. He also stayed with me when he was seeking his seat in Hartlepool (a constituency just next door to mine in Redcar), but unfortunately he left after only one night, as I think my two-up, two-down terrace house in the back streets of Redcar was not quite up to his standards.

I felt sorry for him when he resigned, knowing how he had been so determined to get into the cabinet. A short while after, I took him to the Savoy for breakfast in an attempt to cheer him up. He was his usual mixture of charm and arrogance. Every sentence began with 'I'. He did not ask me one question. He talked about spending more time in Hartlepool and complained about how Tony Blair was unreasonable and had used him, though he said he got on well with Tony. By the end of the breakfast I regretted having asked him. I couldn't tell whether he was saying what he thought I wanted to hear or what he wanted others to hear. What I did know was that he had his actor face on and my effort at friendship had not been received as such. I had been taken to breakfast at the Savoy a number of times and thought how great it was to be able to eat such a good breakfast looking out over the Thames. This was the first time I had paid for it – I had to conceal my horror at the price. I have not been back since.

Christmas eventually arrived. The kids were with their mother this year, so we decided to do something neither of us had done for a long, long time: spend Christmas with the two families. Jon's parents, Liz and John, came, as did my mum, my sister Jean, her husband Rog and their three boys Will, Charles and Tim. All arrived with either girlfriends or other friends. The boys came on the boat in two cars with their girlfriends, while Jean and Rog and friends flew in. I found Jean on Christmas Eve in the big Hillsborough kitchen seeing what she could find to prepare for Christmas Day. The staff, who I had said weren't needed over Christmas, had prepared all the food for us; they had even laid the table as if for a formal dinner. The kids couldn't believe it. Jon cooked Christmas dinner for us all and we had a great time. It was a Christmas none of the family has forgotten. The kids really enjoyed it. Jean's youngest, Will, and his mate Adam made a video, 'The ghost of Hillsborough'. It seemed to consist of cooking bacon sandwiches at four in the morning and jumping out of fridges in their underpants. It only got hairy once when I had to stop go-kart racing in the Queen's throne room. My sister being my sister cleaned up at the end of their stay, leaving everything cleaner than when they had arrived. Sadly my brother and his family couldn't come as they were going to his in-laws.

At the turn of the year I was beginning to feel isolated from what was going on in government and started to think about my position. My conversation with Madeleine Albright came back to me: 'I was too popular for my own good.' But I really didn't want to recognize it – I suppose it was my way of coping. Was I surprised by it? Everyone in cabinet was working hard, but I was top of the polls with the public. I was not voting very much in the House or attending very many committees – I began to think, 'No wonder some people are getting frustrated with me.' To try and make up for this I told Downing Street I was willing to be available for interviews at weekends or to cover over Christmas. I received no response. Like most situations there were two sides to the problem. If I was used when N. Ireland was a current media story, broadcasts might therefore be diverted from the message people wanted to get across. There were also a few stories circulating against me. I was lightweight at the cabinet table and was inclined to make the occasional joke, which was seen as not being serious; I was also accused of not reading my official briefs.

Into the New Year, which began much as the last three months had been. The SDLP and the UUP agreed over the implementation of the pre-Christmas agreement on the government departments and the north–south bodies. But it was not that simple – what's new? The UUP wanted the N. Ireland Assembly simply to debate and to take note of the agreement, whereas the SDLP wanted the parties to formally approve and accept it. Why the difference? Well, David was concerned that if the Assembly approved the 18 December agreement there would be no further barriers to setting up the executive – which he wasn't keen to see happening. But he also didn't want to be seen as the one holding things up. The SDLP saw that too and consequently argued for the exact opposite. They wanted to get moving. The IRA published a New Year message in the republican weekly newspaper *An Phoblacht* which said that the Good Friday Agreement had failed to deliver meaningful changes and that the unionists were pursuing conditions that had contributed to the breakdown of the 1994 ceasefire. It felt to me as if the unionists were willing to slow the process down to avoid outcomes they weren't keen to see. This warning was pretty heavy from the republicans who, like the SDLP, wanted progress. January 1999 was already beginning to feel as difficult as the pre-Christmas period.

We had to find some way to bring things to a head, otherwise I could begin to see this extra 'space' we were giving the parties going on for ever, while the Good Friday Agreement crumbled around our ears. After talking to Tony Blair and officials, both Irish and British, we decided to set 10 March as a deadline for establishing the new N. Ireland government. I knew it was going to be a tough call if we got to 10 March and didn't have everyone on board – what would we do then? Ultimately it was my call as Secretary of State. But I couldn't force people to work together. If I set the process in train to establish the ten ministers and either the unionists or nationalists were not willing to participate then the government would be unbalanced and have to be dissolved again – it simply wouldn't work.

But there was a more sophisticated game in play too – the 'blame game'. I was under pressure from the nationalist side to call David Trimble's bluff and let him stand exposed as the one who had turned down the offer of government in N. Ireland. David, meanwhile, was talking up the prospects of IRA decommissioning so that, if we got to 10 March and it hadn't happened, he could say we hadn't tried hard enough and more time was needed to put pressure on the IRA, thus avoiding the blame himself. It was all getting overly complicated and hard to fathom where to go next. I despise the blame game – it's unproductive. No one gets anywhere. It is much better to sit down and sort out the problem causing the difficulties. To try to collect my thoughts, I went for the weekend at the end of January with Jon to Margaret Jay's house in Glandore. The freshness of the air and the sea and the good food gave me time to think and plan.

George Mitchell returned to London on a visit at the beginning of February and we talked at length about where to go next. He, like me, was concerned that the longer the impasse went on the harder it would be to resolve. Pragmatically he said that regardless of who got the blame for any failure, the unreadiness of the parties to go down the route of trusting one another was at the heart of the problem. I knew that, but it was frustrating my desire to get things moving so we could get the benefits flowing that my daily mailbag told me people wanted to see.

But not everyone. Some people were taking advantage of the lack of political progress to increase their activities as gangsters and thugs. There was a marked upsurge in the level and ferocity of so-called punishment attacks in early 1999. It was deeply depressing both on the level of concern for the victims and on the level of what it said about the communities that supported it; and it also added to the political pressure. People began to say about me, 'How can you go on saying the ceasefires are holding when all these people are getting beaten and tortured?' It gave those that wanted to keep Sinn Fein or the loyalists out of the picture the perfect excuse to say 'I told you so'. The Tories pressed the issue in Westminster, citing cases and quoting statistics provided for them by a Belfast organization called Families Against Intimidation and Terror. During Prime Minister's Questions at the end of January William Hague called on Tony Blair to halt the prisoner releases because of the continuing IRA violence. But here was our dilemma. The Agreement was clear: the prisoner releases and other benefits of the Agreement – like a seat in government – were dependent on the maintenance of ceasefires. So to stop the releases, we would have had to declare the ceasefires at an end – when, despite the activities of a few mindless thugs, they were not. The IRA had not gone back to war, nor were they going to. But if we turned round and said the ceasefires were over, prisoners had to be kept in and Sinn Fein kept out of government, there was every chance that the peace process would be finished and large-scale violence would return and the British government would have broken the terms of the agreement. It was a non-starter. So despite all our revulsion at these attacks, we had to be open and say, 'Yes, it was an imperfect peace, but surely that is better than no peace at all?' William Hague knew this, but he couldn't resist piling on the pressure, buoyed up, no doubt, by regular anti-Sinn Fein stories in the *Daily Telegraph*.

I tried to keep people informed, but it did not always work. I faxed a letter to Norman Tebbit to warn him of the release of the Brighton bomber Patrick Magee, who was responsible for badly disabling his wife. Norman replied,

Thank you for your letter of 21st June informing me of the release of the multiple murderer Magee, which even by fax reached me long after I had been informed by the media. You are wrong that this release caused me any more stress than the previous 276 terrorist releases. Each of these terrorists had victims too. In exchange not a bullet or a bomb has been handed over by the IRA. When you say these releases 'cause difficulties for many of us' I am puzzled. 'Us' must include you. Since you have the power, indeed the responsibility, to suspend the releases in view of the flagrant breaches of the 'ceasefire', the 'difficulty' you are caused could easily be resolved. You simply choose not to do so. Crocodile tears are unbecoming.

Tebbit.

When I informed Margaret Thatcher she wrote to me a similar letter.

Ahead of the 10 March deadline the atmosphere could not have been worse. As the day approached it became increasingly clear that, despite concerted efforts by both British and Irish governments, there would be no movement from either side. So rather than go ahead and set up and launch an executive government with nobody in it, I announced on 8 March that the deadline would be moved back to 2 April – Good Friday, the first anniversary of the Agreement. I was assailed on both sides, with David Trimble saying I had let Sinn Fein off the hook and should have kept the pressure on the IRA to the last minute, and Sinn Fein saying I had let Trimble off the hook and should have forced him to keep his people out of the government.

I took a deep breath and kept going. In fact, at the end of that week, I flew to London to record my *Desert Island Discs* for BBC Radio Four, which was fun and a great honour. I chose my records not just so I sounded good – they were actually ones I listen to. I stuck with my favourite singers, but with Tom Lehrer I changed my first choice from 'Vatican Rag', which given its anti-Catholic content I thought was too controversial, to 'National Brotherhood Week'. I also chose Rod Stewart's 'Blondes Have More Fun', Flanders and Swann's 'A Transport of Delight', a good boogie number from Michael Jackson, 'Don't

Blame It on the Moonlight', and two other favourites, John
Lennon's 'Working-Class Hero' and Cole Porter's 'Don't Fence
Me In'.

By then we were into March and the focus shifted abruptly
to the US for the celebrations around St Patrick's Day on the
17th. It was not a good trip. All seemed okay when I left London
for Washington on Monday the 15th. But by the time I arrived
seven hours later I learnt that a car bomb had exploded in
Lurgan, County Armagh, killing a prominent human rights
lawyer called Rosemary Nelson, who had defended many nationalist and republican suspects. A renegade loyalist group claimed
responsibility for the attack, but there were immediate calls
for a public inquiry, and allegations of collusion aimed at the
RUC.

Straight away in Washington I ran into meetings with human-
rights groups asking me for information and action. Talking to
people back home, we quickly agreed with Ronnie Flanagan
that putting an officer from outside the RUC in charge of the
investigation would help, especially with any witnesses from the
nationalist side who were unwilling to talk to the RUC. That
much I could say to folk in the US to help allay concerns. But
I was in no position then to make any judgements about wider
inquiries while a proper police investigation was under way. I
didn't get a chance to say to anyone that, although Rosemary
had been pushy and difficult, I had respected her and quite liked
her, but because of her combative style she was disliked by many
in the establishment including civil servants, the legal profession
and the police, and anyway her supporters would not have
understood what I was trying to say.

On St Patrick's Day, at the White House party, President
Clinton spoke, urging N. Ireland's party leaders to lift their sights
above short-term difficulties. As usual there was music and the
drinks flowed, but it was an awful night. There were reports of
serious rioting taking place in nationalist areas of Portadown,
including one report saying that Garvaghy Road spokesperson

Breandan MacCionnaith had been seriously injured by the police. We also learned that there had been a killing of a loyalist, Frankie Curry, but details were patchy and it wasn't clear whether this was revenge for Rosemary Nelson's murder. I was anxious and impatient to know what was really happening. Suddenly all the goings-on in Washington seemed a farce and I agreed with my officials that we should cancel the New York leg of our trip and return home. The pressure was getting to everybody.

Back in Belfast, as the end of March approached, we were rapidly running out of time for resolving the devolution and decommissioning problems by the 2 April deadline. It was decided to go for another few days of intensive talks to see if the stalemate could be broken. The last week of March saw all the parties encamped at Hillsborough with the two Prime Ministers holding court in Lady Grey's Room.

The Hillsborough staff could barely cope. We had to set up a makeshift bar and provide regular hot meals for all. At any one time most of the parties were there in large numbers. Sinn Fein held many of their meetings walking in the grounds, believing their rooms to be bugged. Each night we were besieged by anti-Agreement protesters massed outside the gates waving union jacks and hurling abuse at any one they saw inside or come out of the front door. The SDLP had to move rooms because their initial base was too near the front and their conversations were drowned out by the yelling and screaming whenever one of them was visible at the window. The protest was made all the more alarming by the positioning of a very bright searchlight behind the crowd which cast great shadows of their figures and their flags up on to the front of Hillsborough Castle. It was an eerie sight.

On Wednesday, 31 March, the talking went on through the night. David Trimble kept his entire Assembly party there and for a while around midnight there was an almost social atmosphere with people standing around chatting or playing cards while their party leaders filed in and out of the room to engage

with the two PMs. We faced a real dilemma over beds. Hillsborough is big, but not that big. In the end many sacrifices were
made. I remember Nigel giving up his bed to the UUs' Pauline
Armitage; Tony Blair gave up his (saying he would sleep in a
chair) to Ken Maginnis. I discovered Seamus Mallon napping
on the floor in front of the two thrones, where he had to stay
until I could find him a bed elsewhere. The atmosphere was
tired and tense, but the talks were more good-natured than any
of the press reports would have you believe. I remember that
Fred and a couple of his schoolmates were staying there for the
Easter holiday. They were fascinated by all the toings and froings
and kept up a running report to Jon about what was going on.

The all-night session finally produced an outcome – or at least
an outcome that the two governments could accept. In what
was to form a pattern for the future, the two Prime Ministers
produced their best guess at what they thought could succeed
and presented it to the parties to go away and make their own
judgements on. The Hillsborough Declaration, as it was called,
proposed establishing an executive government to be followed
within a month by an 'act of reconciliation' involving all sides.
What this would mean precisely for each party was not spelled
out in detail, but essentially it meant some paramilitary decommissioning on both sides and some kind of symbolic act by us,
the Brits. Ideas around for the latter included making a sculpture
out of the iron legs of a watchtower or some other piece of
British military paraphernalia. It was thought by the Irish that
this would be sufficient to convince the IRA that what they
were doing in terms of decommissioning was not an act of
surrender but a shared moment of reconciliation on both sides.
In fact it posed difficulties for us all – including the loyalists
who opposed the Declaration, partly because they had not been
included in the final discussions on it. Tony and Bertie
announced the Declaration as 'a basis for agreement' to the
world's press assembled on the Hillsborough lawn. Sinn Fein
said nothing. But there was an understanding that they would

go away and consult their membership – with a clear expectation that they would support the deal.

Two days later, in his Easter Sunday address, Gerry Adams said that the Hillsborough Declaration 'may have merit, but it may also be counterproductive if it amounts to an ultimatum to armed groups'. But further indications over the Bank holiday suggested that Sinn Fein were not on board. By the Wednesday, Martin McGuinness made clear that the IRA would not accept decommissioning as a condition to his party's entry into a power-sharing executive in N. Ireland, even in the context of an 'act of reconciliation'.

After all the effort, energy and ingenuity, it was back to the drawing board. But the late-night sessions at Hillsborough left a bitter feeling among the talks parties. Getting together with them the following week, the acrimony flying round the table was vicious. Some people – especially the loyalists – felt excluded from the key discussions. They opposed the Declaration too and 'would have bloody well told the two Prime Ministers that, if they'd been asked, and saved us all a lot of bother'. I felt I had let people down. Despite all my efforts to include everyone and keep them up to speed with what was going on, in the end the process had come down to a three-way conversation between the Prime Ministers and two parties – Sinn Fein and the UUP. I resolved to try to maintain the kind of approach of the original talks which had produced the Agreement the year before. But with no independent chair and two Prime Ministers having limited time it was not going to be easy.

On top of all this, Jon lost his job in April. At the time it was incomprehensible to Jon. He had worked hard to develop business for his bank in the Middle East, and had done so successfully. But he coped with the redundancy amazingly well. He was up and down for a couple of weeks but soon began to focus on different things – a novel, painting, alternative work – and his friends were very supportive, taking him out and doing all they could to help him find something else. He said he wanted to leave full-time work and would look at different part-time options and grab anything he wanted with both hands. I tried to spend more time at home to be available if he wanted to talk. He did very well after twenty-plus years in full-time work. He looked fitter than he had for some time. Both mums would have been happy if they had seen him. And I loved his longer hair! The first weekend after Jon lost his job we went down into the Republic for a weekend off. Despite everything, we had a good break.

Back in London a week or so later, the next round of talks began – with long sessions at No. 10 Downing Street. New proposals emerged which would this time see N. Ireland's government set up, in conjunction with a positive report on decommissioning by John de Chastelain's commission. But it was not a runner: the UUP quickly said they couldn't buy into it, although I know that when David Trimble left Downing Street on 14 May Tony sincerely thought he was on board. When it turned out he was not, I saw the first flash of real annoyance from Tony. The result was a story in the press saying that Tony was 'disappointed' with David Trimble. I don't know exactly what passed between the two men in private, nor what was agreed, but in the eyes of his colleagues the quite hostile outcome made David look a bit foolish and taken in by Tony, which did the UUP leader quite a bit of harm at the time.

The other result of Tony's growing sense of urgency was his announcement of an 'absolute' deadline of 30 June 1999 to resolve the outstanding problems and get the Assembly up and running. He and Bertie Ahern subsequently announced that there would be a series of intensive talks ahead of that date, and that there would be serious consequences for the Agreement if the deadline was not met.

Before that we had another hurdle to get over, the European Parliamentary elections. Although these were very low key across the rest of the UK – which resulted in a very low turnout of voters – in N. Ireland they were another test of strength between the pro- and anti-Agreement parties. The UUP cause was not helped by the leadership virtually disowning their own candidate, Jim Nicholson, amid allegations that he had had an affair. As a consequence, when the election came, their vote slipped back, while Paisley topped the poll once more. The night of the election (10 June) I had a goodbye dinner with Alan and Janet Quilley, who were retiring from life in Belfast. I would be very sad to see them go.

With the Euro-election over, the discussions resumed in Belfast. The existence of an 'absolute deadline' caused a general rumble of dissent around the parties – and among some of the officials. We kept setting deadlines to try to concentrate minds and make progress. But there was a growing feeling, as each one passed without agreement, that people were losing faith in them. One thing I was absolutely sure of: I had, under the Agreement, an obligation to press the button to form the executive at some point. People kept saying that my unwillingness to do this, and take the process to the brink, was giving one or other side an easy way out each time a deadline passed. So this time I was determined to do it. At least then no one could say that the UK government was not honouring the commitments it had made under the Agreement.

The next weekend at Hillsborough, we had Jon's parents, Liz and John, with us. There were also surprise visitors in the form of the comedian Pat Kielty, his girlfriend Amanda from the *Big Breakfast*, and their friend Uncle Eugene. Eugene was a wonderfully funny American who was also a member of the US special branch. He kept everyone amused. On Sunday the comedian Eddie Izzard turned up for lunch. We had invited him to visit us for a meal if he had a moment when he was in Belfast performing. He came with two friends and we had a long discussion over lunch about Europe. He argued passionately that co-operation in Europe and more broadly in the world was going to be necessary if any solutions to some of the serious problems we face are to be found. Some of the more interesting political discussions I had when in government were with comedians or people from the music world. They bring to a discussion a different perspective. Listening to people like Mick Hucknall on what the Labour government should do next or Graham Norton on why the youth are disaffected helped keep me informed and in touch with different worlds.

Monday morning, 28 June, we were prepared for a 'final push' to end the impasse. The parties had been making their positions clear over the weekend, ahead of the intensive negotiations. On the *Frost Programme* on Sunday, David Trimble issued a challenge to Sinn Fein to get a pledge from the IRA to disarm by May 2000. Seamus Mallon said that Trimble's challenge was an indication that the UUP were not expecting their demand – for decommissioning to happen prior to the new government being set up – to be met. On another programme, Martin McGuinness said once again that he could not speak on behalf of the IRA.

Tony Blair and Bertie Ahern flew in to Belfast. Opposition from some of the parties to the kind of hothouse environment there had been at Hillsborough meant that we held all the talks up on the Stormont Estate. This was not ideal because it meant ferrying people, including the two PMs, from buildings on one side of the estate to another. But it was important for some of the party leaders that the talks were seen to come to them rather than the other way around. But, for ease, we all ended up at Castle Buildings (where the Good Friday Agreement had been signed).

The talks were difficult and tortuous. I was very worried; the atmosphere was not good. But both governments continued to give upbeat assessments throughout. This is a usual tactic, which helps to keep a little pressure on the parties, who are all desperate not to be seen as the ones stopping progress being made. We were getting somewhere, but it was still all words and nuances. With the unionists still insisting on what David Trimble called a 'credible start to the process of decommissioning' and the

IRA's public position remaining 'no decommissioning' we were clearly going to get nowhere. But then a chink of light appeared. In talks with the republicans and from our own sources of information we began to understand that the mindset was shifting. We began to sense that there could be progress on decommissioning away from the absolutist stance the IRA had taken at Easter. And while there was nothing we could immediately point to, no clear public statement, let alone action, nevertheless Tony Blair and Bertie Ahern both felt justified in calling it a 'seismic shift' in the position on weapons.

Yet, despite that, the 'absolute' deadline of 30 June came and went. The talking continued. On Friday (2 July) after five solid days of discussions we announced a new proposal from the two governments, which we called the 'Way Forward'. At the same time the Independent Commission produced a report setting out what they considered a credible start to the beginning of the process of decommissioning, and referring to Sinn Fein's 1 July statement that said 'all of us, as participants acting in good faith, could succeed in persuading those with arms to decommission them in accordance with the Agreement'.

Between them, the 'Way Forward' paper and the de Chastelain report gave us something to go on. Tony promised to introduce legislation in Parliament so that if the new government was set up in N. Ireland it could be suspended if the Independent Commission reported at any time that sufficient progress on weapons was not being made. This was an attempt to provide the unionists with a failsafe so that if, contrary to their agreed party position, they did go into government with Sinn Fein ahead of decommissioning starting, they were guaranteed a blame-free get-out if it didn't start very soon. Neither side rejected the proposals at the beginning. But, as the days passed and the legislation was debated in Parliament, it became clear that the Ulster Unionists were deeply divided on whether or not to accept them. There were also rumblings on the Sinn Fein side about the failsafe being outside the terms of the Agreement.

We put our energies into the business of persuading all sides not only that this was a fair way forward and in line with the Agreement but also that it was the only way forward. Articles were drafted and placed in newspapers in the Prime Minister's name. The word on the street was that the IRA was preparing to engage with de Chastelain for the first time. The UUP were still seeking further reassurances but not saying yes or no. The tension at this time was extraordinary: the anticipation of the parties' final responses; the backdrop of violence and disruption over Drumcree '99 (although much less than the year before); and, on top of all that, it was being said that the unionists were demanding my head as the price for accepting the deal.

By July the main point of interest in the media was the impending cabinet reshuffle. The papers were full of speculation about what was going to happen. Bruce Anderson in the *Spectator* and Peter Oborne in the *Express* were both calling for my resignation. The month before, Trimble had come out in public suggesting I should resign or be moved from N. Ireland. He had indicated that Peter Mandelson was a man with whom he could do business. Tony had already been talking to me about moving on when he was over at Hillsborough in late June and was keen to persuade me to go for the London Mayor. If I didn't want that, what about being party Chair, the role Charles Clarke (MP for Norwich South) subsequently took? I made it clear that I wanted to stay, as there was still a lot to be done in N. Ireland, and I wanted to see it through. If I had to be moved, I would be interested in something with a foreign aspect to it.

Soon after this, on Sunday, 4 July, there was more press speculation, with it now being suggested that I would be going to Health, and that Frank Dobson, who held the Health portfolio then, would resign and fight for the London Mayor. This was picked up again in the dailies, particularly *The Times* and the *Telegraph*, the following week.

On Wednesday, 14 July, the Ulster Unionists finally announced that they could not support the 'Way Forward' and would not participate even if the appointment of ministers in N. Ireland went ahead, as I said it must. The result was a moment of high drama and high farce. On the day the new N. Ireland government was due to be formed, the Ulster Unionists didn't turn up at all to take their seats in the Assembly. So once the process of appointment was concluded, we had, for a brief moment, a N. Ireland government composed entirely of nationalists, republicans and the Alliance party. I quickly moved – as I had told the parties I would – to disband the new administration on the grounds that it did not have the necessary cross-community support. Despite my and others' efforts to dissuade him, Seamus Mallon resigned at that point as Deputy First Minister. His patience had come to an end. In an at times angry resignation speech, he accused the UUP of using the crisis to try to 'bleed more concessions out of the governments', of 'dishonouring the Agreement' and of 'insulting its very principles'.

We now had no choice but to evoke a clause under the Agreement to hold a formal review of its implementation – or rather the lack of it. I wanted George Mitchell to come back to conduct the review. It seemed only right, and he remained one of the few people to command respect across the board among the N. Ireland leaders. George was quickly invited to take part in a summit meeting on the peace process between the Taoiseach and the British Prime Minister. At first George was not keen. He had been enjoying his time at home in the US with his young son Andrew. Tony Blair and Bertie Ahern made personal appeals to him; I pleaded with him. He wanted assurances that the review would not drag on and that we would allow him to set it up and stick to a strict deadline for its completion. It was a small price to pay, and eventually he agreed.

Speculation about my position had abated slightly until Saturday, 17 July, when the papers were full of stories that Peter Mandelson was going to be made N. Ireland Secretary, and that I would be given the role of Cabinet Enforcer. It was clear to me that Peter was up to his old tricks. I was asked by an Irish journalist if I wanted to stay in N. Ireland and I said yes. I was angry at what Peter was doing, but I knew I would make matters worse if I said so in public. In my opinion, Peter cared first for himself and only second for the government and what it was trying to do in N. Ireland.

On the Monday I was campaigning in the Eddisbury by-election. That morning the headline in the *Irish News* had been 'Mowlam Fights to Stay on in Stormont'. This led inevitably to me being asked by the journalists in Eddisbury if I wanted to stay as Secretary of State for N. Ireland. I answered that I did, but that as always it was a decision for the Prime Minister. This was viewed as me making it difficult for the Prime Minister to move me. Believe it or not, in my head I believed there was nothing wrong with me having a different view from the Prime Minister. The press immediately got hold of my comments and played them up, so it was very difficult for Tony to do anything other than let me stay. I wanted to continue with the job and saw no harm in saying so, especially when Peter had been so obviously campaigning for my job in the press.

Later that same day I had a prearranged meeting with Tony. I went into No. 10 and said to him what I had said to the press. Throughout my time in government I had tried not to make life tough for Tony. I thought he was doing a good job. I felt justified in saying something in view of what the papers were writing about me. I tried to be helpful and suggested that Peter could be my deputy, if Paul went as Secretary of State to Wales, and could take over from me in six months. I just wanted a little more time to see if I could make progress. He was polite as always – I still assumed we were friends. But Tony did not buy this idea. He wanted me to take a big spending department, such as Education or Health. He also made much of how important I would be at the election. He denied that the stories about me had come from No. 10, and there was no way I was going to be made Enforcer. I again reiterated my interest in matters foreign, but if this was not possible I would go on the backbenches. I felt that going to a big spending department would be like going out of the frying pan into the fire. The meeting ended inconclusively.

Just after I got home the phone rang. It was Peter Mandelson, very distraught, claiming that I had been co-ordinating a press campaign to harm him. We rowed, and I put the phone down on him. I learnt later – from a book written by the journalist Don McIntyre – that No. 10 were trying to work out how to get me out so that Peter Mandelson could have the job. When I refused, Mandelson is quoted in Don's book as saying it was probably no bad thing as I was probably too popular to move at that time – best not to put him in as it was only six months since he had left the Department of Trade and Industry.

On the TV on the morning of Sunday, 25 July Tony Blair talked about the problems in N. Ireland and about the importance of trust. I can remember watching, thinking that if Tony would only trust Ministers and let them do their jobs government would be much better. My position was not helped (although it helped my spirits) when Martin Mansergh, a top Irish official and adviser to Bertie Ahern, let it be known that the Irish would be unhappy if I was moved. If you wanted to be negative you could interpret this as indicating that I was too close to the Irish. But I always believed, and history has shown, that progress in N. Ireland is only really made when the British and the Irish work together. If we are split, then progress slows down or stops.

Partly to get away from all this nonsense, but mainly to brief the US administration on what was happening, I made a short visit over to the US. There was some discussion about whether it was wise for me to go, but I think I was right to. The disappointment in the US about the lack of progress on parts of the Agreement was almost stronger than in the UK or Ireland. It was read by many in Irish America as the beginning of the unravelling of the peace process. There was heavy blame on David Trimble. As ever the Sinn Fein network had got its side of the story out long before anyone else. Martin McGuinness had been in Washington the week before. Despite having set up an office in Washington, the unionists had a much steeper hill to climb.

I wanted to make sure people had the full picture, not one side of it. But I soon ran into a strong feeling in the US that I was leaving the job. People were listening to what I had to say but maybe beginning to think that I was on my way out so they really needed to talk to the person who was going to replace me. That's how easily all the speculation can undermine you. I had lunch in Manhattan with three good friends of mine, Tom Moran, Bill Flynn and Loretta Glucksman, where they made me feel like one of the family – I learnt afterwards that they too thought I was moving on. I also saw Hillary Clinton, who was thinking hard then about whether to run for the New York seat in the Senate. We talked about the enormity of the task ahead of her. We had part of our chat in the pool in the White House grounds where we had a swim in between chatting. But I was confident she had what it took to win and told her so. I wished her the best of luck and gave her a big hug.

IO
Squaring the Circle

Back in Belfast over the summer I just tried to get on with the job – a job that press reports were saying I was not up to. There were suggestions that my health problems had continued. There were also suggestions that I was not a good Minister, and once again it was claimed that I didn't read my briefs from civil servants. I knew this to be untrue because reading them, after the first five pages or so, I often found repetition of basic facts taken from earlier briefings. The final frequent criticism was that I was disliked by the unionists and David Trimble wanted rid of me. It is true we had periods of not getting on but, quite simply put, he did not like all that I was trying to achieve and the easiest way not to move forward was to say I was unworkable with. I wasn't, and, outside of the meetings, many of the more mainstream unionists and I passed the time quite amicably.

I had been there a couple of years and did not think I was doing a bad job. I was slowly making progress. Yes, I was not a typical Minister; yes, some of the unionists found me difficult, as did some colleagues, partly because I was unconventional, partly because I was successful, partly because I was a woman. But that was life. It was after I made it clear that I did not want to move that the counter-briefing against me in the press got worse. I could live with it – you have to as a politician – but what made life impossible was that it was undermining my ability to do the job in N. Ireland. With there being suggestions that I did not have the support of No. 10 – that Jonathan Powell was the person to see if you wanted the Prime Minister to know what you were thinking on N. Ireland issues – my position was becoming unsustainable. Announcements made without me being included, and at times not even being told, made my position even worse. I kept telling myself that I was being treated no better or worse than other Ministers, and on one level that was true. There was not much inclusivity for any Minister, unless you were Jack Straw or Derry Irvine or Gordon Brown.

Jon and I left for our planned summer holiday on the understanding that everything was sorted. Reading the press on our return, my departure had been reported as if I had simply refused to move and had then gone on holiday. The *Sun* banner headline read, 'Mo does a runner'. The press reports were not true, but it did look like I was being a bit independent and bolshie – and in fact that's how I felt. I had said I would call Tony a couple of days into my holiday to find out who my new Ministers were.

We had a great holiday in Turkey. For years we had gone to Greece, but we thought we would give Turkey a try. It lacks the simplicity and warmth of Greece but it was a relaxing holiday nonetheless. We stayed in a wee cottage in the hills above Bodrum, Mulberry Cottage, attached to the main building. The English owners, Michael and Shirley, were very kind to us. They used to get the *Sun* in Turkey and they knew that there was a £10,000 reward if the *Sun* were told where we were. A tribute to their integrity, they did not grass on us, and they did not tell us about the reward. The holiday was spent sleeping, reading, eating and drinking a little. Drink was not high on the agenda as we ate every night in one of the surrounding villages of Turgeish, Torbah or Gummerslick and that meant one of us had to drive. We both came back very healthy.

I remember years ago some Japanese friends in Britain seeing people eating fish and chips out of newspaper and commenting on how poor some people were. A similar cross-cultural misunderstanding happened to Jon and me in Turkey. We saw police with guns entering a villa through a ground-floor window and blocking off the drive with their vans. We assumed it was a raid. Next time we went down the same road they were still there. We soon realized that it was the local police station. They had obviously just locked themselves out.

On our return from holiday I phoned the editor of the *Sun* to claim the £10,000 reward. I had seen myself and knew where I had been on holiday. The editor said it was too late to claim. But I had had a good rest and was looking forward to getting started again. All parties welcomed me back, despite all the rubbish in the press. The parties were all complaining that nothing was happening!

In the eyes of No. 10 little had changed. I had messed up the intended cabinet reshuffle in July and not been willing to go for London Mayor. Before Tony had spoken to me about it I had actually considered it as an option. But I knew I didn't want to leave N. Ireland, although now I was increasingly realizing that my position had been made untenable – I had been undermined to the point that even if Tony had decided to keep me there the counter-briefing had made it impossible for me to do the job. But I was very fed up and depressed at having to leave the job. If people felt that I was harming the chances to move the process forward I would have gone willingly. But I did not think this was the case. My view was yes, the unionists were calling for me to be removed from the job, but the other side had a couple of months before done exactly the same thing. I believe you are not doing the job if you are liked all the time. Many of my predecessors were deeply disliked by one side or the other, but they were left in post to keep pushing ahead.

I had known from the beginning that a major part of my job was to get Sinn Fein to come to the table and put a halt to the constant violence. Then with Sinn Fein in the talks and the violence limited to the extremes on both sides, I needed to keep the unionists in the process without losing the republicans and nationalists all over again. It was never an easy task. What those in the unionist party who objected to the pace of change or the changes, or both, wanted was to try and slow things down. If they could argue and get another person as Secretary of State then they could start the delaying games all over again. Obviously if Sinn Fein thought the process was going against them they would have developed techniques to slow it down too. But the problem for the last thirty years had been to get Sinn Fein to the table in the first place.

In conversations with Tony in the early autumn we discussed a number of options for me. We both tried to be helpful – the meetings were amicable. We talked about the Secretary General of NATO becoming free and it was the United Kingdom's turn. I'd heard this already and said I was hoping that Robin Cook or George Robertson would take it. I understood and accepted that I was not skilled enough to apply for the NATO job and hoped that either Robin or George going would open up other possibilities. What I really wanted was Foreign Secretary, but after discussions I accepted that I needed more experience in government. But then I proposed that if George or Robin went to NATO then Secretary of State for Defence would be open, a job I would like a go at and that would put me in a good place to try later on in my political career for Foreign Secretary. I knew the top brass would not automatically reject me because I had met a fair number of generals in N. Ireland and had worked well with them. Tony indicated it was not on the cards. He wanted to give me Health. My reasons for saying no were the same as earlier in the summer. I had just done a tough job and did not want to go to an equally difficult one. It was going to be very hard to get results in the NHS after the destruction of the Thatcher years.

By now things were getting a little tricky. Tony kept describing me as a friend. I didn't mention it, but if I was he didn't need to keep saying so. He started arguing it was my duty to him as the Prime Minister, to the party and to the country to do what he wanted to enable Labour to get a second term. The trouble was that these arguments no longer had any effect. I was feeling that I was being treated as a girlie – popular as a female commodity who would be useful with the electorate. I no longer

"BUT I DON'T WANT TO GO TO A BALL, I LIKE IT HERE."

felt like I was a comrade-in-arms fighting for the same causes. If it would help I offered to leave government or spend more time with my family. I wasn't being melodramatic, I was just sick of how the leadership were treating people who were in the party or in the unions and I did not like the elitist way that the government was being run. I still believed in the fundamentals of new Labour, the pledges we had set ourselves, but I disagreed with how they were being delivered. Why treat the unions in such a dismissive way when they had helped get us into government and when they were aware themselves that modernization of the union movement was a necessity? Why treat the Parliamentary Labour party in such a dismissive fashion when they had worked for years to achieve this Labour government? I was beginning to feel like a bag of potatoes that they just wanted to dump somewhere so Peter Mandelson could go to N. Ireland.

No one doubted that the Labour party had needed reform. Under the leadership of Neil Kinnock a great deal of work on party reform had taken place. If he hadn't put in the work on internal changes and the driving out of Militant, there would not have been a new Labour government. What I think was difficult was Tony's attitude of how he knows best, and he will prove that he is right. It may have worked at the beginning – people then were so determined not to rock the boat that they went along with him. The sad thing is that we were beginning to make a difference to people's lives with some of our policies and I saw no reason why we couldn't take more people with us along the road to change. Yes, not everyone wanted to go that route, but most would have done so, and more happily, if they had been included and not just told what to do. If a more inclusive and tolerant strategy had been followed, then the unhappiness and unrest in the party and in the unions could have been dealt with and not just left to fester.

I have never lost faith in my socialism. I welcomed new Labour as a way to stick with my principles but change the way we achieve what we want, to a way that takes into account the changes that have taken and are taking place around us. I am not by nature a negative person, I always look on the bright side – one of my characteristics that helped to produce results in N. Ireland. But ever since the campaign for Tony for leader I had felt there was an inner core in the Labour party which was not necessarily part of the cabinet or the party machinery. Nothing formal, but it was there. It was there during the leadership campaign. People like me, Adam Ingram, Peter Kilfoyle and Alun Michael doing the slog work, with Jack Straw seen as the campaign manager for getting voters from the constituency parties round the country and the PLP. But there was also an inner campaign – which I knew about – sorting out strategy, handling criticisms and getting Tony and Labour into power after eighteen years – though I didn't know at the time that this would be the way that government was going to be run too.

I had talked some of this through with Jon on holiday. I always listened to his views but remembered that he was further to the left than the government. He was not a believer in new

Labour and therefore I had to factor in his opposition alongside his wanting the best for me. We talked a lot. At the end I was clear in my support for the Labour government, but equally clear that I was deeply disillusioned by how the government was acting. Jon would have supported me in whatever decision I reached. I sometimes think he would have been happy if I had gone for leader, but in my head that option had never been on the cards.

In between the talks and other meetings I kept up the visits around N. Ireland to reassure people that life and the talks were going on as people hoped. I opened (about a year late) the building and business of a unique company called Forward Emphasis Ltd. I liked it because it was a company that made business work for people. It was staffed by volunteers who operated a call centre to raise funds for charities; they could have been paid, which would have made it a commercial business, but to maximize the take for the charities they worked for nothing. I also launched a new small fast speedboat, the RV *Capitella*, for the Department of Economic Development's Industrial Research and Technology Unit to monitor pollution. I drove it round Bangor Harbour, which was great fun. In addition I presented an Investors in People award to a high-tech IT company, MSC Northern Ireland Ltd. I always doubted the value of these awards, but seeing the effect on the workforce and the management, I had to revise my view.

In my effort to get round most of N. Ireland I had not yet made it to Rathlin Island, just off the north-east coast, so I decided it was time to go. First stop on the way was Ballycastle Police Station on the mainland. It was a really friendly station, so different from police stations I had visited anywhere else in the UK – lots of tea and scones and only two policemen. The big fat Inspector introduced me to the cook, who had come from an outside company to make the tea and scones. The two female traffic wardens were there and apologized for Jenny the cleaner who was too shy to meet me. I was made to feel so welcome I didn't want to leave. I had to explain to Carmel Crystal, who was with me from *Reader's Digest*, that this was not the norm for police stations.

We then took the ferry to the island. At the first house we visited Father McAteer, eighty years old, sitting in the corner. He was a much calmer version of Father Ted. He seemed to be the elder statesman of the island – everyone was very respectful towards him. He organized all the schoolchildren in his parish to play musical instruments or sing. Of those there to greet us three played instruments and the others sang. We visited the Heritage Centre and the old boat house and of course the bar, where we met the eldest resident, a very sprightly eighty-four-year-old Annie. The opening hours are continental, i.e. open all the time. Fred, who came with me, hasn't forgotten the visit – it was so friendly and different from other experiences he had had; he was even asked for his autograph. He also came away with a large brass nail and a funny-shaped old bottle brought up from one of the many wrecks round the island and given to him by one of the residents. They are still in his bedroom today. We had a very enjoyable day out. As I left I hoped the peace and tranquillity that the people there enjoyed would last as long as they did!

While I never stopped enjoying the many opportunities as N. Ireland Secretary to get out and talk to people about the changes in their lives and try to allay their concerns about developments in the peace process, other aspects of the job held only difficulty and anxiety. Often I was called upon to make extraordinarily difficult judgements about issues that caused pain and anguish on all sides. One such case that summer was over the murder of a twenty-two-year-old Belfast taxi driver, Charles Bennett. When his body was found in an alleyway off the Falls Road in West Belfast at the end of July, there were immediate allegations of IRA involvement. I had to study what evidence there was – none of which could most likely be made public or used in court – and make an overall judgement on whether or not this meant an end to the IRA ceasefire. Under the law, if I decided that the ceasefire was at an end, then the prisoner releases had to stop and action be taken against Sinn Fein. It was a tough call. I couldn't say honestly that I thought the ceasefire had broken down. But at the same time I couldn't accept the paramilitaries' definition of a ceasefire which didn't see killings of people on their 'own side', as it were, as a problem. The options open to me were very limited. With the peace process on tenterhooks, the unionists were desperate, along with their supporters in England, to exclude Sinn Fein from the Mitchell review. I was under so much pressure, the easiest option of all would have been to say, 'Okay, a killing has taken place, I can't prove it was the IRA, but enough people say it is so it must be, so the ceasefire is over and Sinn Fein are out.' For a day or two I would have been lauded by most of the British press, with only a few able, hand on heart, to criticize me. But then, a week or a month later, with the peace process going nowhere while everyone waited for Sinn Fein to get back on board – which they would have done unless, after my action, the ceasefire really did break down – where would a day of good feeling and good press for me have got us? Nowhere.

No, I had to tough it out. I stood in front of the cameras in a packed room at the offices of the new Equality Commission in Belfast, where I happened to be visiting that day, and said, 'Although the situation in relation to the IRA is deeply worrying, I do not believe that there is a sufficient basis to conclude that the IRA ceasefire has broken down. Nor do I believe that it is disintegrating, or that these recent events represent a decision by the organization to return to violence. But I want to make clear that I have come very close to judging that the IRA's ceasefire is no longer for real. I will therefore be keeping their position under close review, and will not hesitate to act decisively where I consider that their or any other ceasefire has broken down.'

I wanted to warn the republicans that they were sailing too

close to the wind and that I couldn't accept any further acts like this. I firmly believed that what I had said was true and that eventually most people would accept that. But it was an uncomfortable day – my detractors were many, and there were few who came out to back my decision. The unionists supported immediate court action against my decision – but it failed, without any of the newspapers taking any notice, a few weeks later.

Next on the agenda was the launch of Chris Patten's report into policing in N. Ireland. Studying the early copy we had been sent, I saw that it was a good and thorough report drawn up after wide consultations across the communities, learning from international comparisons, and from Chris Patten's own wide personal experience in N. Ireland as a minister from 1983–5. It avoided the two extremes that were on the table, to disband the RUC or to argue for minimal change. And it addressed two particular concerns I had about the position of the RUC reservists and the older members of the force. As with many problems, money and an understanding of what people had been through were two major ingredients to the report and to its implementation. There were proposals for more money for compensation, for training and for restructuring the service and for a new police college.

I felt very strongly about the Patten Report. Reform of the RUC was an integral part of the Good Friday Agreement. Change was crucial if long-term progress was ever to be made in N. Ireland. A police force that represented the whole community was essential if it was going to be able to serve all the people across N. Ireland. Change was only possible with acknowledgement of some of the progress already made and a proper recognition that the RUC had struggled against the paramilitaries on both sides, in the process losing over 300 brave officers and seeing more than 9000 injured. But, like any change, work has to be done with the people who are going to experience the change before it is implemented. With prior consultation – as there was both before and after publication – implementation should be easier.

So, for me, responding to the Patten Report was less difficult. Chris's Commission was an independent body, set up as part of the Agreement, and it wasn't for me to start picking and choosing which of his conclusions I might like or dislike. I knew from the outset that I had to come out and say that, at least in principle, the government accepted the findings of the Patten Commission. I promised to consult further on the detail of the 175 recommendations, but I wasn't about to announce that all or any of the report's conclusions – which had difficult elements for both unionists and nationalists to accept – were up for renegotiation by me.

I knew that implementing the Patten Report was going to be far from easy. Many of the recommendations were practical and uncontroversial. But symbolic changes to the name of the force, the flying of the union jack and the changing of the badge were big changes for the RUC to handle – and at the same time important for the nationalist community if they were to have confidence in and participate in the police in the future. Real changes in crucial aspects like recruitment were also important to nationalists and republicans as signs that it would no longer be a Protestant- and unionist-dominated force. In the past it had been made worse by the IRA harassing and threatening Catholics who had tried to join the RUC. It was hoped that the Patten changes would make recruitment easier and life in the force a positive experience for Catholics.

The reactions to Patten were fairly predictable, with David Trimble calling it the 'shoddiest piece of work' he had seen in thirty years, and saying the recommendations on the RUC's name and symbols were 'gratuitously offensive'. Sinn Fein were more circumspect but reiterated that they had been seeking 'the disbandment of the RUC'. Only the SDLP welcomed the report in its totality and said that, if 'implemented faithfully and speedily, [it] contains the basis for the objectives of the Good Friday Agreement to be obtained'.

I was impressed with Chris's robust defence of his work. He

quoted the Agreement back to both sides and said he had done what he was asked to do: come up with proposals for a 'new approach' so that 'Northern Ireland has a police service that can enjoy widespread support from, and is seen as an integral part of, the community as a whole'. I was also impressed with Ronnie Flanagan's measured reaction, acknowledging the pain the report's proposals would cause among many of his officers and their families, but saying that the pain would be endured if it meant a new beginning for all. I left N. Ireland with a great deal of respect for Ronnie Flanagan.

I announced that the consultation date would be extended to November to give all sides a chance to reflect on the important changes being proposed, and to give our people time to draw up the necessary legislation. But I was left in no doubt that, despite the fact that criticism for the reforms would shift from Patten on to the British government for following them through, follow them through we must.

Back in London for meetings I spent an evening with my good friend Peter Kilfoyle. We had known each other in the party before we had both got into Parliament, meeting at party events and through the union we were both in, Unison. He was more fed up than I was. We had worked hard together to get Tony elected, Peter being the co-signatory with myself of Tony's nomination to stand as leader of the party. He was just devastated by how Tony was behaving towards him and how he was destroying the party. He kept saying Tony's come-uppance would come in a year or two. He later dealt with his disillusionment by giving up his ministerial job to allow him to speak out on issues important to Labour's core voters, particularly those in the heartlands of the English regions. That same evening the journalist Tony Bevins dropped round. His main contribution was to say that the feelings and views being expressed by Peter were shared by many other MPs he had talked to.

Peter's worrying conclusion for the future was that Gordon Brown was politically too close to Tony, Robin Cook was damaged and the only person with any credibility to challenge Blair was me. I said then, as I have said repeatedly, that I have never had any wish to be leader of the party or to be Prime Minister. Never wanted the job. Being an MP in the Commons, a constituency MP, a cabinet Minister, was more than enough. Having seen how hard Tony had to work for limited returns, how little quality time he got with his family, how vicious the press can be, how quickly he aged, I could see nothing attractive about it.

I relaxed at the weekend by going to the Simply Red concert in Belfast. We had a great time. Keith my security man had got tickets for the staff in the office, so we all danced together and relaxed. I have a wonderful picture in my head of Fred, aged twelve, dancing away with Jon dancing immediately behind him. Father and son without a doubt – I think genes and inherited behaviour are more important than I was taught at school.

The government reshuffle finally happened in early October, after party conference. I knew I would be moved. Frank Dobson resigned to stand for London Mayor; Jack Cunningham resigned from the Cabinet Office, and that's where I went. Peter Mandelson was bound for Belfast.

When Peter was appointed Secretary of State for N. Ireland, he asked if he and his partner Reinaldo could come and talk to me and Jon. He was interested in talking, but primarily the meeting was for Jon to talk to him and Reinaldo about what it was like being 'the wife' of the N. Ireland Secretary in N. Ireland. We dutifully had the two round for a drink. They were late – the reason Peter gave was a different one to the phone message which my security had received. A good honest start to the evening, I thought. Reinaldo was worried about how he would be received and treated. I reassured him that the staff at Hillsborough were fine, good people and would welcome him with no difficulty, as in the event they did. Jon's advice was succinct and to the point: the best thing to do is to stay out of the way. Whatever you say or do will be interpreted in a malign fashion by those who want to do so. At the end of the evening I said I was going over the next morning to Hillsborough to pick up my belongings – we could go at the same time and I would do the introductions. It was agreed and I did the business the next day. I felt I had done my best to facilitate a smooth change-over, though there were moments which I found difficult. I would not miss Hillsborough Castle, even though the grounds are beautiful and we had had some lovely times there as a family and some great parties, but I would miss the staff, particularly Olwyn who had become a good friend. Anyway I left Belfast with my goodies to start my new job in the Cabinet Office. That was the last I heard from Peter during his time in N. Ireland. I had served my purpose for him.

Leaving the people and the place was tough. But so was leaving the peace process so up in the air. I had every confidence in George Mitchell finding a way through, but I was concerned, as I had been over the signing of the Good Friday Agreement, that he wouldn't be left alone long enough to do the job. I saw George a few times before I flew out of Belfast. We had dinner once in his room at the Europa Hotel. Watching him there, tucking into what must have been the millionth hotel chicken dinner, I felt that he was making such a sacrifice in his personal life. I hoped he would succeed quickly and be able to get home to the US again soon.

Now I was watching developments from afar. As George's review continued it was clear that some progress was being made. The parties repaired to Winfield House, the residence of the American Ambassador in London, Philip Lader, for further talks. The eventual deal, which Mitchell thrashed out with the two governments' help, was not a million miles away from what had been on offer in July. If anything, I thought, it offered the unionists less than they had rejected in the summer. But the deal went through and the first ever cross-community government in N. Ireland was finally formed in December.

There were a few surprises in the new government, not least

of which was Sinn Fein's nomination of Martin McGuinness to become Education Minister. The reaction across much of the unionist community to the idea of the 'Godfather of Godfathers' – as Ken Maginnis had once called him – taking charge of their children's education was one of shock and outrage. Martin, after a week in the post, sounded and acted like a Minister who had been in government for years.

That first go at devolved government in N. Ireland was highly significant but very short-lived. Despite the fact that the IRA had, as part of the Mitchell deal, agreed to appoint someone to talk to the Decommissioning Commission, the problem of actually decommissioning the weapons did not go away. To convince his sceptical party to go into government before decommissioning began, David Trimble had given his UUP executive a post-dated letter of resignation. If the IRA didn't deliver by the date set for the first de Chastelain report (31 January 2000), then David's letter would take effect four days later. Progress was made in that short time by the IRA talking to de Chastelain, but it was not enough to save David, and Peter Mandelson unilaterally suspended the fledgling government after just seventy-two days. It was a very anxious time for the people of N. Ireland – especially after expectations had been raised and progress made. I was concerned for them, but I couldn't find it within myself to feel sorry for Peter. He had allowed himself to be filmed drinking champagne in the Department of Foreign Affairs in Dublin before Christmas, and was now finding out how easily and quickly triumph could turn to disaster in N. Ireland. It can and does change so quickly. Sinn Fein would be talking freely with you one minute and then you would take a position they found difficult and they would say your 'British unionism' was showing and get aggressive and leave. The same was true of the other side. Peter soon discovered that when he was outlining further work on the Patten proposals in the House of Commons and Ken Maginnis shouted at him, 'I'm not the betrayer.' What is needed at these difficult times is for Tony to step in with all the authority of the Prime Minister and help out. Tony had done this on numerous times during the negotiations since 1997, and I firmly believe that that level of commitment was crucial to the reaching of the Good Friday Agreement. He put more energy and commitment into N. Ireland than any previous Prime Minister. That was one reason why it was so hard to make progress in the summer before my departure, once people in the talks and the civil servants knew I no longer had his backing.

Our role as Brits in N. Ireland is a difficult one. We are clearly part of the reason why the problem exists. After all, we divided the island under Lloyd George when he was Prime Minister. Because the unionists and loyalists want to stay with the British, and fought as part of the UK in the Second World War, our affinities are closest to them, reinforced through continuing ties among the British establishment. But at the same time our role in the talks was to be arbiter, trying to find an agreement between two communities that both sides could live with. It was not an easy role. The best way to play it, I thought, was to remain shoulder to shoulder with the Irish government, balancing our closeness with unionists against their closeness to the nationalists and the republicans.

Suggestions that Tony Blair had had to step in only because I had lost unionist confidence were clearly wide of the mark as he and Bertie Ahern continued to be fully involved. There were long and tortuous negotiations again at Hillsborough and Stormont. In May 2000 major progress was made on decommissioning when the IRA undertook to open some of its arms dumps for inspection and said it was prepared to 'initiate a process that will completely and verifiably put IRA arms beyond use'. The two-year deadline for progress on decommissioning (which had now expired) was shifted a year to June 2001. David Trimble managed to win the vote he needed among the Ulster Unionist Council, and government was restored to N. Ireland. A process of inspection of IRA arms dumps was begun by the former General Secretary of the South African ANC Cyril Rama-phosa and the former Finnish President Martti Ahtisaari.

To my mind the rest of 2000 looked relatively secure in N. Ireland. My own focus shifted to my work in the Cabinet Office and my plans for the future. But I still kept a watchful eye on progress over the water. I saw that the progress on decom-missioning was painfully slow and that reforms of policing and security in N. Ireland were themselves not taking root as fast as some would like. But I also saw N. Ireland's new government Ministers doing good jobs, taking responsibility and earning respect; unemployment plunging to pre-1970 levels; N. Ireland growing economically faster than any other part of the UK; and my confidence for the future grew.

I also saw the downs: more violence again over Drumcree; David Trimble's party putting more and more pressure on him to act against Sinn Fein over decommissioning; Peter Mandelson's own career taking a nosedive with a second and surely final resignation from government because of his pur-ported involvement in the Hinduja passport application; sec-tarianism and bigotry continuing to rear their heads; internal feuding within loyalism causing more death and pain to families and friends; and bomb attacks by small but lethal renegade republican groups bringing occasional mayhem to the streets of London.

I was pleased when John Reid was made Secretary of State for N. Ireland in January 2001. I knew him from the days when we'd been in the group that supported Neil Kinnock for the party leadership. I was pleased because I knew he was a man of honesty and integrity. Like a number of good Ministers in the government who had been in the Communist party in their youth, he brought to the job strong beliefs as a socialist, a good dose of realism and a desire to see results. Having one Catholic and one Protestant parent and a strong personal supportive relationship, I thought he was the best person in the Parliamen-tary party for the job. He would never have an easy time of it.

Continuing tensions between the Ulster Unionists and Sinn Fein dogged the process. As the deadline for decommissioning loomed again in the summer of 2001 the matter was finally brought to a head. In the absence of actual weapons decommissioning by the IRA, David Trimble resigned as he had said he would, and the process was only saved by John stepping in to suspend the Assembly until a solution could be found. And so there were more talks – this time shifting to the neutral venue of a hotel in Weston Park in Shropshire – and more new proposals.

But it was clear that, in the end, the process could only continue if there was an actual act of decommissioning by the paramilitaries. David Trimble's position was becoming ever weaker – he could not rely on the loyalty of a few in his party – and a few was all it would take to unseat him. The announcement by the IRA on 23 October 2001 that they had made an 'unprecedented move . . . to save the peace process', swiftly followed by a statement from General de Chastelain that he and his fellow commissioners 'have now witnessed an event in which the IRA has put a quantity of arms completely beyond use', was hailed by all but the DUP as a tremendous breakthrough.

Why did they do it? Perhaps it was the pressure of world opinion, especially from America, where the terrible loss of life and destruction wrought by the terrorist attacks on New York of 11 September 2001 focused minds more clearly than ever on the unacceptability of violence as a political tool. Perhaps it was the republicans' own desire to be seen as the saviours of the peace process. Perhaps they made the realistic assessment that David Trimble had gone about as far as he could go and realized that if he were replaced by a more hardline successor it would be even more difficult to make progress. No doubt the proposals from the British government to scale back the security presence – removing some of those watchtowers in South Armagh (hated by local people, as from the towers soldiers could see into their homes), as well as making welcome progress on some of the thorny outstanding issues by inviting an independent judge to investigate allegations of collusion by security forces in the killings of Pat Finucane, Robert Hamill and Rosemary Nelson – helped move the debate on. Perhaps, too, the SDLP's groundbreaking decision to support the revised proposals for bringing in the Patten reforms on policing – Seamus Mallon's concerns having been more or less allayed – made a difference.

For all these reasons and many more, the decommissioning process was begun, and, limping and politically wounded, David Trimble became N. Ireland's First Minister once more. He was joined by the new SDLP leader Mark Durkan, as both John Hume and Seamus had decided to stand down after so many years of working for the peace and progress that had now perhaps, hopefully, finally come to the people of N. Ireland.

At least three external factors still concern me. Firstly, the change of presidency in the US. I paid an early visit to see the new US administration before the 2001 UK general election. I did not see George W. Bush, but I talked to his National Security Adviser, Condoleeza Rice, and to a number of the new officials. I said my bit, but got no real response, as I genuinely think they were uncertain then as to what their strategy was going to be. But it was clear that they were not going to get anywhere near as involved as President Clinton had been, and there is no doubt that his timely interventions were a great help. But in some ways – when I looked, for example, at the kind of military approach the Bush administration were taking in countries like Colombia – I could see that a position of 'not our problem' might be the least bad option for N. Ireland from this presidency.

I also remain concerned about the possible repercussions for N. Ireland from a sustained downturn in the world economy. As yet there are just signs of a possible recession and disagreement between economists over what the future holds. An economic downturn could create problems for the peace process. Hard times for Britain or the Republic would put further strains on the peace process.

The third issue to watch is what happens in the European

With George Mitchell after the Omagh bombing, September 1998

Waiting for news, Hillsborough, April 1999

Hillsborough Declaration, April 1999

Gerry Adams and his Sinn Fein team inside Castle Buildings as the midnight deadline approaches, June 1999

David Trimble and his Ulster Unionist team arriving at Castle Buildings, with the midnight deadline that evening, June 1999

Joke with Ronnie Flanagan at the end of a discussion on security

Goodbye party at the Gay Hussar, 2000

Meeting staff with Hillary Clinton at Hillsborough. Olwyn next to me

Discussions at Hillsborough with Tony Blair and Bill Clinton

RUC renamed,
November 2001

Decomissioning
discussions
continue

NOT AN OUNCE
NOT A BULLET

The watchtowers
that people living
near by and others
wanted dismantled

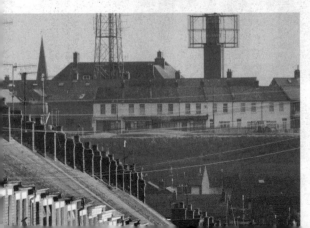

Dove House, Redcar: MIND'S Millennium Mural

Discussions in Colombia with armed forces about drugs

Honorary degree at the University of Teesside with my sister Jean
and my mum Tina

Union, in particular the introduction of the euro and how it affects Britain's role in relation to Europe. As I learnt during my time in N. Ireland, Europe and other European politicians have the potential as a higher level of authority to have a really positive effect on the future of the peace process. Prolonged strains and stresses would be less helpful. Europe, I think, also holds the key to stability in the future. As a level of government above the British and the Irish, it has the chance to help hold the changes in place.

In the end, the biggest influence on the success of the moves towards peace will be the actions and patience of all the people of N. Ireland. The British and Irish governments desperately want peace and the party leaders in N. Ireland need to remain committed and positive about the process. If they are serious about peace and they listen to the people, then lasting peace is possible. If the unionists can make the leap that peace will only come when power is truly shared and the republicans can accept that if real progress is made in the implementing of the Good Friday Agreement then weapons must be a thing of the past, the overwhelming desire for peace among the people of N. Ireland will carry it forward. This will be welcomed by all the other people around the world who care for the people on the island of Ireland.

I am often asked why such progress has been possible in N. Ireland when it proves so elusive elsewhere in the world. I have always been wary of drawing comparisons between N. Ireland and other areas of conflict because I think each conflict has its own peculiarities and origins and unique features. Also I don't know enough about other conflicts to make meaningful comparisons. Nevertheless there are some lessons that I learnt that helped move the process on that might just be helpful elsewhere.

1. *Inclusivity*

For me, 'including people' is one of the first and most important aspects of making any peace process work. Throughout the recent history of N. Ireland, certain groups always felt excluded from attempts to build a peaceful future. Now it is difficult, with such a history of violence, to accept and include people in the process who may themselves have been involved in or have orchestrated acts of violence. But, however difficult, however tough that might be, it is necessary. It is a very first step.

To help establish a ceasefire, we had to take a risk and talk to people. Once there was a commitment to a non-violent way forward, we had to build on it. Of course there had been ceasefires in the past and they had broken down. Just because one is announced doesn't mean it will last or that every single member of the group is committed to it. But over time, with serious engagement on all sides, it can be made to stick. Now there will always be those groups or elements within groups that want to go back to violence. We have those groups in N. Ireland still. There will always be elements in those groups who want to destroy the peace being built. But if they are small and the main groups are observing their ceasefires, then we can work to isolate the renegades.

2. *Trust and Confidence*

Another lesson I learnt is about confidence, which is essential to the process. Confidence makes the difference. Building confidence between the two sides in any conflict is immensely difficult, but is crucial. Every time a step is taken on one side it is important to ask, 'What is this doing to the other side?' What in N. Ireland we called confidence-building measures were a vital part of the jigsaw, as was keeping in touch with people so they knew what was happening. For example, after the Omagh bomb, I was amazed at how much the people did not want to go backwards –

a very positive sign. It followed a pattern. Every tragedy brought untold pain and suffering to families and communities, but the sombre mood across N. Ireland made people more determined that the peace process would work – the exact opposite to what the groups bombing wanted to achieve.

3. *Timing and Momentum*

Timing is key. It is important because confidence can be undermined overnight in a community without people even being aware of it. You need to keep momentum going. Whenever a vacuum is allowed to develop in the political process, you can be damn sure that the militarists will look to fill it with some atrocity or other. Even if you feel you are sometimes pushing people too far, too fast, if you let the pace slip the situation can quickly go backwards. Deadlines help. They give people something to focus on, but they have to be realistic and, if they are not kept to, over time people lose faith in them.

4. *Working Closely with Other Governments*

Another part of making a process succeed is working closely with others, particularly other governments. Over N. Ireland it is clear that throughout history, when Britain and Ireland have worked well together, progress has been achieved; when they have been divided, trouble has started. This was very clear during the summer of the Omagh tragedy, when both governments introduced anti-terrorist legislation – you couldn't put a fag paper between us. That was the best way: it made it harder to hide either side of the border. In our case, working closely with the US government was also important. Before Labour came to power in 1997, Irish republicans were winning the battle for hearts and minds among many of those who cared about Ireland in the US. Over time people like John Hume, who was respected and listened to, did a lot of good work persuading Americans (particularly Democrats) that there was an alternative way forward than through IRA violence. Tony Blair's good relationship with Bill Clinton put us on an entirely different footing. Slowly we made progress on two fronts. First, we convinced opinion-formers that there were two sides to the conflict – i.e. that the unionists had a viable case too. And secondly we showed that the British government were not anti the nationalists, that we were against the violence whether it was republican or loyalist and accepted that there were historic injustices in the society that needed to be remedied. Tony's apology for the London government's inaction during the nineteenth-century Irish famine helped. My efforts to have open, independent inquiries on thorny issues like Bloody Sunday also helped, as did our dogged emphasis on human rights and equality. Slowly, as we worked, suspicious people in the US accepted we were different. We worked hard at it talking to influential politicians, who began to listen to me and realize my perspective was not that of a typical Brit. It was an important change. It began to change people's views and therefore made it harder for Sinn Fein to go to America and be fêted and raise money – although we had no effect on the few folk who were more rabidly Irish republican than Sinn Fein.

5. Involving All Levels in the Community

As well as working with other governments, it is crucial that progress is made at all different levels in a community. The leaders and the people who put their heads above the barricades and talk have to be inclusive of other people involved in the process. If this does not happen progress may be made at one level, which then begins to unravel at another, as David Trimble discovered within his own party and the broader unionist community. Support must come from all levels, not just from the political leaders. The civil-society level, in the form of business, trade unions and the voluntary sector, is crucial. It was particularly noticeable during the period before the talks started and again during the referendum campaign when influential people across civil society made their views known and supported the progress being made.

The voluntary sector always have a lot to offer, but sometimes they can be difficult to work with. Rivalries between groups can present problems. Including as many groups as possible is the best way to deal with rivalries, but you need to keep consultations to a manageable size and to watch out for voluntary groups or non-governmental organizations (NGOs) which are just front groups for one of the parties involved in the negotiations. You can't block such groups, but you need to be aware of what they are up to and try as best you can to involve them.

Unions and the business community can be useful, but are difficult to draw in. They are suffering as much as anyone else in the country but they are not keen to get involved if theirs is a business which is surviving the problems and their workforce is working well together. But this does not mean they are not interested in peace. Time has to be taken to find ways of involving them on their terms. If it is not on their terms, their involvement can be potentially counterproductive. Money and support will come from both if they are included on the terms that they can work with.

The religious community can also be a very positive force for peace as it was in N. Ireland. But, just as business and unions cannot go too far out beyond their customers or their members, so must Church leaders take note of their followers. That does not mean they shouldn't try and take a lead in their communities. But they too have to make judgements about how far to go, taking into account where the flock is as well as where the Church is. A lot depends on the personal strength and beliefs of individual Church leaders. Again one should look at all levels of clergy in the Church. There were many clergy from all denominations in different communities in N. Ireland who made a difference to the peace process. You only have to look at the work of people like the Quakers, the Rev. Roy Magee and the Rev. John Dunlop, Father Alec Reid and Cardinal Daly to see that.

6. Gaining International Support

The interest and involvement of the international community is a tremendous support. External validation of the talks is important because when people are watching from around the world then those involved in the peace process can say, 'If they have belief and confidence, then we can too.'

There is no doubt that money helps. But delivering it in the right way helps even more. For example, when Europe agreed a package of peace and reconciliation money (over £230 million) to use across the communities in N. Ireland, a then Commissioner from Germany, Monica Wulf-Mathies, took charge of how it was to be distributed. She said, 'This money is going to be allocated across twenty-six groups in N. Ireland, and those groups are going to be made up of politicians, business people, trade unionists, community groups, young people. They will decide where the money goes.' This made an incredible impact on the community because money means child care and youth clubs, jobs and environmental improvements. Everyone wanted a bit of the action and, to get it, they had to sit and talk to one another. I can remember going into one of these 'district partnerships' and seeing a big hairy-handed farmer with hardline unionist views sitting and talking to a republican woman. They were discussing what to do with the money. Before they would have spat at each other.

Overseas support helps and visits from foreign figures make a real difference, helping the participants to feel important and to see that what they are doing is being registered elsewhere. This encourages them forward, because they realize that if they are responsible for the failure of a talks process they will be blamed not just in N. Ireland but across the world. During my years in Belfast we were very lucky. We had visits from: Hillary and Bill Clinton; Desmond Tutu and Nelson Mandela; European Commission President Santer and European Parliament President Gil-Robles; Václav Havel, President of the Czech Republic; Canadian Prime Minister Jean Chrétian and many, many other commissioners from Europe and parliamentarians from across the world. We even arranged for a team of Los Angeles rap cricketers to come to N. Ireland as part of their UK tour.

7. Addressing Past Grievances

A painful and bitter conflict like that in N. Ireland throws up all sorts of lasting grievances that need to be dealt with. Otherwise they become running sores that people come back to time and time again. I think it is crucial, in order to create a peaceful situation, whatever the country, never to forget those that have died as a result of the historic trouble. But though you can never forget history, you cannot live in it. If you live in history, you are lost. History must be understood while looking towards the future; but the victims cannot be forgotten, if you are ever to hope to address pain and the suffering that exists among their families and communities. Once those that have suffered the most begin to deal with the pain, they can begin to learn to live together. This cannot happen if the past is ignored. In some way those people have to cope. We, especially Adam Ingram, put a great deal of time and energy into meeting victims' groups and trying to respond to their concerns. It is a vital part of the healing process.

At the same time, underlying grievances must be faced up to. The difficulty in N. Ireland was that both sides felt they had suffered injustices against them. Nationalists would cite examples of past discrimination in jobs or housing and landmark events like Bloody Sunday. The unionists, loyalists in particular, would say, 'They get better treatment than we do from the British government.' There are injustices and inequalities built up over the years on both sides, and they have to be dealt with. When Labour came to power in 1997, the basic principles that guided us about fairness, about justice, about equality fitted well with what was needed in N. Ireland. Therefore the changes that we have made, for example in the anti-discrimination laws, added on to the progress already made by previous governments.

Addressing grievances and supporting those who have lost loved ones is an essential part of winning the support of the wider community. Paramilitary groups thrive in divided and closed communities who may not necessarily approve of the violence but don't see any other way out. If a government is prepared to say, 'Yes, we'll hold an open and fair public inquiry into this concern,' people in the wider community are less likely to say, 'Violence is happening because of how unfairly we have been treated.' The justification is no longer there; you have helped take away the grievance and the cover given to the paramilitaries at the same time.

8. *Dealing with Bread-and-Butter Issues*

Another lesson that I learnt during my time in N. Ireland is that, even though it's the major focus of your work, most people will never connect with the details of a complex peace agreement – 80 or 90 per cent of people in N. Ireland do not give a monkey's about 'paragraph 3 subsection 4' of the Good Friday Agreement, which may have caused us weeks of headaches. What they care about is whether they are going to get a dividend from this in their own lives. Are they going to get a job? Decent health care? Are their kids going to get a good education? These are the issues that cause people to realize that something good is coming from a peace process, over and above the absence of violence. So social and economic policies can't be ignored either. On our business tour of the US in 1999 we stressed more than anything else the message that investing in N. Ireland would bring jobs and hope to young people on both sides, giving the peace process a better chance of working. That trade mission to the US was helped tremendously by the fact that it was led by a unionist and a nationalist, who helped to promote N. Ireland together. They said N. Ireland has changed – and they symbolized that fact. It has a new face not scarred by violence, but marked by hope.

9. Taking Risks

Another lesson is the importance of taking risks. To achieve peace, risks have to be taken by all the participants. Going into the Maze Prison was a particular risk for me. But when the politicians felt and said that violence would return, I saw that as the biggest risk of all. So I went to the prison and talked to the prisoners face to face, and then they could see I was serious. Other party leaders have taken other risks. It is not an easy process, and it might not always work, but it is essential.

10. Go with Your Instincts

Finally, however good the plans and strategy are, you have to be flexible and take a peace process one step at a time. At times you won't have any guidance or precedents to go on, so you have to go with your gut. No one in my position had ever gone in to talk to terrorist prisoners on both sides. I did it, not because it was part of some grand plan, but because it felt the right thing to do at the time. I have made some good decisions and some bad decisions by following my instincts. Sometimes there is nothing else to guide you.

II

Too Rude, Too Rough, Too Sexy

CABINET GOVERNMENT AND THE WHISPERING CAMPAIGN

Entering the door to the Cabinet Office on Whitehall, just up from the gates to Downing Street, felt good. Physically, at least, it does feel like the heart of government. The offices themselves are like a huge rabbit warren with corridors all over the place and people tucked away, sometimes in what looks like a big cupboard, but is called an office. Too many are windowless, which is not healthy. My office in comparison was enormous. My predecessor, Jack Cunningham, had been the first to occupy it and had installed all mod cons including a television and a CD player. One wall was nearly all huge windows with a beautiful view overlooking Horse Guards Parade and St James's Park to the west. One drawback of the positioning was that from about April through to the summer we would have military bands practising on the parade ground each morning for Trooping the Colour or some similar event. It was all very pleasant to start with, but by the time you have heard 'Colonel Bogey' for the tenth time in a week, it begins to jar a little.

When I moved in, I brought my dartboard from Belfast and hung it in the cupboard. I had, over time, chosen numbers on the board to aim at, representing people whom I was finding particularly difficult. I became a whiz shot on certain numbers. I also brought some of my awards from the peace process in N. Ireland as well as my foot-high blow-up doll representing the woman from Munch's picture *The Scream*. Finally I had my prized chess-set of the peace process. I wasn't very keen on Jack's choice of artwork, sort of sciencey-looking pictures of bees and plants. I kept meaning to change them, but never found the time. All cabinet Ministers get to choose from the government art collection to decorate their offices. I had not had very good luck in choosing for my N. Ireland office as I went to the storage place in Soho after everyone else and there was very little left to choose from. I selected one painting for its title, *Discipline over Desire*. It consisted of a white canvas with a foot-long black line to one side. I used it as a test of how grovelly people were when they came to see me. If they commented on it, I used to rave about its beauty. Some raved immediately back, but others were more reticent in their comments. It is possible that some people genuinely liked it, but I tended to have more faith in the judgement of the people who were reticent.

On the first day in the Cabinet Office I did a whistle-stop tour round all the offices. It showed me how spread out into different buildings the Cabinet Office is, as well as giving me a real sense of how big it is. It meant that I had said hi to all my staff, which I think is a good start. The only handicap was they had all told me their names and then, when they came for meetings in my office, while I would have vague face recognition, I felt bad not remembering what to call them. Even worse, with a number of close staff I thought I remembered a name and called them that from then on. For example, Emma in my private office was called Amy by me for the entire time we were together. She didn't seem to mind. I at least got it right when I later went to her marriage celebrations.

After completing the tour, I sat at my very big desk in my very big office, missing Belfast. I had to pull myself together and be positive about what I was about to start doing. If I didn't seem positive, determined to get on and happy, then neither would the people working with me act that way. So I got up from my desk and, smiling, walked towards my private office and asked what next. Then my private secretary John Fuller and my diary secretary Tracey Temple followed me back into my office with piles of paper.

I was on a very steep learning curve, not least because of the number of different policy issues I was involved in: drugs, GM food, deregulation, modernizing government, civil service reform and issues related to deprivation and social exclusion like homelessness, truancy and teenage pregnancy. I was lucky to have two good Ministers – no, it wasn't luck, I'd asked for them – in Ian McCartney (MP for Makerfield) and Graham Stringer (MP for Manchester Blackley). Also on the team were (Lord) Charlie Falconer (who had the misfortune to work on, among many other things, the Millennium Dome) and Margaret Jay, who ran the women's unit and was also Labour Leader in the House of Lords.

I also had to come to terms with the organizational structure of the Cabinet Office, or rather the lack of it. I was given an impressive diagram, called an organogram, of who did what which plainly illustrated the lack of structure in the department, and an attempt by some poor sod to try and define it. My personal adviser Andrew Lappin, who joined me after Anna Healy moved on, brought it in for me to see. We looked at each other and burst out laughing – if this was to help our understanding, it achieved the exact opposite. (Andrew had worked in the Cabinet Office before, so his knowledge was invaluable, as were his writing skills and his sharp mind.) The problem was that, over the years, different Ministers had plucked out of the confusion the bits of the job that interested them, then added them, and chaos reigned. Then even more confusion would arise (and the organogram grow even more randomly) when No. 10 suddenly decided to give new initiatives or responsibilities to the press office or to other parts of the department, often with no consultation with me or the Minister concerned.

It soon became clear that unless No. 10 was prepared to let other government departments do their job and give the Cabinet Office the authority and power to do its job, this confusion would only get worse. As it was, the Cabinet Office risked becoming just a pale shadow of No. 10 with no distinct role at all. With little power and even less money, the office had just developed as best it could, following the issues the different Ministers decided to get their teeth into.

On some issues the Cabinet Office was tasked to try and facilitate greater co-operation between departments, or 'joined-up government' as it was known. This was largely done through a network of committees served by a 'secretariat' of civil servants – who also resided in the Cabinet Office, but seemed to work for the Prime Minister rather than me. We were never allowed to say how often these committees met – even when asked in Parliament – or what they did. To me this created an air of secrecy, which was not necessary as most of them just did the ordinary business of government. Some didn't meet at all and did all their work through correspondence – which meant the civil servants controlled them.

Part of my job was to chair a number of these committees dealing with particular issues, some of which fell to the Cabinet Office because of the need to make sure the different government departments were working properly together; some because they were causing the government problems and there was no one else to take charge of them. As I sat reading the papers on the first day and in the many meetings in the weeks ahead I began to get my head round the issues I was to be involved with.

Since the beginning of time, businesses have been complaining to governments about the 'mountains of red tape' they have to deal with. And governments over the years have gone on churning it out at more or less the same rate. Making new laws and regulations is what governments do, but at the same time the job of the Cabinet Office was to try to simplify, avoid duplication, cancel regulation no longer necessary and get departments to think twice about how they regulate: do they, for example, need legislation or can other methods of regulation be used?

Businesses big and small want as little regulation as possible to keep their costs down so they can remain competitive, grow and, hopefully, employ more people. It is in the interests of government to limit the burden of bureaucracy as much as possible to help create more jobs. But at the same time we need to protect the interests of consumers and workers' basic rights in health, safety, holiday entitlements and so on. The same was true in the public services. People want and deserve to receive good, efficient public services. And the public servants, whether they are doctors, teachers or fire fighters, want to be able to provide a service without excessive rules and regulations hampering them from doing so. Usually the way forward came down to a judgement on what both sides of the debate could live with.

All the different government departments knew this was an issue that had to be addressed and, as both No. 10 and the Treasury frequently told them they had to address it, departments were keen to look like they were co-operating. Now there is something inherently difficult in Ministers and civil servants giving up or amending the rules and regulations they want to introduce. So a system had been introduced to monitor what was coming forward from the departments, which involved me writing more times than was healthy about a proposed new law, 'This piece of legislation is fine but it needs to have a thorough regulatory impact assessment.'

There were lots of 'systems' for dealing with the problem, including a special panel I chaired where we could call Ministers to account for what their departments were doing and an independent deregulatory task force chaired by the Labour-supporting peer Chris Haskins from Northern Foods. And we did make some progress, even though most people, particularly the press, never acknowledged it. This progress was in no mean part due to a good team of civil servants and to Graham Stringer, who did a very competent job. It was all a bit of a slog and a lot of overlapping responsibilities, but at the end of the last parliamentary session in 2001 one of the few new acts of Parliament that actually got passed was a deregulation bill that Graham steered through the Commons. It was a good piece of work that I hoped would make a difference in the future.

One area where we made less headway was over new European regulations. Charlie Falconer was working away on this, but I'm not sure how far he got. Part of the problem arises because our legal system is different from most of the rest of Europe, and we have had a habit of implementing legislation in a more detailed fashion than some of our sister nations in the EU. I sympathized with (Lord) Gus McDonald when I heard that he had been put in charge of this after the 2001 election, but it really does need addressing because it was a constant complaint from business people I met.

None of our jobs were made any easier by the constant input from No. 10 whenever there was a story in a tabloid newspaper or the issue was raised in the House of Commons. Sometimes the intervention was from one civil servant to another, without us Ministers being aware. We didn't question the PM's right to act as he did; rather, more often than not, we agreed with what was being done, but didn't like the cavalier way it was done with complete disregard to what was already going on in the department to tackle the problem. Impatience, short-termism, a knee-jerk reaction, call it what you will, but it made neither our lives in the Cabinet Office nor the lives of other cabinet Ministers any easier.

Another issue which landed on my desk because of the need to co-ordinate across departments was the subject of genetically modified foods. Actually, I think the GM issue had only been shunted on to the Cabinet Office because my predecessor Jack Cunningham was an enthusiast for biotechnology and the government's policy was running into trouble with the public and the press. But one of the causes of the trouble was the open conflict of interest between the then departments of Agriculture and the Environment.

There was a ministerial committee to try to broker an accommodation between the differing views, and I was in the chair. After the talks in N. Ireland I thought this wouldn't be too difficult. But there were tough arguments and strong personalities on both sides. I tried to broker a joint policy statement that everyone could sign up to and would stick to in public. After all, we all agreed that the potential advantages of GM foods and crops ought to be explored. The advantages in medicine, for example, were already being shown in developing better insulin for diabetics, helping cancer patients undergoing chemotherapy and on improving blood products for haemophiliacs. Equally there were potential advantages in GM crops, especially for improving people's nutrition in developing countries. The real issue for us was one of public confidence and whether or not there were any adverse effects on the countryside of growing GM crops on a bigger scale.

Constant opposition from some environmental groups who said we should not be doing any of it and a hostile press talking about 'Frankenstein foods' didn't help to ease the tensions one bit. While there was scientific evidence to back up the claims of the biotech companies that the food and crops were safe, the public didn't trust it. Meanwhile products were being taken off supermarket shelves and removed from sale. It was a good lesson in how little trust there was out there – after BSE and all the other food scares – in what politicians and scientists say. And the only way forward I could see was to establish authoritative independent bodies to look at the evidence and present it in an open informative manner. So, for instance, we had a Scientific Steering Committee – with representatives from non-governmental organizations such as English Nature working together with an industry body (SCIMAC) – identifying field test sites, to assess the impact on the animal and plant life of growing GM crops. Other environmental groups like the Soil Association engaged with us over the separation distances between the crops in these test sites and neighbouring fields. We also set up two independent bodies called the Human Genetics Commission and the Agriculture and Environment Biotechnology Commission to hold investigations and publish reports into the ethical and social dimensions of the new technology as well as the science. Taking a lesson from N. Ireland I knew that in order for these bodies to command as much confidence as possible they had to be as inclusive as possible, even if that meant putting people on them with strongly opposing views, like representatives of green groups, the industry, consumers and scientists. We also had, in the shape of government Chief Scientific Adviser David King, a very able man and a good example of a truly independent voice who could work harmoniously with the system. He well proved his worth during the foot and mouth crisis in the spring of 2001 when he managed to address public concerns in a factual way, criticizing the government sometimes and defending their decisions at others. In my view he usually got the balance right.

At the many ministerial meetings I sought to accommodate the differing views and keep the debate moving forward. The civil servants, who got a little frustrated at times, managed to use their skills in writing the minutes in such a way as not to offend either side and keep the show on the road. We also had representatives on the committees to voice the concerns of the new devolved assemblies and parliaments in Scotland, Wales and N. Ireland. This made it even more difficult – especially when the Welsh Assembly declared Wales a GM-free zone. There was pressure on the Scots to follow suit, which had to be resisted because of the knock-on effect for the trials in England, which were our only way of finding out what the local effects of the crops might be.

We did manage to hold all this together – just. But torn between the powerful environmental lobby on one side and a powerful industry on the other it was never easy. It continued to be an important issue for the government; biotech companies are fought for very hard by all countries for inward investment and it would have been very short-sighted to lose them. As for the general public, our polling showed, as is often the case, that the same individuals held views that could be seen as contradictory. They were worried about the impact of the crops on people and the environment, but at the same time were curious about the possible benefits.

The international dimension was important too. Agri-business, particularly in crop seeds, is an international business but there were lots of disputes between countries about the best way forward. We argued for an international panel to be set up on the safety of GM foods and crops and organized an international conference in Edinburgh in September 2000. I was a little wary. It was crucial that it should be a conference for countries and pressure groups as well as business. I feared it might be overshadowed by the kind of violent protests we had seen at the Seattle World Trade Conference that year and elsewhere. But my fears were unfounded. It went very well. It gave representatives from developing countries the opportunity to express their views. It was particularly useful to hear the importance already put on the potential of GM foods in some of the less developed areas of the world.

GM food is again an issue where, with ministerial co-operation, hard work by good civil servants and the inclusion of independent voices, some progress was made – at least in terms of improving the public debate and killing off some of the scare stories. The progress may not have been fast enough for some in government, but my view remains that while it is important to keep making progress it needs to be at a speed that keeps everyone on board. I think we achieved that. Since I left government, the departments of Environment and Agriculture have been merged into one, so it will be interesting to see whether the debate moves forward, or whether the different officials and Ministers just carry on fighting it out like ferrets in a sack. To start with I was very doubtful about the value of GM foods, but I am now much more positive. The value and advantages to people of products from the biotech industry should be examined – the advantages are potentially staggering.

In other areas of work I didn't chair committees but fronted specific policy or action 'units'. These had grown like Topsy as add-ons to the Cabinet Office over the years. Again the main point was to work with the different interests of the departments on the issues and reach an accommodation – and to get some results on the ground, results people could see and feel. One such unit dealt with the government's anti-drugs strategy. This was an area of major interest and importance to me and to the government. Thousands die each year from drug-related illnesses and overdoses. The impact of drugs, like heroin, on individuals, their families and communities is devastating. Worst of all it was an area where I knew from the letters and comments I had from people nationally and in Redcar that governments in the past had failed to make a significant impact.

Within the anti-drugs unit we had some good officials as well as two outside expert advisers, Keith Hellawell and Mike Trace, to give advice on drugs policy issues. Keith had been dubbed the 'drugs tsar' when he was appointed in 1997, a title that I think was silly. I suppose it was meant to suggest tough, determined leadership, but I thought it an unnecessary Americanism and we could all live without it. Mike and Keith had put together a ten-year strategy to fight both the demand and the supply of drugs. It was a brave attempt to make a number of departments pull together, focusing on the demand for drugs, which involved education programmes (Department of Education), prevention (Home Office) and anti-drug treatment (Health), and cutting the supply of drugs (Home, Customs and Excise, Foreign Office and, importantly, Treasury if any progress was to be made).

It was all progressing okay, but new initiatives kept being added all the time. Some of them were good, like Positive Futures, a national project to give vulnerable young people of about nine to thirteen a chance to try different sports and leisure activities – basically to give them something else to do. It was for the young kids you see hanging around many estates: truants, or kids excluded from school, or those for whom nobody at home had much time. Local sportspeople and the police and probation and social services got together to provide training and facilities helping these kids develop more confidence and get a sense of belonging to something.

I saw one of the pilot schemes operating in my own constituency, which taught basketball. Kids that used to always follow me around when I was out doing visits on a Friday were on the project and when I went to say well done at the end of the scheme, these kids had a sense of self-respect I had never seen before. At last they might have enough sense of self to stay off the drugs and to start making something of their lives. I launched the £1 million national scheme with Trevor Brooking of Sport England and England football manager Kevin Keegan at the Geoffrey Chaucer School in Southwark in South London. The response from the kids there was great and a good indicator of what can be done to help build young people's confidence. The presence of Trevor and Kevin made all the difference. Once again I saw the importance of role models in action.

Other initiatives were less good, responding to the constant pressures to be seen to be tough on all drugs. This to me was counterproductive and increasingly out of step with both public and media opinion. When you had conservative papers like the *Mail on Sunday* and the *Daily Telegraph* saying that government should look again at the whole question of which drugs were illegal and why, I couldn't understand why we had to stick to an outdated 'just say no' approach. It was hypocritical, especially when young people saw adults consuming their legal drugs – cigarettes and alcohol.

I wrote several times to Tony, Jack and other Ministers to try to get some movement, especially on cannabis, and even more especially for people like MS sufferers who use cannabis to relieve their pain and sickness. But sad to say I got nowhere in eighteen months. I wrote to Tony often of my frustration at the lack of progress. I said I thought we were misreading the public mood and missing an opportunity to have a more thorough examination of the law on cannabis use. I believed that using vast amounts of public money handling cannabis-related offences was not the best use of expenditure in support of our

" I MUST SAY MEETING YOU IS QUITE A SURPRISE. DR MOWLAM   YOU'RE MUCH TALLER THAN I WAS EXPECTING."

anti-drugs strategy and called for us to be more radical still and look afresh at the legal position of all currently illegal drugs, in the hope of rationalizing what was clearly a very confusing picture. Our position was far from rational.

But in the end I had to accept that, while the public and press had moved on, many politicians were still stuck in the past. It was frustrating not getting anywhere, but I knew it was a fight that would be won, if not just yet. So I kept talking about it in private, found a form of words I could live with to say in public which didn't make me feel too much like a hypocrite, and concentrated my attention on the problems of hard drugs like heroin. Ministers hid behind 'scientific evidence' that there was a causal link between smoking marijuana and taking heroin. I had seen no such evidence.

I received so many heartrending letters from parents of drug addicts, particularly mums, in a desperate state. One sticks particularly in my memory because it enclosed a note written by her child that said:

Dear Mum thanks for all you've done. You are a great mum. I love
you. I have been trying but I've lost it again. Thanks again. I'm
really sorry about taking the television with me but I need the money.
I Love you . . .

We did introduce a special programme for parents and local
community groups to aid each other and to help their kids
stay away from drugs. We also made progress on treatment
programmes in places like prisons to support addicts in kicking
the habit and going back into society clean. A central pool of
additional money for treatment was agreed too, along with an
independent National Treatment Agency to administer it, which
meant, hopefully, rising above the old inter-departmental
squabbles about who was spending what money and where.
Anti-drug education was expanded too, into nearly every second-
ary and primary school, although I never knew how effective it
was – not very, I suspect. Like so much that happens in the
classroom, it depended on the commitment and personality of
the teacher.

Anyhow, despite this we seemed to be making little progress
in reducing the number of addicts, and the pressure for progress
kept increasing, regardless of what we achieved. It was frustrating for all involved, especially as we didn't know what the total
number of addicts at any one time really was, so it was impossible to measure if we were getting anywhere.

Apart from the cannabis issue, I also faced problems caused
by the fact that there were too many cooks stirring the pot.
There was me, two expert advisers, and then all the Ministers
with their specific departmental interests with a role to play. My
co-ordinating role worked up to a point, but I lacked the leverage
or power to achieve real results. We got general support from
No. 10 but little in terms of real back-up, so when it came to
dealing with those with the actual money and the means to
deliver it was a constant battle. Gordon Brown and the Treasury
gave the money to departments, but then it was up to us to

make sure it was spent on drugs policy. We had to constantly keep chivvying the Ministers and asking the Treasury for more support. It took almost a year, for instance, to get the money out of the Health Department for the National Treatment Agency.

I found the constant fight to increase the power and influence of the department dull. It was a game I was not that interested in playing, much to the disappointment of some of my civil servants. I just wanted to get on with delivering the policies we agreed and I became very frustrated with others who were more interested in empire-building. I found this a real waste of time. To my mind, the best way forward when you came up against a barrier was to have a quick one-day review or get a paper written with options for solutions, rather than play power politics. But I recognize that not seeing the need for this kind of fight was probably one of my political weaknesses.

I decided to stick to my own priorities, focusing on the real need to deal with hard drugs by (a) treating more addicts and (b) increasing international co-operation to cut down the supply of drugs coming into our country. Looking at the supply issue gave me a unique opportunity to work with the governments of other countries, like Colombia, where about 80 per cent of the cocaine that comes into Europe is produced. I first met Colombian President Andres Pastrana at a meeting I was invited to with Tony Blair. Ostensibly I was there to talk about dealing with drugs problems, but we also got into a long discussion about the peace process he was engaged in, and whether there were any parallels with the situation in N. Ireland. I agreed at the end of the meeting that I would go to Colombia to see what I could do to help both on the drugs front and with the peace process.

The Latin America specialists in the Foreign Office took an interest. I think they were pleased to have a high-profile Minister engaged with their issues, and spent a long time briefing me for the visit – everything I wanted to know about Colombia and more. Given that rapidly rising quantities of cocaine were being consumed in the UK and across Europe, my interest in tackling it at source was clearly justified. I made three visits to Colombia in all, over the space of about twelve months. Each time I think a little progress was made on the issues that I continually nagged about. I was never sure about the protocol of nagging another country, especially its President (although I know from personal contacts with Colombian Ministers since that they appreciated it, because it produced results). I always took the view that it was not my country and it was up to them to decide the way forward. My main concern was with the reaction in other countries in Europe and America and how we could best galvanize the international community into action to help both improve the situation in Colombia and reduce the problems we all had with drugs on our streets.

On my first visit to Colombia's capital, Bogotá, I struggled a bit at the start with the altitude. Bogotá is an amazing city, built on a high plateau surrounded by steep mountainsides and cloud forest. The air is pretty thin and damp a lot of the time and the pollution levels are high. I was warned about it and just followed my normal policy when on overseas trips: to sleep as much as you can, and don't drink alcohol – unless it is a celebratory glass with a friend or a glass to say goodbye, and then have a whiskey on the plane back home. But it took a little time to adjust to running out of breath just climbing the stairs to bed.

While I was there I was invited to see a large number of Ministers alongside the heads of the police and the army, as well as talk to some of the soldiers and officers on the ground. My movements, I remember, were organized by a security chief called Bob Marley. I amused myself (and teased him) by humming the other, more famous Bob Marley's songs, 'Get Up Stand Up' and 'No Woman No Cry' as I was being driven around Bogotá, accompanied by the British Ambassador Jeremy Thorpe and my private secretary John Fuller. There were motorbike outriders with us all the time and on each bike there was a second man, riding pillion, with a machine gun ready to fire. It wasn't very reassuring.

I talked to the local non-governmental organizations in Bogotá. I always tried to see the interested NGOs – like CAFOD and Amnesty International – at home before going, so I could have their views alongside the official lines I was being given. Meeting these groups at home and abroad, I learnt, had two advantages: I found out a lot about what was going on in Colombia, and it increased support for my visit from people who knew that I was interested in more than just talking to government and security folk. From a starting point of zero information I had to learn fast. I enjoyed the challenge; I really wished I could have spoken Spanish.

After my first visit I had a good sense of how the drugs problems fitted into the overall picture, which was pretty chaotic and very violent. It was patently obvious that the drugs question could not be dealt with in isolation. There were three main groups fighting with each other and against the government: two revolutionary guerrilla groups, the FARC and the ELN, and a loose alliance of paramilitary gangs, each of which was more or less involved in the drugs trade. People in Colombia said that while the war had been going on for decades, the drugs came later and just made it worse.

The Colombian government's strategy had been to try to bring the FARC and the ELN into a talks process. As an incentive, the FARC had been given an area of Colombia the size of Switzerland, where they could exercise a sort of home rule. The same was being offered to the ELN. The paramilitaries were a different sort of problem, having originally been sanctioned by the state and used by the wealthier landowners as well as the police and army to combat the threat from the guerrillas. But they were now illegal and heavily into the drugs trade too. The FARC and ELN were reluctant to engage with the government until the paramilitary issue was addressed. They said that the army colluded with the paramilitaries, making it easier for them to commit massacres and other human rights abuses. Undoubtedly there was some truth in this, but the level of human rights abuses committed by all sides was absolutely appalling and the government was trying to get it all stopped.

The government strategy had been outlined in a document called 'Plan Colombia' and they were looking for international support for it. President Clinton, faced with the same drug problems in the US as we have, bought into President Pastrana's overall plan and fought a fierce battle against opposition in the US Congress to get approval for a $1.3 billion aid package. Part of the opposition arose because the lion's share of the package was earmarked for military aid. A number of liberals in both the Senate and the House of Representatives opposed the large military element. This view was shared by some but not all the governments in Europe, by some MPs in London, by some folk in the Foreign Office, by many of the NGOs, and of course by many in the press who saw America going back to its old imperialistic ways in Latin America.

The Colombian government were looking to Europe for further help. But the old Europe–USA rivalry and suspicion were getting in the way. I saw part of our role as the UK government as trying to broker a sensible approach between the two camps, while at the same time trying to stop America going over the top. It was true that the military and the police in Colombia were not strong enough to take on all three opposition groups at once and needed strengthening. But they also needed reform, particularly to tackle the collusion issue. There was also a tremendous need for development and economic support. The peasant farmers growing the coca plants (which cocaine is made from) needed to be persuaded that growing something else would provide them with a long-term sustainable future. The US approach was more stick than carrot: build up the army and spray the coca crops with a herbicide to kill it and then encourage the peasants to grow other crops. Europe was much more carrot than stick: give the peasants aid to develop their own economic alternatives to growing coca and stop poisoning their fragile local environment with chemicals.

My view was the Colombian government could not reject the US help because they were in dire financial straits. Whatever we thought, that was a fact of life. This was the point that we had to start from. As a result we had to try and get the Americans to use their military might to spray only where there were large industrial-sized plantations with no permanent population. Then, armed with a commitment from the US not to spray in populated areas, we could argue in Europe for progress on the economic front so that work could be done with the Colombian people on alternative economic development packages.

I was particularly concerned that the part of the plan dealing with economic support wouldn't start early enough with the result that, having had their coca crops destroyed, the peasants would be left with no means of making a living. I said this in my meetings with US State Department officials, particularly Tom Pickering. I promised that we in the UK would try as hard as we could to get the economic support package out of Europe, in return for a US promise to restrict the sprayings to limited areas and to stagger its implementation. I had one worrying meeting with the US General responsible for the project when he agreed with Tom that spraying of populated areas – the peasants' homes – would be avoided, but that he couldn't give the same guarantee for people who had been displaced from their towns and villages by the violence (of whom there are many thousands in Colombia) because they didn't have homes! It was a sort of logic. But surely it would be possible to make an effort to locate the displaced people and take them to safety, where they wouldn't be sprayed with herbicide?

I put in a lot of time with the Americans, arguing these points, keeping in regular contact by letter, phone and, on one occasion, video-conference. I also worked hard on the other side to get the European Union organized to do something that would (a) help keep American excesses in check and (b) rebut criticisms from Washington that we were all carping from the sidelines without lifting a finger to help ourselves. The Spanish felt the same as us and the Foreign Office started working with Spanish officials on getting Ministers from across Europe to work together on a response to 'Plan Colombia'.

We did get somewhere after several meetings in London, Madrid and Brussels and more meetings between the various European Ambassadors stationed in Bogotá. But, God, it was a hard slog. A European aid package totalling some 300 million euros was finally agreed in October 2000, focusing on just the kind of economic packages for the peasants we were talking about. But if I thought Whitehall was slow, I had yet to experience Brussels. They sent one set of officials across to review the situation and to come up with some real projects on the ground to spend the money on. They talked to very few, if any, actual peasants or their representatives to find out what they wanted and came back proposing something nobody seemed to be happy with. So another delegation had to be despatched and this time talked more widely and came up with better ideas. But it all took months, and cost a lot. Meanwhile the Americans were carrying on merrily without us.

It was clear to me that no progress could be made on cutting the supply of cocaine until the violence in Colombia had been brought under control. I offered practical help in the form of police training and sent some individuals out there to advise the negotiators on possible ways to move the talks forward. I had to tread carefully because they were very wary of people coming in and telling them what to do. But after a while when they began to trust me it became clear how much help they needed. I managed, thanks to the help of the N. Ireland Office and the Foreign Office, to get other folk with different expertise sent out to advise the army; we managed to get General Rose, with Bosnia experience, and General Wheeler, with N. Ireland experience. We also got an official from N. Ireland to advise on reform of the police and army. We did a lot, I hope, to help the Colombians function more fairly and effectively.

For me it felt good to get my hands mucky on a real problem again, especially one with so many parallels with the work I had been doing in N. Ireland. But it was also a great opportunity to see a beautiful country and meet some truly lovely people. They were very kind. On one visit we were out in the country at a place called Villavicencio meeting with the army, and seeing for ourselves how impossible the terrain made it for the army to control the traffickers. The security for this visit out of Bogotá was very tight. As we travelled around in a small plane, which was like an oven, I kept going by humming all the Bob Marley songs I could think of.

At the army base, the Commander asked me to address the troops. It was hot and humid and, as I stood up at the table to speak, the gaze of many of the young soldiers was wary and intense. They were very direct in their response to my comments: what was I doing there speaking to them when I should be at home cutting the demand for cocaine? I responded with a long list of what we were doing on that side, but got absolutely no response. As they were showing me around the camp, which was pretty basic, the Commander proudly showed me the doctor's room and the dentist's. I had had toothache for a number of days and so I promptly sat in the dentist's chair and asked him to fix it. The folk travelling with me thought I was taking a big risk – in fact they thought I was mad – but he did a good job.

I left Bogotá thinking what a long way off we were in doing anything to help either them or ourselves with the drugs problem. As is so often the case, there were fundamental barriers that had to be overcome before progress could be made. But it was difficult to see what progress was being made when for so much of the time we were in England rather than Colombia. However, we must have made some waves in the direction of progress because the FARC guerrilla group asked to see me.

The Foreign Office advised against it. As usual I would have just gone in and talked because that is how you move a process forward. After a bit of argy-bargy, the line we eventually agreed was that I would only go if we got something back in return from the guerrillas. But I knew from my experience in N. Ireland that such an approach would not bring results. People who consider themselves freedom fighters see themselves very differently from how they are perceived from the outside. I would have gone with nothing on the table beforehand in the hope of having something on the table when I left them. I would have gone just for a discussion, to build up trust as a precursor to later progress. Sadly I never went.

Other indicators of progress were the views of the neighbouring countries, like Brazil, Peru and Venezuela. They were worried about the effects of developments in Colombia. They feared that peasants, scared by the guerrillas or paramilitaries, or by the US spraying, would leave and cross the border to hide in neighbouring countries. Would not the traffickers then set up in their countries and start planting coca? Equally there was the fear that the growers would just go deeper into the Amazon forests, destroying more of the natural environment by clearing it for growing coca, creating airstrips for planes to transport it out or building factories to process it on the rivers, further polluting the waters – a fear that has proved well-founded.

Because of the concerns of neighbouring countries, on a later visit I stopped off on the way to Colombia to talk with the most powerful neighbour, Brazil. I met a number of groups and Ministers in Rio de Janeiro and Brasília, the capital. The concerns about the drugs and US actions were raised, as well as the need not to forget the neighbouring countries in terms of aid and investment. They needed help with investment too and were fighting the drug menace, although not to the same extent as Colombia. I had a very good meeting with President Cardoso. There had recently been a meeting of Latin American states, and Cardoso was hopeful that if they could work together they could make a difference. This I thought sounded really promising. After discussing the problems of stopping drugs on the border, which were clearly very difficult because of its length, we went on to discuss what efforts could be made in the area of intelligence and security co-operation. Better co-operation was needed both within countries and across national boundaries. We ended with one of the more interesting conversations that I had had for some time, covering Locke, Burke and the fundamentals of what is a democracy.

The Brazilian government had offered to take me to Bogotá by dropping me at the border on the Amazon to be picked up by the Colombians. It was a worthwhile trip, not just because I enjoyed it but also because I learnt a lot. I knew Brazil was a big open country but until I flew over it very low it didn't really hit home. I understood how impossible it was for the police to keep tabs on traffickers. We stopped at a town called Manaus for a break. It was weird, a little area for retail therapy in the middle of the jungle. I bought a very comfortable pair of blue flat shoes, as I did not really have anything for the boat on the Amazon. I now use them for gardening, and while I'm weeding away my shoes make me think about the lush growth in the Amazon, and I think my weed problem is pretty minor compared to that!

When we got to a border town called Leticia, we were warmly greeted and put on a police launch to cross over to Colombia. Before crossing we had a quick trip up the Amazon, which was amazing. The width and power of the river were awesome. Every so often we would pass a bunch of children playing on the banks, and further up the bank you would see a small settlement usually with charity workers or a church to help them out. It was a trip I will never forget. President Cardoso had achieved his aim of showing me the need for better security co-operation as the only way to make progress. The boundary between Brazil and Colombia was so massive and inhospitable it would be nigh impossible to police.

We stayed overnight in Leticia and had a terrific time. We were first treated to a briefing by what seemed like most of the village. Here was a chance to lobby an important person on what they needed. I took it all in and passed it on to President Pastrana when I saw him in Bogotá, as I had promised. The police gave me a guided tour of the village and I saw how extensive the poverty was, but also what, with great ingenuity, folk were doing to make their lives a little more comfortable. The police then returned me to the only hotel in town before the Mayor gave me a meal.

'The Hotel', as it was called, was great. I have stayed at various times in the best hotels that New York or London has to offer. The facilities to swim and enjoy yourself are amazing but they lack any human spirit. Staying in these you could be in any large city in the world. As I write that sentence I suppose that is their attraction. Not for me though. When I entered the hotel in Leticia, there was a large sign declaring that, because of problems with the electricity supply, there was a need at present to choose between light or hot water. The hotel had chosen light. Basic it was, but the greetings and the warmth of the people were better than hot water. I washed very little and went down to the Mayor, who was waiting to take me to eat.

We went to what looked like the only bar and restaurant in town, and ate and drank very well. It was a good fun night. I can remember doing a cross between a salsa, tango and boogie with the chief of the local police. Bearing in mind our different sizes – I being tall and fat and having no real idea what we were doing, although I did it with gusto, and he being short and fat, and knowing exactly what he was doing, and doing it with even more gusto – it was a miracle we lasted so long. But I like to believe that what was most important was that we had a great time. It was an evening I won't forget. It is amazing how wonderful and full of fun the people are even though their country is facing such dire problems. I still miss working with the Colombian government, and the Colombian people.

The other route out of Colombia for large quantities of raw cocaine was on fast boats on the rivers through Venezuela down to the Caribbean, particularly Jamaica, where it was repackaged from small to large boats and transported on to Europe. Jamaica, as a country, is far from happy that because of the demand for cocaine in the UK and Europe its domestic cocaine problem is increasing (local people are paid in kind and often consume the cocaine themselves or sell it on to live) and they have to deal with all the violence and misery the drug trade brings. The Foreign Office were keen for me to go to Jamaica, so off I went. I tried to be clever and go five days early for a holiday and pay for Jon's ticket. It half worked. We had a good time together, but the weather for the whole period was cold and windy like England. In the last two years our short-break holidays of under a week have suffered from the same problem whether it was Jamaica, Spain or France. That's life – but at least it meant more sleep and reading.

I met in the UK with local Jamaican groups and the Jamaican High Commissioner David Muirhead before I left. I outlined what we were doing and planning to do, but they thought we were having no real effect and that much more radical solutions – including the legalization and regulation of drugs – were going to have to be seriously considered in the future. The only meaningful alternative to legalization would be a degree of international co-operation, exchanging security information not just on drugs, but on money laundering and the confiscation of the drug traffickers' assets. The groups also wanted to engage on a number of other issues that they faced in the UK and the difficulties they faced travelling back to Jamaica. It was a pretty hairy meeting, but we made good progress by deciding to list all the issues that had been raised and set up working groups to outline the problems and what they thought the solutions were. I then agreed with them that we would meet again in three weeks, by which time I would have answers from the relevant departments on the questions raised. It inevitably took longer than that, but thanks to my assistant private secretary Robert Cayzer, who worked with me on Jamaica, we got there in the end. On the issue of drugs the groups were united. The traffickers from the gangs in Jamaica were coming to the UK, operating in areas where Jamaicans lived and causing enormous problems of violence and addiction. There was also concern about what effects an increase in drug trafficking and the accompanying violence would have in Jamaica.

On arriving in Jamaica I couldn't help but fall in love with the country, its beauty and its people, even though I knew that there were parts of it where it was not safe for me to go. I visited the centre of Kingston's Trenchtown and saw the same poverty I came across later in rural areas, people packed into small rickety structures with a family of six living in a room no bigger than my bathroom. It is an image that will always stay with me, as will the people's resilience and determination to keep their spirits up and bring up their children in the best way possible in desperate living conditions. I visited a community centre there where I was shown round by the local residents and a friendly guy called Ziggy, who was doing his best to help as a community worker. The centre, partly funded by the British government, was just like a playschool over here but with about a fifth of the equipment and able to take in only a minuscule number of children from the area. Drug consumption was a problem that exacerbated an already almost impossible situation.

Immediately the residents knew I was from London they wanted to thank 'Mrs Clare' for her help. On my return home I phoned Clare Short at the Department for International Development to pass the message on. I talked to a number of Jamaican Ministers and learnt what efforts they were trying to make to combat the drugs trade. Their attitude was that western demand for drugs was at the root of the problem – much like in Colombia. We were asked for help with training the police and to continue with assistance for projects like the one that I had visited in Trenchtown. I took the requests back to the relevant departments and they did all they could. But, again like Colombia, any help given to Jamaica would have repercussions for the other islands in the Caribbean. It could result in displacement of the drug traffickers to other islands such as Guadeloupe or Antigua, which was only passing the buck.

What was terrifying was the lack of money that the Jamaican government had at its disposal. A very small amount of its national income was spent on services for the people – some estimates were as low as 10 per cent. All the rest was used to service the national debt. Such poverty and lack of resources meant that progress on the drugs issue was dependent on progress in many other areas. The Jamaicans are understandably a very proud people and were trying to do many things to help themselves. The most constructive action we could take was to continue to write off our share of their national debt and encourage other countries to do the same. Then there were development projects that the Jamaican government were working on, like the one down the coast from Montego Bay at Port Royal, which needed financial backing rather than grants or charity. They put together a tourist attraction of shops, a bit of antiquities and entertainment. To my untrained eye it looked like a good idea, particularly because it had guaranteed thousands of visitors a day from cruise ships, which at the moment have only a very limited number of places to dock. Port Royal was an ambitious project. It had deep water and needed a pier. I would have thought with the guaranteed customers it was a worthwhile investment. I came home with details that I discussed with, among others, Richard Branson. He suggested I approach Air Jamaica as a possible source of help, which I did.

I know a group from Port Royal came over to London to find investors. I hope they were successful because it was a fine example of a project that would make such a difference in terms of jobs and therefore the level of poverty and would be (with support) an excellent investment for a Jamaican-led project. It would be an enormous help in fighting the drugs problem too, because a decent job is the best guarantee to stop people turning to drugs and crime as a way of life.

With a very rugged coastline, the Jamaican coastguards had an almost impossible job trying to stop the drugs coming in. The traffickers had fast, modern speedboats; the coastguards had only two boats in all, one of which – when I was there – was in the dry dock getting repaired. Frustratingly, the coastguards had numerous high-quality boats tied up in their port, which they had captured from the traffickers. But they couldn't use them; they could only keep them for a while in case they were claimed, and then by law they had to auction them off. Sometimes they were bought back by the drug traffickers! I chatted with the Jamaican Prime Minister, P. J. Patterson, about the problems the coastguards were facing and suggested that it might be a good idea to change this law so as to allow the coastguards to use the fast boats they had captured. When he agreed, I offered to ask a UK civil servant to go over and help redraw the law to make the changes possible. Since British colonialism had left Jamaica with a bureaucracy not dissimilar from our own, I thought it was the most useful thing I could offer.

While in Jamaica I also went to the women's prison at a place called Fort Augusta. After seeing the sleeping quarters (dark and grim), and the head of the Jamaican Prison Service, John Prescod (a very competent and impressive person), I met with a group of English and Jamaican women who had been caught drug trafficking between the two countries. I was introduced and spoke briefly. The faces that greeted me were mainly sullen and untrusting. I managed not to comment, but what I found most amazing was that there were women there who looked just like my granny used to. I know old people can be carriers of drugs (mules as they are called) too, but it brings it home when you see the miserable life these grannies are leading in a place like Fort Augusta.

We had a good discussion with the women, and I know the

prison head listened because some of the complaints they made about the food were solved by having the prisoners themselves working in the kitchen to cook it how they liked it. They had other complaints they addressed to me too. Many of them had trouble getting home when they had finished their prison sentences, because their return tickets were invalid. They were told they had to try and raise the money for their tickets from their families. I took this up with our High Commissioner, Tony Smith, who said the embassy did not have the money to start paying (where would such a policy stop?), but inevitably if the situation was dire they would consider it. I said I would contact the airlines concerned to see what could be done. All the relevant airlines eventually agreed to make the tickets good if the embassy acted as a filter so that they weren't taken for a ride.

I tried to talk with the women about what we were doing as a government to warn people against risking their health, their children's futures and the lives of others by smuggling drugs. I talked about the education programmes we were putting into our schools and community projects like Positive Futures. But the answers I gave met with blank faces. The women wanted more done. And they wanted to help. We agreed we would try and make a video for a television slot and for use in schools with them talking straight to camera about what had happened to them. A number of those who didn't mind going public about their cases agreed to contact me on returning to the UK. I spent a fair amount of time trying to get people to help put this video together. I eventually found a man called Rick Elgood from Geejam Studios in London who was willing to do it for us. I tried to raise some money but with no luck. When I left government this was the one thing I really left without a parent politician to nurse it to conclusion. It turns out that it did not stay in government. It took on a life of its own. I used to get regular calls from the folk engaged on it. I hope they see it through.

After travelling west, I also went east in my determination to improve international co-operation against drugs. In particular I went to Iran, where their problem was now a familiar one to me: their country was being used as a transit route for drugs – this time heroin. Most of the world's heroin at the time came from the poppies grown in Afghanistan, with most of it then taken through Iran or Pakistan and onward to Europe. Like in Jamaica, the Iranians feel, rightly in a sense, that they are being used and that their problem stems from the demand for drugs in the west.

There were signs that the efforts being made by Iranian President Khatami to open things up a bit with governments in Europe were bearing fruit. Business was returning and many governments were beginning to take steps to open up dialogue on different issues. In London I had met with the Iranian Ambassador, who had extended the official invitation to me to visit and see part of the country and discuss our mutual concerns about the drugs trade. I also met a group of prominent Iranians living in London before I went out. I was the first British woman Minister to go there since the Islamic revolution in 1979. I had to shop first to buy the required garment – called a rapoche – to cover my hair and body in line with Islamic law.

The Iranians pulled out a lot of stops for my visit and I got to see the Speaker of the Iranian Parliament, Mr Karroubi, Vice-President Hashemi, Interior Minister Moussavi-Lari, Foreign Secretary Kharazzi and finally President Khatami himself. All were wary of me to begin with. But we talked a lot and made some progress on sharing information on our fight against drugs domestically. Their problem was growing, and we looked to see what further co-operation there could be in the future between Iran and the UK. I knew we were making progress when during my meeting with President Khatami we began talking in a more relaxed manner – well, as relaxed as you can be with two long lines of officials extending from where we sat. At times like that, the number of officials present can be a real handicap to progress, when personal chemistry is so important. In our conversation we moved from our two countries to a general discussion of politics and political philosophy. It was a good discussion and helped to establish a working relationship. He asked me how I was coping being dressed from head to toe in black, as is expected of women in Iran. I said I was enjoying it. I had been able all week to wear trousers and not wash my hair. I was enjoying a break from living in a suit. He smiled at me and said the form of dress, the rapoche, had many advantages. I decided wisely, I think, not to take the conversation any further. The Englishwomen in the embassy said they were okay to wear in the winter but in the summer they were very uncomfortable. I now use mine as a dressing gown. The postman has learnt to cope when I go downstairs in the early morning for a parcel too big for the letterbox, but I have had some interesting conversations with Muslims that come to the door.

Looking back on all the meetings in all the countries that I visited, I believed we had the start of some good working relationships. Where the UK could assist in small ways, it helped a common understanding to grow as to how we could begin tackling the international drugs trade together. But the groups involved in the trade are very rich, very powerful and very violent, and, unless countries come together with a unity of purpose, there is never going to be any hope of stopping them. Lines between drug-producing and drug-consuming countries are becoming ever more blurred, but each still blames the other for the problem. I think the sand is shifting slightly. When I was in Washington in March 2001 President Bush made an important statement recognizing that those countries where the demand for drugs was high had a big responsibility towards those where it was produced. It was an important shift from the old 'war on the drug barons' rhetoric. But I have to say that my meetings with, among others, Condoleeza Rice didn't inspire me to believe that the US was ready to take a more enlightened approach. Nevertheless across the world there is a greater recognition today than ever before that we are all in this together and if there are to be solutions then they have to be forged together without playing the blame game.

I took a special interest in drugs policy because I cared about it and understood the issues well. I tried to make progress across the board. I saw my main job as being to nag, chivvy, encourage and make sure goals were reached. It was also to support the civil servants and people delivering policy on the ground so that when they were doing a good job I could reinforce and encourage them, and give them more confidence; as a result I did a fair number of visits to drug centres. These were very useful as I could see for myself what was working or not. The main lesson that I learnt was that every addict is different, and the centres that were making most progress were ones that were flexible and had the resources to respond to the individual needs of each of their clients.

My attitude in all the areas I worked on was the same. I firmly believe in talking to as many people as possible about the policy under consideration, with as many different views as possible. I obviously didn't agree with everyone but it does make a difference if people have had the opportunity to share their experience and opinions. What was interesting with the pressure groups – the non-governmental organizations – was their surprise that I wanted to talk to all the groups, even those vehemently opposed to government policy. Because pressure groups have few resources they need to maximize the benefit of every event. So I had to be very cautious not to overstate my case, particularly with regard to what was going to happen or what I could deliver. I am not criticizing pressure groups – in fact I have a lot of respect for them and consider the work they do to be an important part of a democracy.

The problem for the civil servants is that the system is not built to move quickly: minutes have to be circulated, decisions taken cannot be acted upon until they have been sent up to the permanent secretary and then laterally to other relevant Ministers. Even in times of national emergency it still takes time and a great deal of personal effort to get things moving. I remember on one occasion being asked to take part in government action to help deal with the awful problems people in the South of England were having with flooding. It was winter 2001. I got in the car and drove down there, to Lewes in Sussex. I went to an old people's home and around the local shops and houses. People were really miserable and increasingly angry at what they saw as the lack of government action. I came back to London with a long list for each of a number of different departments, including the suggestion that we needed a task force quickly. Eventually a task force was set up under Countryside Minister Elliot Morley to take it all forward. But the time and the energy everyone had to devote just to make basic things – like getting in supplies of sandbags – happen was exhausting.

Nothing moves quickly in government unless you sit on it and make it happen. I tried to sit on as many decisions as possible by having my lists. Every morning I checked with John my private secretary what progress had been made on a host of issues. If he was not there, one of the assistant private secretaries, Miles or Robert, or Tracey or Graham from my office, were treated to the list. Then I would rewrite it at night with issues crossed off if they had been completed and others added. The special advisers, Nigel and Andrew, would some mornings look at me as if to say, 'Oh God, not the list treatment again.' The civil servants, I now know, thought the same, but were too polite or too well trained to say so. But now they joke with me and say they are thinking of having one of their own.

Throughout my working life, I found that with the demands being made on me it was only by lists that I could keep track of all the different bits of my life. For example some days I would have a list for immediate action in the office, another for work that was under way or requests for information that I did not want to ask for every day but did not want to forget. I had a list of things that I needed to do both at home in London and at work. I had a shopping list for food and other bits, a list for

Jon of things to remind him about or to say to him, because if I didn't see him for a couple of days I didn't want to forget things. You will be pleased to hear that now I am working independently the number of lists has declined considerably.

I enjoyed my time in the Cabinet Office. The staff are bright and good fun, and we worked well together. I think some of the frustrations I felt were shared by them. Until the cabinet structure and its role with No. 10 is clarified, the Cabinet Office will always be a difficult place to get results. The structure of government, and many of its functions, like policy making, do need modernizing urgently, as does the civil service, but it can only be done by strong leadership from the centre and with the buy-in of the other departments and the unions. The unions know it has to happen and are keen to be part of it. But there is an enormous job to be done if central government is ever going to do its job properly and make sure that the services people pay for through their taxes are delivered efficiently and effectively for everyone. I think the bottom line is good management. Are the civil servants trained to be proactive and manage? No. Can politicians manage? Some can, but many have no idea. I am not arguing for bringing businessmen into government – many that I meet are not effective managers. Management in government is about being cost-effective, but also about delivering a public good which has to be evaluated against criteria other than just value for money. This I think is a central problem for modern-day governments that want to get results. Delivery of policy does not come without proper management and careful thought about what is needed. Sadly this does not always take place.

12

Wait A Mo, I Haven't Gone Yet

THE FUTURE

I had made myself a promise when I entered the House of Commons: after five Parliaments, approximately twenty years, I would leave. I believed that that was long enough to achieve some results in Parliamentary politics and that after that I wanted to try and do something else. I certainly wasn't going to let myself become a pensioner and still be in the House of Commons. I was leaving Parliament, but I certainly wasn't leaving politics.

My decision to leave Parliament came earlier than planned in the summer of 2000. I was actually bounced into announcing my decision in September that year by my constituency agent in Redcar who had a tendency to chat to the local press on my behalf. He made a statement that was interpreted as me saying I was going. It was all over the national press the next day. I had not discussed it with him, but, as I was thinking of it, when the media were on to me to confirm or deny the story I wasn't going to lie. Some of the newspaper headlines were ones of surprise and shock at the events. Others speculated that something had been going on – page one of the *Independent* that morning had 'Mowlam to quit, but the whispers continue'.

But before I said anything publicly I wanted to talk to Tony Blair. He had seen the story and assumed I would dismiss it. He was shocked when I told him I wanted to go. I told him that I was leaving Parliament at the next election, but also that I wanted to resign immediately from the cabinet and from my job as Cabinet Office Minister. I felt I was duty bound to do so, and that if I did not go I would be a bit of a lame duck. Tony tried to persuade me to stay in Parliament, but eventually he accepted my decision. He would not however accept my resignation from the cabinet. Only Nigel, I, Tony and Alistair were in the room, and we all spoke frankly. In fact I was relieved, as I had been trying to think for some time of the best way to go, causing the least damage possible to the government. At the end of the meeting Nigel and Alistair discussed the best way to handle it with the press and that was that.

My relationship with Ali has had its ups and downs. I think he certainly overdid it on the spinning and became a very powerful non-elected figure. He is tough but you need to be in his job, working with a tough media. He probably did some spinning against me, but he was good at the job he was paid to do and I don't dislike him for it. He went over the top at times, but who doesn't? Throughout my time in government I had a good relationship with most people in Tony's office, including Angie Hunter, who served Tony well, and I think of her as a friend. And I had all right but rather distant relationships with Cherie and Jonathan Powell – they're not really my kind of soulmates. Cherie and I chat amiably when our paths cross at social events. We are not of the same social circle and have never got to know each other. I feel I know enough lawyers. Jonathan has been around the party and I have never really got to know him either. I felt on his arrival he had a poor grasp of the politics of the Labour party and didn't seem to think it mattered.

My relationship with Tony had, I think, begun to get rocky at the party conference in Brighton in 1998. Getting a standing ovation for someone else in the middle of your speech would be a little too much for any speaker – although, as I have said, I think it affected some of those around Tony a lot more than it affected him. Clearly me digging in over staying in the N. Ireland job in the summer of 1999 did not please No. 10, especially as they were seen to back off. Not something a Prime Minister likes to be seen to do. I made no secret of the fact that I was not happy in the way I left N. Ireland. I said at the time that I knew that I would have to go soon, but for me it was too early. There was still a lot to do. I knew it was not possible to stay in the same job for ever, but there were Ministers in other governments and in the Blair government that were to stay in the same job for more than one Parliament. But I also knew it was ultimately the PM's decision.

I felt frustrated about leaving N. Ireland at such a crucial stage in the peace process. I had stood up to unionism and loyalism over Drumcree in the face of concerted opposition from many people including David Trimble. But I had been right to do so, because it can never be right or fair to back down in the face of unacceptable pressure. I felt it was also necessary to stand up to the negative forces within unionism again over the implementation of the Good Friday Agreement. David Trimble was as much a hostage as the rest of us to those in the Ulster Unionist party who opposed the progress that the Agreement represented.

It almost seemed towards the end of my time in N. Ireland that some of the people around me, who had made so much over the years of the importance of the history, were now in danger of ignoring it. They were fighting endless battles over issues that paled into insignificance in the light of the tremendous steps forward that the Agreement represented. It was such a momentous opportunity – with ceasefires in place and many ancient, bitter political quarrels settled – and yet the risk was really there that it would all be squandered. Yes, weapons decommissioning is an important part of the peace process, but it was the wrong issue to get stuck on – all or nothing – with very little room for compromise on either side. That's never a wise place to be in any negotiation. But we were where we were, and we had to work with it, despite the fact that, in my book, it put back the possibility of implementing the Agreement by years rather than months.

I believed that Sinn Fein and the republicans were willing to take the peaceful route. Yes, of course they would try to make what gains they could towards their ambition of a united Ireland, but this would be through democratic not violent means. If, as many thought, they were playing a double game and did return to violence, I would have been proved wrong. But in the process many hundreds of lives would have been saved, and any remnants of support from the Irish, British and American governments for Sinn Fein would have evaporated. Perhaps even more importantly the response of the people north and south on the island of Ireland would have been so negative that it would have done Sinn Fein irreparable damage.

So I believed that we had little to lose and everything to gain by keeping going forward. And if the unionist leadership at that time had played the game they could have co-operated and at the same time reinforced their position. This was exactly how the Agreement was constructed, and it would have been in their interests to implement it because it would have protected their position. Sensible heads in the Ulster Unionist party knew this at the time. But by then the hardline tail was wagging the moderate dog, and the British government was not willing to stand up to the hardline element in unionism, as I believe we should have done. To be honest, towards the end, I did not even bother to put my views on the table because of my deteriorating position with No. 10. I felt I was not being listened to, and, as I have said, my position in N. Ireland was undermined, not just in my view – many other people thought the same. As one N. Ireland politician said to me, he thought it better to talk to the organ grinder or his staff at No. 10 than to me the monkey.

Not taking the job at the Department of Health in the 1999 autumn reshuffle was, I'm sure, another mistake on my part in Tony's eyes. It led to firm statements from No. 10 that I had not even been offered the job. I had already decided that I did not want to go straight from one extremely tough job to another, but my decision was reinforced by a chance meeting with Ken Clarke, who told me, 'Don't take Health, it's a nightmare.' But my rejecting what Tony wanted to do with me, for a second time, I'm sure did not help our relationship.

Another job suggested for me, about which at times there was much press speculation, was that of Mayor of London. All during 1999 there had been various attempts to get me to take the opportunity of standing to be Mayor, something that continued well into my time in the Cabinet Office. One of the most startling attempts was as early as March 1999. I was woken up by a call from Radio Cleveland with the news that the *Guardian* was saying on its front page that I was going to stand for election as Mayor, and could I give an interview on this dramatic event. I called the journalist that had written it. He said the story had first appeared in the *Mirror* and he understood it to be a story floating about, and the source was Jonathan Powell at No. 10. I spoke to other journalists who said the same thing.

I had actually thought about it as a possible future option if I was going to have to leave N. Ireland. When however I looked at the powers and the funds for doing the job, I decided no. The powers were limited and the money even more so. Much of the funding had to be negotiated with the Treasury. As there was no sign of Gordon moving from the Treasury I could only see obtaining money as a constant nightmare. 'No thank you' was my first thought and a very wise one it proved to be, particularly when I later watched all the problems over funding the London Underground. I would have backed Ken Livingstone and Bob Kiley on that. Ken had in my view the most economic way of getting the money and Kiley, whom I had met, had restructured the New York subway and struck me as an effective operator and a competent manager.

When Tony and I discussed it many times during 1999, I said why I thought it was not doable, but he was convinced it was. It was a good job from his point of view and an exciting one with potential. I also argued that I was not identified as a Londoner and there were plenty of good competent candidates from among the London Labour MPs, such as Glenda Jackson, Nick Raynsford and Ken Livingstone. I can't remember when I said to Tony that I thought Ken would do a good job, as the whole thrust of No. 10's thoughts and actions was to stop Ken. I wasn't in agreement because not only did I think he would do a reasonable job but the voters of London were keen on him and I didn't think he could be beaten. This was not what No. 10 wanted to hear, but I thought the people of London would make the decision in the end.

I weakened in March 2000 and said I would give it a go. But after a couple of days' reflection I changed my mind and said I wasn't prepared to do it. Anyway, by this time Frank Dobson had been the No. 10 preferred candidate for six months and was out campaigning and doing his best. We were all out speaking on platforms with him to try and increase his support, but the pressure behind the scenes for me to stand had continued since the beginning of the year. And odd stories kept cropping up in the press about me 'making a late entry into the contest' and quoting 'senior insiders' in Downing Street as saying, 'She might yet be the only one that can save our bacon.' Simultaneously pressure was put on Frank Dobson to stand down by a number of people. For example, in January 2000 Margaret McDonagh, General Secretary of the Labour party, and the MP Tessa Jowell were despatched to see him to say he could not win and should stand down – an act of gross unfairness as he was only standing because Tony had convinced him it was necessary for the good of the party. But I think my refusal to stand was just about the last straw for Tony and Ali in relation to me.

Was it a coincidence that it was around this time that the most aggressive of the off-the-record briefing against me began? True, I had set the cat among the pigeons again by admitting in January that I had smoked cannabis as a student. The question 'Have you ever smoked dope?' was asked of anyone in government who worked in the anti-drugs field. Since becoming the co-ordinator of government's anti-drugs policy in November 1999, I knew that sooner or later I would be asked outright. I had been holding to a line agreed with No. 10 that basically meant not answering the question directly at all. It was pointed out quite forcibly to me that it was not helpful to my cabinet colleagues, that they would now be asked if they had smoked it and what their views were. In effect it would become a witch-hunt.

I was doing a pretty good job of avoiding the question until one Sunday newspaper found a woman from my student days at Iowa State University in the US, who said she had seen me 'holding a cannabis cigarette'. As soon as I heard about it, I was determined to be honest and nail the story then and there. So I did a couple of Sunday TV interviews just to get my version of events out there. I said I had tried marijuana, but hadn't liked it particularly and unlike President Clinton I did inhale, but it wasn't part of my life. I didn't see that it would in any way affect my fight against the drugs that were killing people, like heroin and cocaine, and I said so. I also said that I would continue to say to young people that taking drugs is not within the law and is not a sensible thing to do in your life.

Despite the high level of official paranoia, my cabinet colleagues did a good job of handling it. Jack Straw was on the Sunday programmes too and he said, 'Good for Mo in making this clear.' Keith Hellawell said, 'I think we've got to stop this idea of witch-hunts and pointing the finger. The debate needs to be at a much higher level than that. If there continues to be a label on people – you know, "you are a bad person if you ever took drugs" – then we'll never move forward. There needs to be more openness.' The level of support I got across the political spectrum in the press – from the *Guardian* to the *Telegraph* – for being open and honest and not afraid to debate the issues was astonishing. But I think the fact that I went ahead and said what I wanted anyway despite what Downing Street had wanted was just another example for them of how I wouldn't toe the line.

The most vicious of the whispering against me began a week or so later. On 30 January 2000 the *Independent on Sunday* ran a story quoting a 'senior government aide' as saying that my battle with a brain tumour had left me 'without the intellectual rigour' to do my job. (What had I just achieved in N. Ireland?) Again, a senior government aide was quoted as saying, 'The illness appears to have affected her, and she doesn't appear to be able to do the job in the same way. That deft touch has gone.' Later on it got worse with an article in the *New Statesman* quoting a 'leering adviser' as saying 'and then there was the time that Mo had attended a trade unions conference and had a good time with the whole executive, one by one'. At first it was hurtful. But I decided that the only way to beat it was to not read it and ignore it. There was a lot of debate, which friends tried to engage me in, about who was doing it. I did not take part in that because that would have only kept the stories running.

On the one hand I was still seeing very positive opinion polls, like the one on Channel Four that month which had viewers voting me the most popular politician in the country. Yet the press were still getting plenty of what they wanted on the quiet from 'government sources' or 'senior Labour figures'. As the *Daily Express* put it, 'Not a day goes by without a so-called "senior government aide" or "insider" badmouthing her. Yesterday alone we were told she's a "loose cannon", "has only herself to blame", misses vital strategy meetings, refuses to talk to Peter Mandelson, gave up her bodyguard voluntarily and then started to complain, and isn't trusted by Blair or Millbank with interviews".'

I managed throughout what were a difficult first few months of that year to keep going. I remember going on *Woman's Hour* in February when the attacks were heavy, saying that I did not know who was putting the knife in, it hurt a lot but I wasn't going to be beaten. It was then said that I was the one keeping the story going by acknowledging that it was happening and commenting on it. But what was I supposed to do? Agree with it, say I had lost, and accept all the other lies? That's just not me. And in the middle of all this crap in the press about how I was not up to the job, No. 10 were still trying to get me to run for London Mayor!

I didn't consciously fight back, but I did do the odd interview and when asked questions about what was going on continued to answer them honestly. I did that in an interview in March with Colin Brown of the *Independent*, when I said that the answer to the criticisms that I was unwell and not up to the job was just to get on with it and show that I was. I explained that I had given up reading the stupid bits about me in the press, leaving that to my husband, Jon, who just relayed a sense of what was going on.

It was getting to the point where I just didn't know who to believe. The *Sun* ran a front-page 'exclusive' in April saying that Blair was making plans to pull Mandelson out of N. Ireland and put him in the Cabinet Office, a move 'which would spell the end of popular Dr Mowlam's cabinet career'. I had flu that month and on my return to work I found that some of the work I had been doing on drugs was being shifted to the drugs tsar, Keith Hellawell, and a new head had been appointed to my press office. The *Sunday Times* reported these facts under the heading, 'Isolated Mo is elbowed out to the Labour sidelines'.

But despite all the rubbish being written I managed to keep my spirits up, and to keep doing the job. I remember one press conference that month when I was interrupted by the trill of a journalist's mobile phone. 'Whoever's phone that is,' I announced calmly, 'will be beaten.' I was still getting plenty of support. One poll in the *Guardian* in May led the paper to write that 'Mo Mowlam continues to prove the popular success story of the Labour Government' and that 'she remains Labour's strongest electoral card'. I think the journalist was Alan Travis and he rather optimistically wrote afterwards that the news was 'likely to lay to rest the whispering campaign against her'. No such luck, Alan. A week later *The Times* reported that a 'very senior colleague' had said I was about to have a nervous breakdown!

That same May Suzanne Moore wrote in the *Mail on Sunday*:

How annoying it must be when you set out to destroy someone, orchestrate a vicious whispering campaign against them, imply they are incompetent, out of control and mentally unbalanced – and the damn silly public don't take a blind bit of notice. Despite demoting her, and publically sidelining her, the personality-free zone that has done the Government's dirty work on Mo Mowlam has failed spectacularly. We still like her. She is still more popular than the PM. What will they do now? Say sorry, promote her, or continue to pretend she has gone barmy?

I was beginning to think very seriously about the future and why this had become a government that I no longer wanted to be a part of. When I announced I was leaving Parliament, at the beginning of September, one of my most positive supporters was Barbara Castle, the former Labour Cabinet Minister and beloved of the party. She went public saying how badly she thought I had been treated. She said, 'I'm very pro-Mo. If it hadn't been for Mo, there wouldn't have been a Good Friday Agreement. Then, unfortunately, Tony Blair stepped in and started making deals with the unionists and she was edged out.' Barbara went on, 'I think she was being humiliated. The Cabinet Office is a non-job. No self-respecting woman would stay in a non-job. She's her own woman and isn't going to pretend she's something she isn't. I think Mo's a successful politician in her own right and more successful than most men. It's a very sad day for the Labour party.'

What was sad was that in spite of the support of Barbara and several other MPs I was still trying to protect Tony Blair by saying, yes, sexism in politics exists but it is a problem across Europe, not just here in Britain. What I couldn't or didn't want to see then, but it is so clear to me now, was that I was being forced out of the cabinet. I was too popular to sack, so I had to be 'persuaded to leave'. I desperately didn't want to believe there had been a campaign, and denied it to myself even when the evidence was staring me in the face. I have now accepted it and dealt with the anger at what they did to my life.

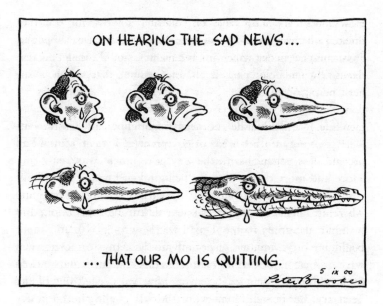

I still can't bring myself to think Tony Blair okayed it. I like to think it was the young arrogant set in Downing Street and some at the Labour party headquarters at Millbank who liked talking to journalists and wanted to sound important. I was an easy target, as were other women. Harriet Harman was driven out, Ann Taylor and Margaret Beckett often dismissed, and Margaret Jay had a very rough time. In the end, misogyny may be part of the explanation. Another view was expressed by Roy Hattersley, who said in *The Times* in the middle of the year:

I think Downing Street have a vision of their sort of people. And if a Minister is not their sort of person then that Minister is beyond the pale. The young men who surround the PM are a pretty extreme bunch in one way or another, who want to create an atmosphere of the laager, the South African laager in which everyone who was of a right mind was inside, and everyone who is of an unlike mind is outside. She may have Blairite philosophies but she doesn't have a Blairite character and personality. Blairites don't walk about party conferences with their shoes off. Blairites don't admit that they smoked whatever it was she smoked. Blairites don't swear in public. So because her performance and behaviour is not like them, because she isn't a female Stephen Byers, they assume that somehow she must be excluded.

While I could handle the negative briefing, my frustrations were growing in other areas of government. I was finding I had less and less patience with the way government was being run. More and more decisions were being taken by No. 10 without consultation with the relevant Minister or Secretary of State. There are plenty of examples scattered through this book, and it didn't just apply to me. Don't get me wrong: No. 10's input could be very valuable, especially if the Ministers concerned were properly included in the discussions and particularly when we were having problems getting what we needed out of the Treasury. But it is different when the first you learn of a policy change or decision that affects the job you are doing is through your civil servants or, even worse, though the press. It doesn't do a lot for your standing as a member of the government, or for perceptions of how your relations are with the centre of government.

This was a problem for me in N. Ireland, but at the Cabinet Office it became even worse. I think part of it was that the Cabinet Office was seen by Tony and his inner circle as just an extension of the Downing Street operation. So if they had work on a new policy they wanted developed, they would just create a new unit in the Cabinet Office to deal with it. The people who ended up working in the units often believed they had a direct line to the PM, even if it was just to the policy-making part of No. 10. This was very undermining and not the kind of supportive role I expected. The Cabinet Office press office was on occasion used in the same way.

As I say, I did not disagree with much of the policy. I had always been a strong advocate of new Labour from the time of

Neil Kinnock and had worked strenuously to help achieve reform – speaking, writing, working on committees and later as a member of the National Executive of the party. What I found difficult was the way policies were being implemented and people were being dealt with. I believe, whatever you are doing, you should try as hard as possible to take people with you, particularly if you want the policy to work.

Changes in the public services, for example, necessarily involve the trade unions, and despite the fact that there will always be some resistance to change, if people are included in the policy formulation and implementation then they can be moved onside. The trade unions are as keen to see a Labour government stay in power and make progress as the politicians. I believe they could have been more helpful if they had been more included. Perhaps we might have avoided some of the mistakes of that first new Labour government – like the insulting 75p increase given to pensioners – if there had been more consultation with Labour members and trade unionists, who would have argued strongly against it.

When we arrived in government, Labour party members both inside and outside the trade union movement were as ecstatic as everyone else. We could have captured and built on that feeling much more if the style had been more inclusive from the beginning. Instead we were seen to be cosying up to big business, in a one-sided manner. Being seen to do more to listen to both sides would have made us stronger, and helped us to move forward on necessary reforms. By the time I left government our relations with the unions as a government were not in good shape. One big union had withheld some of its funding support and the leader of one of the unions closest to the Prime Minister was openly criticizing him. The General Secretary of the Trades Union Congress, John Monks, was doing his best to represent his members' views and at the same time temper his language, in the hope of getting Tony to see his point of view. I know the relationship between the Labour party and the trade unions has always blown hot and cold, and there is always a lot of low-level politicking going on. But I would have felt better about it if it hadn't been so clear some of the time that the people around Tony Blair were looking to pick a fight with the unions in order to please business and to get a good headline in the *Sun*.

I knew as well as any Minister that making an effort to include people is very time-consuming and certainly will not produce a result that pleases everyone. But in my experience if talks and discussions with interested groups – the voluntary sector, trade unions and business – have taken place prior to decisions being made then their objections, if they have not been met in discussions, are usually less aggressively voiced. Equally, inclusivity becomes more possible if the centre – i.e. No. 10 – trusts Ministers more, and actually delegates some of the decision-making to them.

Both the trade union movement and the Labour party have been important parts of my life. I worked a lot with the trade unions when I was at Northern College in Barnsley and made many good friends who are still friends today. For much of my life the Labour party has been an integral part – again many friends from twenty years ago whom I met in the party are still close. I think this was another distinction between Tony and me. As someone once put it, I hugged the party and the union movement, and Tony shook their hand. I was right with Tony on the need for reform of both. Within both there were a large number of folk that knew change and modernization were on the cards. Where we differed was on how to get change. I was for praising and inclusivity, and Tony wanted to work out what was needed and then go about achieving it – no great difference, but a difference that folk recognized. Perhaps if we had worked together better, we could have made a lot of progress.

But I was as guilty as any other Minister in not taking enough time talking to backbench MPs in our own party. I briefed the spokespeople of the other parties and did an information sheet regularly for my Parliamentary colleagues, but I failed to do enough face-to-face meetings to include them. After all, this was their government too and more effort to consult on policy matters before they are introduced means you have a government that ultimately faces less antagonism among its Parliamentary colleagues and makes better decisions as a result. Of course there would still be rows and rebellions, but a more open and accommodating atmosphere would make all the difference in the world.

Part of the answer to this problem is a radical review of how our Parliamentary system works. At the start of the twenty-first century the demands on MPs and in particular Ministers are much greater than they were thirty years ago. To be a good constituency MP means time spent in the constituency visiting and answering letters; a reasonable attendance at the House of Commons for votes; and listening to and participating in the odd debate. Being a Minister in addition means that all parts of the MP's job get done less well than one would hope. To have a family life as well is a real struggle. The whole structure ought to be looked at hard.

Reading this through it feels like an extended moan. It should not be read as that. I am proud of having been a cabinet Minister in the Labour government and proud of what it has achieved, which in many areas is considerable. Looking at the dodgy state of the Tories in recent years it's all too easy to see what the alternative could be. I just feel that with more inclusiveness, more trust between players, even more progress could have been made. This goes in particular for the differences between Tony Blair and Gordon Brown. If Tony cannot sort out a working relationship with Gordon, then I think he has no choice but to move him. The trouble over the timing of the 2001 election was because Gordon and Tony argued for weeks over whether the election should be called in May as Gordon wanted, to get foot and mouth off the headlines, or in June as Tony wanted. During the election campaign the tensions at party headquarters resulted in a cabinet Minister saying to me, 'Gordon is trying to run this campaign with himself and a few cronies, and is excluding people close to Tony and full-time officials.' The difficulties over differences over the policy on the euro and personal animosity is hampering the work of government. Watching the body language of the two of them in cabinet is an education. Frosty would be an understatement. When criticisms surface in the press they claim that they are the best of friends. The public aren't taken in.

The decision I took to leave the government was the toughest of my life. It was a long time coming and in the end I was more concerned that my departure couldn't be interpreted as any kind of slight on the Labour party. That is why I campaigned so hard in the 2001 general election. The demand for me to go with prospective candidates and press the flesh in their local high street was very strong. I campaigned in fifty-two constituencies and have seen enough high streets, market places and shopping centres in towns across Britain to write a book. Immediately after the general election I went away, but had lobbied before leaving – as I did so often into what seemed a vacuum at No. 10 – for Adam Ingram to be given something if he was moved from N. Ireland. He was moved to be Minister of State at Defence, which was a job I knew he would love and also could do well at.

When I announced my decision to go, my main thoughts were about the friends I would miss in the Cabinet Office, among MPs and in Ireland north and south. I knew I would go back in years ahead to visit my favourite spots on the island of Ireland. So why did I leave? I still support the Labour government and consider on balance that Tony is the best leader we have for the Labour party and government. Progress in N. Ireland would not have been possible without him.

There is no one thing that made me leave the government. It was not an easy decision. The Labour party in some shape or form had been a dominant feature for most of my life. I will continue to be a political animal in some form. I disliked intensely the centralizing tendency and arrogance of No. 10. I think their lack of inclusiveness of the cabinet, MPs, party members and the unions leads to bad decisions. Try as I might, I got no indication that their views or behaviour would change. I found the briefings against me cruel and unfair but would have weathered them if they had not undermined my ability to do the job both in N. Ireland and in the Cabinet Office. Why stay if it has been made impossible to do the job? Yes, there is part of me that feels on reflection that I was driven out. I think I did a good job in N. Ireland and made progress and not to be allowed to continue was a crying shame. I am no longer bitter, only sad that I was not able to stay and work at it.

After I had announced that I would be leaving Parliament and the government, Sir John Kerr, permanent secretary at the Foreign Office (whom I got on with since his time as Ambassador in Washington), was given the task by No. 10 of finding something for me to do. It was felt that this would soften my leaving the government. A number of options were entertained in the international sphere, but there was really not much available. One option discussed, which I have taken up, was to become a member of the International Crisis Group. This is an organization made up of individuals from many different countries with an interest in conflict management who come together to produce good, clear, independent reports on conflicts around the world. I have enjoyed my role in this since the first meeting in Brussels in September 2001. I learnt a lot from experts on other conflicts around the world and had good discussions with people that knew more than me, which is always stimulating. John Kerr and Tony put in a lot of effort to get me membership of the ICG. It is a positive organization and gives me an arena in which I can continue my interest in Latin America, particularly the drug problems and the conflict in Colombia.

It was always frustrating in government not having enough time to think or write. Soon after the general election I took on a weekly newspaper column, partly to help pay the day-to-day bills but more because I enjoy writing and doing it keeps me engaged with current issues. Friends would phone with ideas – some of which I would exclude, interesting though they were, because they were too London-centric, like problems with bus lanes or with minicabs. A frequent question was how did I cope with no longer being in government? The truth is I haven't really noticed much of a difference in terms of workload. Yes, there are fewer meetings and no evening voting, but I still work regularly six days a week. I write for the first four or five hours every morning. Then, in the afternoon, I prepare and read material for writing my book the next day, have the odd meeting and sometimes a nap. I then try and relax and spend time with family in the limited evening time left.

On finishing this book I have lots of other things I want to do. The first is to involve myself in cross-community – or integrated – education in N. Ireland in a fund-raising capacity. It was one of the issues I considered focusing on at the start of my time as Secretary of State, but it soon became clear that the talks were the most important thing, and that is what I concentrated on. I was sad not to make more progress on supporting these pioneering schools, but I knew it was much more than just an issue that you did on the side.

In principle there is a lot of support for integrated education in N. Ireland. Encouraging children from both sides of the religious divide to be educated together at the same school is one of those issues which it is difficult to oppose. The problem is that it can be seen to undermine the Church schools, of all denominations. This is especially true when Churches are desperately trying to hold on to their congregations – although not so desperately in N. Ireland, which has a church-going population higher than anywhere else in the UK or Ireland. Nonetheless Church schools are important to all religions in N. Ireland, and therefore support for integrated education among the clergy on all sides is low. Similarly, among the majority of political parties, excluding the Women's Coalition and the Alliance party, all are lukewarm about integrated education, partly because it would begin to break down a clear voting block for each of their parties.

Out of government, with no particular role in N. Ireland apart from a deep personal interest in what happens, I knew it would be tough to really make a difference in the development of integrated education. Also I would defend a parent's right to make their own choice as to the school for their child. But when I began planning a fund-raising visit to five US cities it was on the basis of improving the facilities at the existing integrated schools to help them compete for pupils on a level playing field with other schools. My sponsors, the Integrated Education Fund in N. Ireland, helped select a number of schools with particular needs – schools which in many cases were started on amazingly small amounts of money, itself an indication of the strength of desire among some parents to have their children educated together. My first fund-raising attempt had to be postponed because of the appalling events in New York of 11 September. But when it becomes possible I will be off to the United States to see what I can raise among the Irish American community.

The other idea I want to develop is what has been nicknamed Mo-Mo homes. From my time in government and when I was in opposition there was one constant problem, which was very depressing because there was nothing that I could do to help. That was when parents, usually in their sixties, came to talk to me about the problems they were having coping with their severely disabled child. Often such 'children' could be a strapping man of nearly forty – he could be too heavy to lift if he fell over. All I felt I could do was talk to them, suggest they shared their problems with their doctor or their social worker, and give them some addresses of residential homes where they could try and get a place. I spent most of the time counselling them that it was all right to put their child in a home. They had done a sterling job and it would be better to move him now so they would know he was happily settled before the whole situation became untenable. More residential accommodation for disabled people is desperately needed, and I believe it is a government responsibility to help to provide it. But what I want to see is some way of giving the parents a rest, some kind of life for the many, many years that they have put in looking after their child. There are not many facilities that cater for a family with a disabled child, but the number of holiday facilities is increasing. Nevertheless there are very few that will take a child without the parents for a week or two, to give the parents a much deserved rest.

I want to try and increase the number of holiday homes for disabled people who are brought up by their parents. Talking to people already working in the field the biggest problem they face is finding a regular supply of volunteers to work with the trained staff, because disabled people need one-to-one care. To pay for more staff makes the whole exercise very costly.

There is another vulnerable group of people I would like to help. Working as I have in government with many drug addicts and ex-addicts I have met some of the most decent, kind and giving people. Many whom I have met in halfway homes across the country, lovely though they are as human beings, do not have the confidence or self-respect to go back into their communities. If they go home their families may continue to treat them as addicts, as many families will have gone through years of the addict trying to give up and failing and will be wary of money or goods going missing from the house again. Also returning to their peer group, unless they are feeling really confident about being clean, can put heavy and unhelpful pressures on the young person to return to drugs.

For an ex-addict to get their self-respect back they need loving. Unfortunately you cannot legislate for love. But what is so true about many of the people I know with disabilities is that they are good friends and respond to care and friendship warmly and really make you feel wanted. Perhaps because of what they have been through or are going through themselves, their first instinct is not to think, 'Why are your teeth in such bad shape as a result of heroin?' or 'Why are you so horribly thin?' but rather to give the ex-addict a cuddle.

What I want to try and achieve is a disabled holiday home next to a halfway house for ex-addicts who are clean but are not yet strong enough to go out into their communities. They need more time in sheltered accommodation; they need someone there to help them find training for a job. In return they work in the holiday home with the disabled folk. This is as yet an idea, but it will be one of my priorities for the future.

I also would like to give talks and accept a few of the many invitations to attend events I receive. Then I will find a proper job. I don't know what it will be and have not really thought about it yet. All I know is I would like it to include working with diverse groups of people, dealing with specific problems like helping in one of the many conflict areas around the world. I also know I like a challenge, so I have not cancelled out trying to help run a business. I would not mind trying a bit of television work which included talking to or interviewing people. Some-time in the next few years I would also like to do some fund-raising work for a cancer charity that I have chosen, to acknowledge the help I received when I had my tumour.

I am also looking to increase my leisure-time activities, which at the moment consist of jigsaws and knitting. I started knitting when I stayed with the Irish President Mary McAleese and her family for a weekend. She sits and knits without even thinking about it. It was very handy, as when my mother died in Novem-ber 2000 I was left a half-made blanket of coloured woollen squares all sewn together. I decided to finish it, so I started knitting. However, I had forgotten how Mary had said to cast off, so I started looking for someone who could knit and eventu-ally found that Carole, one of the tea ladies in the Cabinet Office, could. I am now knitting away and the wool blanket of many squares is growing from a small cover to a much larger cover. I'm aiming for a double bed. I want to learn how to take photos so that when we go on holiday my snaps are not always the boring ones with the thumb in the corner. I am also going to learn something I have always wanted to do, fly-fishing. Being out surrounded by water, nature and quiet sounds like a dream to me. Finally I would like to take more holidays – and particularly exotic holidays. Jon has promised to do the organizing and I have promised to keep him to it. I would also like some holiday time with my stepchildren before they are too old. They may be too old already.

And I will find a job. Whatever I do it will be political in some shape or form. Politics and the Labour movement have been central to my adult life. The values of justice, fairness and equality that drove me into politics are still with me today. A future job may not be in a party political form because I think that the nature of politics is beginning to change, and that the kinds of problems ahead of us are different from some that we have faced in the past, and Parliament may not be the place to deal with them. What follows are a few thoughts on the major issues which I think we are all going to have to get to grips with in the future.

There has been a great deal of discussion in recent years about how global markets dominated by global companies have affected people across the world. Many argue that we can do nothing about it, despite all the problems and inequalities it brings with it. Others argue that greater free trade will integrate all peoples within a world economic market, and that open markets will over time help spread liberal democracy. The dominance of one way of thinking, the dominance of global corporations always makes me feel uncomfortable. I agree with it insofar as there is no other economic model apart from capitalism really functioning in the world. I believe that with greater international co-operation between governments we have a chance to put a social side, policies on health and education, alongside the economic. I also believe that if governments and people work together they can make the power of global capitalism work better for everyone. There are world problems that can only be dealt with on a global and political level. The free market is too crude and volatile to be able to solve the problems we face – problems which are many, especially the widening gap between rich and poor, the international drugs business, the frightening increase in AIDS and the problems of the deteriorating world environment.

Since 11 September 2001 my concern that the importance of politics was being underestimated has been savagely reversed. The war on terrorism has brought politics back to centre-stage, not just in the form of war and the need for international co-operation, but also in the form of an appreciation that not all people around the world share the west's view of the world, a belief in free-market economics and liberal democratic forms of government. We have had to take into account the religious dimension of people and societies, something that has been in general decline in the west's political thinking for many years. So we have a lot of hard thinking to do.

It was in my dealing with the drugs problem that I had been particularly impressed by this need for political action both on a domestic and an international level. Drugs are the third largest business in the world, with estimated sales in excess of US$500 billion. They devastate many lives, both in the west and in the less developed countries where they are produced or through which they are transported. They criminalize large areas of our societies, whether through users, dealers, producers or money launderers.

As I have described above, I spent a lot of time while I was in office visiting other countries which were suffering such problems either as a supplier, such as Colombia, or as a transit route, such as Iran and Jamaica. All of these countries blamed the west for being the cause of their own particular woes, the argument being that if we didn't buy the stuff it would not be produced and shipped around the world. This is a persuasive argument and, given the failure of western governments to kill off demand, it is difficult if not impossible to disagree with. The main thing

I learnt from these visits was that what we see as our own very difficult domestic issue, with the drug dealers in the pub, the local crime caused by addicts stealing to pay for their habit, is also global. It is something that we have to address in a global way.

I also learnt that to have a war against drugs does not work, for it is in effect a war against ourselves – it is too crude a response. Drugs are not like an external enemy, they are part of our own social, political and economic body. By trying to kill the problem we may kill ourselves. It was like the problem of the IRA in Ireland: the use of force did not ultimately solve the problem. Members of the IRA survived because they were an extension of the actual communities they lived in. If there hadn't been support for them they would not have been able to survive. This is an uncomfortable truth, but a similar truth to the one that has to be faced about drugs. Drugs are popular, people want to take them. They will pay a lot of money and take a lot of risks to get hold of them. We have tried through education and intimidation to change this but it has not worked. A different approach has to be adopted both to help in the west and to end the devastation the trade is causing in the developing world.

The demand which is fuelling the drugs trade comes mainly from the west, and it is here we will have to take a lead. From this perspective I have been drawn to what might be seen as a radical solution. We need to legalize all drugs. We can then regulate the trade, tax the drugs, decriminalize the whole process around the world. The results of this would be significantly beneficial domestically, but would also revolutionize the problem for such countries as Iran, Jamaica and Colombia. It would replace corrosive political activity with dollar-earning businesses. This would help to clean up government, reduce corruption and diminish addiction in these countries, where today workers in the drugs trade are often paid in drugs themselves. A legal monthly salary would be much better. It would not be easy, and it is something that will require global co-operation, but – as we have seen since the events of 11 September 2001 – international political will can be brought to bear on these difficult global issues.

But like many of the issues that afflict the world the core of the problem is to be found in our own societies. In particular the growing gap between rich and poor can be attributed to the way the world economy is managed by the west. The damage to the world's environment can also be put at the door of the west, not least the excessive and wasteful energy-users, especially in the United States. We have to face up to our own culpability if we are going to be able to work with less developed nations on a global scale. As those at the bottom of the pile, they often see much more clearly than we do the damage that actions cause, often because the consequences are felt by them rather than by us.

Although this is changing, the resentments that led to the attack on the World Trade Center in New York were an evil manifestation of a resentment against such inequality of power and wealth between the United States and many in the Muslim world. Of more immediate impact in the UK is the growing number of asylum seekers reaching our shores. The present war against terrorism will do nothing to diminish this. In many ways we now face on a global scale the same problems that confronted our forebears in Victorian Britain on a national scale. Despite our wealth we have reached a point where we can no longer isolate ourselves from the poverty that exists side by side with our affluence. So as Edward, Prince of Wales said in the 1930s, 'Something must be done.' Just as he saw the poverty in Britain, so we must recognize the same plight among people around the world. But because it is so often global in its reach it is difficult to address.

I believe we can all do something at home through our domestic politics and as consumers in what we buy, and thus start to solve the problems. But this will not be enough. International co-operation is essential, and supranational bodies such as the European Union are vital. That is why we should join the euro:

a united Europe is more important politically than just a narrow argument about economic advantage. But such a united Europe should not be inward looking, it should not say 'we're all right, Jack', and leave the poorer parts of the world to pick up the pieces in the wake of our excesses. We must look to work with the world to solve problems together. As 11 September showed, no country can isolate itself from global politics. We now have a new definition of globalization.

Of course there are also changes that are peculiar to Britain – some having a connection with what is happening globally (such as the increasing multiculturalism of Britain), others (such as the changing of our family units or attitudes to women) being caused by domestic social and economic pressures. Other important issues include the ageing population, coping with structural economic change, often caused by multinational companies shifting their production around or out of the UK, and Englishness and our sense of national identity.

These may seem to be disparate issues, but there is something common to all of them. They all require us to face up to a new reality; they all require us to be honest about the nature of our society, and how it works so that we can best manage it. Bad policies and bad government are often caused by politicians trying to solve problems of the past. This is an easy trap for governments to fall into when they are constantly harangued by a press which usually thinks it is representing what the people think. What is needed from politicians is leadership. What is needed from the press is greater responsibility, waking up to the fact that it has a role in moulding our society, not just reporting gossip. People cling to the past for security, but unfortunately only by recognizing reality can greater security be found. This is a strain and a problem in all democratic politics – another problem with which we must grapple.

The ageing of the population is an interesting example of how we must confront reality. After the Second World War people wanted to have children – a natural reaction to the ravages of war. This created a wave of people who will in the next decade become pensioners. The challenge this is presenting us with is that the young, who usually pay for the costs of the ageing part of society through taxation, are getting fewer in proportion to the number of the old. The situation is made worse by better medicine, which is increasingly costing more (medical inflation is about three times more than the general rate) and enabling people to live longer. We have to face this reality and attempt to find solutions.

I would suggest one key answer would be to shift perceptions of age. Yes, there are more old people, but those people on the whole are far fitter than in the past. Many can and still want to work. Let's change employment and pension laws to allow them to do so. Let's work at trying to change the cult of youth in companies so that more experienced people can be employed for longer. This may mean that salaries have to fall as people get older, rather than inevitably rising as they do now. It would reflect reality, and create a more flexible and realistic job market. Of course there are many other things that must be addressed such as the health service, transport and housing policy. But all of the issues are interwoven. Our concerns with asylum seekers should be tied to our need for more young people to pay taxes to pay for the old. But then this puts strains on our already multicultural society. Different lifestyle choices, more working women, divorce and later marriage are all leading to more single people and fewer babies, only making more complex any government's policy responses.

None of this is easy, but I would urge us all to look at these things realistically and with goodwill, and not pine for some golden past, when marriage and morality held our nation together. It was never like that – the problems were just different.

And finally, what it is to be English. Events in recent history, the growth of the idea of Europe and devolution in the United Kingdom have meant that a subject that has not been questioned for a long time rises up the agenda of important political issues.

The problem is that a national identity often lies in the past, so many still look to our empire, to our success in world wars, to the pomp and circumstance of the monarchy. But increasingly these are becoming irrelevant as more and more young people know little of these things and care even less. But it is important that we can all share a sense of national identity that is not just about football, for it is only through this that a nation can work together, support the poor and the weak and maintain a credible legal system. We must trust in our institutions – they are what holds our society, our country together. But to gain that trust they must be relevant to the reality of our society. We need to remember our past, but we must not live in it.

Sadly I have a long list of problems I think we are going to face but no equivalent list of solutions. All I can offer is on the national level: that the government should face up to the difficult problems ahead, that the public should practise some tolerance in the face of these issues and try and help the politicians make progress, and that the media should examine problems in the context of today and not in the light of past prejudices. Internationally our task is clearer. Unless there is a greater effort to tackle globalization and work together as nations, we will continue to make life harder for the vast majority of people on this planet. And we are not exempted from difficult times in the future unless we start recognizing the problems that lie ahead.

To end on this gloomy note is not what I want to do. Although life does contain many difficulties and there is not always a 'happy ending', I hope the story I have told shows more hope than despair – shows that people working together can overcome many obstacles, often within themselves, and by doing so can make the world a better place.

Glossary

AIS	**Anglo-Irish Intergovernmental Secretariat.** The permanent secretariat, staffed by officials of the British and Irish governments, set up to service the structures created by the Anglo-Irish Agreement in 1985.
All	**Alliance Party.** Founded in 1970 it draws support from both sides of the community. Its share of the vote is usually in single figures.
ANC	**African National Congress.**
CAFOD	**Catholic Agency for Overseas Development.** International aid and development charity.
CDU	**Campaign for Democracy in Ulster.** London-based group, supported by members of the Labour party, that pressed for reforms in N. Ireland during the late 1960s.
CIRA	**Continuity Irish Republican Army.** The military wing of republican Sinn Fein.
CLMC	**Combined Loyalist Military Command.** Established in 1991 as an umbrella group for the main loyalist paramilitary organizations. Announced ceasefire on 13 October 1994.
DUP	**Democratic Unionist Party.** Founded in 1971 by the Reverend Ian Paisley and other unionists opposed to what they saw as the 'weakness' of the Ulster Unionist party.
ELN	**National Liberation Army.** Colombian guerilla group founded in 1964.
FARC	**The Revolutionary Armed Forces of Colombia.** Largest guerilla group, officially formed in 1964.
INLA	**Irish National Liberation Army.** The military wing of the Irish Republican Socialist Party. Notorious for its unpredictability and ruthlessness.
IRA	**Irish Republican Army.** Paramilitary organization formed in 1919 and dedicated to the removal of the British presence from Ireland. Split in two in 1969/70 when the majority of its members left to form the Provisional IRA. Those that remained styled themselves the Official IRA (OIRA).
IRSP	**Irish Republican Socialist Party.** Founded in 1974 by disaffected members of Official and Provisional Sinn Fein.
LOCC	**Lower Ormeau Concerned Citizens.** Residents' group in South Belfast, opposed to marches through their area by the Orange and other 'loyal' orders.
LVF	**Loyalist Volunteer Force.** Loyalist paramilitary organization, formed by dissident members of the Ulster Volunteer Force in 1996.
NGO	**Non-governmental organization.**
NI	**Northern Ireland.** 'Northern Ireland' is the correct description of that part of the United Kingdom. It is widely used by unionists, who

also describe the political entity as 'The Province' or 'Ulster'. Some nationalists prefer to use 'The North of Ireland' or 'The Six Counties', signifying a close association with the Irish Republic.

NILP   **Northern Ireland Labour Party**. Founded in 1924 it struggled to find support throughout most of its history, and was finally wound up in 1987. Since then the labour banner in N. Ireland has been carried by a variety of small groupings and individuals.

NIO   **Northern Ireland Office**. The United Kingdom government department established in March 1972 to administer Direct Rule in N. Ireland.

NIWC   **Northern Ireland Women's Coalition**. Political party founded in 1996 on a cross-community basis. Strongly supportive of the peace process and progressive social and economic policies.

PANI   **Police Authority for Northern Ireland**. The body established in 1970 to provide independent oversight of the Royal Ulster Constabulary and ensure an effective and efficient police force. Succeeded by the Northern Ireland Policing Board in November 2001.

PIRA   **Provisional IRA**. Republican paramilitary organization formed in 1969/70 by breakaway members of the Irish Republican Army.

PLP   **Parliamentary Labour Party**.

PUP   **Progressive Unionist Party**. Loyalist party founded in 1979. Closely associated with the Ulster Volunteer Force.

RIRA   **Real IRA**. Dissident republican group that emerged following the Provisional IRA's ceasefires of 1994 and 1997. Responsible for the Omagh bomb in August 1998. Its political wing, the 32-County Sovereignty Committee, is comprised mainly of ex-members of Sinn Fein.

RSF   **Republican Sinn Fein**. Founded in 1986 by members of Sinn Fein who left that party in protest at its decision to end its policy of abstention from the Irish Parliament. Maintains support for the 'armed struggle'.

RUC   **Royal Ulster Constabulary**. The police force in N. Ireland between 1922 and 2001.

SDLP   **Social Democratic and Labour Party**. Radical, left of centre, nationalist party founded in 1970, principally by supporters of several small nationalist/social-democratic parties. Virtually unchallenged for the nationalist vote for many years, it lost ground to Sinn Fein in the 1990s and early 2000s.

SF   **Sinn Fein**. Republican party formed after the break-up of 'old' Sinn Fein in 1970. Dedicated to a United Ireland and closely associated with the Provisional IRA.

UDA   **Ulster Defence Association**. Loyalist paramilitary organization formed in 1971 from various local vigilante groups. It is believed to have been responsible for several hundred murders, many carried out under the cover-name of the Ulster Freedom Fighters.

UDP   **Ulster Democratic Party**. Founded in 1989 in succession to the Ulster Loyalist Democratic Party, the political wing of the UDA. Wound up at the end of 2001 having failed to gain significant political support.

UFF   **Ulster Freedom Fighters**. A cover-name for members of the Ulster Defence Association.

UKUP   **United Kingdom Unionist Party**. Strongly anti-Good Friday Agreement unionist party founded and led by Robert McCartney QC.

UUP   **Ulster Unionist Party.** The largest unionist party in N. Ireland, it provided the government of N. Ireland from 1921 until March 1972. Throughout the succeeding 30 years it competed for votes with the Democratic Unionist Party, at some times – such as after the signing of the Anglo-Irish Agreement in 1985 – in loose coalition with the DUP, and at others – such as since the Good Friday Agreement – in acrimonious political conflict.

UVF   **Ulster Volunteer Force.** Loyalist paramilitary organization formed in 1966.

Chronology

There are as many different versions of this chronology as there are people who write about N. Ireland. This is by no means an exhaustive account of events, but rather what I think are the most significant developments that have shaped the peace process over the last thirty-five years.

1967
January   Northern Ireland Civil Rights Association formed.

1969
August   Widespread rioting in Derry and Belfast. British troops arrive on the streets of Northern Ireland.

1971
August   Internment introduced in N. Ireland.

1972
January   Bloody Sunday – 13 men were shot dead by the British Army.

March   Direct Rule from London introduced.

July   Bloody Friday. 22 IRA bombs in Belfast kill eleven people.

1973
December   Conference at Sunningdale in England leads to power-sharing government being set up in N. Ireland in January 1974

1974
May   Ulster Workers Council strike begins in opposition to power-sharing government. Loyalist car bombs in Irish Republic kill 30. New N. Ireland arrangements collapse.

October   IRA bombs kill five in pubs in Guildford, Surrey, England.

November   IRA bombs kill 21 people in bars in Birmingham, England.

1978
January   European Court of Human Rights rules that interrogation methods used on internees in 1971 amounted to 'inhuman and degrading treatment'.

Chronology

1979

August   IRA bombs kill 18 British soldiers at Warrenpoint,
              Co. Down. Lord Mountbatten and companions killed by
              IRA bomb on boat off Co. Sligo.

1980

October   Republican prisoners in N.Ireland begin hunger strike –
              called off in December.

1981

March   Second hunger strike begins. IRA prison leader Bobby Sands
              dies in May – by October called off after ten deaths.

1983

March   Irish government announces the setting up of the New
              Ireland Forum to discuss nationalist aims.

1984

October   IRA bomb at Conservative party conference in Brighton kills
              five people.

1985

November   Margaret Thatcher and Garret FitzGerald sign Anglo-Irish
              Agreement.

1986

April   Ulster Unionist Party announces it is ending links with the
              British Conservative Party.

November   Sinn Fein votes to allow successful candidates to take their
              seats in the Irish Parliament. Major demonstrations in
              N. Ireland against the Anglo-Irish Agreement.

1987

November   IRA bomb in Enniskillen, Co. Fermanagh kills 11 people
              during Remembrance Day service.

1988

January   John Hume and Gerry Adams meet.

March   Three IRA members killed in Gibraltar.

              Loyalist Michael Stone launches grenade attack killing three
              at funerals of those killed in Gibraltar.

August   Eight British soldiers killed travelling on a bus in
              Ballygawley, Co. Tyrone. Three IRA members killed by
              soldiers in Co. Tyrone.

1989

September   IRA bomb kills 11 military bandsmen at Deal in Kent.

November   N. Ireland Secretary, Peter Brooke, says the IRA cannot be beaten militarily and that the British government will have to respond imaginatively to an IRA ceasefire.

1990

April   Gerry Adams says an unannounced IRA ceasefire could be a reality if the British government enters into talks with Sinn Fein.

July   Conservative MP, Ian Gow, killed by IRA at his home in Sussex, England.

November   Peter Brooke says Britain has 'no selfish strategic or economic interest' in N. Ireland. His attempts to make progress on talks and launch of the 'three-stranded' approach are crucial to future progress.

December   For first time in 15 years IRA holds Christmas ceasefire for three days – to be repeated in the years ahead.

1991

February   IRA fire three mortars into the garden at the back of 10 Downing Street.

December   IRA bomb attacks in London.

1992

January   IRA kills eight Protestant workers repairing a police station at Teebane, Co. Tyrone.

February   Loyalists kill five Catholics in gun attack on bookmakers on Ormeau Road, Belfast.

1993

March   Johnathan Ball and Tim Parry killed by IRA bomb in Warrington, England.

April   News emerges that John Hume and Gerry Adams have been in secret talks.

IRA bomb Bishopsgate in City of London causing extensive damage.

May   John Hume continues to talk despite bombs in a number of towns in N. Ireland.

September   IRA observes undeclared ceasefire for a week to coincide with a trip to N. Ireland of prominent Irish Americans.

October   Gerry Adams says he will be able to persuade the IRA to end its campaign if the British respond positively to the Hume–Adams talks.

IRA bomb in fish shop on Shankhill Road kills 10.

UDA kills seven people in bar at Greysteel, Co. Derry.

November	John Major rules out John Hume initiative.
	Evidence emerges of secret contact between British government and IRA.
December	Downing Street Declaration released in London by John Major and Albert Reynolds.

1994

January	Broadcasting ban on Sinn Fein lifted in Irish Republic. Bill Clinton grants visa to Gerry Adams.
March	IRA mortar attack at Heathrow. IRA call three-day ceasefire.
June	Six Catholics killed in loyalist attack on bar in Loughinisland, Co. Down.
July	N. Ireland Secretary Patrick Mayhew calls for the scrapping of Articles two and three of Irish constitution.
	IRA kills three loyalists and bombs loyalist pubs in Belfast.
August	IRA calls 'complete cessation' of its military campaign.
September	John Hume, Gerry Adams and Albert Reynolds shake hands in public. John Major lifts broadcasting ban on Sinn Fein and says IRA has to abandon violence for good. Bill Clinton lifts White House ban on contact with Sinn Fein.
October	Loyalist groups announce ceasefire, declaring union with Britain to be safe. John Major says he will make a working assumption that the IRA ceasefire was intended to be permanent.
November	Bill Clinton announces aid package to N. Ireland. Post Office worker Frank Kerr killed by IRA during armed robbery. Gerry Adams expresses regret.
December	British government announces exploratory dialogue with Sinn Fein. Bill Clinton appoints Senator George Mitchell as his economic envoy in N. Ireland.

1995

January	British government announces end of ban on Ministers meeting Sinn Fein and loyalist groups.
February	British and Irish governments release joint 'Framework Documents'.
May	Patrick Mayhew meets Gerry Adams in Washington after outlining conditions for Sinn Fein to enter all-party talks which include 'actual decommissioning' of IRA arms.
August	James Molyneaux resigns as leader of the official Unionist party. David Trimble is elected to succeed him in September.
November	British government publishes 'Building Blocks' document proposing all-party preparatory talks and an international

body to address the decommissioning issue. Bill Clinton
shakes hands with Gerry Adams in Belfast.

1996

January	British and Irish Ministers meet Sinn Fein in Stormont. George Mitchell recommends that talks and decommissioning should occur in parallel. John Major announces plans for elections to precede talks in N. Ireland.
February	IRA ceasefire ends with Canary Wharf bomb.
May	Elections held in N. Ireland.
June	Talks begin in N. Ireland without Sinn Fein.
October	IRA bomb army headquarters in Lisburn, Co. Down.

1997

February	Bombardier Stephen Restorick killed by IRA in South Armagh.
May	Labour wins UK general election. Tony Blair becomes Prime Minister and appoints Mo Mowlam as N. Ireland Secretary. Go-ahead given for British officials to meet with Sinn Fein.
July	IRA restores its ceasefire. Ian Paisley and Robert McCartney withdraw their parties from the talks.
August	Mo Mowlam meets Sinn Fein. Sinn Fein invited to attend all-party talks.
September	General John De Chastelain announced as chair of international body to oversee decommissioning issue. On entering the talks Sinn Fein sign up to Mitchell Principles of non-violence; IRA later says it has 'problems' with some of them. UUP and loyalist parties rejoin talks.
October	Talks begin. Tony Blair meets Gerry Adams in Belfast.
December	Loyalist paramilitary leader, Billy Wright, killed in Maze Prison by INLA inmates.

1998

January	Mo Mowlam meets loyalist prisoners in Maze to encourage them to support peace talks. In London, UDP suspended from peace talks due to UDA/UFF announcement of involvement in recent violence.
February	In Dublin, Sinn Fein suspended from talks because of IRA violence. UDP return to talks.
March	Talks resume in Belfast. Sinn Fein return.
April	George Mitchell hands draft agreement to parties. UUP, loyalists and Alliance reject. Tony Blair and Bertie Ahern join talks in Belfast. Discussions on north–south arrangements conclude. UUP and SDLP resolve differences over Northern Ireland Assembly. After all-night discussions,

agreement on all outstanding issues reached by 4.45 p.m. on April 10th. UUP Ruling Council votes to support agreement.

May	Sinn Fein vote to allow party members to take their seats in Northern Ireland Assembly for first time. Referendums in N. Ireland and Irish Republic show overwhelming public support for Good Friday Agreement.
June	Elections to Northern Ireland Assembly – 80 seats won by pro-Agreement parties, 28 by opponents of the deal.
July	David Trimble and Seamus Mallon elected as First and Deputy First Ministers.
August	Bomb planted by republican splinter group, the Real IRA, kills 29 in Omagh, Co. Tyrone.
December	John Hume and David Trimble receive Nobel Peace Prize. Agreement reached on detailed structure of new arrangements for north–south co-operation.

1999

February	Assembly approves new north–south bodies and government departments in N. Ireland.
April	Talks at Hillsborough attempt to resolve impasse over decommissioning and the formation of executive government in N. Ireland.
July	British and Irish governments propose The Way Forward to resolve outstanding difficulties. When unsuccessful, Seamus Mallon resigns as Deputy First Minister. Formal Review of Good Friday Agreement announced. George Mitchell agrees to return to chair it.
September	Patten report on future of policing in N. Ireland published.
October	Mo Mowlam replaced as N. Ireland Secretary by Peter Mandelson.
November	Mitchell review concludes. N. Ireland government formed and devolution follows.

2000

February	Peter Mandelson announces suspension of devolution citing insufficient progress on decommissioning.
May	Negotiations at Hillsborough and Stormont lead to IRA undertaking to open some of its arms dumps for inspection, saying it is prepared to 'initiate a process that will completely and verifiably put IRA arms beyond use'. David Trimble wins support of Ulster Unionist Council to return to government in N. Ireland.
	Process of inspection of IRA arms dumps begun by former General Secretary of the South African ANC Cyril Ramaphosa and former Finnish President Martti Ahtisaari.

2001

January	Peter Mandelson resigns and John Reid becomes N. Ireland Secretary.
May	David Trimble announces he will resign as N. Ireland's First Minister unless IRA decommissioning begins.
July	David Trimble resigns. N. Ireland government suspended to avoid complete collapse.
August	Following talks in Shropshire, England, British government produce new proposals for implementing Patten police reforms and scaling down security apparatus in N. Ireland. SDLP announce support for policing plan.
October	IRA decommissioning begins.
November	David Trimble re-elected as N. Ireland's First Minister; new SDLP leader Mark Durkan becomes Deputy First Minister.

Index

Acknowledgements

PICTURE ACKNOWLEDGEMENTS

Section 1

Author's collection: page 7 below, page 8. © *Evening Gazette* Teesside: page 1 below, page 5 above. © *Daily Mail* 1997/Atlantic Syndication: page 3. John Harrison, Harrison Photography Belfast: page 5 below. © *The Independent*/ photo Peter Macdiarmid: page 6 above. © North News and Pictures Middlesbrough: page 1 above, page 2 below, page 4. PA News Photo Library: page 2 above, page 6 below, page 7 above.

Section 2

Author's collection: page 16 below. John Harrison, Harrison Photography Belfast: page 11 below, page 13 below. PA News Photo Library: page 9 below, page 10, page 11 above, page 12 above, page 13 above, page 14, page 15, page 16 above. Pacemaker Belfast: page 12 below. © Telegraph Group Limited 2002: page 9 above.

Section 3

Author's collection: page 18 above, page 20, page 23 below. © *Evening Gazette* Teesside: page 23 above. John Harrison, John Harrison Belfast: page 17, page 21 below. Judy Hume/University of Teesside: page 24. PA News Photo Library: page 18 below, page 19, page 22. White House official photograph: page 21 above.

CARTOON ACKNOWLEDGEMENTS

Steve Bell: text pages 96, 187. Peter Brookes/©Times Newspapers Ltd, London 1995 and 2000: text pages 19, 355. Garland/©Telegraph Group Limited 2002: text page 288. Louis Hellman/*Evening Standard* 1998 text page 228. MAC/©*Daily Mail*/Atlantic Syndication: text pages 204, 323. Martyn Turner/*The Irish Times*: text page 262.